Sacred Music as Public Image for
Holy Roman Emperor Ferdinand III

For Dan
I.L.D.E.U.E.

Sacred Music as Public Image for Holy Roman Emperor Ferdinand III
Representing the Counter-Reformation Monarch at the End of the Thirty Years' War

ANDREW H. WEAVER
The Catholic University of America, USA

ASHGATE

© Andrew H. Weaver 2012

All rights reserved. No part of this publication may be reproduced, stored in a retrieval system or transmitted in any form or by any means, electronic, mechanical, photocopying, recording or otherwise without the prior permission of the publisher.

Andrew H. Weaver has asserted his moral right under the Copyright, Designs and Patents Act, 1988, to be identified as the author of this work.

Published by
Ashgate Publishing Limited
Wey Court East
Union Road
Farnham
Surrey, GU9 7PT
England

Ashgate Publishing Company
Suite 420
101 Cherry Street
Burlington
VT 05401-4405
USA

www.ashgate.com

British Library Cataloguing in Publication Data
Weaver, Andrew H.
   Sacred Music as Public Image for Holy Roman Emperor Ferdinand III: Representing the Counter-Reformation Monarch at the End of the Thirty Years' War. –
(Catholic Christendom, 1300–1700)
   1. Ferdinand III, Holy Roman Emperor, 1608-1657 – Arts patronage. 2. Ferdinand III, Holy Roman Emperor, 1608–1657 – Public opinion. 3. Church music – Holy Roman Empire – 17th century. 4. Church music – Catholic Church – 17th century. 5. Music patronage – Holy Roman Empire – History – 17th century. 6. Music and state – Holy Roman Empire. 7. Holy Roman Empire – Kings and rulers – Biography. 8. Holy Roman Empire – History – 1517–1648. 9. Public opinion – Holy Roman Empire.
I. Title II. Series
781.7'1'00943'09032–dc22

Library of Congress Cataloging-in-Publication Data
Weaver, Andrew H.
   Sacred Music as Public Image for Holy Roman Emperor Ferdinand III: Representing the Counter-Reformation Monarch at the End of the Thirty Years' War / Andrew H. Weaver.
      p.   cm. – (Catholic Christendom, 1300–1700)
   Includes bibliographical references and index.
   1. Music – Political aspects – Holy Roman Empire – History – 17th century.
   2. Ferdinand III, Holy Roman Emperor, 1608–1657. I. Title.
   ML3917.H65W43 2011
   780.943'09032–dc23
                                                                     2011024577

ISBN   9781409421191 (hbk)
ISBN   9781409421207 (ebk)

Printed and bound in Great Britain by the MPG Books Group, UK

Contents

List of Figures — *vii*
List of Tables — *xi*
List of Music Examples — *xiii*
List of Abbreviations — *xv*
Series Editor's Preface — *xvii*
Acknowledgements — *xix*

Introduction — 1

PART I: SETTING THE STAGE

1   Ferdinand III's Public Image and the Thirty Years' War — 15

2   *Justitia et Pietas*: A Portrait of Ferdinand III — 43

PART II: MEANS OF PRODUCTION

3   Emblematic Sound: Musical Performance as a Mirror of Imperial Majesty and Piety — 67

4   The Politics of Printing: The Print Program of Giovanni Felice Sances — 121

PART III: MUSIC AS REPRESENTATION

5   Musical Portraiture: Representations of the Emperor in Sound — 159

6   Mirrors and Models: Piety and Spirituality in the Service of the Crown — 193

7   *Maria Patrona Ferdinandi (et Austriae)*: Ferdinand III's Marian Devotion as Public Image — 223

Epilogue: Ferdinand III's Image after the War — 251

Appendix: Dedicatory Texts of Music Prints Dedicated to the Emperor and Other Imperial Figures   *265*
Bibliography   *291*
Index   *317*

List of Figures

1.1 Peter Paul Rubens, *The Meeting before the Battle of Nördlingen*, 328 × 388 cm, oil on canvas, ca. 1634–35, Kunsthistorisches Museum, Vienna (used by permission) — 18
1.2 Cornelius Schut, *Victory at Nördlingen*, 226 × 160 cm, oil on canvas, 1635, STAM, Ghent, inv. 711 (used by permission) — 19
1.3 Frans Luyckx, *Ferdinand III*, 214 × 141 cm, oil on canvas, ca. 1639, © the Nationalmuseum, Stockholm (used by permission) — 21
1.4 Medal honoring the Battle of Nördlingen, 4 cm, 1634 (Kunsthistorisches Museum, Vienna, Münzkabinett, used by permission) — 22
1.5 Lucas Schnitzer, *Ferdinand III*, engraving, 1634 (Österreichische Nationalbibliothek, Vienna, Bildarchiv, Pg 149 137/3 in Ptf 123: I (66), used by permission) — 23
1.6 Anonymous engraving of Ferdinand III, 1634 (Österreichische Nationalbibliothek, Vienna, Bildarchiv, Pg 149 137/3 in Ptf 123: I (4c), used by permission) — 24
1.7 Frontispiece of Antonino Collurafi, *L'aquila coronata*, 1637 (Österreichische Nationalbibliothek, Vienna, 79.B.51, used by permission) — 26
1.8 "Dagger of Providence," from Matthias Jacobus, *Arma virtutum* (Universitätsbibliothek, Vienna, Hauptbibliothek, Sign.: I 245631, used by permission) — 28
1.9 Jan van den Hoecke, *Emperor Ferdinand III*, 74.5 × 61 cm, oil on canvas, ca. 1644–47, Kunsthistorisches Museum, Vienna (used by permission) — 35
2.1 Georg Urllmayr, frontispiece of *Nomenclatur oder Namen der .. Religions Reformation im Ertzherzogtumb Österreich …*, color engraving, after 1654 (Österreichische Nationalbibliothek, Vienna, Bildarchiv, 302.955-B, used by permission) — 47
2.2 Lukas Vorsterman after a painting by Cornelius Schut, Ferdinand III depicted as a patron of the arts and sciences, engraving, 1633 (© Albertina, Vienna, Holländische DG n.m. GM, used by permission) — 58

2.3	Michael Frommer, frontispiece of Andreas Rauch, *Currus triumphalis musici*, engraving, 1648 (Bibliothèque nationale de France, used by permission)	62
3.1	Giovanni Burnacini, staged tournament in *La Gara*, engraving from the libretto, 1652 (Österreichische Nationalbibliothek, Vienna, Bildarchiv, NB 606942-C, used by permission)	80
3.2	Lucas Schnitzer, scenes from Ferdinand III's coronation as King of the Romans (detail), engraving, 1636–37 (Österreichische Nationalbibliothek, Vienna, Bildarchiv, 238.572-B, used by permission)	83
3.3	Peter Paul van Mildert and Jacob Bruynel, scene from the 1654 production of *Theodosius*, engraving from the libretto, 1654 (Österreichische Nationalbibliothek, Vienna, *35.O.64, used by permission)	96
4.1	Title page of Giovanni Felice Sances, *Motetti a 2, 3, 4, e cinque voci*, 1642 (Archivio Musicale del Duomo, Como, used by permission)	136
4.2	Table of contents of Andreas Rauch, *Currus triumphalis musici*, 1648 (Bibliothèque nationale de France, used by permission)	150
5.1	Wolfgang Kilian, triumphal arch erected in Regensburg for Ferdinand III (detail), engraving, 1653 (Österreichische Nationalbibliothek, Vienna, 7.P.26, used by permission)	180
7.1	Procession from the *Schottenkirche* to St Stephen's Cathedral on March 29, 1645, anonymous engraving (© Albertina, Vienna, Historische Blätter Wien 1, used by permission)	237
7.2	Sebastian Jenet, engraving of the *Mariensäule* from Matthias Bastianschiz, *Oliva Pacis*, 1650 (Österreichische Nationalbibliothek, Vienna, 296.331-A. Adl. 4 Alt. Mag., used by permission)	240
E.1	Medal honoring the Peace of Westphalia (reverse), 4 cm, 1648 (Kunsthistorisches Museum, Vienna, Münzkabinett, used by permission)	253
E.2	Franciscus van den Steen after a painting by Joachim von Sandrart, *The Triumph of Ferdinand III*, engraving, 1653 (© Albertina, Vienna, Ö.K. fol. 4–5 Nr. 5+6, used by permission)	255

E.3	Wolfgang Kilian, triumphal arch erected in Regensburg for Ferdinand III (front), engraving, 1653 (Österreichische Nationalbibliothek, Vienna, 7.P.26, used by permission)	258
E.4	Wolfgang Kilian, triumphal arch erected in Regensburg for Ferdinand III (back), engraving, 1653 (Österreichische Nationalbibliothek, Vienna, 7.P.26, used by permission)	259

List of Tables

I.1	The arrangement of hexachords in *cantus durus*	12
3.1	Italian operas and oratorios performed at court during Ferdinand III's reign	72
3.2	Jesuit dramas performed in Vienna for the imperial family during Ferdinand III's reign	88
5.1	Texts of the three imperial motets in Rolla's *Teatro musicale*	186
6.1	Surviving Eucharistic motets by composers employed by Ferdinand III	200
6.2	Lost Eucharistic motets by composers employed by Ferdinand III	200
6.3	Valentini, *Salve tremendum*	208
6.4	Valentini, *Deus qui pro redemptione mundi*	209
6.5	Texts of two mystical motets from Sances's *Motetti a una, due, tre, e quattro voci*	214
7.1	Texts of Sances's O *Domina gloriae* and O *dulcis Virgo*	245

List of Music Examples

3.1	Ferdinand III, *Humanae salutis sator*, bars 101–10	112
3.2	Ferdinand III, *Humanae salutis sator*, bars 132–9	113
3.3	Ferdinand III, *Deus misereatur nostri*, bars 48–51	114
3.4	Sances, *O bone Jesu* (1642), bars 21–3	116
3.5	Sances, *O vos omnes* (1638), bars 72–9	116
3.6	Bertali, *Exultate et cantate* (1649), bars 47–51	117
5.1	Sances, *Judica me Deus*, bars 1–8	162
5.2	Sances, *Judica me Deus*, bars 19–26	163
5.3	Sances, *Laetamini in Domino*, bars 64–75	165
5.4	Sances, *Audi Domine*, bars 1–27	175
5.5	Sances, *Audi Domine*, bars 53–60	181
5.6	Sances, *Honestum fecit*, bars 56–62	184
5.7	Sances, *Miserere servorum tuorum*, bars 121–8	188
5.8	Sances, *Excita furorem*, bars 1–8	189
6.1	Valentini, *Mensa sacra*, bars 21–9	202
6.2	Valentini, *Salve tremendum*, bars 16–22	210
6.3	Sances, *Dulcis Amor Jesu*, bars 19–27	216
6.4	Sances, *O Crux benedicta*, bars 23–32	217
6.5	Sances, *O Domine guttae tui sanguinis*, bars 1–7	218
6.6	Sances, *O Domine Jesu*, bars 26–33	219
6.7	Sances, *O Domine Jesu*, bars 96–101	219
7.1	Sances, *Ardet cor meum*, bars 1–12	232
7.2	Sances, *Ardet cor meum*, bars 25–34	233
7.3	Sances, *Ardet cor meum*, bars 84–103	234
7.4	Sances, *O dulcis Virgo*, bars 48–55	246
7.5	Sances, *O Domina gloriae*, bars 71–85	247

List of Abbreviations

A-Kr	Kremsmünster, Benediktinerstift
A-Wn	Vienna, Österreichische Nationalbibliothek
CS-KRa	Kroměříž, Státni Zámek a Zahrady
D-Lr	Lüneburg, Ratsbücherei
HHStA	Vienna, Haus-, Hof- und Staatsarchiv
HKA	Vienna, Hofkammerarchiv
I-MOe	Modena, Biblioteca Estense e Universitaria
KHM	Vienna, Kunsthistorisches Museum
NÖHA	Niederösterreichische Herrschaftsakten
RRMBE	Recent Researches in the Music of the Baroque Era
S-Skma	Stockholm, Statens Musikbibliotek
WSLA	Vienna, Wiener Stadt- und Landesarchiv

Series Editor's Preface

The still-usual emphasis on medieval (or Catholic) and reformation (or Protestant) religious history has meant neglect of the middle ground, both chronological and ideological. As a result, continuities between the middle ages and early modern Europe have been overlooked in favor of emphasis on radical discontinuities. Further, especially in the later period, the identification of 'reformation' with various kinds of Protestantism means that the vitality and creativity of the established church, whether in its Roman or local manifestations, has been left out of account. In the last few years, an upsurge of interest in the history of traditional (or catholic) religion makes these inadequacies in received scholarship even more glaring and in need of systematic correction. The series will attempt this by covering all varieties of religious behavior, broadly interpreted, not just (or even especially) traditional institutional and doctrinal church history. It will to the maximum degree possible be interdisciplinary, comparative and global, as well as non-confessional. The goal is to understand religion, primarily of the 'Catholic' variety, as a broadly human phenomenon, rather than as a privileged mode of access to superhuman realms, even implicitly.

The period covered, 1300–1700, embraces the moment which saw an almost complete transformation of the place of religion in the life of Europeans, whether considered as a system of beliefs, as an institution, or as a set of social and cultural practices. In 1300, vast numbers of Europeans, from the pope down, fully expected Jesus's return and the beginning of His reign on earth. By 1700, very few Europeans, of whatever level of education, would have subscribed to such chiliastic beliefs. Pierre Bayle's notorious sarcasms about signs and portents are not idiosyncratic. Likewise, in 1300 the vast majority of Europeans probably regarded the pope as their spiritual head; the institution he headed was probably the most tightly integrated and effective bureaucracy in Europe. Most Europeans were at least nominally Christian, and the pope had at least nominal knowledge of that fact. The papacy, as an institution, played a central role in high politics, and the clergy in general formed an integral part of most governments, whether central or local. By 1700, Europe was divided into a myriad of different religious allegiances, and even those areas officially subordinate to the pope were both more nominally Catholic in belief (despite colossal efforts at imposing uniformity) and also in allegiance than they had been four hundred years earlier. The pope had become only one political factor, and not one of the first rank. The clergy, for its part, had virtually disappeared from secular governments as well as losing much of its local authority. The stage was set for the Enlightenment.

Thomas F. Mayer,
Augustana College

Acknowledgements

This book began life as my Ph.D. dissertation, and in my many years of working with this material I have been aided by numerous institutions and people, whom I am pleased to thank here. Work on the dissertation was funded by fellowships from the Mellon Foundation, The Mrs Giles Whiting Foundation, the John Perry Miller Fund of the Yale University Graduate School of Arts and Sciences, and the Miriam U. Christman Travel Fellowship from the Society for Reformation Research. More recently, work on the book was made possible by two Grants-in-Aid from the Catholic University of America, one that funded a graduate student research assistant in 2007 and one that funded a research trip to Prague, Milan, and Vienna in 2009. I am also indebted to the American Musicological Society for providing two subventions that helped cover publication costs: one from the Margarita M. Hanson Endowment and the other from the AMS 75 PAYS Endowment (funded in part by the National Endowment for the Humanities and the Andrew W. Mellon Foundation).

I have been fortunate to work in many libraries and archives during the course of this project, and I am grateful to the helpful staffs of the Hofkammerarchiv, the Haus-, Hof- und Staatsarchiv, the Abteilung für alte und wertvolle Bestände of the Universitätsbibliothek, the Münzkabinett of the Kunsthistorisches Museum, and the Österreichische Nationalbibliothek (especially the Bildarchiv, Musiksammlung, and Sammlung von Handschriften und alten Drucken) in Vienna; the National Library of the Czech Republic in Prague; and, closer to home, the Performing Arts Reading Room of the Library of Congress and Catholic University's Mullen Library and Music Library. For providing me with materials, I must also thank the Bayerische Staatsbibliothek in Munich, the Bibliothèque nationale de France in Paris, the Archivio musicale del Duomo in Como, the Nationalmuseum and the Statens musikbibliotek in Stockholm, the Stadsmuseum in Ghent, as well as the Kunsthistorisches Museum, Albertina, and Österreichische Nationalbibliothek in Vienna. Many thanks are also due to those among these institutions who granted permission for the reproduction of items from their collections.

None of this work would have been possible without the generous assistance of numerous colleagues, mentors, and friends. First and foremost, I must express my deepest gratitude to Steven Saunders. Not only did his pioneering work lay a firm foundation for all of my work on seventeenth-century Vienna, but from the moment I first contacted him as a young graduate student considering a dissertation on Ferdinand III, he has never been anything but generous, encouraging, supportive, and helpful. He was the first to read every chapter of this book, and his discerning eye and superb insights have made it immeasurably better than it would have been otherwise. Other colleagues who have contributed to the book—by sharing materials, suggesting sources, looking things up, answering questions, and providing ideas—include Micaela Baranello, Claudio Bernardi, Tassilo Erhardt, Alexander Fisher, Mary Frandsen, Roger Freitas, Denise Gallo, Robert Holzer, Dr Elisabeth Klecker, Jeffrey Kurtzman, Caitlin Miller, Janet Page, Johannes Prominczel, Robert Rawson, Geraldine Rohling, and Grayson Wagstaff (with many apologies to anyone I left out!). Finally, I would have never been able to reach this point without the unflagging support of my two most important mentors: my dissertation adviser Ellen Rosand and my undergraduate adviser Honey Meconi, both of whom have been instrumental in shaping me as a scholar.

When working on music that is unfamiliar to most performers (and even scholars!), it is always rewarding to find colleagues who are willing to perform the music, thereby providing a much more satisfying experience than plunking out the music on the piano or listening to a MIDI file on Finale. In this regard, I am deeply grateful to Richard Lalli, director of the Yale University Collegium Musicum, and Stephen Alltop, director of the Northwestern University Alice Millar Chapel Choir, both of whom indulged me by programming concerts of this music.

I am very fortunate to be a faculty member in a vibrant graduate program in musicology, and my interactions with Ph.D. and M.A. students at Catholic University have enriched this book immeasurably. Kathleen Anders-Musser was a diligent research assistant, tirelessly transcribing music into Finale and saving me countless hours of busy work. Ken Stilwell, although he never received financial remuneration, has also been a superb assistant, helping with such mundane tasks as digitizing microfilms but, more importantly, engaging in long conversations, letting me bounce ideas off of him, and providing insights that appear in this book. I am also grateful to the following students enrolled in my Fall 2008 musicology seminar, who indulged me by letting me teach basically the entirety of this book and all of whom contributed ideas that have found their way into it: Jessica Bachicha, Katerina Lichtenwalter, Marilyn Maturani, Janet McKinney, Jami Moore, and Nelson Niño.

For checking my translations and offering insights into the texts, I am grateful to Valeria Garino (for Italian) and Fernando Gracia García and Sarah Ferrario (for Latin); I am especially grateful for Sarah's insights into Classical allusions. Of course only I am to blame for any errors that remain in the translations. Rachel Barham also deserves my thanks for reading the entire typescript with a careful editorial eye, offering insights, helping to weed out the remaining pesky typos and infelicitous word repetitions, and in general contributing the final layer of polish to the text.

It is always best to end on a personal note. Although they may not realize it, my parents have contributed to this work in countless ways with their constant love, support, and encouragement. And last but never least, my husband Dan has been part of my life since the very inception of this project. It may not have always been the easiest road, but I cannot imagine what it would have been like to work on this book without him by my side. For everything from his Photoshop wizardry to his patience, understanding, and emotional support I am forever grateful. Thank you, Dan, for making room in your life not just for me but also for Ferdinand III.

Introduction

Studies of the artistic representations of early modern monarchs tend to focus primarily on either those who spectacularly succeeded (Elizabeth I, Louis XIV) or those who spectacularly failed (Charles I). But what of the whole range of rulers who occupy the middle ground between these two poles, those who muddled through difficult circumstances and achieved a moderate level of success, only to be overshadowed by their mightier contemporaries? Can we not learn just as much—if not more—about the nature of early modern monarchy by examining those who rallied against the odds and persevered in the face of debilitating crises, even if in doing so they failed to achieve a prominent place in the grand narratives of European history?

Holy Roman Emperor Ferdinand III (r. 1637–57) is one such ruler who can offer valuable lessons to the scholar of the early modern era. One of the most neglected figures within the pantheon of Habsburg emperors, Ferdinand III was overlooked by historians already in his own day: aside from an unfinished biography published in 1656, the Emperor did not receive a book-length biography until 2008, 400 years after his birth.[1] This neglect is not difficult to fathom. In contrast to the undisputed triumphs of the emperors flanking his reign, Ferdinand III never saw a major victory during his years on the imperial throne; his reign instead corresponded to the most harrowing decade of the Thirty Years' War, and his lasting legacy is the brokering of a peace treaty that was decidedly unfavorable to the Habsburgs. Ignored not just in the larger histories of Western Europe, Ferdinand III barely has a place in the grand narratives of the Habsburg monarchy.

But it is precisely Ferdinand III's overshadowed position between two giants that makes his reign worthy of closer attention. Ferdinand II (r. 1619–37) and Leopold I (r. 1658–1705) were different emperors with different accomplishments and correspondingly contrasting legacies. Ferdinand II stands out as the militant Counter-Reformer pursuing an unrelenting course of re-Catholicization in the Empire, the success of which was bolstered by military triumphs at the battles of White Mountain (1620) and Nördlingen (1634) and confirmed (albeit temporarily) by the

---

[1] Lothar Höbelt, *Ferdinand III. (1608–1657): Friedenskaiser wider Willen* (Graz, 2008). The unfinished biography is Galeazzo Gualdo Priorato, *Historia di Ferdinando Terzo Imperatore* (n.p., 1656; reprint, Vienna, 1672).

Peace of Prague (1635).[2] Leopold I, on the other hand, ascended the throne during a time of relative peace; although no less devoted to the Counter-Reformation cause, his lasting image is that of the peaceful foil to the ambitious expansionist Louis XIV, as well as the patron of (and frequent performer in) lavish operatic spectacles.[3] Leopold's greatest triumph, moreover, was the successful repulsion of the Turkish siege of Vienna in 1683, which led to the deliverance of Western Europe from the Turkish threat and helped elevate the Habsburgs back to the position of important players on the European stage.

So dissimilar was Leopold from Ferdinand II that his successes could have never followed directly upon the latter's reign. The elder Ferdinand's projects were unfinished at his death; the Peace of Prague was quickly undermined by France's declaration of war against the Habsburgs, which initiated the final phase of the Thirty Years' War. Ferdinand III's burden was the need to finish everything his father had started; although his maneuvering through the last decade of the war and the Peace of Westphalia may have weakened the Habsburgs' claims to world power, at the same time he managed to bring Ferdinand II's unfinished projects to a close with a relatively (and surprisingly) high degree of success, establishing within the Habsburg hereditary lands a sturdy foundation upon which Leopold could build.[4]

To borrow a popular and much debated trope from historians of the early modern era, Ferdinand III's reign coincides with a definite "crisis" in seventeenth-century Austria. From the Habsburg perspective, this was first and foremost a crisis of authority, as the dynasty struggled to maintain its position as a powerful political leader in the face of a losing war and changing balance of powers within the Holy Roman Empire and Europe as a whole.[5] The very crux of the Austrian crisis occurred precisely during

---

[2] Important monographs on Ferdinand II's reign include Robert Bireley, *Religion and Politics in the Age of the Counterreformation: Emperor Ferdinand II, William Lamormaini, S. J., and the Formation of Imperial Policy* (Chapel Hill, 1981) and Steven Saunders, *Cross, Sword and Lyre: Sacred Music at the Imperial Court of Ferdinand II of Habsburg (1619–1637)* (Oxford, 1995).

[3] See especially Maria Goloubeva, *The Glorification of Emperor Leopold I in Image, Spectacle, and Text* (Mainz, 2000).

[4] This point is made in (among other places) Robert Bireley, "Confessional Absolutism in the Habsburg Lands in the Seventeenth Century," in Charles W. Ingrao (ed.), *State and Society in Early Modern Austria* (West Lafayette, 1994), pp. 36–53 and Bireley, "Ferdinand II: Founder of the Habsburg Monarchy," in R.J.W. Evans and T.V. Thomas (eds), *Crown, Church and Estates: Central European Politics in the Sixteenth and Seventeenth Centuries* (London, 1991), pp. 226–44.

[5] The idea that the seventeenth-century "crisis" was essentially one of absolutism has been argued in Niels Steensgard, "The Seventeenth-Century Crisis," in Geoffrey Parker and Lesley M. Smith (eds), *The General Crisis of the Seventeenth Century*, 2nd edn (London,

Ferdinand III's reign; because he forms a crucial bridge between Ferdinand II and Leopold I, a close examination of his reign is necessary for a fuller understanding of the Habsburg dynasty during a critical time in European history.

A main premise of this book is that Ferdinand III's achievement was primarily a cultural one, a point that has been eloquently sustained in R.J.W. Evans's classic monograph *The Making of the Habsburg Monarchy*.[6] Instead of asserting and consolidating authority through increasingly bloated and ineffective government institutions,[7] the Habsburgs were best able to strengthen their authority through the promotion of a distinctive court culture dominated by the Catholic faith. Although this culture manifested itself in many ways, one important locus for all cultural activity at court, especially as related directly to the Habsburgs' political power, was the Emperor's public image.

Ferdinand III provides an especially fascinating case study in monarchical representation, for the circumstances of the war forced him to revise the image he had cultivated at the beginning of his reign: that of a mighty, victorious warrior. By examining the revision of Ferdinand's image in the face of increasingly dire political and military circumstances, this book seeks to gain insight into the means by which Habsburg power was secured and stabilized in the troubled decade of the 1640s. In the process, it offers a new perspective on the representation of early modern monarchs, going beyond the well-known examples of such rulers as Elizabeth I and Louis XIV; this is especially true in that the main focus of inquiry, Latin-texted sacred music, has not been explored by scholars as a significant means of monarchical representation.

In recent years, scholars have argued that the representations of early modern monarchs were more than mere projections of a ruler's actual, perceived, or desired power and authority. Rather, in light of a wide range of studies that construe power not "simply as the capacity of sovereign agents to enact their will, but as complex negotiations between rulers

---

1997), pp. 32–56 and Theodore K. Rabb, *The Struggle for Stability in Early Modern Europe* (Oxford and New York, 1975), pp. 33–4.

[6] R.J.W. Evans, *The Making of the Habsburg Monarchy, 1550–1700: An Interpretation* (Oxford, 1979). This point is also made in Howard Louthan, *Converting Bohemia: Force and Persuasion in the Catholic Reformation* (Cambridge, 2009), pp. 19–20.

[7] On the imperial government, see Jeroen Duindam, *Vienna and Versailles: The Courts of Europe's Dynastic Rivals, 1550–1780* (Cambridge, 2003), pp. 223–97; Evans, pp. 146–51; Henry Frederick Schwarz, *The Imperial Privy Council in the Seventeenth Century* (Cambridge, MA, 1943); John P. Spielman, *The City and the Crown: Vienna and the Imperial Court, 1600–1740* (West Lafayette, 1993), pp. 53–74.

and subjects,"[8] scholars such as Kevin Sharpe and Louis Montrose have identified monarchical representations as an important site of such negotiations, one of the primary means through which rulers sought both to maintain and also to actively construct their power.[9] The ruler's image thus not only reflected perceptions but also shaped them, in a complex process that flowed in both directions between rulers and subjects, mediated by the people in charge of creating the artworks. Representations acted as a dialogue within the shared discourse of power, projecting the monarch's desired authority while simultaneously responding to the needs of his subjects.[10] In order to maintain his power, a typical early modern ruler could not be a blind autocrat but needed to use his image to address his subjects' concerns, justify his actions, and demonstrate how he served the people's best interests, thereby securing good relations with the elites on whom he depended to finance his government, fill the ranks of his army, and keep his state running smoothly. The royal image was thus not only an assertion of power controlled by the monarch but also a means by which the monarch himself was controlled; it set expectations and limits, impressed but also reassured, and above all presented a model for the ruler to follow.

A corollary to the idea of representation as a negotiation between ruler and subjects is the idea that representations were also inherently unstable and open to diverse interpretations, that they held as much potential to undermine as to sustain authority. As Sharpe has written,

> Authority in all ages has needed—and still needs—to be performed, written and displayed: to be publicized. But publication and publicization render authority public, that is constructed and determined by public audiences as well as communicated to them. By authoring and presenting themselves, rulers made themselves available to interpretation and so made readers and spectators of the scripts and spectacles of state into critics of government.[11]

---

[8] Kevin Sharpe, *Selling the Tudor Monarchy: Authority and Image in Sixteenth-Century England* (New Haven and London, 2009), p. 9.

[9] Sharpe, *Selling*; Sharpe, "Sacralization and Demystification: The Publicization of Monarchy in Early Modern England," in Jeroen Deploige and Gita Deneckere (eds), *Mystifying the Monarch: Studies on Discourse, Power, and History* (Amsterdam, 2006), pp. 99–115; Sharpe, "Representations and Negotiations: Texts, Images, and Authority in Early Modern England," *Historical Journal*, 42 (1999): pp. 853–81; Louis Montrose, *The Subject of Elizabeth: Authority, Gender and Representation* (Chicago, 2006).

[10] Kevin Sharpe, "'So Hard a Text'? Images of Charles I, 1612–1700," *Historical Journal*, 43 (2000): p. 384.

[11] Sharpe, *Selling*, p. 18.

This phenomenon impressed upon early modern rulers the importance of persuasion, in service of which the *form* of an artwork and the manner in which it was presented were equally important as its intended meaning. The type of media (medal, canvas, engraving, panegyric, theater, firework, music), the context in which it was presented (court festivity, joyous entry, religious procession, liturgical service), the means by which it was distributed (public exhibition, the commercial marketplace, a gift), the very style of an artwork (overwhelmingly elaborate, classically ordered and balanced, straightforward and popularizing, large scale or intimate); all of this directly impacted how audiences consumed and interpreted the image and to what extent they accepted or contested the ruler's power.[12] Regardless of the specific images on a triumphal arch or the words of a sermon, the sheer experience of being present at a joyous entry and at a coronation mass could announce a city's acceptance of the ruler's power and the divine nature of kingship, respectively; if, however, a picture of the arch or the text of the sermon were disseminated via print, what may have seemed to a spectator an ancillary embellishment could take on a life of its own and assume a new persuasive function for someone who had not been present at the original occasion. A large portrait hanging in a richly decorated antechamber conveyed power through its surroundings, while the same image reproduced in an inexpensive printed engraving could be given an entirely new context and function with a richly decorated frame.[13] The same piece of music, furthermore, could be received differently when heard in either a private devotional service in the royal chapel or a public liturgy in a large cathedral, which in turn is different from reading the music in the pages of a commercial print.

To achieve success, the ruler thus needed to negotiate carefully between the many means of representation and the contexts in which they could be received, two concerns that will guide my readings of artworks throughout this book. Yet despite this need to direct the audience's interpretation as much as possible, no ruler ever had total control in the creation and distribution of his representations. The most well-known paradigm today is the conscious "fabrication" of Louis XIV through a carefully planned program under the auspices of centralized artistic academies,[14] but that model was neither as "absolute" as is widely claimed nor applicable to the great majority of early modern monarchs. In most cases, a ruler's

---

[12] The importance of the type of media is discussed in Montrose, pp. 5–6 and Sharpe, *Selling*, pp. 41–52.

[13] On allegorical frames in engraved portraits, see Elisabeth von Hagenow, *Bildniskommentare: Allegorisch gerahmte Herrscherbildnisse in der Graphik des Barock: Entstehung und Bedeutung* (Hildesheim, 1999).

[14] Peter Burke, *The Fabrication of Louis XIV* (New Haven, 1992).

representation was conceived not by a single centralized authority but by a diverse, heterogeneous group consisting of the ruler, his family, government officials, courtiers, ecclesiastical figures, and other elites (including those not specifically attached to the court), all of whom had their own motivations and goals and for whom the glorification of the ruler could serve to legitimize their own power as much as it enhanced the monarch's.[15] To this must be added the plethora of "unofficial" representations stemming from outside the court, including those created by foreign courts and artists as an homage to the ruler; appropriations of the official image for purposes unintended by the court; as well as underground, subversive images, which had the potential to have as great an effect on a ruler's representation as the laudatory representations authorized by the court. The image was also controlled to no small extent by the artists themselves: the writers, composers, painters, sculptors, architects, engineers, and other artisans and laborers, as well as the musicians, actors, and dancers who brought many of the creations to life. All of these creators could have their own motivations and agendas that affected the inception and reception of the work, and the effect is only multiplied in the case of the grand state spectacles (operas, processions, entries) conceived, created, and performed by epic numbers of people.

As the elected ruler of the large, disjointed Holy Roman Empire, Ferdinand III directly experienced these challenges of successful representation. Even without taking into account the crisis of the Thirty Years' War, the political constitution of Ferdinand's various realms demonstrates the precarious balancing act inherent in any representation. Within his hereditary lands Ferdinand acted as direct sovereign, but he depended on the estate assemblies for the day-to-day governing of his realm and the implementation of his political decrees.[16] His political power as construed by his public image was directed primarily to the estates, whose best interest was served by supporting the Emperor's image in that it helped maintain their own (often considerable) political power. To support his imperial identity, the Emperor had also to use the same image to negotiate power with the electors and other principalities of the Empire, a much trickier proposition considering the varying levels of sovereignty enjoyed by the territories, not to mention the multiplicity of confessional loyalties throughout the realm. This audience, while respecting the institutions of the Empire, had different expectations of the reach of the Emperor's power. On top of this, Ferdinand III, like any other European monarch, had to be mindful of diplomatic relations with foreign powers throughout Europe, for which his image served yet another function.

---

[15] Sharpe, *Selling*, pp. 20–21, 40; Montrose, p. 105; Goloubeva, pp. 2–3.
[16] Duindam, pp. 274–9.

In all of these cases, the negotiations of power were mediated through the court, which played a significant, multifaceted role in the creation and consumption of the Emperor's image. On one hand, as the main agents through which the image was passed on to the estates and other sovereigns, individual ambassadors, administrators, and other courtiers served as the primary audience for whom official representations were intended. On the other hand, Ferdinand III regularly presented himself outside the walls of the Hofburg, through both processions and religious services in the city of Vienna and frequent travels to other cities of the Empire. On these occasions, the court as an entity served as the main vehicle of the Emperor's representation, together presenting through collective ceremonial actions Ferdinand's image to a broad audience comprising everybody from wealthy merchants to illiterate peasants. Even on these occasions, however, specific messages could be directed to the elites who comprised the Emperor's entourage. The court thus served a unique function as both audience and agent, which emphasizes the fluid, dynamic process through which the Emperor's image was created and consumed.

In light of this conception of the Emperor's representation as a negotiated, unstable commodity over which he could never exert complete control, it may come as a surprise that, throughout the book, I analyze Ferdinand III's image from a primarily "top–down" perspective—as a creation by the court with specific intended meanings—and pay little attention to reception and effectiveness. This approach, however, is grounded in specific practical, methodological, and conceptual circumstances. From the practical perspective, the surviving evidence almost demands a top–down approach; due to the relative paucity of documents (stemming no doubt from the neglect of Ferdinand III by later generations), the vast majority of surviving artifacts presenting the Emperor's image (especially during the 1640s) comes from official court sources, with little to no documentation of the behind-the-scenes machinations that went into their creation: publications (opera libretti, panegyrics, reports of court festivities) issued by the official court printer and other publishers under court auspices, music prints by court musicians, paintings and engravings by artists employed by the Habsburgs, and the like. The dearth of evidence of the reception of these works (in the form of eyewitness accounts of musical performances and court festivities, sales records of commercial products, and extensive evidence of the distribution of works throughout the realm) also creates a circumstance in which we have little choice but to analyze from the top down rather than the bottom up.[17] Due to these limitations

---

[17] In *Music and Wonder at the Medici Court: The 1589 Interludes for* La Pellegrina (Bloomington, 2008), Nina Treadwell analyzes the work's reception and effectiveness by

(on account of which we can often not be entirely sure who instigated an image), I have occasionally found it convenient to use the terms "the Emperor" and "Ferdinand III" as shorthand for the main agent behind the creation of imperial representations, but in most cases this needs to be understood as a synecdoche for the entire political establishment that had a stake in the image.

This is not to say, however, that I ignore the issue of the negotiation of the Emperor's image or the malleability of interpretations. For one thing, in instances in which the author of a work is known—especially in the case of the music prints by Giovanni Felice Sances that serve as the main source for much of the music discussed in the book—consideration is always given to the author's background and possible motivations, with an eye to how those motivations (which may or may not be in line with the goals of the Emperor and his court) may have affected the presentation and reception of the image. For another thing, in regard to published texts, Sharpe has drawn attention to the concept (originating with scholarship on the history of the book) of the "imagined reader" as an agent in their creation, for whom the author devises strategies to guide interpretation and ensure the intended reception of the text.[18] This concept applies directly to the various printed materials discussed in this book, including Sances's prints. By paying close attention to paratexts and other aspects of a print that add context and meaning to the works it contains, we can explore how the court approached the challenge of negotiating with a diffuse anonymous audience and directing the reader's attention to an official interpretation. By reading between the lines of paratexts, approaching artworks as multivalent creations, and always keeping in mind the many possible interpretations that audiences may have brought to works, I aim to bring the audience into the construction of the representation as much as possible given the available evidence.

My top–down approach, moreover, accords with the larger goals I have set out for the book. Because I aim to elucidate the means through which Ferdinand III sought to maintain Habsburg authority at the end of a disastrous war, the *strategies* through which his public image was revised serve as more valuable avenues for inquiry than the reception and effectiveness of the resulting artworks. Even if audiences failed to grasp the meaning of an artwork, the meaning that the court intended

---

comparing the misinterpretations and misreadings in the various unofficial eyewitness accounts with the printed musical score and the official prose description of the event. Such an approach is not possible for me, given the available documents for the artworks I discuss in this book.

[18] Sharpe, *Selling*, pp. 22–6.

it to communicate is still valuable.[19] In the short run, one can easily dismiss Ferdinand III's representational efforts as a failure, judging by the absence of critical reactions to the artworks, the sparse evidence of their dissemination, and the rapid disappearance of the Emperor from the collective European memory. Viewed from a broader perspective, however, the strategies that I identify as guiding Ferdinand's representations lived on beyond his reign; as we will see, they seemed to guide aspects of later rulers' representations. Thus, even if the strategies did not bring Ferdinand III lasting posterity, they were still considered a valid model for later generations, from which fact we can deduce that they must have had some measure of success in promoting the image intended by the court. By examining imperial artworks in light of their presumed function during a critical time of transition for the Habsburg monarchy, I provide new insights into the ways that the arts, and especially sacred music, were marshaled in the service of monarchical representation.

This book falls into seven chapters divided into three parts plus an epilogue. Part I ("Setting the Stage") provides the necessary background for the investigation of Ferdinand III's representation during the 1640s. Chapter 1 sets up the central problem, providing a detailed look at Ferdinand's image as military victor during the late 1630s followed by a discussion of the events of the Thirty Years' War until 1643, during which time the imperial forces succumbed to increasingly disastrous defeats on the battlefield and the Emperor sought unsuccessfully to negotiate peace. This is then followed by an introduction to the main strategy through which the Emperor's image was revised, along with an explanation as to why sacred music proved to be the optimal medium through which to enact this revision. Chapter 2 provides a portrait of the main subject of the book, not through a biographical sketch but through detailed examinations of three important aspects of the Emperor's public life: his roles as Counter-Reformer, politician, and patron of the arts. These discussions, which include examinations of representations that relate to each role, provide a foundation upon which we can better understand the representations discussed in Part III. Chapter 2 also elucidates important concepts that ground my understanding of the Emperor's religious and political policies, most importantly the *Pietas Austriaca*, "anti-Machiavellianism," and "confessionalization."

---

[19] In this regard, I follow Tatiana C. String, *Art and Communication in the Reign of Henry VIII* (Aldershot: Ashgate, 2008), pp. 4–5: "What this book studies in particular is the *intent* to communicate. It is not a study of the *impact* of works of art in the communication process."

As music (and especially sacred music) has hitherto been little studied as a means of monarchical representation, Part II ("Means of Production") examines the primary ways in which this ephemeral art was able to contribute to a monarch's public image, with specific examples drawn from Ferdinand III's musical patronage. Chapter 3 focuses on the musical performance. It first examines the main contexts in which music was heard at the Habsburg court—opera, Jesuit drama, and the Catholic liturgy—with an eye to how the combined effect of sensory stimuli helped present the Emperor's image. The final section focuses on the music itself, discussing how sacred music was able to communicate to different listeners. Chapter 4 discusses the representational function of music when disseminated via the commercial print. After a general discussion of the means by which music prints could serve as representation, the bulk of the chapter discusses Sances's substantial body of publications. The chapter concludes by considering additional prints by non-court composers that also contributed to Ferdinand III's image during the 1640s.

Part III ("Music as Representation") examines specific musical works that represented Ferdinand III and helped enact the revision of his public image. Chapter 5 discusses the phenomenon of musical portraiture, pieces of sacred music that present images of the Emperor and communicate the same sorts of messages found in painted or engraved images. Divided into two chronological sections, one focusing on music published in 1638 and the other on music published in the 1640s, the chapter also provides concrete evidence of the revision of Ferdinand's image. Chapter 6 focuses on two seemingly contrasting aspects of the Emperor's religious life: his Eucharistic piety and his adherence to mystical theology. The former manifested itself primarily in public displays of piety to a large audience, while the latter resided in the Emperor's inner spirituality, presented primarily to the educated elites close to him. By examining imperial sacred music composed for these devotions, we learn that, despite differences in style, performance context, and dissemination, both Eucharistic and mystical motets served the same representational functions: providing a mirror of Ferdinand's devout soul and a model for his subjects (and himself) to follow. Chapter 7 ties together many of threads discussed throughout the book with a discussion of the most important aspect of Ferdinand III's public image: his devotion to the Blessed Virgin of the Immaculate Conception. Although in the early years of his reign the Emperor's Marian devotion was of a private, personal nature, by transforming his private devotion into a public cult in the face of a siege of Vienna in 1645, Ferdinand brilliantly used his image to bind his subjects to him and assert his authority. This public cult was exemplified not only by the music of his chapel but by the construction of the *Mariensäule* (Marian column) in

Vienna's *Platz am Hof*, a monument that set an important precedent for Ferdinand's successors.

The book concludes with an Epilogue that provides an overview of the flourishing of artistic representations in many media during the 1650s, which constituted yet another revision of Ferdinand III's image after the Peace of Westphalia. The Epilogue also provides an assessment of the significance of Ferdinand's image and a consideration of the legacy that his representational strategies left for later rulers.

Before concluding this Introduction, I must discuss a few technical matters. When analyzing the harmonic language of music composed before 1660, the conceptual framework of our major–minor system of tonality is inadequate for describing the music's expressive effect. In this regard, I have found especially useful the modal–hexachordal system as explicated by Eric Chafe and elaborated upon by later scholars.[20] In this system, the harmonic framework of a composition is conceptualized via the hexachord, a scalar sequence of six pitches that correspond to the first six notes of our major scale. The Middle Ages acknowledged the existence of three hexachords (which served as pedagogical devices): the natural hexachord beginning on C, the soft (or *mollis*) hexachord beginning on F and featuring a B-flat, and the hard (or *durus*) hexachord beginning on G and featuring a B-natural. If the pitches of a hexachord are ordered not as a scale but in fifths from flattest to sharpest (that is, the hexachord C–D–E–F–G–A rearranged to F–C–G–D–A–E), they create a system of three interlocking hexachords, in which the natural hexachord is flanked by the other two hexachords, each extending a fifth beyond the central hexachord (see Table I.1). This system, or *cantus*, serves as a harmonic framework within which we can understand the music from Ferdinand III's court. The entire harmonic language of the composition is provided by the notes of the three hexachords, each of which can serve as the root of a triad. Only the six pitches of the central hexachord, however, serve as the available cadence points.

---

[20] Eric Chafe, *Monteverdi's Tonal Language* (New York, 1992); Beverly Stein, "Between Key and Mode: Tonal Practice in the Music of Giacomo Carissimi" (Ph.D. diss., Brandeis University, 1994); Susan Shimp, "The Art of Persuasion: Domenico Mazzocchi and the Counter-Reformation" (Ph.D. diss., Yale University, 2000).

Table I.1   The arrangement of hexachords in *cantus durus*

soft hexachord	B-flat	F	C	G	D	A	
natural hexachord		F	C	G	D	A	E
hard hexachord			C	G	D	A	E	B

The beauty of this system is that it allowed composers to exploit the sharp and flat ends of the *cantus* for expressive effect, for example by harmonizing one section of a composition with chords based on the flattest notes (B-flat, F, C) and then harmonizing the next section with chords on the sharpest notes (A, E, B-natural). Composers could also create new systems by adding hexachords based on sharper or flatter pitches to either end of the basic system. The most common other system is the *cantus mollis*, which is centered on the *mollis* hexachord and flanked on the flat end by the hexachord containing two flats (E-flat, B-flat, F, C, G, D) and on the sharp end by the natural hexachord. One of the most expressive ways that composers employed the modal–hexachordal system was to switch during the course of a work between *cantus mollis* and *cantus durus*.

In my music examples, I have endeavored to remain true to the original source, which entailed reproducing all accidentals as they appear, even when this produces accidentals that are redundant according to modern practice. The editorial methods employed are those currently favored by A-R Editions in the series "Recent Researches in the Music of the Baroque Era" and include regularizing barlines and placing in angle brackets text repetitions indicated in the source by "ij."[21] Obvious errors in the source have been tacitly emended, and editorial accidentals and figured bass have been added in square brackets only when absolutely necessary. In the presentation of the texts of musical works, spelling and capitalization have been standardized, and punctuation has been added. The sources for individual lines in the motet texts are cited in endnotes at the conclusion of the chapter. In the transcriptions of the texts of all other documents, spelling, capitalization, and punctuation are reproduced exactly as in the original source. Unless stated otherwise, all translations are my own.

---

[21] See Giovanni Felice Sances, *Motetti a 2, 3, 4, e cinque voci (1642)*, ed. Andrew H. Weaver, RRMBE, vol. 148 (Middleton, 2008), pp. 217–19.

PART I
Setting the Stage

CHAPTER 1

Ferdinand III's Public Image and the Thirty Years' War

Amid a brilliant trumpet fanfare, Emperor Ferdinand II and his 28-year-old son Ferdinand III entered the richly decorated imperial hall of the Regensburg Rathaus. Five days earlier the younger Ferdinand had been crowned King of the Romans (ensuring that he would succeed his father as emperor), and now, on January 4, 1637, they were celebrating the coronation with a grand ballet organized by the Emperor's wife Eleonora Gonzaga.[1] The King and the Emperor took their seats next to their wives in a box placed directly in front of a newly constructed theater fitted with stage machinery and decorated with a curtain of silver and red silk, gleaming in the light of many torches. Strategically positioned on both sides of the box were platforms on which sat important political figures. On the right sat the Catholic electors of Mainz and Bavaria and Ferdinand III's younger brother Archduke Leopold Wilhelm, with the ambassadors to the Papal and Spanish courts positioned on a separate platform further to their right. To the left of the Emperor's box sat the Elector of Cologne, the wife of the Bavarian elector, and Ferdinand III's sister Archduchess Cecilia Renata, while further to their left sat the ambassadors of the Protestant electors of Saxony and Brandenburg. Behind these eminent spectators were benches and chairs holding about a hundred additional princes, ambassadors, and other nobles; only people of the highest quality had been permitted to enter the Rathaus that evening.

Suddenly from behind the theater came marvelous music played by many instruments. As the spectators marveled at the melodious strains, onto the stage rolled a triumphal chariot containing six singers from the imperial chapel, superbly dressed in a variety of colors and bearing insignia representing the Habsburg realms. The musicians sang of their great pleasure at the coronation of "the Austrian Hero," and once the chariot reached its destination, they rose and took turns paying homage to the new King. The first to sing was the musician representing the kingdom of Hungary (which Ferdinand III ruled), who thanked God for providing the strength with which

---

[1] This discussion is based on *Le quattro Relazioni seguite in Ratisbona nelli tempi sotto notati ... Terza del Balleto fatto nella Casa del Consiglio di detta Città li 4. Gennaro 1637 ...* (Vienna, 1637). A transcription of excerpts from this report is in Herbert Seifert, *Die Oper am Wiener Kaiserhof im 17. Jahrhundert* (Tützing, 1985), pp. 626–7. A manuscript libretto of the ballet (written by Valeriano Bonvicino) is A-Wn, Cod. 9931.

the pious Ferdinand was able to protect the country from cruel enemies. As he sang in his concluding aria, "Cosi lieto, e contento, / O mio Regno, / Vedrai spento, / l'Hoste indegno [Thus happy and content, O my Kingdom, you will see the unworthy enemy subdued]."[2] Hungary was followed by another kingdom that Ferdinand III ruled, Bohemia, who sang directly to the Emperor, joyfully thanking him for providing such a glorious, strong, invincible King of the Romans. The two kingdoms were then followed by Austria, Styria, and Alsace. Austria addressed Ferdinand III, extolling the happiness and prosperity he brought to the land; Styria addressed the electors, thanking them for choosing such a strong and pious hero; and Alsace congratulated the entire Empire for the security promised by the new King: "Egli, potente, e invitto, / Mostrerà quanto vale / Virtù, contro furrore, / Contro rabbia, valore, / Contro l'Invidia livida, e malvaggia, / Merto sovrano, e con il ferro ignudo, / Sarà difesa tua, tuo schermo, e scudo [He, powerful and invincible, shall demonstrate so much true virtue against the furious, valor against the angry, sovereign merit against the livid and evil Envy, and with the naked sword he will be your defense and your shield]."[3] For, as Alsace concluded in his final aria, "è un Re guerriero, / Pio, Vincitore, e Giusto."[4]

Following these praises, the sixth musician, representing Tyrol, congratulated the other hereditary lands on their good fortune to be ruled by the Habsburgs. Tyrol's aria had barely finished when a great eagle descended from the top of the theater, upon which sat a seventh singer (the most virtuosic of all of them), representing the Holy Roman Empire. From above the center of the stage, this singer praised Ferdinand III's piety and strength and congratulated the electors for restoring the ancient majesty and splendor of the Empire.[5] Tyrol then invited the other singers and their noble citizens to join in a celebratory dance, thus initiating a splendid ballet performed by 20 of the Emperor's pages and 20 of the highest ladies of the court led by Cecilia Renata, which led to an hour-long communal ball that brought the marvelous evening to a close. In this way, through a spectacular, costly multi-media theatrical extravaganza organized by the Empress, written by one of her chaplains, and performed by the Emperor's musical establishment together with members of the imperial court, the Emperor-elect was glorified to the noble audience, branded with the image of a just ruler, a pious man, and especially a powerful, brave, victorious warrior.

---

[2] A-Wn, Cod. 9931, fol. 11r.
[3] Ibid., fols 16v–17r.
[4] "He is a warlike King, Pious, Victorious, and Just" (ibid., fol. 17r).
[5] Ibid., fol. 19v.

Public Image: Ferdinand the Military Victor

That the prevailing component of Ferdinand III's image celebrated in the 1637 ballet was his strength as a powerful, undefeated warrior should come as no surprise when the event is placed into the context of this particular juncture of the Thirty Years' War. Although by 1637 the war had been dragging on for nearly twenty years, it was still going relatively well for the Habsburgs, and they were perhaps somewhat justified in believing that it might soon be over. This optimism was due primarily to the triumphant imperial victory at the Battle of Nördlingen on September 6, 1634, which had resulted in the Peace of Prague (May 30, 1635), an important (albeit compromised) win for the Emperor's Catholic cause that simultaneously managed to placate—if only temporarily—his German adversaries.[6] Although France had declared war on the Habsburgs shortly after the signing of the peace treaty, the French army's initial forays on the battlefield were decidedly not successful,[7] and the imperial forces were able to keep the powerful Swedish army at bay.[8] Nördlingen was thus still fresh in the historical memory, not having yet been tarnished with devastating military setbacks.

The Battle of Nördlingen, together with the siege and re-conquest of Regensburg that preceded it, were especially crucial for Ferdinand III's public image. In May 1634, after the death of the notorious General Albrecht von Wallenstein, Emperor Ferdinand II had appointed his eldest son as General of the imperial army. The future Emperor thus had a direct hand in the battle, to the extent that he could claim full responsibility for the victory. This personal involvement in the most significant imperial victory to date became the foundation of Ferdinand's martial image, and it was celebrated in artworks in a variety of media as early as the year of the battle itself. The most monumental of these is a huge canvas by Rubens that now hangs in Vienna's

---

[6] Geoffrey Parker (ed.), *The Thirty Years' War*, 2nd edn (London and Boston, 1997), pp. 127–8. A detailed discussion of the Battle of Nördlingen is in William P. Guthrie, *Battles of the Thirty Years War: From White Mountain to Nordlingen, 1618–1635* (Westport, 2002), pp. 259–96. For excellent discussions of the Peace of Prague (from two different perspectives) see Ronald G. Asch, *The Thirty Years' War: The Holy Roman Empire and Europe, 1618–48* (New York, 1997), pp. 110–17 and Robert Bireley, *Religion and Politics in the Age of the Counterreformation: Emperor Ferdinand II, William Lamormaini, S. J., and the Formation of Imperial Policy* (Chapel Hill, 1981), pp. 209–29.

[7] Richard J. Bonney, "France's 'War by Diversion,'" in Parker, *Thirty Years' War*, pp. 129–37.

[8] In October 1636, the Swedes defeated the imperial forces at the nearly indecisive Battle of Wittstock, but by June 1637 they were forced to retreat north to Pomerania, and by spring 1638 they had lost almost all the gains won at Wittstock; William P. Guthrie, *The Later Thirty Years War: From the Battle of Wittstock to the Treaty of Westphalia* (Westport, 2003), pp. 54–61.

Figure 1.1 Peter Paul Rubens, *The Meeting before the Battle of Nördlingen*, 328 × 388 cm, oil on canvas, ca. 1634–35, Kunsthistorisches Museum, Vienna

Kunsthistorisches Museum (Figure 1.1).[9] The painting depicts a moment just prior to the battle as the future Emperor (on the left) greets his cousin and ally, the Cardinal-Infante Ferdinand of Spain, an event that Rubens has transformed into one of timeless significance. Observing the two generals are allegorical figures of the Danube and Germania; their forms are larger than those of the mortals and fill the bottom third of the canvas. Though the battle has not yet occurred, the inevitability of the victory is signaled by the eagles swooping down to crown the men with the laurel wreaths reserved for great heroes. To viewers of this painting, the imperial army's triumph was preordained by God himself. Another celebration of the battle that makes even more explicit the role of divine providence in assuring the victory is a painting by Cornelius Schut depicting the two generals on horseback and carrying batons (the conventional symbol for military command), riding over

---

[9] Peter Paul Rubens, *The Meeting before the Battle of Nördlingen*, oil painting on canvas, ca. 1634–35, KHM; reproduced in color in Wilfried Seipel (ed.), *Kunsthistorisches Museum Wien: The Picture Gallery*, trans. Gitta Holroyd-Reece (Innsbruck, 1996), pp. 206–7.

Figure 1.2   Cornelius Schut, *Victory at Nördlingen*, 226 × 160 cm, oil on canvas, 1635, STAM, Ghent, inv. 711

the bodies of slain enemies while the Virgin Mary and baby Jesus smile down from heaven (Figure 1.2).[10]

As powerful as these paintings are in projecting Ferdinand III's military might, neither was created specifically with the future Emperor's glorification in mind. Rather, they were painted for the Cardinal-Infante, to decorate triumphal arches for his joyous entries into Ghent (January 27, 1635) and Antwerp (April 17, 1635) as the new Governor of the Spanish Netherlands.[11] More significant are those images that were commissioned by Ferdinand III himself. One famous example is a portrait painted ca. 1639 by the Emperor's court artist Frans Luyckx (Figure 1.3).[12] In this full-length portrait, the Emperor stands in gilded armor, looking directly out at the viewers and engaging us with a firm, confident gaze. To his left is a table holding his helmet, along with a map diagramming the Battle of Nördlingen.

The battle and Ferdinand's role in it were also celebrated in a number of more ephemeral media disseminated by the imperial court. Among the medals created in 1634 in commemoration of the victory is one that explicitly references Nördlingen and Ferdinand's participation in the battle (Figure 1.4).[13] One side shows a full riding portrait, with the General in full armor holding a command baton with the city of Nördlingen in the background. The reverse illustrates the battle itself, with a German inscription, "Victory at Nördlingen."

The court also commissioned a number of printed portrait engravings that celebrate Ferdinand III's military prowess. In one picture made by the German engraver Lucas Schnitzer in 1634, the future Emperor, in full armor and carrying his baton, mounts a rearing horse (Figure 1.5).[14] He is perched on a hillside before a panoramic view of a battle, labeled in the lower right corner as Nördlingen. The re-conquest of Regensburg is celebrated in an anonymous

---

[10] Cornelius Schut, *Victory at Nördlingen*, oil painting on canvas, 1635, Ghent, STAM; color reproduction in Klaus Bussmann and Heinz Schilling (eds.), *1648: War and Peace in Europe* (3 vols, [Münster], 1998), Catalogue, p. 119 (fig. 353).

[11] Schut's painting was for Ghent and Rubens's for Antwerp. For more information on the Antwerp entry and the artworks created for it, see ibid., pp. 133–7.

[12] Frans Luyckx, *Ferdinand III*, oil painting on canvas, ca. 1639, Stockholm, Nationalmuseum, Gripsholm; color reproduction in Bussmann and Schilling, Catalogue, p. 73 (fig. 151). The Flemish Luyckx (1604–68) became court painter to Ferdinand III in 1638; the Emperor favored him greatly and ennobled him in 1652.

[13] KHM, Münzkabinett, #b 1001.

[14] A-Wn, Bildarchiv, Pg 149 137/3 in Ptf 123: I (66). Schnitzer (active 1630–71) worked primarily in Nuremberg; his favorite subjects were images from battles and cityscapes, and he also issued a series of imperial portraits. See Ursula Mielke and Tilman Falk (eds), *Johann Schnitzer to Lucas Schnitzer*, Hollstein's German Engravings, Etchings, and Woodcuts, 1400–1700, vol. 46 (Rotterdam, 1999), p. 5.

Figure 1.3 Frans Luyckx, *Ferdinand III*, 214 × 141 cm, oil on canvas, ca. 1639, © the Nationalmuseum, Stockholm

Figure 1.4   Medal honoring the Battle of Nördlingen, 4 cm, 1634

engraving from 1634 (Figure 1.6).[15] Although Ferdinand is not dressed in military garb (he instead wears the mantle and turban of the Hungarian king), the rich frame surrounding the oval portrait proclaims his military might. On the lower right a subjugated enemy falls backwards, while on the left a map illustrates the victory at Regensburg. Atop the picture, a laurel wreath and two trumpets announce Ferdinand's glory, while below a Latin inscription proclaims:

> Here stands FERDINAND THE THIRD of the lineage of the Throne of Austria, under whom the fortunate Line of his FATHER is now born anew to the Empire: whom the happy region of Hungary reveres as King, and before whom Bohemia truly trembles, and whose illustrious deeds the brave citizens of Regensburg and Norica [a region of the Empire comprising Central Austria and Bavaria] witnessed in war.

Ferdinand's powerful military image was also celebrated in a variety of works that appeared throughout Europe without the imperial family's initiative. Such "unofficial" works must always be approached with caution, for they resulted from a tangled web of motivations that can often be difficult to decipher. On the most basic level, the creator of the work was ingratiating himself to the new ruler, but more often a third party (such as the artist's patron) mediated this interaction between addresser and addressee; in many cases, the work could have had more meaning to this third party than to Ferdinand himself. This is especially true for works that, although praising Ferdinand, bear a dedication to someone else. Did the dedicatee commission the work from the artist in order to ingratiate himself to the new ruler? Did

---

[15]   A-Wn, Bildarchiv, Pg 149 137/3 in Ptf 123: I (4c).

Figure 1.5   Lucas Schnitzer, *Ferdinand III*, engraving, 1634

the artist include the dedication in order to add visibility to his work, making it more likely that Ferdinand would pay attention to it? To what extent were artist and/or dedicatee trying to admonish and control the ruler as opposed to simply glorifying him? Because of these and similar questions, the circumstances behind each of these artworks must be closely examined on a case-by-case basis, a task that lies outside the scope of this chapter. Nevertheless, such

Figure 1.6   Anonymous engraving of Ferdinand III, 1634

works, even if Ferdinand III never saw them, were important contributions to his public image.[16] Peter Burke has pointed out that works by foreign artists were of much value to a monarch, demonstrating to the viewer the great honor with which a ruler was held outside of his immediate circle and homeland.[17] These works are also important for demonstrating the extent to which the "official" image promulgated by the court was recognized and accepted throughout Europe.

In this regard, it is significant that in all of the sources that I have examined, two themes dominate: Ferdinand's military valor and his immense piety; these are often connected in that the latter is usually praised as a main reason for triumphs on the battlefield. These two themes converge, for example, in the illustrated frontispiece of the Venetian Antonino Collurafi's *L'aquila coronata*, a panegyric to Ferdinand III on the occasion of his ascension to the imperial throne (see Figure 1.7).[18] The unmistakable imperial symbol of the double-headed eagle dominates the engraving; behind the eagle stand allegorical representations of piety (in a veil and carrying a cross) on the left and of war (wearing a helmet and carrying lance and shield) on the right, which together are crowning the eagle with a (not very accurate) rendering of the imperial crown. The 44-page text is devoted entirely to glorifying Ferdinand's military valor and piety, with perhaps slightly more emphasis on the latter. This comes through in a list provided halfway through the work of who is rejoicing at the new Emperor's ascension: in order, God, the angels, the Church, Virtue, Peace, War, the army, Fortune, and the entire world, including of course the Pope and Venice.[19] Ferdinand's military valor is practically the sole subject of an eight-page panegyric by the Milanese Guglielmo Plati, published with a dedication to the Captain General and Governor of Milan, Diego Felipez de Guzmán, Marquis of Leganés.[20] This hyperbolic encomium offers effusive praise of Ferdinand's military might, including references to Nördlingen and frequent comparisons with illustrious Classical and mythical figures; a long list of character traits, for instance, states (among other things) that Ferdinand is as magnanimous as Alexander the Great, as just as Trajan, as learned as Caesar Augustus, as faithful as Constantine, as strong as Ajax, as invincible

---

[16] Almost all of the books discussed here, however, appear in manuscript catalogues of the imperial library prepared during the reigns of Ferdinand III (A-Wn, Cod. 13555, Cod. 13556, Cod. 13557, Cod. Ser. n. 4450) and Leopold I (A-Wn, Cod. 12590, Cod. 12592).

[17] Peter Burke, *The Fabrication of Louis XIV* (New Haven, 1992), pp. 52–3.

[18] Antonino Collurafi, *L'aquila coronata overo la felicita sospirata dall'universo* (Venice, 1637).

[19] Ibid., pp. 22–3.

[20] Guglielmo Plati, *La Gloria, Panegirico per le Grandezze di Ferdinando III. Re de' Romani eletto* (Milan, 1637). The emphasis on military valor may well be due to the tastes of the dedicatee, who was renowned for his military exploits.

Figure 1.7   Frontispiece of Antonino Collurafi, *L'aquila coronata*, 1637

as Hercules, and as ingenious as Ulysses.[21] A fascinating work published by the Silesian Matthias Jacobus celebrates Ferdinand's military might through a series of images created by cleverly positioned Latin words, most of which feature acrostics of the Emperor's name (see, for example, the "dagger of providence" illustrated in Figure 1.8).[22]

The foreign center that saw the largest number of celebrations of Ferdinand's powerful, pious image was Rome, for during these critical years of the war it was deemed crucial that Rome and the Empire appear to form a united front against both the threat of Protestant heresy and the danger posed by the bellicose Turks.[23] For the entire month of January 1637, the eternal city saw countless spectacular festivities celebrating the new King of the Romans, including spoken and sung dramatic productions, speeches, and fireworks. All of these were sponsored by people or institutions closely connected to imperial politics: the Spanish ambassador, the imperial ambassador, the German judge on the Papal Rota, the Cardinal Protector of the Holy Roman Empire (whose job was to protect imperial interests at the Papal court), the Jesuit *Collegio Germanico*, and the churches of the German and Spanish communities in Rome.[24] One of the fireworks presented by the Spanish ambassador featured a square tower that split down the middle to reveal a round tower. This round tower then broke apart to reveal a larger-than-life statue of Ferdinand III in full armor on horseback, carrying the command baton and wearing the imperial crown. The many stages of this grand display were captured in a series of engravings by Claude Lorrain.[25] Of the many publications commemorating

[21] Ibid., sigs A5–A5v: "Voi sete Magnanimo come Alessandro, Giusto come Traiano, Dotto come Cesare, Fedele come Constantino, Pietoso come Antonino, Augusto come Ottaviano, Provido come Tiberio, Liberale come Tito, Animoso come Temistocle, Indefesso come Agesilao, Sagace come Annibale, Intrepido come Ciro, Severo come Galba, Affabile come Pirro, Famigliare come Silla, Eloquente come Epaminonda, Solerte come Sertorio, Modesto come Scipione, Honesto come Zenofonte, Forte come Aiace, Invitto come Alcide, & Ingegnoso come Ulisse."

[22] Matthias Jacobus, *Arma virtutum quae Serenissimo, Potentissimo, et Invictissimo Principi ac Domino, Domino Ferdinando Tertio ...* (Breslau, n.d.).

[23] Peter Rietbergen, *Power and Religion in Baroque Rome: Barberini Cultural Policies* (London, 2006), p. 182.

[24] For discussions of these events and the publications issued to commemorate them, see ibid., pp. 183–5; Laurie Nussdorfer, "Print and Pageantry in Baroque Rome," *Sixteenth-Century Journal*, 29 (1998): pp. 454–7; Frederick Hammond, *Music and Spectacle in Baroque Rome: Barberini Patronage Under Urban VIII* (New Haven and London, 1994), pp. 227–30, 272–3. For a list of the fourteen Roman publications describing the various events celebrating Ferdinand's coronation, see Maurizio Fagiolo dell'Arco, *Bibliografia della festa barocca a Roma* (Rome, 1994), pp. 40–42 (nos. 129–42).

[25] The full series of nine engravings is reproduced in Lino Mannocci, *The Etchings of Claude Lorrain* (New Haven and London, 1988), pp. 178–203. Four of the tower images are also reproduced in Hammond, pp. 228–30.

PARAZONIUM PROVIDENTIAE.

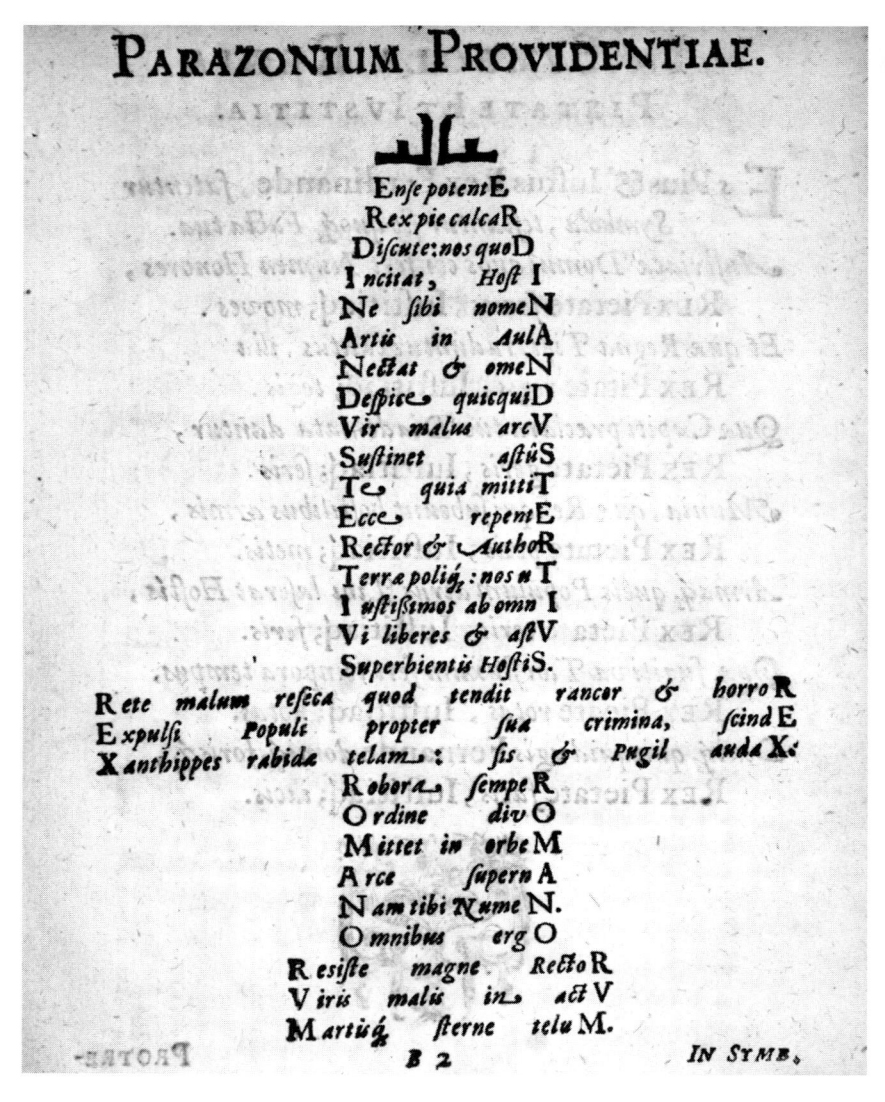

E nse potent E
R ex pie calca R
D iscute: nos quo D
I ncitat,   Host I
N e sibi   nome N
A rtis in   Aul A
N ectat &   ome N
D espice   quicqui D
V ir malus   arc V
S ustinet   astu S
T e   quia mitti T
E cce   repent E
R ector &   Autho R
T erra polig,: nos u T
I ustissimos ab omn I
V i liberes & ast V
S uperbientis Hosti S.

R ete malum reseca quod tendit rancor & horro R
E xpulsi Populi propter sua crimina, scind E
X anthippes rabidæ telam : sis & Pugil auda X
R obora sempe R
O rdine div O
M ittet in orbe M
A rce supern A
N am tibi Nume N.
O mnibus erg O
R esiste magne Recto R
V iris malis in act V
M artisq sterne telu M.

B 2   IN SYMB.

Figure 1.8 "Dagger of Providence," from Matthias Jacobus, *Arma virtutum*

events in Rome, the most sumptuous is a book of more than 160 pages by Luigi Manzini describing the events hosted by the Cardinal Protector, Maurizio of Savoy.[26] The first 90 pages describe the occasions and include 11 engravings

---

[26] Luigi Manzoni, *Applausi festivi fatti in Roma per l'elezzione di Ferdinando III al Regno de' Romani* (Rome, 1637). An in-depth discussion of this print is Wendy Maria

(of various architectural creations and three firework displays), as well as the full libretto of an opera titled *Il Trionfo*. This is followed by 70 pages of Italian and Latin poems in praise of Ferdinand III by a variety of authors; the main themes of all of these poems are piety and military triumph.

Works by German Catholics tended to emphasize Ferdinand's piety over his military strength, yet warlike themes are still present in many of these works. A book of 12 emblems published in honor of Ferdinand's coronation by the Jesuit College of the Bavarian town of Dillingen, for instance, begins with two unmistakably triumphant militant images, labeled respectively "Christus regnant, vincit, triumphant" and "De caelo victoria."[27] A 20-page Latin panegyric by Albertus Pallantius published in Cologne, also celebrating Ferdinand's coronation as King of the Romans, focuses almost entirely on the role of divine providence in securing the new ruler's power, including at his military victory in Nördlingen.[28]

The most well-known and widely disseminated contribution to Ferdinand III's image during the late 1630s was neither published specifically to commemorate his coronation nor even initially conceived for him, yet it did much to spread his image as a mighty warrior: Claudio Monteverdi's Eighth Book of Madrigals, the *Madrigali guerrieri, et amorosi* of 1638.[29] Although the composer had originally intended to dedicate the book to Ferdinand II (which is apparent from the text of dedication), after the elder Ferdinand's death Monteverdi went to great lengths to craft a book that honored the new Emperor and supported his martial image.[30] This comes through from the title of the book alone, for only a powerful, invincible warrior could be deemed

---

Attanasio, "Fiery Art: Festival Decorations for the Election of Ferdinand III as King of the Romans in 1637" (M.A. thesis, University of California Riverside, 1999).

[27] *Regiae virtutis, et felicitatis XII symbola ... Ferdinando III ... cum Rex Romanorum inauguraretur, coronaretur ... in humillimae gratulationis, venerationis, et gratissimi animi argumentum offerebat Collegium Societatis Jesu Dilinganum* (n.p., 1637), sigs A3–A4.

[28] Albertus Pallantius, *Serenissimo, Potentissimo Principi, ac Domino, Domino Ferdinando III. ... cum Rex Romanorum eligeretur, inauguraretur et coronaretur Panegyricus* (Cologne, 1637). Nördlingen is mentioned on p. 7.

[29] Claudio Monteverdi, *Madrigals, Book 8: Madrigali guerrieri et amorosi*, ed. Gian Francesco Malipiero and Stanley Appelbaum (New York, 1991). The translations of the madrigals in this section are adapted from this edition.

[30] See the Appendix for the text of the dedication. On the origins of this madrigal book, which extend back to 1633, see Steven Saunders, "New Light on the Genesis of Monteverdi's Eighth Book of Madrigals," *Music & Letters*, 77 (1996): pp. 183–93. Monteverdi had enjoyed a long and profitable relationship with the Habsburgs, and it makes sense that he would want to maintain this relationship by honoring the new Emperor with his publication. On Monteverdi's relationship with the Habsburgs, see Andrew H. Weaver, "Divine Wisdom and Dolorous Mysteries: Habsburg Marian Devotion in Two Motets from Monteverdi's *Selva morale et spirituale*," *Journal of Musicology*, 24 (2007): pp. 243–5.

worthy of a publication that glorifies war (regardless of whatever the true "war" represented by the primarily amorous madrigal texts may be).[31]

Monteverdi incorporated the Emperor's triumphant image into the texts of the madrigals themselves; the entire section of warlike madrigals, in fact, is framed by proclamations of Ferdinand's triumph. The opening work of the volume, *Altri canti d'Amore*, sets an anonymous sonnet that serves essentially as a second dedication to the Emperor. The final sestet of the poem addresses Ferdinand by name, alludes to his recent coronation, and asks him to accept the publication, the contents of which, so the poem promises, "Del tuo sommo valor canta."[32] The *ballo* that closes the *madrigali guerrieri* is introduced by an adaptation of a sonnet that Ottavio Rinuccini had written to honor King Henry IV of France. The octet of the sonnet concludes with, "Rimbombi il mondo / L'opre di Ferdinando eccelse e belle,"[33] which is followed by a sestet that recounts generic military victories. Another powerful representation of the Emperor's military might comes in the long sixth madrigal, *Ogni amante è guerrier*, another adaptation of a Rinuccini poem for Henry IV. The lengthy second section of this madrigal serves as an encomium to the recently crowned Emperor:

> O pur la dove innuda i larghi campi / L'Istro real, cinto di ferro il busto, / Seguir tra l'armi il chiaro e nobil sangue / Di quel gran re ch'or su la sacra testa / Posa il splendor del diadema augusto; / Di quel gran re ch'alle corone, ai lauri, / Alle spoglie, ai trionfi il ciel destina.

> [there where the broad fields are flooded by the regal Danube, my breastplate enclosed in steel, I follow into battle the famous and noble blood of that great King who now upon his sacred head wears the splendor of the august diadem, that great King destined by heaven for all of the crowns, laurels, spoils, and triumphs.]

---

[31] For a provocative interpretation of Monteverdi's warlike madrigals, see Robert Holzer, "'Ma invan la tento et impossibil parmi,' or How guerrieri are Monteverdi's madrigali guerrieri?" in Francesco Guardiani (ed.), *The Sense of Marino* (New York, Ottawa, and Toronto, 1994), pp. 429–50. By privileging the warlike texts in my reading here, I do not discount other Habsburg-specific interpretations of the book that draw upon the amorous texts. Tim Carter, for instance, has connected the print to the well-known motto, "Bella gerant alii, tu felix Austria nube"; "The Venetian Secular Music," in John Whenham and Richard Wistreich (eds), *The Cambridge Companion to Monteverdi* (Cambridge, 2007), pp. 184–6.

[32] "Sing of your matchless valor." The entire text of the sestet is: "Tu cui tessuta han di cesareo alloro / La corona immortal mentre Bellona, / Gradite il verde ancor novo lavoro / Che mentre guerre canta e guerre sona, / O gran Fernando, l'orgoglioso choro / Del tuo sommo valor canta e ragiona."

[33] "Let the world resound with the lofty and beautiful deeds of Ferdinand."

The reference to the Danube is clearly a way to personalize the text for the Emperor, but the fact that not only Vienna but also Regensburg lie along that river could have also reminded some listeners of Ferdinand's earlier victories at Regensburg and Nördlingen. The text continues with a celebration of military victories and concludes with a final address to the Emperor, using his full name: "O gran Fernando Ernesto, / S'inchineranno alla tua invitta spada, / Vinti cedendo le corone e i regni [O great Ferdinand Ernst, [your enemies] shall bow before your invincible sword, vanquished and yielding their crowns and realms]."

By 1640, then, a vast array of art forms—music, text, painting, engraving, numismatics, fireworks, dance, drama, and spectacle—were working together to create a clearly defined image of the new Emperor: a powerful, undefeated warrior whose strength stemmed primarily from divine providence, granted on account of his deep Catholic piety. Although this image was authorized by the imperial court, it was not something over which the Emperor maintained exclusive control; as with the representations of many early modern monarchs, it was the result not of a consciously unified system or "program" but of a loose network of artworks produced over a span of several years by a wide number of people with varied (even possibly conflicting) motivations.[34] Taking this into account, it is all the more remarkable that Ferdinand's image as a strong, pious military victor seems to have been consistent among his allies and peers. This was of course a great boon for the new Emperor asserting his power upon ascending the throne; at the same time, however, it posed a challenge to Ferdinand III, setting up enormous expectations for him to maintain this image as the Thirty Years' War entered its tumultuous final decade.

Private Reality: Failed Battles and the Quest for Peace

Although Ferdinand III scarcely could have known in 1637 that the pinnacle of Habsburg success in the war was over, he undoubtedly would have sensed that the tide was slowly turning against him.[35] His first major military setback came

---

[34] The idea of "hybrid, improvisatory" representation vs. a unified system is discussed in Louis Montrose, *The Subject of Elizabeth: Authority, Gender and Representation* (Chicago, 2006), p. 104 and Kevin Sharpe, "Representations and Negotiations: Texts, Images, and Authority in Early Modern England," *Historical Journal*, 42 (1999): p. 869. Maria Goloubeva has also discussed the lack of a consistent "program" or "policy" for glorifications of Leopold I: *The Glorification of Emperor Leopold I in Image, Spectacle, and Text* (Mainz, 2000), p. 9.

[35] For further information on the events discussed in this section, see Guthrie, *Later*, pp. 58–122; Parker, pp. 145–52; Konrad Repgen, "Ferdinand III., 1637–1657," in Anton Schindling and Walter Ziegler (eds), *Die Kaiser der Neuzeit, 1519–1918: Heiliges Römisches Reich, Österreich, Deutschland* (Munich, 1990), pp. 149–57.

in March 1638 with the French victory at the Second Battle of Rheinfelden, which encouraged the French to claim the important area along the Rhine. In December of that year, the strategically positioned fortress of Breisach fell into enemy hands, and by the end of 1639 the French had conquered much of the Rhineland. Trouble was simultaneously brewing up north. In late 1638 the Swedish army began pushing into the Empire, and in April 1639 they defeated the Saxon and imperial armies at the Battle of Chemnitz, giving the Swedes access to Silesia and Bohemia. Soon Bohemia was occupied by the Swedes; Prague was bombarded (but not outright attacked), and over the next year countless Bohemian towns were ruthlessly plundered. Things came to a head in late 1642, by which point the Swedish army had conquered most of Silesia and had also captured Olomouc (Olmütz), the capital of Moravia (which remained under Swedish control until the end of the war). With the enemy dangerously close to Vienna, the Emperor sent troops to protect Austria, but instead of repelling the Swedes he experienced the first in a series of truly crushing blows. On November 2, 1642 the Swedes laid waste to the imperial army (under the leadership of Archduke Leopold Wilhelm) at the Second Battle of Breitenfeld. The costs to the imperial forces were devastating, including over 5000 casualties and 5000 prisoners.[36]

With his military situation rapidly deteriorating, Ferdinand III realized that the time had come to turn his thoughts away from battle and toward reconciliation. In contrast to his mighty public image, private letters to his brother of 1641–43 betray anxiety and a strong yearning for peace. In March 1641, for instance, he expressed hope that God would, through his grace, provide the "so lang verlangten friden,"[37] and scarcely two years later he was praying earnestly for God and the Virgin Mary to offer "alleß zu einem glikhligen endt gedein solle, amen."[38] Compounding Ferdinand's worries was the fact that he was losing the financial and military support of his allies. The Spanish Habsburgs, without whose assistance the victory at Nördlingen would have been impossible, were becoming too embroiled in their own troubles to offer substantial assistance in the Empire.[39] Ferdinand III's German supporters

---

[36] Parker, p. 152; Guthrie, *Later*, pp. 105–22.

[37] "So long yearned for peace." HHStA, Familienarchiv, Familienkorrespondenz A, Karton 11, fol. 66r (March 27, 1641): "Gott verleihe verners sein genad und dermal eins den so lang verlangten friden"

[38] "A happy ending to all of this, amen." Ibid., fol. 245r (n.d. [late December 1642 or early January 1643]): "und ist wol billich Gott und Unser Fraun darumb zu dankhen, denn es khin menschlih, sundern gettlihes werkh ist, hoffe auch, sein allmacht solle noch ferners sein gnad geben, daß alleß zu einem glikhligen endt gedein solle, amen."

[39] In October 1639 the Dutch navy destroyed a vast Spanish armada at The Downs, Spain experienced two internal revolts the following year (Catalonia in May and Portugal in December), and France inflicted heavy losses on the Spanish army at the Battle of Rocroi on May 19, 1643 (Parker, pp. 152–3).

were also slowly turning their backs on him. In January 1640 the Emperor's closest German ally, the Elector of Bavaria (who had enjoyed a place of honor at the 1637 ballet honoring Ferdinand's coronation), held secret (albeit unsuccessful) peace negotiations with France, and by spring 1642 Bavaria and the other Catholic electors were considering further negotiations with France at the exclusion of the Emperor.[40]

After participating in failed peace talks during the late 1630s (which the Emperor did not initiate), Ferdinand's first step in his own tentative bid for peace was to call an electoral meeting, which was held in Nuremberg from February to June 1640.[41] When these talks proved futile, the Emperor went a step further and proposed a full imperial diet to be held in Regensburg, the first such meeting since 1613.[42] The Diet opened on September 13, 1640 and met in over 360 formal sessions throughout the following year, continuing to convene even when in January 1641 the Swedish army briefly besieged the city. Facing increasingly dire circumstances, Ferdinand became willing to make concessions in order to preserve peace within the Empire; he even went so far as to fully abandon his father's controversial Edict of Restitution of 1629. Despite his increased willingness to make concessions, however, by the final meeting of the Diet on October 10, 1641 very little headway had been made toward achieving a permanent peace.

The reasons for the European powers' inability to successfully negotiate peace in the late 1630s and early 1640s are too complex to enumerate here. It is certain, though, that the Emperor himself contributed to this deadlock. Despite his ardent desire for peace, his openness to negotiations, and even his willingness to make concessions, he remained convinced that peace could be reached on his own terms. Throughout the Diet of Regensburg and beyond, he refused to relinquish the hope that he could arrange separate peace deals with each of his enemies. While he was willing to make concessions to the German Protestants, France, and Sweden individually, he was not yet ready to bow down to the collective demands of all his enemies working together. And such would his frame of mind remain as long as he had a viable fighting force. Even as the final Westphalian peace negotiations opened in the summer of 1643, Ferdinand held his ground, establishing separate meetings for the Catholic and Protestant powers and allowing only limited representation of the states within the Empire. By this point, however, he was in a completely different position from where he had been in 1637, one that demanded not only new political and diplomatic responses but new artistic ones as well.

---

[40] Ibid., p. 152.
[41] On these talks, see ibid., pp. 148–9.
[42] Kathrin Bierther, *Der Regensburger Reichstag von 1640/1641* (Kallmünz, 1971); Parker, pp. 149–50.

A Crisis of Representation

The early 1640s marked a critical turning point in Ferdinand III's reign, a true crisis that required a significant rethinking of political policy if the Emperor were to successfully end the war with his reputation and sovereignty intact. This political crisis was accompanied by a corresponding crisis in the Emperor's representation. On the most practical level, the rising costs of the war were making it increasingly difficult for Ferdinand to spend money on the lavish artworks and theatrical events that had helped craft his image in the 1630s. It is telling that, after a medal issued to commemorate the Regensburg Diet in 1641, there are no known medals bearing the Emperor's image until the end of the war in 1648.[43] Similarly, after June 1642 there were no full-scale operas or ballets planned at court until 1648.[44] Nor are there any grand paintings or even engravings that can be securely dated to the mid-1640s. Foreign glorifications of Ferdinand's image also seem to have come to an end; with no major military victories or political events to commemorate, there was clearly no need for other rulers or nobles to spend money to propagate the Emperor's image as a powerful warrior.

The artworks that *were* produced at court during the first half of the 1640s, moreover, are strikingly different from those of the 1630s. The only portrait of Ferdinand III securely datable to this time, by the Flemish artist Jan van den Hoecke, could hardly differ more from the militant images of the 1630s (see Figure 1.9).[45] This painting (measuring only 74.5 by 61 cm) is as austere as the earlier paintings are sumptuous: against an unadorned, neutral background, marked by only a hint of color from the red drapery in the upper left corner, sits a bare-headed emperor wearing only plain black garments, a white lace collar, and the pendant of the Order of the Golden Fleece. The dramatic musical productions at court also changed strikingly: the only opera produced in 1642, *Lo Specchio di Virtù*, is an austere moral allegory in which human pleasures and vices are sent to Hell and "Free Will" concedes victory to Virtue,[46] and the only other dramatic productions until the end of the war

---

[43] The medal commemorating the Diet is KHM, Münzkabinett, #b 971.

[44] See Table 3.1.

[45] Jan van den Hoecke, *Emperor Ferdinand III*, oil painting on canvas, ca. 1644–47, KHM. The painting was most likely completed between Hoecke's entrance into Archduke Leopold Wilhelm's service in 1644 and his move with the Archduke to the Spanish Netherlands in 1647. Color reproduction in Bussman and Schilling, Catalogue, p. 424.

[46] Only a printed libretto survives: Horatio Persiani, *Lo Specchio di Virtù* (Vienna, 1642). For a discussion of this work, see Herbert Seifert, "The Beginnings of Sacred Dramatic Musical Works at the Imperial Court of Vienna: Sacred and Moral Opera, Oratorio, and Sepolcro," in Paola Besutti (ed.), *L'oratorio musicale italiano e i suoi contesti (secc. XVII–XVIII): Atti del convegno internazionale, Perugia, Sagra musicale umbra, 18–20 settembre 1997* (Florence, 2002), pp. 501–2.

Figure 1.9   Jan van den Hoecke, *Emperor Ferdinand III*, 74.5 × 61 cm, oil on canvas, ca. 1644–47, Kunsthistorisches Museum, Vienna

are two unstaged oratorios from 1643, one commemorating the Passion and one recounting the life of a martyred saint.[47] Also telling is an opera performed

---

[47]   These works, for which only printed libretti survive, are Giovanni Valentini, *Santi Risorti nel Giorno della Passione di Christo* (Vienna, 1643) and Valentini, *La Vita di Santo*

in Regensburg on July 14, 1641 in celebration of the Emperor's birthday. The plot recounts Tasso's well-known tale from *Gerusalemme liberata* of the Christian soldier Rinaldo's encounter with the sorceress Armida.[48] Considering that the work was performed during the Diet, presumably before an audience consisting of representatives from the Protestant realms of the Empire, a story celebrating a Christian warrior fighting in the Crusades seems especially apt. Perhaps more significant, however, is that the tale ends (as in Tasso) not with military subjugation but with Rinaldo (the obvious stand-in for Ferdinand III) convincing Armida to cease waging war in Egypt for the sake of his love for her.

Especially striking is the one surviving medal issued during the years 1642–47.[49] Instead of featuring a portrait of the Emperor, one side shows a shovel crossing a sword and other implements of war, surrounded by the inscription, "strena auspiciis anni Christi M DC XXXX IIII dicata."[50] On the back of the coin a German inscription encircles the Hebrew word "Jehova": "Gott gib Fried in deinem Lande Gluck und Heil zu allem Stande."[51] Another overt call for peace is seen in an engraving of the Emperor by the Flemish printer Pieter van Sompel from the same year.[52] Underneath an image of the bare-headed Emperor in his coronation mantle, a long inscription recounts important dates in Ferdinand's reign, ending with, "Vivat, aureaque nos pace reficiat, vovemus id. April. CIƆ IƆ CXLIV [we pray on April 13, 1644 that he may live, and that he may restore us with a golden peace]."[53] A call for peace is the guiding theme of one of the few foreign writings in Ferdinand III's honor from the 1640s, which was published in Frankfurt in May 1641 in anticipation that a peace treaty would emerge from the Diet of Regensburg.[54]

Agapito (Vienna, 1643).

[48] Only a manuscript libretto survives for this work, A-Wn, Cod. 13349, which offers no clues as to the author, composer, or any circumstances surrounding the performance (aside from the date); not even a title is provided.

[49] KHM, Münzkabinett, #1411 1914/B.

[50] "A good omen consecrated by the leadership in the year 1644."

[51] "God, grant peace in your lands, and good fortune and safety to all the estates."

[52] A-Wn, Bildarchiv, Pg 149 137/3 in Ptf 123: I (17). This image was published as part of a series of imperial portraits titled *Effigies Imperatorum Domus Austriacae*; Dieuwke de Hoop Scheffer, George S. Keys, and K.G. Boon (eds), *Christoffel van Sichen I to Herman Specht*, Hollstein's Dutch and Flemish Etchings, Engravings and Woodcuts, ca. 1450–1700, vol. 27 (Amsterdam, 1983), pp. 203–14. The imperial series of images appear as Nos. 14–24 (pp. 209–13).

[53] The full text of the inscription is: "Ferdinandus III, Ferdinandi II filius, natus III id. Jul. CIƆ I ƆC VIII. Hungar. Bohem ac demum XII kal. Januar. CIƆ IƆ CXXXVII Romanor. Rex. Patri, XV kal. Mart. vita defuncto, succedit Imperator laudatiss. Vivat, aureaque nos pace reficiat, vovemus id. April. CIƆ IƆ CXLIV."

[54] Johannes Angelius Werdenhagen, *Germania supplex, Divo Ferdinando III. Caesari invictissimo, et Imperii Romano-Germanici semper Augusto, omnem sceptri beatifilicitatem*

From these existing artworks, it seems clear that Ferdinand recognized that his militant, victorious image of the 1630s was no longer tenable during the troubled years of the 1640s. This is, of course, perfectly understandable. With no military victories since Nördlingen, the Emperor no longer had the political capital to back up this image. Not only did he know this, but so did all of the other European powers; if Ferdinand wanted to avoid embarrassment in the eyes of his peers and rivals, not to mention a loss of authority over his subjects, his only option was to stop celebrating long-past triumphs and revise his victorious image into something more closely resembling his decidedly unvictorious reality.

Revising the image of a reigning monarch, however, was easier said than done. For as dire as the 1640s were becoming and as much as Ferdinand needed to change his image, one of the most important requirements for any successful monarchical representation is a sense of continuity.[55] Most scholars have discussed the need for continuity across generations, the idea that the image of a dynasty needed to remain constant regardless of whichever specific individual was wearing the crown. Continuity was just as crucial within the reign of a single ruler. Sudden changes in a monarch's widely accepted image would invite an array of criticisms: instability, indecisiveness, fickleness, capriciousness, weakness, and especially lack of control and authority. While a successful representation always acted as a dialogue (projecting the monarch's desires while also responding to the needs of his subjects), absolute rulers—especially those in precarious elected positions—still needed to always appear to have the upper hand. Ferdinand III thus needed to find a way to reshape his image while still seeming to be the one in control, the one in the position of authority who knew what was best for the realm. Along the same lines, it was also crucial for Ferdinand to maintain his image as a strong leader. As Maria Goloubeva has argued, successful representations did more than merely repeat a positive image in a vacuum; rather, they related recent events to the permanent concept of a good ruler.[56] This being the case, what was Ferdinand to do in the face of such disastrous events as the Second Battle of Breitenfeld? How was he to maintain the image of a strong, capable leader if he could no longer celebrate his triumphant leadership on the battlefield (or even at the negotiating table)? A final complication was the role of the Emperor's Catholic piety in his image. If his earlier military triumphs had been the result of divine providence, then how could one explain God's apparent abandonment of the Emperor during the 1640s? How could Ferdinand

---

cum pace saluberrima optans (Frankfurt am Main, 1641).

[55] The need for continuity in representations of a monarch's image is discussed, in a Habsburg context, in Goloubeva, pp. 7–10.

[56] Ibid., p. 10.

continue to assert that he was favored by God when it seemed that He was no longer providing protection and support, let alone victory?

The strategy through which Ferdinand III's image was revised while addressing the need for continuity was to gradually morph his image as a powerful warrior into that of a comforting, protective father, someone whose every actions were for the sake of keeping his subjects safe. In this way he sought to maintain not only his position of authority but also the image of a strong leader, someone who knew what needed to be done in order to end the war and restore safety and security to his realm. This safety could be ensured, moreover, by Ferdinand's continued prayers to God for assistance, even during this difficult time when it may have seemed that the Lord had turned His back on the Empire. By exuding complete confidence that God was still on his side, the Emperor hoped to prove that his reign was still blessed by the guiding hand of divine providence.

This strategy can be seen to guide one of the few laudatory writings about Ferdinand III issued in the 1640s, a panegyric by Everhard Wassenberg published in Cologne "cum privilegio Caesareo" in 1647.[57] Little is known of Wassenberg's life; we know only from his own writings that he was born in 1610 and that by 1667 he had served as librarian and Latin secretary to Emperor Ferdinand III, Archduke Leopold Wilhelm, King Philip IV of Spain, and King Władysław IV of Poland.[58] Wassenberg was no stranger to pro-Catholic, pro-Habsburg propaganda; his best-known work, the *Commentariorum de bello inter invictissimos Imperatores Ferdinandos II. et III. et eorum hostes* (first published in 1637), was a commentary on the Thirty Years' War told entirely from the perspective of the imperial forces, praising the Catholic cause and scolding the Protestants.[59] So popular was the *Commentariorum* that it appeared in new, updated editions almost every year until 1648 from presses in Frankfurt, Cologne, Hamburg, Antwerp, and Gdansk; some later editions were given the catchier title *Florus Germanicus*, and a German translation appeared beginning in 1643. In addition to the 1647 panegyric to Ferdinand III, Wassenberg also published two later works in honor of Archduke Leopold

---

[57] Everhard Wassenberg, *Panegyricus, Sacratiss. Imperatori Ferdinando III. dictus* (Cologne, 1647).

[58] Mayr-Deisinger, "Wassenberg, Eberhard," in *Allgemeine Deutsche Biographie*, vol. 41 (Leipzig, 1896), pp. 233–4. Mayr-Deisinger does not mention Wassenberg's service to Archduke Leopold Wilhelm, which is listed on the title page of Wassenberg's *Theatrum gloriae, Serenissimo Principi Leopoldo Guilielmo, Archiduci Austriae ... post expeditionem Belgicam anni 1649 ab Everhardo Wassenbergio, ejusdem Archiducis Bibliothecario et Historiographo, extractum et consecratum* (Brussels, 1650).

[59] I have been unable to locate a copy of the 1637 edition of the *Commentariorum*. The earliest I have found is Everhard Wassenberg, *Commentariorum de bello inter invictissimos imperatores Ferdinandos II. et III. et eorum hostes, praesertim Fredericum Palatinum, Gabrielem Bethlenum, Daniae, Sueciae, Franciae reges liber singularis* (Frankfurt, 1638).

Wilhelm, as well as writings celebrating Ferdinand IV's coronation as King of the Romans in 1653 and Leopold I's coronation as emperor in 1658.

Wassenberg's 1647 panegyric begins in a similar manner as his popular *Commentariorum*, relating a history of the Thirty Years' War beginning with the Defenestration of Prague and the Catholic victory at the Battle of White Mountain. Upon reaching the point in the narrative when Ferdinand III is appointed General of the imperial army, the book features lengthy asides that praise the Emperor's virtues in war (pp. 51–2), his faith in God (pp. 52–3), and his military discipline (p. 54). During the discussion of Ferdinand's successes at Regensburg and Nördlingen (pp. 54–69), Wassenberg continues to stress, as writers had done in the 1630s, that Ferdinand's faith played an important role in the victories; Wassenberg even draws a comparison between Ferdinand and the ancient Roman Emperor Constantine, who had famously achieved victory under the sign of the cross (p. 61). Thus, even at this late date, Wassenberg still saw it fit to praise the Emperor for his military valor and for the strong faith in God that had helped make his victories possible.

Nevertheless, Wassenberg could not avoid the fact that the war had taken a turn for the worse. After a discussion of Ferdinand's coronation as King of the Romans (pp. 69–82), the book launches into a discussion of Leopold Wilhelm's military campaigns (pp. 82–103). Although it leaves out specific details (in fact, the narrative essentially stops), the book does not hide the Habsburgs' military misfortunes. Especially telling is the treatment of the worst years of the war, which is folded into a lengthy encomium commending the Emperor for his constancy in the face of adversity (pp. 103–9):

> Divisum, laceratum, scissum, a Te partim & alienatum, in Te partim etiam armatum, Tuum Imperium vidisti; & Tu tamen integer modis omnibus permansisti. Sweinitzio Lipsia, Lipsiae Bernburgum, Bernburgo Janckovium successit; & Tu, tot cladium arietibus quassatus, non cessisti.

> [You saw Your Empire divided, lacerated, split up, part of it alienated from you and part of it even armed against you; yet you persisted, unaffected in every way. Leipzig followed Schweidnitz, Bernburg followed Leipzig, Jankov followed Bernburg; yet you, shattered by the battering ram of so many defeats, did not give up.][60]

This is followed by five pages praising Ferdinand's faith in God and the divine providence that continues to protect him, even during his current trials (pp.

---

[60] Wassenberg, *Panegyricus*, p. 106. The town of Schweidnitz fell to the Swedish army in June 1642, Leipzig in December. The Swedes captured Bernburg in late 1644 (practically decimating the imperial army in the process), and Jankov was the site of a devastating imperial defeat in March 1645 (see Chapter 7).

109–13). Within this section Wassenberg compares the Emperor to Abraham (whom God had tested by ordering him to sacrifice his only son Isaac), and he brings the section to a close with an adage, in all capital letters, "Qui confidit in Domino sicut Mons Sion non commovebitur in aeternum [he who has confidence in the Lord shall, like the Mount of Zion, not be disturbed in eternity]."[61] The panegyric concludes by offering three reasons why it makes sense for Ferdinand to continue waging war (pp. 113–27), only to finish with a lengthy seven-page peroration that praises the Emperor for his perseverance in the quest for peace (pp. 127–33).

By 1647, then, Ferdinand III's faith in God and his protection by divine providence were still important aspects of his public image, with, however, a new emphasis. While the triumphant military victories of the 1630s were certainly not forgotten, the Emperor's piety was now being praised not as a source of military might but as a source of constancy when faced with difficulties. The focus on the Emperor's piety has actually increased since the 1630s; Wassenberg devotes considerably more pages to the troubled years of the 1640s than to Ferdinand's earlier victorious exploits on the battlefield, with the result that the most prominent element of the Emperor's public image now seems to be his unshakable faith that God's divine hand was still protecting him and his people. The inevitable conclusion is that this trust in God guided the Emperor's actions and that this trust, far more than his earlier military triumphs, made him a good, wise, and strong leader.[62] Nothing spoke louder to this change in emphasis than the fact, so stressed by Wassenberg at the end of his panegyric, that Ferdinand was no longer focusing on waging battles but was earnestly seeking peace.

While Wassenberg's work helps illuminate the revision to Ferdinand III's public image, this one Latin writing, published so late in the war, was not in itself enough to successfully enact the shift in focus. This work instead reflects and confirms a change that had started occurring already as early as 1638, even when monuments to the Emperor's military valor (such as Monteverdi's madrigal book and Luyckx's portrait) were still being created. In the absence of other writings or visual artworks reflecting the transition in the Emperor's representations, one remaining art form stands as the ideal medium through which we can trace this revision in action. This art form is the one upon which Ferdinand had always lavished the greatest attention, the one in which he participated personally, and the one that he never relinquished even

---

[61] Ibid., p. 113. The comparison to Abraham appears on p. 111.

[62] A similar strategy in Leopold I's public image during times of difficulty is discussed in Goloubeva, pp. 198–201; as she puts it, "In most laudatory texts of the reign, various afflictions are shown to contribute (or expected to contribute in the end) to his ever greater triumph, as his Christian patience is rewarded" (p. 199).

during the lowest points of the war: music, especially the Latin liturgical and paraliturgical genres of mass and motet.

There are many reasons why sacred music proved the best medium through which Ferdinand could achieve a successful revision of his public image. From a thematic point of view, few art forms could have done more to help move the Emperor's piety into the forefront of his representations. By concentrating on the patronage of sacred music, Ferdinand consequently drew attention to his participation in liturgical observances and other pious activities. Sacred music also had the advantage of being less potentially subversive than other media. An opera, for instance, with its grand, multisensory display, its profusion of characters, and its often complex plots, left much scope for individual interpretation, which rulers needed to counter through written descriptions that promulgated the "authorized" interpretation of the work.[63] Many other media, especially more ephemeral ones such as engravings and medals, could also take on a variety of meanings depending on the context in which they were received. Sacred music, however, had a secure narrative context within the long-established liturgy of the Catholic Church and its equally long-established symbolic systems. Although Ferdinand could not, of course, control the contexts in which musical works would be performed once they were disseminated beyond the confines of his court, the sacred nature of the music nevertheless allowed for a good possibility that it would still be performed within a religious (if not strictly liturgical) context. Of course, this was also a hurdle, in that the religious context might potentially obscure the representational message of a work (especially if the Emperor were not present during the performance), but imperial composers were able to ingeniously craft multivalent sacred works that simultaneously served liturgical, devotional, and political ends.

From the perspective of means of production, sacred music offered the advantage that the Emperor could exert more control—or at least perceive that he exerted more control—than he could with the types of artworks produced in the 1630s. By focusing on an art form that was created almost solely by the musicians in his employ, in terms of both composition and performance, Ferdinand was able to maintain a level of supervision over the works that far surpassed what was possible with media such as opera and visual artworks, which included the participation of countless artisans and craftsmen. Because of this, it in fact seems possible to speak of a coherent (if still somewhat diffuse) "program" guiding the revision of Ferdinand III's image in the 1640s, whereas it is not possible to say the same of his representations in the 1630s or after the war. By focusing on fewer media, fewer artworks, and fewer artists, Ferdinand allowed himself the possibility of a stronger, more cohesive message. Not only could he maintain control by commissioning specific works

---

[63] See Chapter 3.

from his musicians, but he could also exert influence over which works were disseminated to a broader public via print.[64]

Sacred music provided not only a more cohesive message, but, from a purely practical perspective, a *cheaper* one as well. Ferdinand's focus on sacred music meant that he needed to expend virtually no additional costs in order to promote his image. The musicians were already in his employ, and his love of music assured that he was always going to spend the money to hire them anyway. Moreover, the liturgical and devotional services at which the music was performed were also going to happen regardless, and unlike theatrical events that required the creation of new sets, costumes, machinery, and countless other expensive accoutrements, the spectacle that was a Catholic service was already provided by the Church itself. Sacred music also allowed for many opportunities as to when Ferdinand's image was promulgated: not only weekly public Mass and Vespers but also the profusion of special feasts during the liturgical year, as well as the busy schedule of processions, pilgrimages, and other events that filled the calendar, most of which featured musical performances by the imperial chapel in addition to a rich mantle of dynastic traditions, symbols, and ritual that helped emphasize political messages.[65]

Finally, of all artistic media, music was the one most able to reach the widest number of people in the widest variety of ways. Whether as a mere sonic emblem of grandeur, as an embellished sermon or oration, or even as a printed text, music was capable of spreading Ferdinand's image to a larger audience than was possible with any other art form.[66] Even a single musical work was capable of reaching different audiences through different means and communicating a message specific to each audience: what an illiterate commoner experienced as an impressive sonic display of the Emperor's magnificence upon hearing a motet performed by the imperial chapel during Mass at St Stephen's Cathedral could have an entirely different meaning to a noble courtier attending the same Mass, who could understand the Latin words and glean a specific message based on his knowledge of recent political events. The same work might then appear in a printed collection of music, where it could be accompanied by rubrics, dedications, and other texts that emphasized yet another meaning. This is not to say that music always succeeded in providing exactly the image that Ferdinand III needed it to portray (a common problem with any means of monarchical representation), but through his patronage of sacred music the Emperor was able to address his crisis of representation, which in turn helped make it that much easier for him to successfully resolve the political crisis that was the Thirty Years' War.

[64] On the role of musical prints in Ferdinand's representations, see Chapter 4.
[65] See Chapter 3.
[66] The means by which music accomplished this are explored in Part II.

CHAPTER 2

Justitia et Pietas: A Portrait of Ferdinand III

Who exactly was Ferdinand III? As with most early modern monarchs, it is difficult—if not impossible—to answer this question definitively. Ferdinand III was many things to many people, and accordingly, his representation was a heterogeneous amalgam of his various roles and responsibilities as Holy Roman Emperor, combined with his own personal interests. Without claiming to uncover the "true" Ferdinand, this chapter offers a portrait of the Emperor through individual examinations of three important components of his public life—his roles as zealous Counter-Reformer, prudent politician, and lavish patron of the arts—thereby providing a foundation from which we can better understand the manifestations (and the motivations behind the manifestations) of his official image as it was revised and promulgated during the 1640s. Our discussions must of course also include examinations of representations that focus on each role.

Although we will never be able to discover Ferdinand's personality, we can nevertheless glean from such sources as private letters and ambassador reports that he does not seem to have been naturally predisposed to the role thrust upon him of a powerful military general.[1] The Venetian ambassadors, for instance, frequently mention his piety, intelligence, political acumen, and especially his passion for music, science, and the hunt, but they say little of his physical or mental aptitude for battle.[2] Ferdinand's letters to his brother Archduke Leopold Wilhelm, written when Leopold Wilhelm was general of the imperial army, contain much talk of war (as expected) but nevertheless present the portrait of an artistic, sensitive, caring individual deeply concerned with the emotional and physical welfare of his brother, other family members, and even court employees.[3] The Emperor

---

[1]   Reports of the Venetian ambassadors to the Viennese court are in Joseph Fiedler (ed.), *Die Relationen der Botschafter Venedigs über Deutschland und Österreich im siebzehnten Jahrhundert* (2 vols, Vienna, 1866–67), vol. 1, pp. 179–408. Ferdinand III's letters are collected in HHStA, Familienarchiv, Familienkorrespondenz A, Karton 11; an overview of them is in Kathrin Ledel, "Private Briefe Kaiser Ferdinands III. an Erzherzog Leopold Wilhelm 1640–1643, 1645: Eine Studie" (Diploma-Arbeit, University of Vienna, 1995).

[2]   For more details, see Andrew H. Weaver, "Piety, Politics, and Patronage: Motets at the Habsburg Court in Vienna During the Reign of Ferdinand III (1637–1657)" (Ph.D. diss., Yale University, 2002), pp. 41–6.

[3]   Ibid., pp. 43–5.

also suffered from the familiar curse of many generations of Habsburg inbreeding, giving him a weak physical constitution that did not hold great promise for a long life, let alone daring military exploits.[4] Ferdinand III and his father thus faced an immense challenge from the moment the younger Ferdinand received his first crown (as King of Hungary) in 1625. Not only did they need to construct the powerful image discussed in the previous chapter and convince the world that this was indeed a man able to overpower enemies on the battlefield, but they also needed to negotiate skillfully between fact and fiction. An important aspect of this negotiation was crafting representations that capitalized on the young ruler's strengths and cast those strengths in the most positive light possible while also appropriating them for the Habsburgs' needs.

Ferdinand the Counter-Reformer

If Ferdinand III was not naturally inclined to be a military warrior, he was nevertheless perfectly suited to play the part of a staunch champion of the Catholic Church. Like his father before him, Ferdinand received a solid education from the Society of Jesus, from whom he would have absorbed the missionary zeal of the order, and throughout his reign he retained as his confessor a Jesuit priest, Johannes Gans.[5] He also publicly supported the Jesuits and their militant agenda throughout his life, for example by aiding in the establishment of Jesuit colleges and universities and by frequently attending Jesuit dramas, even providing financial support for some of the productions.[6] As discussed in Chapter 3, one of the most visible and highly publicized aspects of Ferdinand III's life was his participation in religious observances, which included Mass and Vespers on all feast days and Sundays, in addition to daily private Masses. There is also no evidence arguing against the fact that Ferdinand led anything but an exemplary moral lifestyle; Charles Ingrao and Andrew Thomas have pointed out, for instance, that the total absence of any record (even in ambassador reports) of imperial mistresses or illegitimate children during the reigns of Ferdinand II, Ferdinand III, and Leopold I suggests that they actually

---

[4] Lothar Höbelt, *Ferdinand III. (1608–1657): Friedenskaiser wider Willen* (Graz, 2008); Ernst Tomek, *Kirchengeschichte Österreichs* (3 vols, Innsbruck and Vienna, 1935–59), vol. 2, p. 542. On this issue for the Habsburg dynasty as a whole, see Karl Vocelka and Lynne Heller, *Die private Welt der Habsburger: Leben und Alltag einer Familie* (Graz, Vienna, and Cologne, 1998), pp. 28–48.

[5] On Gans and his influence on Ferdinand III (which was not as great as the influence wielded by Ferdinand II's Jesuit confessor), see Robert Bireley, *The Jesuits and the Thirty Years War: Kings, Courts, and Confessors* (Cambridge, 2003), pp. 209–11.

[6] Ferdinand's support of Jesuit drama is discussed in Chapter 3.

practiced the moral virtues that they preached.[7] There is thus no reason to doubt either the sincerity of the Emperor's very public displays of deep Catholic piety or his belief that by working to stamp out Protestantism and re-establish Catholicism as the sole religion in his lands he was saving his subjects' souls.

The most outward sign of Ferdinand III's piety was indeed his efforts to re-Catholicize his realm. The goal of unifying his hereditary lands under the banner of the Catholic Church was a top priority for Ferdinand III throughout his reign, and in continuing the work of the Counter-Reformation, he followed the example of his father before him. To this day the elder Ferdinand's greatest legacy remains his tireless efforts as the most militant defender of Catholicism of all the Habsburg emperors. Even before assuming the imperial throne in 1619, Ferdinand II had achieved great success in purging Inner Austria of Protestants during his tenure as Archduke of Styria in the early years of the century.[8] The 1620 victory at the Battle of White Mountain only strengthened his resolve to continue this work in other realms of the Empire, culminating in the notorious Edict of Restitution of 1629, a controversial and inflammatory proclamation in which Ferdinand II stepped beyond the bounds of the imperial constitution by issuing a new law (without consulting the imperial Diet) that in addition to outlawing Calvinism stripped many Protestant rulers of land and reclaimed it for the Catholic Church.[9]

That Ferdinand II expected his heir to continue this work was expressed in a number of documents and artworks. In May 1621, for instance, the Emperor signed his testament, which repeatedly stresses the importance of achieving confessional unity and urges Ferdinand III to continue the work of re-Catholicization.[10] In the first codicil of the testament, signed

---

[7] Charles W. Ingrao and Andrew L. Thomas, "Piety and Patronage: The Empresses-Consort of the High Baroque," *German History*, 20 (2002): p. 36.

[8] Robert Bireley, *Religion and Politics in the Age of the Counterreformation: Emperor Ferdinand II, William Lamormaini, S. J., and the Formation of Imperial Policy* (Chapel Hill, 1981), p. 14; Bireley, "Ferdinand II: Founder of the Habsburg Monarchy," in R.J.W. Evans and T.V. Thomas (eds), *Crown, Church, and Estates: Central European Politics in the Sixteenth and Seventeenth Centuries* (London, 1991), pp. 233–4, 236; Bireley, "Confessional Absolutism in the Habsburg Lands in the Seventeenth Century," in Charles W. Ingrao (ed.), *State and Society in Early Modern Austria* (West Lafayette, 1994), pp. 39–41.

[9] On the Edict and its political ramifications, see Bireley, *Religion*, pp. 52–61, 74–94; Gerhard Benecke, "The Practice of Absolutism II: 1626–1629," in Geoffrey Parker (ed.), *The Thirty Years' War*, 2nd edn (London and New York, 1997), pp. 88–9; Ronald G. Asch, *The Thirty Years' War: The Holy Roman Empire and Europe, 1618–48* (New York, 1997), pp. 76–7, 94–8.

[10] This will, along with its first codicil signed on the same day and its second codicil signed in August 1635, is transcribed in Gustav Turba, *Die Grundlagen der Pragmatischen Sanktion* (2 vols, Leipzig and Vienna, 1911–12), vol. 2, pp. 335–55, 359–61.

on the same day, he instructed his heir to maintain a close connection to the Jesuits:

> we earnestly commend to you the well-deserving Society of Jesus and its priests. Through their skill, their instruction of our dear youth, and their exemplary manner of life, they do much good in the Christian Catholic Churches and more than others loyally work and exert themselves to maintain and propagate the Catholic religion not only in our Inner Austrian lands but in all our kingdoms and territories and throughout Christendom. In this ungrateful and perverse world they encounter more hatred and persecution than others and so are more in need of protection, help, and assistance.[11]

A broader public was informed of the expectation for Ferdinand III to follow in his father's footsteps by a medal issued in 1627, shortly after the younger Ferdinand's coronation as King of Bohemia.[12] One side presents a conventional profile portrait of the young King, while the other features an illustration of two eagles flying toward the sun, with the inscription, "Imitabor parentem."[13]

That Ferdinand III willingly took on this role as an ardent Counter-Reformer, allowing it to become as much a part of his own image as that of his father, is superbly illustrated by a full-color thesis title page issued sometime after 1654, during the final years of his reign (Figure 2.1).[14] In front of a map of Habsburg territories stand Ferdinand III on the left and his heir apparent Leopold I on the right, both sumptuously clad in full regalia. In chains on the ground in front of the men is an exotically dressed representation of Heresy, lying atop scattered books, one of which is ascribed to Luther and another to Calvin. At the top of the page, smiling down upon the vanquishers of heresy, are allegorical representations of those who benefited the most from Ferdinand's efforts: the Church (on the left) and Theology (on the right). Giving the pair of Counter-Reformers their blessing are the enthroned Virgin Mary holding the baby Jesus, the Holy Spirit (represented by the dove), and God the Father (represented by the Hebrew word "Jehova"). The presence of Leopold I in this picture shows that, just as Ferdinand II had expected his heir to assume his mantle of militant Counter-Reformer, so too did Ferdinand III expect the same of his son.

Indeed, throughout his reign Ferdinand III followed his father's lead by overseeing within his hereditary lands the same actions that Ferdinand

---

[11] Translation from Bireley, *Religion*, p. 8. Original in Turba, vol. 2, pp. 354–5.
[12] KHM, Münzkabinett, #b 996.
[13] "I will imitate my father."
[14] A-Wn, Bildarchiv, NB 10772.

Figure 2.1 Georg Urllmayr, frontispiece of *Nomenclatur oder Namen der ... Religions Reformation im Ertzherzogtumb Österreich ...*, color engraving, after 1654

II had successfully implemented to suppress Protestant practices. These included imperial edicts, enforced conversions among the nobles, and the banishment of Protestant ministers and schoolmasters and their replacement with "exemplary" and "capable" Catholic priests.[15] Ferdinand III also continued the practice of imperially sanctioned visitations (or "Reformation Commissions") that supervised the proper running of Catholic parishes and instructed the local population in the faith, with force if necessary.[16] But for Catholicism to truly take root, the void left by the banishment of Protestantism needed to be filled with a firm Catholic identity and a sincere love for the Church and its traditions. This is not something that can be achieved through legislation and control, and for this reason, some scholars have questioned whether "top–down" re-Catholicization efforts were ever truly successful in reaching and converting the bulk of early modern society, especially the lowest classes.[17] While the imperial government was unable to directly provide the sort of nurturing experiences necessary to sway the hearts and minds of the entire populace, one strategy that was considered a viable method of instilling in people a devout Catholic spirit was to use the Emperor's public image as a means of persuasion. During the final decade of the Thirty Years' War, Ferdinand III's pious image thus served a dual purpose: in addition to helping maintain the Emperor's authority in the face of military defeat, it was simultaneously a tool in the re-Catholicization process, directed specifically at Protestant subjects. Whether or not the Emperor's representation actually succeeded in converting Protestants does not diminish the insights we gain by acknowledging that the Habsburgs intended it to serve this purpose.

There were a number of ways in which the Emperor's image was thought to aid in re-Catholicization. The main method was that it offered an exemplary model for imperial citizens to follow. While it was surely understood that the lower classes would not have had enough access to the image (or even the comprehension of it) to truly imitate it, it was at least hoped that as those closest to the court—the nobles and other elite political figures who comprised the main intended audience and who had more direct control over the lower classes—supported the Emperor's pious

---

[15] Robert Douglas Chesler, "Crown, Lords, and God: The Establishment of Secular Authority and the Pacification in Lower Austria, 1618–1648" (Ph.D. diss., Princeton University, 1979), pp. 300–318. See also Kurt Piringer, "Ferdinand des Dritten Katholische Restauration" (Ph.D. diss., University of Vienna, 1950).

[16] Bireley, "Confessional Absolutism," pp. 45–7; Bireley, "Ferdinand II," pp. 237–9; R.J.W. Evans, *The Making of the Habsburg Monarchy, 1550–1700: An Interpretation* (Oxford, 1979), pp. 118–21.

[17] See, for instance, Marc R. Forster, "The Thirty Years' War and the Failure of Catholicization," in David M. Luebke (ed.), *The Counter-Reformation: The Essential Readings* (Oxford and Malden, 1999), pp. 163–97.

image and followed his example, the effects would gradually trickle down to all levels of society. Even on the most superficial level, however, if an image presented the Emperor as a powerful person whom God favored because of his piety, this could be seen as an attraction that might potentially draw others to the Church in search of similar benefits. A painting such as Schut's *Victory at Nördlingen* (Figure 1.2), for instance, might persuade people that if the Virgin had aided the Emperor in battle she could likewise help them overcome their own adversities. Furthermore, because much of the Emperor's image was connected to the splendor of public religious occurrences, the sheer spectacle created by Ferdinand's (and his chapel's) presence at Mass and Vespers could attract people to the Church and keep them coming back until the Catholic ritual became engrained in their lives.

A successful re-Catholicization effort thus not only depended on the Emperor's maintenance of an untarnished reputation; it was also crucial that the court project an image that was *attractive* enough to win people over to the Church. To aid in this, as well as to help construct a pious image that was unique to the imperial dynasty, the Habsburgs adhered to a moral and religious code known as the *Pietas Austriaca*.[18] This piety had its origins in Habsburg legends stretching back to their first ruler Rudolph I (r. 1273–91), and it reached its climax during the Counter-Reformatory years of the seventeenth century, when it was frequently lauded in printed historical works.[19] Strongly influenced by the Jesuits, this *Pietas* consisted of four main pillars: devotion to the Eucharist, faith in the cross, Marian piety, and veneration of saints. By capitalizing on some of the most popular Catholic symbols that were either downplayed or outright eschewed by the Protestant faiths, especially those with miraculous or magical aspects, the Habsburgs sought to use the *Pietas* as a means of attracting people back to the Church. The fact that the *Pietas Austriaca* was part of a long dynastic tradition allowed for continuity among images of the Habsburg emperors, yet it was at the same time multifaceted enough to allow each emperor to craft his own distinctive image by emphasizing specific elements more than others. The *Pietas Austriaca* thus shaped the Habsburg public image while simultaneously functioning as a valuable Counter-Reformation weapon.

---

[18] Anna Coreth, *Pietas Austriaca*, trans. William D. Bowman and Anna Maria Leitgeb (West Lafayette, 2004).

[19] Examples include Nikolaus Vernulz, *Virtutum augustissimae gentis Austriace libri tres* (Louvain, 1640); Johann Peter Lotichus, *Austrias Parva: id est, gloriae Austriacae, et belli nuper Germanici, sub divo Matthia, Ferdinandis II. et III. Impp. gesti, compendaria* (Frankfurt, 1653); Didacus Lequille, *De rebus Austriacis tomus tribus: Piissima atque augustissima Domus Austria* (Innsbruck, 1660); *Phosphorus Austriacus de Gente Austriaca libri tres, in quibus gentis illius prima origo, magnitudo, imperium, ac virtus asseritur, et probatur* (Louvain, 1665); Wenceslaus Adalbert Czerwenka, *Annales et acta pietatis augustissimae ac serenissimae Domus Habspurgo-Austriacae* (Prague, 1694).

Indeed, it formed the foundation of every Habsburg representation during the early modern era and left its mark on almost every cultural artifact produced by the court.[20] Ferdinand III was no exception, and we shall continually return to the *Pietas Austriaca* in Part III.

Ferdinand the Politician

Despite the apparent veracity of Ferdinand III's deep Catholic piety and his earnest efforts at re-Catholicization, there is nevertheless a disparity between his image as an ardent Counter-Reformer and the political reality of the final decade of the Thirty Years' War. As discussed in Chapter 1, as the 1640s dragged on and Ferdinand became increasingly desperate to end the war, he offered more and more concessions to his Protestant enemies. In this respect, he was not the militant Counter-Reformer his father had been but a moderate who relinquished the desire to reconvert the entire Empire. Ferdinand concentrated his Counter-Reformation efforts instead on his own hereditary lands, and in this regard he was indeed quite successful; scholars unanimously agree that Austria and Bohemia emerged from the Peace of Westphalia as solidly Catholic lands, which is confirmed by the pervasive Catholicism in Austria to this day.

The more limited focus of the Emperor's efforts had consequences for both the nature of the war and his public image. As Robert Bireley has pointed out, for Ferdinand II the Thirty Years' War had been a true "holy war" (rather than a mere "religious war") in that the language discussing it in official court documents was characterized by "the belief in a summons from God to take up the fight and a promise of divine aid that would lead to victory even in the face of great odds."[21] Once the Peace of Prague was signed in 1635, however, this myth could not be sustained, for those fighting in a holy war need to be so confident in their protection by divine providence that there is no need whatsoever for the concessions granted to the Protestants in the peace treaty.[22] As discussed in Chapter 1, however, the belief that Ferdinand III was constantly protected by divine providence continued to play an important role in both his militant image as victor

---

[20] For examples, see Adam Wandruszka, "Ein Freskenzyklus der 'Pietas Austriaca' in Florenz," *Mitteilungen des Österreichischen Staatsarchivs*, 15 (1962): pp. 495–9; Franz Matsche, *Die Kunst im Dienst der Staatsidee Kaiser Karls VI.: Ikonographie, Ikonologie und Programmatik des "Kaiserstils,"* (2 vols, Berlin and New York, 1981), vol. 1, pp. 108–212; Steven Saunders, *Cross, Sword and Lyre: Sacred Music at the Imperial Court of Ferdinand II of Habsburg (1619–1637)* (Oxford, 1995), pp. 178–222.

[21] Bireley, *Jesuits*, p. 61.

[22] Ibid., p. 164.

at Nördlingen and his image as a protective father whom the Lord would deliver from his current tribulations. Ferdinand III's responsibilities as a political leader were thus decidedly at odds with his need to continue presenting himself as a pious Counter-Reformer protected by God, forcing him to navigate carefully between his desire to spread Catholicism and the reality of the fact that he ruled a vast, heterogeneous political system that could never be made to conform with his vision of the ideal Catholic state. In the larger scheme of things, however, his more moderate approach to re-Catholicization was not incompatible with his view of Catholic statecraft.

In his political policy, Ferdinand III adhered to a belief system that was common among Catholic rulers of the early modern era, what modern scholars have labeled "anti-Machiavellianism."[23] In opposition to Machiavelli's theory of political power, which was denounced as immoral and un-Christian, anti-Machiavellian writers sought to prove not only that Christianity and political leadership were not incompatible but also that only by adhering to Christian principles could any ruler be successful. Anti-Machiavellianism, which flourished throughout the seventeenth century, originated in two treatises published independently in 1589: Giovanni Botero's *Ragion di stato* and Justus Lipsius' *Politicorum sive civilis doctrinae libri sex*, the former of which was especially influential on Habsburg political thought. Botero's theory of successful political rule was based on the concept of virtue, which is what gave the monarch the consent of the people to be ruled; as Bireley has explained it, "*Virtù* produced reputation, understood as the support of the people, and reputation constituted the cardinal element in the ruler's power, which in turn augmented his reputation."[24] Political power thus resided ultimately in the ruler's adherence to a moral lifestyle, which could come only from a life of pious devotion to the Catholic Church. Botero further identified three pairs of virtues that every ruler had to cultivate: valor and prudence (the most important virtues, in that they secured reputation), justice and liberality (with which the ruler gained the love of his subjects), and temperance and religion (which needed to be possessed by both the ruler and his people).

Evidence for Ferdinand III's knowledge of anti-Machiavellian political theory (and Botero's in particular) comes from various documents that served as educational tools in his and his siblings' upbringing. These include Ferdinand II's above-mentioned 1621 testament as well as two additional writings: the anonymous *Princeps in compendio*, first published in 1632, and an unpublished didactic work written by the nobleman Gundakar

---

[23] Robert Bireley, *The Counter-Reformation Prince: Anti-Machiavellianism or Catholic Statecraft in Early Modern Europe* (Chapel Hill and London, 1990).

[24] Ibid., p. 54. Bireley discusses Botero's concept of virtue on pp. 53–63.

von Liechtenstein in 1639 for Archduke Leopold Wilhelm.[25] Of these, the most important is the *Princeps in compendio*, both because it was written precisely during Ferdinand III's formative years as he was being groomed for the imperial crown, and also because as a published work it served as nothing less than a public portrait of the ruler he would become. Its importance as a mirror of the Habsburg monarchy is confirmed by the fact that Leopold I saw fit to reissue it in 1668.

The *Princeps* begins by immediately impressing upon the reader how vital it is for the ruler to maintain a close relationship to God. The first section, titled "Quomodo cum Deo se princeps gerere debeat,"[26] opens with a quotation from Proverbs 8:15: "Per me reges regnant."[27] This quote brings to mind the divine right of kings while also instructing the ruler to trust in divine assistance. As the text continues: "Ideo ante omnia necesse est, ut eundem Deum, a quo munus istud accepit, ante oculos sibi ponat et nihil contra mandata eius agat nec unquam ab eiusdem voluntate recedat [therefore, it is necessary that above all things he place before his eyes God, from whom he receives his office, and neither do anything against His commands nor at any time recede from His will]."[28] The ruler is also explicitly instructed to follow the strategies that guided Ferdinand's representations as warrior and protective father: rejoicing in God's providence and trusting in the Lord in times of trouble. Later sections form a virtual compendium of the virtues enumerated by Botero: "De iustitia et clementia principis" (Section 4), "De oeconomia et liberalitate principis" (Section 5), and "De affabilitate, gravitate et auctoritate principis" (Section 6).[29] Evidence that Ferdinand III took these anti-Machiavellian mandates seriously and passed them on to his sons comes from a funeral oration given by the Jesuit preacher Thomas Dueller after Ferdinand IV's

---

[25] *Princeps in compendio, hoc est puncta aliquot compendiosa, quae circa gubernationem reipublicae observanda videntur* (Vienna, 1632; reprint, Vienna, 1668). A recent edition of *Princeps in compendio* is ed. Franz Bosbach in Konrad Repgen (ed.), *Das Herrscherbild im 17. Jahrhundert*, Schriftenreihe der Vereinigung zur Erforschung der Neueren Geschichte, vol. 19 (Münster, 1991), pp. 79–114. Gundacker von Liechtestein's work is edited in Wenzel Eymer, *Gutachten des Fürsten Gundacker von Liechtenstein über Education eines jungen Fürsten und gute Bestellung des Geheimen Rates* (Leitmeritz, 1905). An overview of both works is in Konrad Repgen, "Ferdinand III., 1637–1657," in Anton Schindling and Walter Ziegler (eds), *Die Kaiser der Neuzeit, 1519–1918: Heiliges Römisches Reich, Österreich, Deutschland* (Munich, 1990), pp. 144–9. Overviews of the *Princeps in compendio* are also in Coreth, pp. 1–3 and Maria Goloubeva, *The Glorification of Emperor Leopold I in Image, Spectacle, and Text* (Mainz, 2000), pp. 37–8.

[26] "How the prince should conduct himself before God."

[27] "Through me kings reign."

[28] Repgen, *Herrscherbild*, p. 89.

[29] "Concerning the justice and clemency of the prince"; "Concerning the economy and liberality of the prince"; "Concerning the courtesy, dignity, and authority of the prince."

untimely death in 1654.[30] In discussing the potential that the younger Ferdinand had shown for the imperial throne, Dueller relates that, when the 14-year-old heir had been asked in 1647 to describe the foundation for a strong rule, he replied, "Die steiffe und beständige Andacht zu GOTT dem Allmächtigen."[31]

In addition to the importance of an unblemished, pious reputation, another crucial aspect of anti-Machiavellian thought, present in both Botero and the *Princeps in compendio*, is the necessity of promoting Catholicism and achieving religious unity within one's realm; the co-existence of multiple confessions in a single realm, it was argued, could sow nothing but discord and rebellion.[32] The second section of the *Princeps*, titled "De cultu divino promovendo,"[33] explicitly states that it is the ruler's duty to establish Catholicism and stamp out dissenting Christian faiths:

> Bonus princeps animum suum semper et primario ad Dei cultum et honorem ante omnia promovendum intendet. Ac primo quidem sedulo curabit, ut religionem Catholicam, ubi ea fuerit, sartam tectam conservet et magis magisque promoveat ac nullas haereses illabi patiatur.

> [The good prince will above all things always and primarily exert his spirit to the promotion of the cult and honor of God. And indeed he will carefully see to it that he restore, defend, preserve, and to a greater and greater extent promote the Catholic religion wherever it may be and never suffer nor sink to heresy.][34]

It is thus apparent that the Counter-Reformation zeal and pious image discussed in the previous section served far more than just the Church, for they were also intimately connected to Habsburg political policy and the consolidation of the Emperor's central authority. As Robert Chesler has pointed out, "Catholicism, with its stress on hierarchy and tradition, was a perfect instrument for the re-assertion of order and the acceptance of

---

[30] Thomas Dueller, *Oesterreichischer Phoenix oder Ferdinandus Quartus ... nebest allgemeinen Wehemut diser Welt abgestorbem ... Durch gegenwertige Klag Rede beweinet* (Vienna, 1654).

[31] "The strong and steadfast devotion to God the Almighty." Ibid., sig. Dr: "Er war gefragt den 23. Weinmonats 1647. Jahrs, seines Alters im 14. Quae essent Regnorum firmamenta, durch waß die Königreich befestiget werden? und gleich sprach Er, zuforderist, Die steiffe und beständige Andacht zu GOTT dem Allmächtigen. Er verstunde nemblich auch schon damahls, waß er mit der Muttermilch gesogen, gleich wie den Vögelein der Lufft, den Fischen das Wasser, also denen Fürsten das angeborne Element sey die Andacht."

[32] On this point in Botero, see Bireley, *Counter-Reformation*, pp. 62–3.

[33] "Concerning the promotion of religion."

[34] Repgen, *Herrscherbild*, p. 90.

authority,"[35] words that echo Botero himself: "No law is more favorable to princes than the Christian one, because it submits to them not only the bodies and means of the subjects, but their souls and consciences, too, and it binds not only the hands, but also the feelings and thoughts."[36]

This belief that re-Catholicization was directly connected to effective governance corresponds to the much debated modern concept of "confessionalization." As generally understood today, confessionalization is a complex "fundamental social process" that comprised two related historical phenomena.[37] The first is the hardening of the distinctions between the Christian denominations (from both doctrinal and ritual perspectives), which brought with it not only religious but also cultural, social, and political ramifications.[38] The second is the more controversial idea that this delineation of the confessions played an important role in state-building and the emerging modern world, in that each denomination relied upon secular authorities to help impose its brand of orthodox piety, from which the state enjoyed the benefit of more loyal and disciplined subjects. Originally formulated in the 1970s and '80s by Heinz Schilling and Wolfgang Reinhard (from the Protestant and Catholic perspectives respectively), the concept of confessionalization has found general acceptance among scholars of early modern Germany and has begun to be applied to non-German lands. It is not, however, without its critics, especially those who challenge Reinhard and Schilling's decidedly "top–

---

[35] Chesler, "Crown, Lords, and God," p. 290. Bireley offers a similar view in *Counter-Reformation*, p. 231: "Christianity was a stalwart support of the state because it insisted upon the divine origin of authority and the subjects' duty of obedience and allegiance... ."

[36] Quoted in Wolfgang Reinhard, "Reformation, Counter-Reformation, and the Early Modern State: A Reassessment," *The Catholic Historical Review*, 75 (1989): p. 403.

[37] For excellent overviews of the many facets of confessionalization, see Heinz Schilling, "Confessionalisation in Europe: Causes and Effects for Church, State, Society, and Culture," in Klaus Bussmann and Heinz Schilling (eds), *1648: War and Peace in Europe* (3 vols, [Münster], 1998), vol. 1, pp. 219–28 (he uses the phrase "fundamental social process" on p. 219) and Reinhard, "Reformation, Counter-Reformation." Superb historiographical discussions of the concept include Thomas A. Brady, Jr., "Confessionalization: The Career of a Concept" and Heinz Schilling, "Confessionalization: Historical and Scholarly Perspectives of a Comparative and Interdisciplinary Paradigm," both in John M. Headley et al. (eds), *Confessionalization in Europe, 1555–1700: Essays in Honor and Memory of Bodo Nischan* (Aldershot, 2004), pp. 1–20 and 21–35 and Ute Lotz-Heumann, "The Concept of 'Confessionalization': A Historiographical Paradigm in Dispute," *Memoria y Civilización*, 4 (2001): pp. 93–114. An application of confessionalization to musicological scholarship is Alexander J. Fisher, *Music and Religious Identity in Counter-Reformation Augsburg, 1580–1630* (Aldershot, 2004).

[38] First developed by Ernst Walter Zeeden in the 1950s and '60s, this idea of *Konfessionsbildung* ("formation of the confessions") is narrower in scope than confessionalization and thus often considered separately from it; on this point, see Schilling, "Confessionalization," pp. 22–4.

down" approach that posits the main agents of confessionalization to be the educated elite of ecclesiastical and state institutions. One of the most ardent critics has been Marc Forster, who has both pointed to the complete failure of top–down confessionalization in Speyer and has eloquently argued that the decidedly successful re-Catholicization of southwest Germany was the result of the negotiation between elite and popular culture, with the bulk of the success coming "from below."[39] Others have attempted to mediate between the top–down and bottom–up perspectives; for instance, Howard Louthan's examination of the successful re-Catholicization of Bohemia equally emphasizes both the elite agents of reform and the role of popular piety,[40] while Trevor Johnson has argued that the re-Catholicization of the Upper Palatinate succeeded because of both the elite culture's accommodation of popular religious traditions and the rural culture's adaptation of orthodox Catholicism.[41] What has become clear is that confessionalization is a complex, multifaceted phenomenon that must be examined on a case-by-case basis in light of the unique political, cultural, and social contexts of each early modern state.

There can be little doubt that Ferdinand III believed in the viability of confessionalization "from above," even if the success of his efforts must undoubtedly be attributed as much to other levels of society as to his court.[42] In our examination of the Emperor's representation throughout this book, this top–down perspective serves as an important frame of reference for understanding how the court intended others to interpret the Emperor's

---

[39] Marc R. Forster, *The Counter-Reformation in the Villages: Religion and Reform in the Bishopric of Speyer, 1560–1720* (Ithaca, 1992) and *Catholic Revival in the Age of the Baroque: Religious Identity in Southwest Germany, 1550–1750* (Cambridge, 2001). Other critiques of top-down confessionalization are Heinrich Richard Schmidt, "Sozialdisziplinierung? Ein Plädoyer für das Ende des Etatismus in der Konfessionalisierungsforschung," *Historische Zeitschrift*, 265 (1997): pp. 639–82; Stefan Ehrenpreis, "Konfessionalisierung von unten: Konzeption und Thematik eines bergischen Modells?" in Burkhard Dietz and Stefan Ehrenpreis (eds), *Drei Konfessionen in einer Region: Beiträge zur Geschichte der Konfessionalisierung im Herzogtum Berg vom 16. bis zum 18. Jahrhundert* (Cologne, 1999), pp. 3–13; Luise Schorn-Schütte, "Konfessionalisierung als wissenschaftliches Paradigma?" in Joachim Bahlcke and Arno Strohmeyer (eds), *Konfessionalisierung in Ostmitteleuropa: Wirkungen des religiösen Wandels im 16. und 17. Jahrhundert in Staat, Gesellschaft und Kultur* (Stuttgart, 1999), pp. 63–77.

[40] Howard Louthan, *Converting Bohemia: Force and Persuasion in the Catholic Reformation* (Cambridge, 2009).

[41] Trevor Johnson, *Magistrates, Madonnas, and Miracles: The Counter Reformation in the Upper Palatinate* (Aldershot, 2009).

[42] Even Marc Forster discusses Habsburg confessionalization after 1650 as an essentially top–down phenomenon; see his "Catholic Confessionalism in Germany after 1650," in *Confessionalization*, pp. 239–41. Other discussions of imperial Habsburg confessionalization include Bireley's "Confessional Absolutism" and "Ferdinand II."

representations. We can only understand how Ferdinand III's image was expected to help maintain his authority in the final years of the war by realizing that it was part of a larger project through which the Emperor sought to draw people to the Catholic Church and strengthen the hold of Catholicism in his lands, all in the service of his political aims. Simply put, the Emperor believed that, if he could secure his subjects' adherence to the Catholic Church, and especially to the unique brand of Catholic piety defined by the *Pietas Austriaca*, he was simultaneously securing their allegiance to him; the Catholic identity of the Habsburg hereditary lands thus came first and foremost from the Emperor's image. This makes an exclusively top–down perspective a viable avenue of inquiry, even if the Emperor was not the active agent in promulgating and imposing this Catholic identity, or if the Catholicism as practiced and understood by the masses did not conform entirely to his.

Despite the obvious interconnection between church and state, in which the two existed in a symbiotic relationship, the fact remained that Ferdinand III was a secular and not an ecclesiastical authority, with the result that politics continued to maintain some autonomy from religion (and vice versa). Schilling has stressed the significance of the dualistic rather than monistic relationship between church and state in early modern Europe, which allowed the two institutions to operate independently when necessary and kept them in balance, never giving one absolute domination over the other.[43] Significantly for Ferdinand III, this gave him the opportunity he needed to wisely navigate toward the Peace of Westphalia. A fundamentalist, monistic state would never have been able to recognize the rights of heretical governments, which would have defeated the Westphalian negotiations even before they began. Ferdinand, however, recognized that a setback for the Catholic Church would nevertheless be a victory for Europe, which was what allowed him to relinquish his father's desire to re-Catholicize the entire Empire and focus instead on his hereditary lands (which in turn was a victory for him). This also led him to less overtly stress the Counter-Reformatory aspects of his representations that were promulgated beyond the hereditary lands, thereby making it easier for Protestant nobles to accept his image and his (limited) power over them.

This does not mean, however, that Ferdinand III was not a good Catholic ruler or that representations celebrating his faith in divine providence were a blatant lie. In this regard, the Emperor was again aided by anti-Machiavellian political theory, which recognized, in addition to

---

[43] See, for instance, Schilling, "Confessionalization," pp. 27–8 and "War and Peace at the Emergence of Modernity: Europe Between State Belligerence, Religious Wars and the Desire for Peace," in Bussmann and Schilling, vol. 1, pp. 18–19.

"providentialist pragmatism" (in which success was bestowed directly by God), what Bireley has called "intrinsic pragmatism," in which success stemmed from moral action guided by reason.[44] By recognizing a larger good (the end of disastrous warfare) that would result from his otherwise unacceptable religious tolerance, Ferdinand III was able to justify concessions to heretics and focus his energies where they really mattered and would serve him better. This willingness to act independently of religious interests for the good of the state distinguished Ferdinand III from his more militant father and is what made him a good politician. The fact that these decisions relied on intrinsic pragmatism no doubt also permitted him to continue believing in his image of the pious Catholic ruler working in concert with God's will.

Ferdinand the Patron of the Arts

One of Ferdinand III's greatest legacies, in his own day as well as ours, was his passion for the arts. While European rulers had long made a public show of their artistic patronage for political purposes, in the 1630s the young Ferdinand's obvious penchant for the arts was potentially detrimental to the Habsburg cause, as it could easily be considered a superfluous distraction from war that made him seem too weak to be the mighty warrior able to overcome infidels on the battlefield. Even Ferdinand II had been derided by enemies for his conspicuous expenditure on music during the Thirty Years' War.[45] Already in the early 1630s, therefore, the court made a conscious effort to cast Ferdinand III's artistic bent in the most positive light possible, by using it as evidence for his erudition and wisdom. Figure 2.2, an engraving from a 1633 thesis title page based on a lost painting by Cornelius Schut, shows allegorical representations of the various arts and sciences paying homage the young King while three saints (all former kings of Hungary) watch approvingly from heaven.[46] The saints make it clear that Ferdinand's patronage of the arts is perfectly compatible with his Catholic kingship, which is further reinforced by the banner on the left featuring the Virgin Mary and by the lions flanking Ferdinand's throne. The lions, a standard iconographic reference to the throne of King Solomon, equate the young ruler with the biblical King, assuring the viewer that his role as artistic patron contributes to his wise

---

[44] Bireley, *Counter-Reformation*, pp. 30–33 (see also pp. 51–2 on Botero's emphasis on intrinsic rather than providentialist pragmatism).

[45] For an example, see Saunders, *Cross*, p. 3.

[46] Albertina, Vienna, Holländische DG n.m. GM. The saints are identified as St Stephen, his son St Emeric, and St Ladislaus.

Figure 2.2   Lukas Vorsterman after a painting by Cornelius Schut, Ferdinand III depicted as patron of the arts and sciences, engraving, 1633

and just rule (and also introducing a representational trope that would become significant in the later years of the war; see Chapter 5).

Ferdinand III showed a clear preference for some arts over others. He was not, for instance, an extravagant patron of the visual arts. He did not initiate any impressive new building projects, and the structures he did commission were generally austere, with no resemblance to the overwhelmingly monumental *Kaiserstil* of the late Baroque (as epitomized, for instance, by the eighteenth-century *Karlskirche*).[47] The only substantial public sculpture that Ferdinand commissioned in Vienna is the *Mariensäule* in the *Platz am Hof* (see Chapter 7). Nor was the Emperor a lavish collector of paintings, despite the fact that he retained court painters and

---

[47] The generally un-ostentatious character of Viennese architecture under Ferdinand III and his father is examined in Hellmut Lorenz, "The Imperial Hofburg: The Theory and Practice of Architectural Representation in Baroque Vienna," in Ingrao, *State and Society*, pp. 93–109. On the *Kaiserstil*, see Matsche.

is known to have purchased canvases by famous artists.[48] The bulk of the seventeenth-century collection at Vienna's Kunsthistorisches Museum was assembled not by Ferdinand III but by Archduke Leopold Wilhelm, who was by far the more passionate art collector of the two brothers.[49]

What Ferdinand III's court culture lacked in obvious opulence was made up for by his patronage of the less visually ostentatious arts of literature and music. The Emperor avidly cultivated Italian literature and poetry, to such an extent that Italian became one of the most common languages spoken at his court.[50] This emphasis on Italian culture is not surprising; not only did the Italian brides of Ferdinand II and Ferdinand III (both named Eleonora Gonzaga) contribute much to the cultivation of an Italianate court culture, but the continued eminence of Italy in the seventeenth-century cultural world also made it the natural choice for northern European rulers seeking to endow their courts with a radiant luster. By the end of his reign, Ferdinand III had established a literary academy in the Italian manner, as had his brother and the second Eleonora Gonzaga.[51] The Emperor and Leopold Wilhelm were even active as writers of Italian poetry, and each of them published books of their poems.[52]

It was above all as a patron of music for which Ferdinand III was most well known. While he followed his father's lead in this regard, Ferdinand III's interest in music surpassed Ferdinand II's to the extent that he was active as a composer himself, passing his compositional gift on to Leopold

---

[48] In letters to Leopold Wilhelm from 1641 and 1642 Ferdinand mentions recent purchases of works by such well-known masters as Corregio, Titian, and Rubens; HHStA, Familienarchiv, Familienkorrespondenz A, Karton 11, fols 78 (July 14, 1641), 182 (October 26, 1642), and 235 (December 27, 1642) (see also Ledel, "Private Briefe," pp. 40, 63, 73).

[49] Karl Schütz, "The Collection of Archduke Leopold Wilhelm," in Bussmann and Schilling, vol. 2, pp. 181–90.

[50] On Habsburg patronage of Italian literature, see especially Erika Kanduth, "Italienische Dichtung am Wiener Hof im 17. Jahrhundert," in Alberto Martino (ed.), *Beiträge zur Aufnahme der italienischen und spanischen Literatur in Deutschland im 16. und 17. Jahrhundert*, Chloe, vol. 9 (Amsterdam and Atlanta, 1990), pp. 171–207 and Umberto de Bin. "Leopoldo I. imperatore e la sua corte nella letteratura italiana," in *Bolletino del Circolo Accademico Italiano, 1908–09* (Trieste, 1910), pp. 1–78.

[51] On academies at the imperial court, see Theophil Antonicek, "Italienische Akademien am Kaiserhof," *Notring Jahrbuch* (1972): pp. 75–6; de Bin, "Leopoldo I. imperatore"; Ulrike Hofmann, "Die Accademia am Wiener Kaiserhof unter der Regierung Kaiser Leopolds I.," *Musicologia Austriaca*, 2 (1979): pp. 76–84; Herbert Seifert, "Akademien am Wiener Kaiserhof der Barockzeit," in Wolf Frobenius et al. (eds), *Akademie und Musik* (Saarbrücken, 1993), pp. 215–23.

[52] Ferdinand III, *Poesie diverse composte in hore rubate d'Academico Occupato* (n.p., n.d.) and Leopold Wilhelm, *Diporti del Crescente, divisi in rime morali, devote, heroiche, amorose* (Brussels, 1656). On poetry by members of the imperial family, see Kanduth, "Italienische Dichtung," pp. 180–83; de Bin, "Leopoldo I. imperatore," pp. 21–6; Saunders, *Cross*, pp. 183–4.

I.[53] Ferdinand III's affinity for music was widely known in his day and frequently mentioned by writers. The Venetian ambassador Girolamo Giustinani, for example, commented that "La musica è l'unica sua deletatione, compone bene, e giudica delle voci e dell'arte equisitamente [music is his sole delight; he composes well and exquisitely judges voices and the art]."[54] One of the poems in Leopold Wilhelm's published poetry book lauds his brother by proclaiming that Ferdinand ruled with both sword and plectrum.[55] Musicians throughout Europe knew of the Emperor's passion for their art and frequently honored him with dedications.[56] Even well over a hundred years after his death a dictionary entry related that Ferdinand was "praised by all writers of his time as a great connoisseur and patron of music."[57]

Ferdinand III's love for music was apparent just from the size of his musical establishment. Upon his ascension to the imperial throne, the total number of people in the imperial chapel exceeded 90, of which 54 were adult male musicians (25 singers and 29 instrumentalists); the rest consisted of at least 15 trumpeters, ten choirboys, nine female singers, and various other personnel.[58] Ferdinand continued to maintain a chapel of

---

[53] For details on Ferdinand III as a composer, see Steven Saunders, "The Emperor as Artist: New Discoveries Concerning Ferdinand III's Musical Compositions," *Studien zur Musikwissenschaft*, 45 (1996): pp. 7–31; Theophil Antonicek, "Die italienischen Textvertonungen Kaiser Ferdinands III.," in Martino, *Beiträge*, pp. 209–33; H.V.F. Somerset, "The Habsburg Emperors as Musicians," *Music and Letters*, 30 (1949): pp. 204–15; Guido Adler (ed.), *Musikalische Werke der Kaiser Ferdinand III., Leopold I. und Joseph I.* (2 vols, Vienna, 1892; reprint, Westmead, 1972). On Ferdinand II's musical patronage, see especially Saunders, *Cross* and "Sacred Music at the Hapsburg Court of Ferdinand II (1615–1637): The Latin Vocal Works of Giovanni Priuli and Giovanni Valentini" (2 vols, Ph.D. diss., University of Pittsburgh, 1990). Important studies of Ferdinand III's musical patronage include Theophil Antonicek, "Musik und italienische Poesie am Hofe Kaiser Ferdinands III.," *Mitteilungen der Kommission für Musikforschung*, 42 (1990): pp. 1–22; Steven Saunders, "Der Kaiser als Künstler: Ferdinand III and the Politicization of Sacred Music at the Habsburg Court," in Max Reinhart (ed.), *Infinite Boundaries: Order, Disorder, and Reorder in Early Modern German Culture*, Sixteenth-Century Essays and Studies, vol. 40 (Kirksville, 1998), pp. 187–208; Weaver, "Piety, Politics, and Patronage."

[54] Fiedler, vol. 1, p. 337.

[55] Leopold Wilhelm, p. 98: "Fonda Cesare il scettro, / E sù la spada, & sul canoro plettro."

[56] For a list of 19 musical works dedicated to Ferdinand III, see Weaver, "Piety, Politics, and Patronage," pp. 45–6, fn. 25.

[57] Cited in Saunders, "Kaiser als Künstler," p. 188. The original source is Ernst Ludwig Gerber, *Historisch-biographisches Lexikon der Tonkünstler* (Leipzig, 1790–92; reprint, Graz, 1977), col. 404.

[58] For a detailed discussion of the composition of Ferdinand III's chapel, including comprehensive lists enumerating the membership by year, see Weaver, "Piety, Politics, and Patronage," pp. 54–75, 83–90.

this size for as long as possible. Only in 1645, at the nadir of the Thirty Years' War when Vienna was besieged by the Swedish army, did the Emperor deem it necessary to reduce the chapel. Three singers and eight instrumentalists left his service in that year alone, decreasing the chapel to a mere 30 musicians.[59] As soon as he was able, Ferdinand began to rebuild the chapel; by 1650 the number of musicians had increased to 36, and the numbers went up every year thereafter. Significantly, the vast majority of the musicians in the imperial chapel (especially the singers) were Italian, and much of the music they performed was in the latest Italianate styles.[60] As with his cultivation of literature, the Emperor looked to the Italian peninsula for the best musicians and the most cutting-edge compositions in order to enrich the prestige of his court.

Both of these features of the chapel—its Italianate nature as well as its size—were important means by which Ferdinand III could proclaim his magnificence. Indeed, public appearances by the chapel constituted a crucial aspect of his public image (see Chapter 3). The splendor of the imperial musical establishment was also announced in other ways. No published report of a Habsburg ceremony, for instance, is complete without mentioning the awe-inspiring performance by the imperial musicians, ensuring that even those who were not there knew about the Emperor's spectacular music.[61] Even something as straightforward as a published list of chapel members could do much to impress upon readers the grandeur of the imperial musical establishment. One such list, published in 1655, provides the name and musical specialty of each musician as well as the city from which most of them hailed, thereby boasting not only the size but also the Italianate nature of the chapel.[62] A superb pictorial representation of the chapel's magnificence appeared in the frontispiece of a musical publication dedicated to the Emperor in 1648, in which Ferdinand rides in a triumphal chariot atop a vast array of heavenly musicians (Figure 2.3).[63] Despite the

---

[59] Ferdinand, however, recompensed them for all back wages and let them live in their quarters for as long as necessary. Many of the musicians moved immediately into the chapel of Leopold Wilhelm, who informed one of his officials in a letter dated March 1, 1645 that due to "the reform of the *Hofstatt*" he would be taking on the services of several of his brother's musicians; see Saunders, "Sacred Music," vol. 1, p. 55 and vol. 2, p. 866 (Documents 16 and 17).

[60] See Chapter 3 for a discussion of musical styles in imperial sacred music.

[61] For examples, see Weaver, "Piety, Politics, and Patronage," pp. 31–4 and Saunders, "Kaiser als Künstler," pp. 189–90.

[62] Gabriel Bucelinus, *Germania topo- chrono- stemmato-graphica sacra et profana* (2 vols, Ulm, 1655–57), vol. 1, pp. 279–80.

[63] Andreas Rauch, *Currus triumphalis musici, Imperatorum Romanorum Tredecim ex Augustissima Archiducali Domo Austriaca* (Vienna, 1648). This print is discussed in detail in Chapter 4 and the Epilogue.

Figure 2.3 Michael Frommer, frontispiece of Andreas Rauch, *Currus triumphalis musici*, engraving, 1648 (Bibliothèque nationale de France)

obviously fantastical nature of this image, it nevertheless conveys well the awe a seventeenth-century listener experienced upon hearing the chapel perform, and it also illustrates the great variety of instrumental forces that the chapel encompassed.

There is plentiful evidence that Ferdinand III was no passive employer but enjoyed a close relationship with his musicians and was actively involved in the workings of the chapel. A series of letters to Leopold Wilhelm, for instance, demonstrates that the Emperor personally auditioned prospective musicians, especially the much sought-after castrati. In December 1641 he heard with much anticipation the singing of a newly arrived Roman castrato named Giuseppino (most likely Giuseppe Bianchi, who served in Ferdinand's chapel in 1641–43 and 1654–57), and he complained to Leopold Wilhelm that the singer's disappointing voice did not live up to his expectations.[64] Other musicians (and Giuseppino himself) assured Ferdinand that the voice would soon improve, but two weeks later the Emperor was still grumbling that Giuseppino's voice was not yet up to his standards.[65] The Emperor also fostered close personal relationships with his musicians. One such chapel member was Giovanni Valentini, who had been *maestro di cappella* of Ferdinand II's chapel and remained in this post after Ferdinand III's ascension. In his youth Ferdinand III had studied music and Italian poetry with Valentini, and as an adult the Emperor continued to seek artistic advice from the composer and share completed works with him, taking close heed of the *maestro*'s criticism and praise.[66] Valentini enjoyed special status with the Emperor and could speak freely about matters of concern. In a fascinating letter from November 11, 1642, Ferdinand scolded his brother for taking musicians into battle, for the Emperor's vice chapel master Pietro Verdina (who was temporarily serving Leopold Wilhelm) had been taken prisoner during the disastrous Second Battle of Breitenfeld. Tellingly, Ferdinand expressed this disapproval as coming from Valentini.[67] Verdina, who had served as chapel master of

---

[64] HHStA, Familienarchiv, Familienkorrespondenz A, Karton 11, fol. 116 (December 14, 1641); Saunders, "Sacred Music," vol. 2, p. 902 (Document 101).

[65] HHStA, Familienarchiv, Familienkorrespondenz A, Karton 11, fol. 126 (December 28, 1641); Ledel, "Private Briefe," p. 50.

[66] In a number of letters Ferdinand mentions showing musical and poetic works to Valentini and comments on changes suggested by the composer. See, for example, HHStA, Familienarchiv, Familienkorrespondenz, Karton 11, fols 148–150 (August 16, 1642) and 153 (August 24, 1642); see also Ledel, "Private Briefe," pp. 55–6 and Saunders, "Sacred Music," vol. 2, pp. 903 (Document 103), 904 (Document 105). On Valentini's relationship with Ferdinand III, see also ibid., vol. 1, pp. 468–79.

[67] HHStA, Familienarchiv, Familienkorrespondenz A, Karton 11, fol. 190r: "Umb die Musici ist mir wol laidt und absunderlich umb den Verdina wegen seines weibs und khinder. Der Valentin hallt nichts darauf daß die Musici in Krieg ziehen."

Ferdinand's small personal chapel in the years before he became emperor,[68] was another composer to whom the Emperor was apparently close. When Verdina died in July 1643, shortly after being released by the Swedes, Ferdinand commented sadly to his brother, "Umb den Verdina ist mir wol laid, wir haben alle baide in suo genere wol einen gueten diner verlohrn [I'm especially upset over Verdina; we've both lost an especially good servant in this man]."[69]

Music was by far the art form about which Ferdinand III was the most passionate. Through his personal experience as a composer and his close interaction with the workings of the chapel, it was also the art form over which he exerted the most direct influence. It should thus come as no surprise that of all the arts it was primarily music that the Emperor put to political use as an important means through which he sought to promulgate his public image and communicate important messages throughout his realm and to other nations. We therefore turn now to an examination of the specific ways that this ephemeral, performative art was able to serve as a means of monarchical representation.

---

[68] On this chapel, which was established in 1631, see Weaver, "Piety, Politics, and Patronage," pp. 54–5.

[69] HHStA, Familienarchiv, Familienkorrespondenz A, Karton 11, fol. 272r (July 29, 1643).

PART II
Means of Production

CHAPTER 3

Emblematic Sound: Musical Performance as a Mirror of Imperial Majesty and Piety

Among the means of monarchical representation in the early modern era, some artistic media, such as engravings, medals, and books, were produced in many copies and therefore could be perused at leisure, anytime and anywhere one chose. Others, such as paintings, sculptures, and architecture, existed in single copies that were tied to a specific location but could nevertheless be enjoyed for unspecified amounts of time. Music, however, was limited by both place and time in that it needed to exist within the confines of a specific occasion in order to serve a purpose towards the representation of a monarch.[1]

Ferdinand III, like so many other early modern monarchs, knew how to take advantage of such occasions, and he organized, attended, and participated in a myriad of grand events (both secular and sacred) that helped present his image in spectacular fashion. Music played a role in almost all of these occasions; however, it was just one of many other sensory spectacles, and scholars have tended to focus on more concrete mementos, such as pictures and texts, when discussing the ways these events helped represent monarchs.[2] This is perhaps understandable; not only has much seventeenth-century music been lost, but it is also easier today to assess artistic media that still exist in their original forms rather than one that must be recreated through notation and for which we usually have only vague descriptions and emotional reactions from those who experienced it at its original performance. Nevertheless, music was far more than just an ornament decorating an already overwhelming sensory

---

[1] I am considering here only music in performance and not musical notation, which is discussed in Chapter 4.

[2] Maria Goloubeva, for instance, admits that although she included opera in her study of Leopold I's representations, she chose to discuss only the texts, feeling that they were more significant than music in projecting the Emperor's image; *The Glorification of Leopold I in Image, Spectacle, and Text* (Mainz, 2000), p. 24. Two studies that superbly draw connections between the actual music of operas and the representation of the patron's image are Nina Treadwell, *Music and Wonder at the Medici Court: The 1589 Interludes for* La Pellegrina (Bloomington and Indianapolis, 2008) and Kelley Harness, *Echoes of Women's Voices: Music, Art, and Female Patronage in Early Modern Florence* (Chicago and London, 2006).

occasion, and it too could play an active role in promoting the monarch's image, communicating messages beyond those present in texts, pictures, and actions.

Before we can discuss the music itself, however, it is crucial to understand the larger contexts in which it would have been heard, for the other sensory stimuli played an indispensible role in the listener's interpretation of the music. This chapter accordingly examines three important types of ceremonial occasions in which music contributed to Ferdinand III's image: secular theatrical events, Jesuit drama, and liturgy. After discussing how the events as a whole contributed to the Emperor's representation, the final section explicates how sacred music in particular (regardless of the specific context) could communicate messages to listeners.

Opera

No musical art form has been discussed as a significant means of monarchical representation more than opera.[3] This is not surprising, for from its inception at the turn of the seventeenth century, opera (like its sister genre the intermedio) was designed as an extravagant multimedia spectacle intended to showcase the splendor and magnificence of secular courts.[4] Indeed, with no other single artistic event could a noble patron show off more of the artistic talent cultivated at his court: not only the singers, instrumentalists, actors, dancers, composers, and poets, but also the architects, engineers, painters, seamstresses, wigmakers, and the like. This was an art form whose extravagant costs limited its appearance to only the wealthiest courts,[5] and the exclusive, invitation-only nature of these (usually) one-time-only events helped foster a sense of privilege among those lucky enough to attend.[6] The dissemination of libretti,

---

[3] See, for instance, Kristiaan P. Aercke, *Gods of Play: Baroque Festival Performances as Rhetorical Discourse* (Albany, 1994); Peter Burke, *The Fabrication of Louis XIV* (New Haven and London, 1992); Hubert Christian Ehalt, *Ausdrucksformen absolutischer Herrschaft: Der Wiener Hof im 17. und 18. Jahrhundert*, Sozial- und Wirtschafthistorische Studien, vol. 14 (Munich, 1980), pp. 147–60; Goloubeva; Frederick Hammond, *Music and Spectacle in Baroque Rome: Barberini Patronage Under Urban VIII* (New Haven and London, 1994); Treadwell; Harness.

[4] A seminal work on the purpose of seventeenth-century opera is Lorenzo Bianconi and Thomas Walker, "Production, Consumption and Political Function of Seventeenth-Century Opera," *Early Music History*, 4 (1984): pp. 209–96.

[5] That is, until the advent of public opera in Venice in 1637, but even then the high price of tickets ensured that this remained an exclusive, noble event.

[6] On the extreme importance attached to theatrical invitations (and the competition for invitations) at Leopold I's court, see Goloubeva, pp. 70–73.

scenarii, engravings, and other written descriptions of the events helped add a sense of permanence to the occasion and also ensured that those who were not in attendance could experience at least a small taste of the patron's magnificence. Through the use of both subtle and overt references in the textual, visual, and musical elements of the opera, moreover, the genre served as a perfect vehicle for the glorification of the person paying the bill.

Nevertheless, the study of opera as a means of monarchical representation poses challenges. Foremost among these is the fact that much of the music of these works has been lost; because these were one-time events, the manuscript copies of the music were often not retained in court libraries, and (with notable exceptions) it seems that the commemorative value of printed musical scores was not considered to be as high as that of other printed memorabilia.[7] Ferdinand III's court was no different, and unfortunately we do not have a single piece of music from the operatic productions at court during his reign.[8]

Another challenge posed by opera is that of interpretation. Although in most cases it is clear that the protagonist of the opera is meant to stand in for the patron, there are still many aspects of every opera that elude clear explanation. It is in fact often easy to discover elements of an opera that undermine the patron rather than glorify him.[9] This was as much a problem in the seventeenth century as it is for modern scholars; in fact, an opera could potentially cause diplomatic tensions if it was felt that a certain character or situation reflected poorly on another court.[10]

---

[7] The most famous exception is Monteverdi's *Orfeo*, published in 1609 and reprinted in 1615.

[8] For a discussion of the types of poetry in opera libretti from Ferdinand III's reign and speculation about how they would have been set to music, see Herbert Seifert, *Die Oper am Wiener Kaiserhof im 17. Jahrhundert* (Tützing, 1985), pp. 288–94. One Italian dramatic work for which music does survive (but for which we have no record of a performance) is Ferdinand III's unnamed "Drama Musicum," which exists in at least five manuscript sources, listed in Steven Saunders, "The Emperor as Artist: New Discoveries Concerning Ferdinand III's Musical Compositions," *Studien zur Musikwissenschaft*, 45 (1996): p. 28. Excerpts from this work are in Guido Adler (ed.), *Musikalische Werke der Kaiser Ferdinand III., Leopold I., und Joseph I.* (2 vols, Vienna, 1892; reprint, Westmead, 1972), vol. 2, pp. 5–26. For more information on the Drama Musicum, see Theophil Antonicek, "Die italienischen Textvertonungen Kaiser Ferdinands III," in Alberto Martino (ed.), *Beiträge zur Aufnahme der italienischen und spanischen Literatur in Deutschland im 16. und 17. Jahrhundert*, Chloe, vol. 9 (Amsterdam and Atlanta, 1990), pp. 209–33.

[9] On this point, see especially Georgia J. Cowart, *The Triumph of Pleasure: Louis XIV and the Politics of Spectacle* (Chicago, 2008).

[10] For an excellent example, see Harness, pp. 1–2. Treadwell's basic approach in *Music and Wonder* is to use the misinterpretations reported in unofficial accounts of the performance as a key to understanding how the audience discerned meaning in the work.

This resulted in a plethora of *argomenti*, letters to the readers, and other explanatory texts included with the libretto or scenario, which clarified the exact message that the audience was expected to take away from the work; unfortunately, these do not exist for every work produced at the imperial court.

A final problem when considering opera as a means of representation is that the sheer number of people involved in a single production has led scholars to question the extent to which some patrons were actively involved in the creative process and to which extent they exerted control over the production.[11] While we unfortunately know little about the planning process for operatic productions at Ferdinand III's court, one surviving document sheds some light on the Emperor's role in mounting productions. In 1648, an opera titled *I Trionfi d'Amore* (with music by Giovanni Felice Sances) was planned to commemorate the Emperor's marriage to his second wife Maria Leopoldine of Tyrol; the premiere, planned for Prague, was canceled at the last minute because of the death of King Władysław IV of Poland less than two months before the wedding, and although another performance was planned for Bratislava (Preßburg) the following year, it seems that it never took place.[12] The only surviving record of this work is a manuscript libretto; this is clearly a working document, with frequent corrections made to the text in another hand.[13] Appended to the end of the libretto is a bifolio in a different hand and on different paper, which was sewn into the manuscript at a later date.[14] This document, addressed to the Emperor, offers a glimpse of the behind-the-scenes preparations for the Bratislava production. The first page contains a list of the scenic requirements for the work, at the bottom of which is written, "Il tutto rimettendosi al benigno volere, et comando di V Maesta."[15] The inner two pages contain a list of the singers who had

---

[11] Harness, pp. 3–5.

[12] Seifert, *Oper*, pp. 39–40; Seifert, *Der Sig-prangende Hochzeit-Gott: Hochzeitsfeste am Wiener Hof der Habsburger und ihre Allegorik 1622–1699*, Dramma per musica, vol. 2 (Vienna, 1988), p. 21.

[13] A-Wn, Cod. 13182.

[14] This document is transcribed in full in Egon Wellesz, "Einige handschriftliche Libretti aus der Frühzeit der Wiener Oper," *Zeitschrift für Musikwissenschaft*, 1 (1918–19): pp. 280–81; a slightly different transcription of the inner two pages is in Elisabeth Charlotte Salzer, "Le grandi rappresentazioni del teatro italiano a Vienna barocca," trans. L. Cavalcoli, *Revista italiana del dramma*, 3 (1939): pp. 163–5. A facsimile of the document is in Peter Webhofer, *Giovanni Felice Sances, ca. 1600–1679: Biographisch-bibliographische Untersuchung und Studie über sein Motettenwerk* (Rome, 1964), pp. 26–8; Webhofer suggests that the document is in Sances's hand (p. 25).

[15] "All of this is being put on again at the benign will and command of Your Majesty" (A-Wn, Cod. 13182, fol. 48r).

prepared the roles for Prague, together with a consideration of different singers for some parts. In debating cast changes, the writer makes a point of mentioning twice that the Emperor has the final word and will be the one to judge which singers will perform.[16] From the existence of this document and the deference paid to the Emperor's decisions (in addition to Ferdinand's close relationship with his musicians discussed in Chapter 2), it seems reasonable to infer that Ferdinand III exerted a fair amount of control over the sights and sounds that comprised his operas.[17]

Keeping in mind that there is still much that we do not and cannot know about the operatic productions at court, this section provides an overview of these events during Ferdinand III's reign.[18] It discusses both the physical atmosphere of the theater and the types of subjects covered in the libretti, keeping an eye to how all of this contributed to the Emperor's representation. All known operatic performances (and related events) during Ferdinand III's reign are detailed in Table 3.1; not included in the table are theatrical presentations for which we have only scant evidence and that were most likely spoken comedies in the *Commedia dell'arte* tradition.[19]

---

[16] Ibid., fol. 49v (in debating between two singers for two different roles): "à Praga doveva Recitar d'Amore Bartolomeo, ma hora mi par troppo grande però giudicherei, che la parte di Amore la facesse Adamo et quella di Mirtia Ninfa, Bartolomeo, se però la M.V. giudicherà che sia ben aplicata." Ibid., fol. 50r (at the end of the document): "Rimettendomi al voler di V. M^ta. per poter far rescriver le parti a quelli che doveranno impararle, et che dalla M.V. sarà desposto."

[17] Evidence of Leopold I's close participation in the planning of operas during his reign is in Goloubeva, p. 47. An exception to operas over which Ferdinand III would have exerted control are those that were organized by Archduke Leopold Wilhelm and performed by his musicians. These include an opera produced in 1638 for King Władysław IV of Poland, *Lo Specchio di Virtù* from 1642, and two unknown Carnival operas from 1657.

[18] The definitive work on operas at the Habsburg court in the seventeenth century is Seifert, *Oper*, to which this discussion owes much.

[19] For information on these comedies, for which there is evidence from 1639, 1652–54, and 1656–57, see ibid., pp. 171–2, 438–43.

Table 3.1 Italian operas and oratorios performed at court during Ferdinand III's reign

Title	Authors	Date	Location	Occasion	Acts	Sources
Unnamed ballet with sung introduction	Valeriano Bonvicino (text)	Jan. 4, 1637	Regensburg, Rathaus, Reichssaal	Ferdinand's coronation as Roman King	1	MS libretto (A-Wn, Cod. 9931); printed description (Vienna, Gelbhaar)
Intermedio, *Il Faneto*, for an unknown opera[a]	Prospero Bonarelli (text)	Oct. 14, 1638	Vienna, Hofburg	Visit from King Wladyslaw IV of Poland	4	MS libretto (A-Wn, Cod. 13310)
Unknown ballet		March 1639	Vienna, Hofburg	Carnival		
Unknown sung passion	Giovanni Valentini (music)	Apr. 1640	Vienna, Hofburgkapelle	Holy Week		
Unnamed opera ("comedia") about Armida and Rinaldo		July 14, 1641	Regensburg	Emperor's birthday; imperial diet	3	MS libretto (A-Wn, Cod. 13349)

Opera ("comedia"), *Ariadne abbandonata da Theseo*	Francesco Bonacossi (text)	Aug. 18, 1641	Regensburg, a garden	Empress's birthday; imperial diet	3	Printed scenario (n.p.); MS libretto (A-Wn, Cod 13349)
Oratorio, *Ragionamento sovra il Santissimo*	Giovanni Valentini (text, probably music)	Apr. 10, 1642	Vienna, Hofburg (Hofburgkapelle?)	Lent (Holy Week?)[b]	3	Printed libretto (Vienna, Cosmerovius)
Oratorio, *Rime sovra la Colonna, Flagello, Corona di Spine, Croce, e Lancia di Christo*	Giovanni Valentini (text, probably music)	Apr. 18, 1642	Vienna, Hofburg?	Holy Week		Printed libretto (Vienna, Cosmerovius)
Opera ("drammatica"), *Lo Specchio di Virtù*	Horatio Persiani (text)[c]	June 15, 1642	Vienna, Hofburg	Emperor's birthday (given a month early)	3	Printed libretto (Vienna, Gelbhaar)
Opera (oratorio?), *Santi Risorti nel Giorno della Passione di Christo*	Giovanni Valentini (text and music)	Apr. 1643	Vienna, Hofburg (Hofburgkapelle?)	Holy Week		Printed libretto (Vienna, Cosmerovius)

Oratorio ("dialogo"), *La Vita di Santo Agapito*	Giovanni Valentini (text, probably music)	Aug. 18, 1643	Vienna, Hofburg	Empress's birthday	1	Printed libretto (Vienna, Cosmerovius)
Unknown ballet		May 3, 1648	Vienna, Hofburg	Spanish re-conquest of Naples		
Opera ("dramma imperfetta"), *I Trionfi d'Amore*	Giovanni Felice Sances (music)	1649 (between March and June?)	Bratislava[d]	Emperor's marriage	5	MS libretto (A-Wn, Cod. 13182)
Unnamed moral "drama musicum"	Ferdinand III (music)	composed by 1649	No record of a performance exists		1	at least 5 MS sources[e]
Unknown "demonstration" by costumed musicians		1651 (before March 22)	Vienna, Hofburg			
Unnamed opera ("attione") with tournament and ballet		July 13, 1651	Vienna, Hofburg	Emperor's birthday	3	Printed libretto (Vienna, Cosmerovius)

Opera ("dramatica") with tournament, *La Gara*	Alberto Vimina (text)	Jan. 8, 1652 (plus 3 more performances until Jan. 18)	Vienna, Hofburg, large dancehall	Birth of Infanta Margarita Teresa	3	Printed libretto (Vienna, Rickhes); printed German libretto (Vienna, Rickhes)
Introduction to a ballet, *Dafne in Alloro*	Benedetto Ferrari (text)	Feb. 12, 1652	Vienna, Hofburg	Monday before Ash Wednesday	1	MS text (I-MOe, ms. ital. 33)
Unknown ballet		Feb. 13, 1652	Vienna, Hofburg	Tuesday before Ash Wednesday		
Opera ("dramma"), *L'Inganno d'Amore*	Benedetto Ferrari (text); Antonio Bertali (music)	Feb. 24, 1653 (plus another performance March 2)	Regensburg, temporary theatre near the Capuchin cloister	Monday before Ash Wednesday; imperial diet	3	Printed libretto (Regensburg, Fischer); printed German scenario (Regensburg, Fischer)
Unnamed oratorio	Archduke Leopold Wilhelm (text)?	Apr. 4, 1654	Regensburg or Vienna, Hofburgkapelle	Holy Week	1	MS libretto (A-Wn, Cod. Ser. n. 4270); printed text (Brussels, 1656)
Unknown ballet		Feb. 9, 1655	Vienna, Hofburg	Tuesday before Ash Wednesday		

Unknown comedy ("burletta")		Feb. 7, 1656	Vienna, Hofburg, private chamber		
Unknown ballet		Feb. 28, 1656	Vienna, Hofburg	Tuesday before Ash Wednesday	
Unknown sacred opera ("sacra rappresentatione")		Apr. 14, 1656	Vienna, Hofburg	Holy Week	
Opera ("drama"), *Theti*	Diamante Gabrielli (text); Antonio Bertali (music)	July 13, 1656	Vienna, Hofburg, large dancehall	Emperor's birthday	5	Printed libretto (Vienna, Cosmerovius)
Unknown opera ("pastorale")		Jan. 28, 1657	Vienna, Hofburg	Carnival	
Unknown opera		Feb. 4, 1657	Vienna, Hofburg	Carnival	
Unknown ballet with sung introduction		Feb. 8, 1657	Vienna, Hofburg, large dancehall	Carnival	

| Oratorio, L'Ave Maria Addolorata col Morto Giesu | "L'incognito Ottuso" (text) | No date (1640s or 50s?);[e] the author also mentions the performance of a similar work the previous year. | Vienna? (Hofburgkapelle?) | Holy Week | 1 | MS libretto (A-Wn, Cod. 13278) |

Most information in this table, especially on the unknown works, is drawn from Seifert, *Oper*, pp. 37–42, 132–5, 438–43. Information on the sacred dramatic works is primarily from Seifert, "Beginnings of Sacred Dramatic Musical Works."

[a] Seifert has proposed that the opera was Bonarelli's five-act *L'Imeneo* (*Oper*, pp. 37–8, 170).

[b] The date of Easter in 1642 was April 20; April 10 is when the dedication of the libretto was signed and was not necessarily the date of the performance.

[c] Seifert has speculated that the music may have been composed by Giacinto Cornacchioli ("Beginnings of Sacred Dramatic Musical Works," p. 502).

[d] The performance, originally planned for Prague in 1648, may have never taken place (Seifert, *Oper*, pp. 39–40).

[e] See the list of sources in Saunders, "Emperor as Artist," p. 28. Excerpts of the work are published in Adler, *Musikalische Werke*, vol. 2, pp. 5–26. See also Antonicek, "italienischen Textvertonungen."

[f] Seifert has argued that Ferdinand III may have composed the music for this work ("Beginnings of Sacred Dramatic Works," pp. 499–500).

[g] Seifert has argued, based on the watermark of the manuscript libretto, that the work was performed in the 1640s ("Beginnings of Sacred Dramatic Musical Works," p. 498), while Saunders has speculated that this work could be the unknown "sacra rappresentatione" from April 1656 ("Antecedents," p. 77).

The Setting

Due to its nature as a festive spectacle (as well as the high production costs), an opera could not be a regular event; rather, to secure the prestigious, commemorative value of these works, operas were planned in conjunction with other special events or during especially festive times of the year such as Carnival. One of the most common uses of the genre throughout Europe was to celebrate weddings. However, although wedding operas were an important element of Habsburg court spectacle throughout the seventeenth century, the only wedding opera produced at court during Ferdinand III's reign is the above-mentioned *I Trionfi d'Amore* for his second marriage.[20] The most common occasions for which operas were presented at Ferdinand's court were birthdays; a total of five operas during his reign commemorated birthdays, four for him and one for his first wife Maria of Spain. Operas were also planned to coincide with important political gatherings, at which it was crucial for Ferdinand to assert his power; two birthday operas from the summer of 1641 occurred during the Diet of Regensburg, and an opera was given in 1653 during the second Regensburg Diet of Ferdinand's reign, at which his eldest son Ferdinand IV was crowned King of the Romans. Operas could also be planned for diplomatic purposes outside of any specific occasion; for instance, an opera was presented by Archduke Leopold Wilhelm in 1638 in honor of a visit from King Władysław IV, who in September of the previous year had married Ferdinand III's sister Cecilia Renata.[21]

Indeed, the very multivalence of an opera meant that in most cases the work served more than one function. This is true, for instance, of the two operas from 1641 mentioned above, which ostensibly celebrated birthdays but also glorified the Habsburgs for the attendees of the Regensburg Diet. It is also true of the most spectacular opera produced at court during Ferdinand's reign, *La Gara* from January 1652 (for which also the most

---

[20] Ferdinand III's first wedding, however, had been celebrated at court in 1631 with a variety of festive theatrical events over the space of almost two weeks: three ballets on February 27, March 4 (a horse ballet), and March 9; two dramas on March 1 and 3; and an opera on March 9. For more information on these works, see Seifert, *Oper*, pp. 30–33, 434–5 and Seifert, *Sig-prangende*, pp. 13–18.

[21] The only document of this occasion that survives in Vienna is a manuscript libretto by Prospero Bonarelli of a four-part intermedio, *Il Faneto* (A-Wn, Cod. 13310). Seifert convincingly argues that the opera was Bonarelli's five-act *L'Imeneo*, a work consisting of both sung and spoken roles (*Oper*, pp. 37–8, 170). This work about the early history of Hymen, the Greek god of marriage, would have been appropriate for the occasion. See also Seifert, *Sig-prangende*, pp. 19–20.

lavish printed libretto survives).[22] On the most basic level, this was a birthday work, celebrating the birth in July 1651 of the Spanish Infanta Margarita Teresa. However, considering the long tradition of marriages between the Austrian and Spanish Habsburgs, this work could very well have also been the first step in arranging Margarita Teresa's betrothal to Ferdinand's son (she eventually married Leopold I in 1666). On a larger level, this opera could have also served other diplomatic purposes. Ferdinand III had been forced by the Peace of Westphalia to end all military alliances with the Spanish Habsburgs, leaving Philip IV at the mercy of France for another 11 years; perhaps this celebration of the Spanish King's new daughter was an attempt by Ferdinand III to soothe relations between the two Habsburg powers.

Even before the curtain went up, the very atmosphere of the opera theater contributed to the Emperor's representation. As has been discussed by scholars of seventeenth-century opera at Italian courts, great significance was attached to the seating arrangements in the hall.[23] Pride of place was given, of course, to the Emperor himself. His was literally the best seat in the house; not only was it perfectly positioned directly opposite the center of the stage to give him the ideal view of the single-point stage perspective (and also to give other attendees a clear view of him),[24] but it was also often lavishly decorated to emphasize his privileged status and sometimes to provide commentary on his character. For *La Gara*, for instance, the imperial throne was placed on a raised platform underneath a grand baldacchino supported by two statues representing Peace and Virtue (see Figure 3.1).[25] To ensure that everyone noticed the Emperor's arrival, and to introduce him with the proper pomp and majesty, he entered the hall to a trumpet fanfare, a fact that is noted in several libretti.[26] The placement of the other guests in relation to the Emperor also made an important

---

[22] Alberto Vimina, *La Gara* (Vienna, 1652). The libretto was also published in a German translation (*Der Welt-Streit*). For more information on the planning of this production (which was initially planned for November 1651), see Seifert, *Oper*, pp. 40–41.

[23] Harness, pp. 13–14.

[24] Ibid., pp. 13–14. The focus of the stage on only the eyes of the ruler has been interpreted as reinforcing the idea of absolutism; see Roy Strong, *Art and Power: Renaissance Festivals, 1450–1650* (Berkeley and Los Angeles, 1984), pp. 32–5 and Aercke, pp. 33–4.

[25] Vimino, *La Gara*, sig. A2v: "S'incaminarono verso il Maestoso Trono, e si posero a sedere. Era questo situato nel centro del Teatro in altezza di cinque gradini cinto di balaustrata molto vaga. Ne gli angoli esteriori del piano sopremo s'ergevano su i suoi piedestalli due statoe dorate della maggior grandezza naturale, una delle quali rappresentava la pace, e l'altra la virtù. Si mostravano in atto di sostenere con le braccia aperte, & ellevate il pomposo baldacchino delle loro Auguste Maestà, a fronte delle quali si mirava il Prosenio non men maestoso, che ben' inteso."

[26] Ibid., sig. A2v; Benedetto Ferrari, *L'Inganno d'Amore* (Regensburg, 1653), sig. X3v.

Figure 3.1 Giovanni Burnacini, staged tournament in *La Gara*, engraving from the libretto, 1652

statement; at the 1637 ballet celebrating Ferdinand III's coronation in Regensburg, for example, the Bavarian Duke Maximilian I, an important political and military ally whom Ferdinand II had recently elevated to the position of elector, was given a prominent position on the platform directly to the Emperor's right, while the representatives of the Protestant electors were positioned further away on the left.[27]

Nothing spoke more to the Emperor's magnificence, however, than the production itself. Everything from the elaborate sets and luxurious costumes to the beautiful voices and instruments spoke of his superior taste, while specific stage images and even colors could help reinforce the allegorical interpretation of the work as a representation of the Emperor. Especially important was the stage machinery, an expected element of any Baroque opera.[28] If, for example, Jove wore imperial colors, or if he made his appearance riding an eagle in majestic splendor (as in the final act of

---

[27] See p. 15.

[28] For a summary of the stage machinery in operas from Ferdinand III's reign, see Seifert, *Oper*, 369–75.

La Gara), any audience member would have realized that the Roman god represented the Emperor.[29] An additional element of grandeur was added to Habsburg operas by the inclusion of grand set pieces such as ballets and staged tournaments, many of which featured the participation of members of the imperial family.[30] The libretto for *La Gara*—the centerpiece of which was a tournament led (and won) by Ferdinand IV (pictured in Figure 3.1)—lists in its opening pages a total of 22 machines used throughout the production, as well as six scene changes (which occurred in an instant right before the spectators' eyes) and other scenic effects such as a drawbridge and eight chandeliers in the shape of an eagle.[31] The last page of the libretto for *Theti*, the final surviving opera produced during Ferdinand III's reign, lists 16 machines (including one that transformed the protagonist Thetis into a stone, a lion, and a bird), six scene changes, and three ballets, the last of which featured a performance by the future Emperor Leopold I. The actual substance of *Theti* was apparently not particularly well received, but everyone in the audience was stunned by the scenic effects and dancing; one Florentine observer remarked that the opera served merely as scaffolding for the splendid work of Ferdinand III's engineer Lodovico Ottavio Burnacini.[32]

The Plots

As important as the staging was for producing a mirror of Ferdinand III's majesty and power, it was the libretto that most directly presented a specific image of the Emperor. This could be explicit and unambiguous, as in the 1637 coronation ballet in which representations of Ferdinand's realms praised him directly, but more often the image was presented obliquely through the guise of a well-known story or allegorical characters, almost always introduced with an explicit explanation in the prologue. The types of plots found in court operas during Ferdinand's reign varied considerably, demonstrating that there was by no means any set "formula" that court artists were expected to follow when creating a work for the Emperor.

Like most Italian opera of the first half of the seventeenth century, the most popular sources for the plots of Habsburg court operas were ancient

---

[29] Jove's entrance in *La Gara* is described in Vimina, *La Gara*, sig. O: "Quando si vedea più frequente la folla del Torneo, prendendo i spettatori sommo diletto, fù subito il guardo di ciascuno allettato a mirare la comparsa di Giove. Si lasciò questa Deità vedere asciša sull'aquila in forma maestosa da vaghissimo splendore circondata, originato da lumi invisibili ingegnosamente collocati."

[30] On the tradition of court tournaments, see Strong, pp. 11–16, 50–57.

[31] Vimina, *La Gara*, sig. B. The chandeliers are probably those visible in Figure 3.1.

[32] Seifert, *Oper*, pp. 42, 215, 642.

Roman mythology and epic literature. Three works draw upon mythology (including two tales that had already served as the basis of renowned operas elsewhere)—*Ariadne abbandonata da Theseo* (1641), *Dafne in Alloro* (1652), and *Theti* (1656, about Achilles' mother Thetis)—while two are based on epic poems (the unnamed Armida opera from 1641, based on Tasso, and the 1648/49 *I Trionfi d'Amore*, which tells the tale of Ulysses and Circe from Homer's *Odyssey*). Even the operas that have freely invented plots draw upon well-known figures from Roman mythology, including Jove, Apollo, Minerva, Mars, Venus, and Cupid. Some operas also follow the conventions of Venetian public opera. Examples include *L'Inganno d'Amore*, performed at the Diet of Regensburg in 1653,[33] and *I Trionfi d'Amore*, a fanciful capriccioso featuring two completely separate plots: the Ulysses story (told in the second and fourth acts) framed in Acts 1, 3, and 5 by a frothy pastoral tale of two shepherds and two nymphs who swear off love but end up happily together.

More numerous than these works on well-known stories or following conventional plot formulas are those featuring allegorical characters and a thin plot that serves only as an excuse to praise the Emperor. In addition to the 1637 coronation ballet and the 1642 moral opera *Lo Specchio di Virtù*, which features the triumph of Virtue over a variety of sins and concludes with Good Wishes (*Augurio*) singing Ferdinand III's praises, an unnamed opera of 1651 and *La Gara* of 1652 both explicitly glorify the house of Habsburg. Act I of *La Gara* features Religion defeating Envy, to the praise of Apollo and the nine Muses, while the remaining two acts are centered around the tournament between the four parts of the world that concludes with Jove (representing the Emperor) ending the battle and declaring the winner. The opera of the previous year also features a tournament, this one between Mars (whose squad consists of Valor, Fury, and Scorn) and Minerva (whose squad includes Prudence, Hope, and Strength), who are fighting over which of them better exemplifies Ferdinand III.[34] It is perhaps no accident that these two blatantly laudatory operas were the first ones produced at court after the war (not including the aborted *I Trionfi d'Amore*), at a time when Ferdinand III was in the most desperate need to rebuild his powerful image.

---

[33] Seifert comments that this libretto marks the appearance in Vienna of "ein neuer venezianischer Typus," pointing out that the librettist Benedetto Ferrari had previously written operas for the Venetian stage (*Oper*, pp. 212–15).

[34] The libretto refers to Minerva as Bellona, but it is clear that the character is meant to represent the prudent, wise aspect of the Roman Goddess, not the wild, furious, irrational Goddess of War. On the features of Minerva vs. Bellona, see Jane Kromm, "The Bellona Factor: Political Allegories and the Conflicting Claims of Martial Imagery," in Cristelle Baskins and Lisa Rosenthal (eds), *Early Modern Visual Allegory: Embodying Meaning* (Aldershot, 2007), pp. 175–95.

EMBLEMATIC SOUND 83

Figure 3.2   Lucas Schnitzer, scenes from Ferdinand III's coronation as King of the Romans (detail), engraving, 1636–37

Other Musical Events at Court

A consideration of the theatrical spectacles at Ferdinand's court would not be complete without mentioning a number of other types of works. Unstaged oratorios, always on a religious subject but sung in Italian, were common beginning in 1640. Many of these are obvious precursors to the *sepolcro*, an Italian oratorio-like genre performed during Holy Week before a painted representation of the Holy Sepulcher, a genre that was institutionalized as regular practice only during Leopold I's reign.[35] At least six oratorios—four with libretti (and probably music) by Giovanni Valentini (1640, 1642, 1643), one with a libretto by Ferdinand's brother Archduke Leopold Wilhelm (1654), and one with a libretto by an anonymous author identified only as "L'incognito Ottuso" (unknown year)—are known to have been performed during Holy Week and deal with themes on the Passion of Christ.[36] Another oratorio by Valentini shows an additional purpose this genre could serve at court. *La Vita di Santo Agapito*, a work celebrating the child martyr Agapitus, was performed in August 1643 on the birthday of Ferdinand's first wife Maria, whose middle name was Agapita. The representational function of all these oratorios lay primarily in that they served as mirrors of the patron's devout soul (as discussed in Chapter 6).[37]

Another type of dramatic production popular at court was the ballet. Many of these, such as works for Ferdinand's 1631 marriage and 1637 coronation, are essentially miniature, one-act operas in that they begin with lengthy sung introductions that make explicit the commemorative nature of the work. The same is true of *Dafne in Alloro* of 1652, and it may also very well be the case for the other ballets performed at court, but very few documents survive for many of them, aside from general

---

[35] On the early history of the sepolcro, see Herbert Seifert, "The Beginnings of Sacred Dramatic Musical Works at the Imperial Court of Vienna: Sacred and Moral Opera, Oratorio, and *Sepolcro*," in Paola Besutti (ed.), *L'oratorio musicale italiano e i suoi contesti (secc. XVII–XVIII): Atti del convegno internazionale, Perugia, Sagra musicale umbra, 18–20 settembre 1997* (Florence, 2002), pp. 489–511 and Steven Saunders, "The Antecedents of the Viennese Sepolcro," in Alberto Colzani et al. (eds), *Relazioni musicali tra Italia e Germania nell'età barocca: Atti del VI convegno internazionale sulla muisca italiana nei secoli XVII–XVIII* (Como, 1997), pp. 63–83. For more information on the sepolcro, see especially Gernot Gruber, *Das Wiener Sepolcro und Johann Joseph Fux, 1. Teil* (Graz, 1972) and Howard Smither, *A History of the Oratorio, Volume 1: The Oratorio in the Baroque Era, Italy, Vienna, Paris* (Chapel Hill, 1977), pp. 364–415.

[36] We know precious little about the 1640 work; our only evidence comes from a brief mention in a letter by Ferdinand III to Leopold Wilhelm, in which he refers to it as a passion (Saunders, "The Antecedents," p. 64). The dedication (to the Emperor) of the libretto by L'incognito Ottuso mentions that a similar work had been performed the year before (A-Wn, Cod. 13278, fol. 2r: "Hor non potranno su i pulpiti le troppo mordaci lingue ferirla, come fecero l'anno passato, che nè le Birgitte, nè i più antichi pennelli, ne i torchi più frequenti valsero a raffrenarle"; see also Seifert, "Beginnings," p. 498).

[37] Another oratorio-like (though not necessarily dramatic) work from Ferdinand III's reign is a "dialogo" for Christmas with text by Leopold Wilhelm and music by Ferdinand III, listed in HKA, NÖHA, W61/A/32, fol. 9v; the text was published in Leopold Wilhelm, *Diporti del Crescente, divisi in rime morali, devote, heroiche, amorose* (Brussels, 1656), pp. 53–8. No record of a performance of this work at court exists.

descriptions in court records.[38] These works functioned as representation in the same manner as court operas, and they often also represented in the most obvious sense by featuring members of the imperial family as performers.

One final type of performance that should be mentioned are those occasions when the chapel performed as an accompaniment to another secular event at court, such as a ball or banquet. Although not theatrical events, these occasions nevertheless maintained a level of decorum and social protocol (centered around the person of the Emperor) similar to that encountered at an opera performance. A broadsheet illustrating events from Ferdinand III's coronation as King of the Romans, for instance, includes an image of the banquet that followed the ceremony (see Figure 3.2).[39] The picture shows a formally arranged room with the guests seated at individual tables positioned on raised platforms along the walls, radiating outward from a higher platform centered along the far wall, at which sit the Emperor and the new King.[40] Although musicians are not pictured in the engraving, we know from a published account of the Regensburg events that both vocal and instrumental music was performed.[41] This music would have added a sense of grandeur to the event and would probably have included texts that explicitly praised the Habsburgs. As the seating arrangement pictured in Figure 3.2 does not seem to have fostered conversation, it is reasonable to assume that (unlike at banquets and wedding receptions today) the dinner guests would have actually paid attention to the music as they ate.[42]

---

[38] For more information on ballets at the Habsburg court (including those performed in conjunction with operas), see Seifert, *Oper*, pp. 127–64.

[39] A full illustration of the broadsheet, which was published by the Nuremberg engraver Lucas Schnitzer, is in Ursula Mielke and Tilman Falk (eds), *Johann Schnitzer to Lucas Schnitzer*, Hollstein's German Engravings, Etchings, and Woodcuts, 1400–1700, vol. 46 (Rotterdam, 1999), p. 51 (No. 52) and Jeroen Duindam, *Vienna and Versailles: The Courts of Europe's Dynastic Rivals, 1550–1780* (Cambridge, 2003), frontispiece.

[40] A similar seating arrangement appears in an anonymous engraving of the banquet following Ferdinand IV's coronation as King of the Romans in Regensburg in 1653, reproduced in Seifert, *Oper*, p. 1004 (Abb. 46).

[41] *Le quattro Relazioni seguite in Ratisbona nelli tempi sotto notati ... Seconda della Incoronatione dell'istessa Maestà li 30. Decembre 1636 ...* (Vienna, 1637), sig. Dr: "Tutto il tempo che durò il Conuito, i musici Casarei fecero lor belli concerti, e simfonie, massime alcuni novamente composti dal Sig. Gio. Valentini."

[42] An engraving from a court banquet in the Hofburg in 1651, however, shows groups of people sitting at 11 large banquet tables; see Duindam, fig. 11.

Jesuit Drama

Although not official court events, fully staged Latin dramas presented by the students of the Jesuit College and University in Vienna were transformed into court occasions when attended by the Emperor and/or other members of the imperial family. If the loss of information about operas poses challenges in studying them as means of monarchical representation, the same is true to an even greater extent of Jesuit dramas. Not only is music lacking for all of these works, but there is also precious little surviving information about the planning of these events and the people involved, including the identities of the composers and librettists; we only know which works are by Nicholas Avancini because he included the texts in his later collected works edition.[43]

Staged theatrical productions featuring music and dance were produced at Jesuit colleges already in the 1550s, within the first two decades of the founding of the order.[44] Although not everyone felt that these productions were the best use of the Society's time and money, most Jesuits enthusiastically supported them on account of their excellent educational value (for both performers and spectators) and their ability to impart moral and spiritual lessons just as (if not more) effectively as a sermon. As the Jesuits spread throughout Europe, they brought the Latin dramas with them; the earliest record of Jesuit drama in Vienna dates as far back as 1555.[45] We unfortunately know very little about the role that music played in the productions; however, it seems clear that the plays almost always consisted of both spoken and sung parts. Most of the Viennese dramas conclude each act (or part) with a chorus, and two libretti (from 1643 and 1644) specifically label each one as a "chorus musicus."[46] A report of the 1640 performance of Avancini's *Zelus sive Franciscus Xaverius Indiarum*

---

[43] Nicholas Avancini, *Poesis dramatica*, vols 1 and 2 (Cologne, 1675).

[44] General overviews of Jesuit drama include William H. McCabe, *An Introduction to the Jesuit Theater: A Posthumous Work*, ed. Louis J. Oldani (St Louis, 1983); Jean-Marie Valentin, "Gegenreformation und Literatur: Das Jesuitendrama im Dienste der religiösen und moralischen Erziehung," *Historisches Jahrbuch*, 100 (1980): pp. 240–56; Valentin, *Les Jésuites et le théâtre (1554–1680): Contribution à l'histoire culturelle du monde catholique dans le Saint-Empire romain germanique* (Paris, 2001); Valentin, *Le théâtre des Jésuites dans les pays de langue allemande (1554–1680): Salut des âmes et ordre des cités* (3 vols, Bern, 1978). On Jesuit drama specifically in Vienna, see Bernhard Duhr, *Geschichte der Jesuiten in den Ländern deutscher Zunge* (4 vols, Freiburg: Herder, 1907–28), vol. 2, part 1, pp. 657–703 and vol. 3, pp. 459–501; Willi Flemming, *Geschichte des Jesuitentheaters in den Landen Deutscher Zunge*, Schriften der Gesellschaft für Theaterwissenschaft, vol. 32 (Berlin, 1923); Kurt Adel, *Das Wiener Jesuitentheater und die europäische Barockdramatik* (Vienna, 1960).

[45] McCabe, p. 38; Adel, pp. 16–17.

[46] A-Wn, Cod. 13347 and Cod. 13275.

Apostolus mentions the singing of the Te Deum and other hymns by a hundred boys, the singing of angels, and the use of trumpets and tympani, in addition to fireworks.[47]

A list of Jesuit dramas known to have been performed in Vienna during Ferdinand III's reign is provided in Table 3.2; this is not a comprehensive list but only includes those that we know (or can reasonably infer) were attended by the imperial family.[48] Only those family members for whom we have solid evidence of their attendance are listed, although others quite likely also attended. That many of these performances were specifically intended as glorifications of the Emperor is evident from the titles alone; a number of them feature some version of the word "Austria," while others incorporate Ferdinand III's motto, "Justitia et Pietas." Two titles also include the motto "Consilio et Industria," which was used by Ferdinand IV and taken up by Leopold I after his brother's death. Because these were not official court events, we cannot assume that Ferdinand III exerted much, if any, control over them; however, there is evidence that the Emperor sometimes offered financial support for productions,[49] which would likely have given him some input in the creative process. All the same, in many cases these works may have been intended not only to glorify the Emperor but also to teach or subtly admonish him, and/or to provide a model that the Jesuits felt he should strive to emulate.

---

[47] Duhr, vol. 2, p. 665. For evidence of the use of music in sixteenth-century Jesuit dramas, see Franz Körndle, "'Ad te perenne gaudium': Lassos Musik zum 'Vltimum Judicium,'" *Die Musikforschung*, 53 (2000): pp. 68–71.

[48] Included in Table 3.2 are all dramas known to be performed during Corpus Christi (as this was an especially important feast for the Habsburgs) and all dramas by Avancini, even if we do not have evidence that the imperial family attended. Bibliographies of Jesuit dramas include Jean-Marie Valentin, *Le théâtre des Jésuites dans les pays de langue allemande: Répertoire chronologique des pièces représentées et des documents conservés (1555–1773)* (2 vols, Stuttgart, 1983–84); Kurt Adel, "Handschriften von Jesuitendrama in der Österreichischen National-Bibliothek in Wien," *Jahrbuch der Gesellschaft für Wiener Theaterforschung*, 12 (1960): pp. 83–112; Johannes Müller, *Das Jesuitendrama in den Ländern deutscher Zunge vom Anfang (1555) bis zum Hochbarock (1665)* (2 vols, Augsburg, 1930), vol. 2, pp. 43–87; Carlos Sommervogel (ed.), *Bibliothèque de la Compagnie de Jésus* (10 vols, Brussels and Paris, 1890–1909).

[49] McCabe, p. 39.

Table 3.2 Jesuit dramas performed in Vienna for the imperial family during Ferdinand III's reign

Title (and author, if known)	Date	Acts/Parts	Source of Plot	Known Attendees	Sources (sources are in Latin, unless otherwise specified)
David sitiens	June 1638 (Corpus Christi)		Old Testament		No surviving sources; mentioned in Duhr, *Geschichte der Jesuiten*, vol. 2/1, p. 671
Zelus, sive Franciscus Xaverius Indiarum Apostolus, by Nicholas Avancini	1640	5	Allegory, based on hagiography	Emperor, Empress	Printed scenario (Vienna, Formica); printed text in Avancini, *Poesis dramatica*, vol. 2 (Cologne, 1675)[a]
Suspicio, sive Pomum Theodosii, by Nicholas Avancini	1641	8	History		Printed text in Avancini, *Poesis dramatica*, vol. 1 (Cologne, 1675)
Unnamed Drama	1643 (Holy Week)[b]	3	Allegory, based on Songs 4:4	Emperor	MS libretto (A-Wn, Cod. 13347)
Fortunae Tragoedia, sive Emmanuel Sosa naufragus, by Nicholas Avancini	Spring 1643; performed twice, the second time at Ferdinand III's request[c]	5	History		Printed scenario (Vienna, Cosmerovius);[d] printed text in Avancini, *Poesis dramatica*, vol. 1 (Cologne, 1675)
Fiducia in Deum, sive Bethulia liberata, by Nicholas Avancini	1643 (spring?)	5	Old Testament (Judith)	Emperor	Printed text in Avancini, *Poesis dramatica*, vol. 2 (Cologne, 1675)
Amor et Timor Eucharistiae	June 1643[e] (Corpus Christi)	7	Allegory		MS libretto (A-Wn, Cod. 13309)

Felix Annus 1644	Jan. 1, 1644	6	Allegory, based on recent history	Emperor, and the "entire house of Austria"	MS libretto (A-Wn, Cod. 13242)
SS. Eucharistia, Certum Piis in necessitate subsidium in D. Maximiliano Austriaco	May or June 1644?[f] (Corpus Christi)	3	History/Habsburg legend (reign of Maximilian I)		MS libretto (A-Wn, Cod. 13275)
Curae Caesarum pro Deo pro populo, sive Theodius Magnus Pius et Justus Imperator, by Nicholas Avancini	1644	5	History		Printed text in Avancini, Poesis dramatica, vol. 1 (Cologne, 1675)
Arma Austriaca Eucharistica, sive Lapis David de Goliath victor	June 18, 1645 (within Corpus Christi octave)	2	Old Testament (1 Samuel 17:19–51)	Emperor	MS libretto (A-Wn, Cod. 13923)
Belisaurius, sive Speculum utriusque Fortunae, hoc est Prosperae et adversae	Feb. 28, 1647[g]	3	History		Printed scenario (Vienna, Rickhes)
Franciscus Fernandus Japoniae Rex Animatus defensus sublevatus	June 23, 1647 (within Corpus Christi octave)	6	History	Ferdinand IV, Maria Anna[h]	MS scenario (A-Wn, Cod. 13911)
Saxonia Conversa, sive Clodoaldus Daniae Princeps, cum tota familia a Carolo Magno superato Vitigindo, conversus, by Nicholas Avancini	Aug. 22, 1647	5	History	Ferdinand IV, Maria Anna, Leopold I	Printed German scenario (Vienna, Cosmerovius); printed Latin scenario (Vienna); printed text in Avancini, Poesis dramatica, vol. 1 (Cologne, 1675)
Jason, by Nicholas Avancini	1648?		History/Mythology		No surviving sources; mentioned in Müller, Jesuitendrama, vol. 2, pp. 32–3

Christus Eucharisticus Portus Afflictorum	June 1648 (Corpus Christi)			No surviving sources; mentioned in Duhr, *Geschichte der Jesuiten*, vol. 2/1, p. 671
Fortuna Eucharistico-Austriaca Pietati et Justitiae	No Date (1648–1654)[j]	5	Allegory, based on history and the Bible: Psalm 71:7, Baruch. 5:14, Isaiah 32:17	Emperor, Ferdinand IV	Printed scenario (Vienna, Cosmerovius); MS libretto (A-Wn, Cod. 13341)
Morandus Cultu Eucharistico	1650 (June or July 4)[k]	4	Hagiography (St Elizabeth of Portugal)	Emperor, Ferdinand IV, Leopold I, Sigismund[l]	Printed scenario (Vienna, Rickhes; MS libretto (A-Wn, Cod. 13281)
Pax Imperii, sive Joseph a Fratribus recognitus, by Nicholas Avancini	Sept. 1650	5	Old Testament (Genesis 41–5)		Printed German scenario (Vienna, Cosmerovius);[m] printed text in Avancini, *Poesis dramatica*, vol. 1 (Cologne, 1675)
Increata et incarnata Dei Sapientia. Ludens in orbe terrarum	Jan. 1, 1651	3	Allegory, based on Proverbs 8	Emperor	Printed scenario (Vienna, Cosmerovius); MS libretto (A-Wn, Cod. 13284)[n]
Bacchanalia fortunae aulicae, sic olim ab Aegyptiis appellata	Carnival 1651	4	History	Emperor, Ferdinand IV, Leopold I, Sigismund	Printed scenario (Vienna, Cosmerovius)
Sacrificium Pacificum Melchisedech Regis Salem, hoc est, Regis Justitiae et Pacis in pane et vino Deo libatum: Abrae autem de V. Regibus victori oblatum	June 11, 1651° (Sunday within the octave of Corpus Christi)	2	Old Testament (Genesis 14–15)	Emperor, Empress, Ferdinand IV, Leopold I, Sigismund	Printed scenario (Vienna, Cosmerovius); MS libretto (A-Wn, Cod. 13359)

Zelus Ignatianus a divini nominis et gloriae zelo accensus	July 13, 1651	6	Allegory, based on hagiography and Psalm 8:3	Emperor, Empress, Ferdinand IV, Leopold I	Printed scenario (Vienna, Cosmerovius); MS libretto (A-Wn, Cod. 13258)
Sanctus Franciscus Xaverius, by Nicholas Avancini	July 31, 1651	5	Allegory, based on hagiography		Revival of the work first performed in 1640 (see above); no scenario from this production survives
Phlebotomia languentis Jesu	Jan. 1, 1652	7	Allegory (praise of the imperial family)	Emperor, Empress, Ferdinand IV, Leopold I, Charles Joseph[p]	Printed scenario (Vienna, Cosmerovius)
Liga Pietatis Austriacae cum Consilio et Industria contra arma invidiae	Jan. 1, 1652?	9	Allegory (praise of the imperial family)	Emperor, Ferdinand IV[q]	MS libretto (A-Wn, Cod. 13285)
Bertulphus durch Ansberta von Ottomani Gefängnuß das Römisch Reich durch Oesterreich vom Joch Martis erlöset[r]	1652	3	A play by Jacob Bidermann (1578–1639) relating an old legend	Emperor, Empress, Ferdinand IV, Leopold I, Charles Joseph	Printed German scenario (Vienna, Kürner)
Theodosius Magnus Justus et Pius Imperator, by Nicholas Avancini	1654, between May 24 and July 9[s]	5	History	Emperor, Empress, Ferdinand IV	Revival of work first performed in 1644 (see above); printed libretto (Vienna, Cosmerovius)

Regiae Virtutes, seu Initia Regni Salomonis Pietate et Justitia, Consilio et Industria, Duce Sapientia semper felicia	Feb. 20, 1656	5	Old Testament (1Kings 2, 3, 8, 10)	Emperor, Empress, Leopold I, Duke and Duchess of Bavaria	Printed Latin and German scenario (Vienna, Kürner)[f]
Hymenaeus Theandri et Psyches, sive Nuptiae Dei-Hominis et Animae	1656	15	Allegory	Emperor, Empress, Leopold I, Duke and Duchess of Bavaria	Printed scenario (Vienna: Kürner)
Pax in Passione Christi	No date (Holy Week?)	3	Passion	Emperor	MS libretto (A-Wn, Cod. 13352)

[a] A modern edition of the scenario is in Valentin, "Programme von Avancinis Stücken," pp. 3–7. The scenic organization of the printed text differs from the scenario and most likely reflects revisions made by Avancini for the 1651 revival; for a side-by-side comparison, see *ibid.*, pp. 6–7.

[b] According to the title page of the libretto, this drama was performed when Ferdinand III visited the Holy Sepulchre in the Jesuit church am Hof.

[c] Duhr, *Geschichte der Jesuiten*, vol. 2/1, p. 687.

[d] A modern edition of the scenario is in Valentin, "Zur Wiener Aufführung des Avancinischen 'Sosa Naufragus' (1643)," pp. 223–7.

[e] The 1643 date and relationship to the Habsburgs is proposed in Adel, "Handschriften von Jesuitendrama," p. 100.

[f] Date proposed by Adel, "Handschriften von Jesuitendrama," p. 98.

[g] Sommervogel (*Bibliothèque de la Compagnie de Jésus*, vol. 8, p. 693) and Müller (*Jesuitendrama*, vol. 2, p. 74) list the year as 1642, but the date is clearly given as 1647 in the scenario. Valentin (*Le théâtre des Jesuites dans les pays de langue allemande: Répertoire bibliographique*, vol. 1, p. 159) also gives the year as 1642, but he is only following Sommervogel and admits that he did not check the original source.

h Maria Anna (1634–96) was the second child of Ferdinand III and his first wife.

i The drama was clearly performed after the war and before Ferdinand IV's death.

j Only Ferdinand III is mentioned in the printed scenario, but the MS libretto is dedicated to both Ferdinand III and Ferdinand IV.

k Valentin (*Le théâtre des Jésuites dans les pays de langue allemande: Répertoire bibliographique*, vol. 1, p. 193) lists the date as Corpus Christi, but this may be only based on the appearance of the word "Eucharistico" in the title. July 4 was the feast day of St Elizabeth of Portugal.

l This is probably Archduke Sigismund Francis (1630–65), brother of Ferdinand III's recently deceased second wife Maria Leopoldine (whose father was one of Ferdinand II's brothers).

m A modern edition of the scenario is in Valentin, "Programme von Avancinis Stücken," pp. 7–14.

n Valentin (*Le théâtre des Jésuites dans les pays de langue allemande: Répertoire bibliographique*, vol. 1, p. 198) incorrectly gives the call number of the manuscript as 13282.

o Scholars have been uncertain about the date of this play; although the publication date given in the scenario is 1651, the title page includes two chronographs that add up to 1650. However, the play could only have been performed in June 1651, as the title page of the scenario lists one of the audience members as Ferdinand III's wife Eleonora Gonzaga, who married the emperor in April 1651.

p Charles Joseph (1649–64) was the only child of Ferdinand III and Maria Leopoldine.

q Ferdinand IV is not listed in the libretto, but "Consilio et Industria" was his personal motto; considering the message of the work, it is hard to imagine that he was not in attendance.

r Some scholars (including Sommervogel and Müller) have incorrectly surmised that this is the same play as Avancini's *Fides coniugalis, sive Ansberta, sui coniugis Bertulphi e dura captivitate liberatrix* (performed for Leopold I's wedding in 1667 and included in Avancini, *Poesis dramatica*, vol. 2).

s The drama must have been performed between the family's return from Regensburg on May 24 and Ferdinand IV's death on July 9.

t A facsimile edition of the scenario is in Szarota, *Jesuitendrama im deutschen Sprachgebiet*, vol. 2/1, pp. 51–62.

The Setting

Evidence of the imperial family's frequent attendance at Jesuit dramas during Ferdinand III's reign begins only in the year 1643, which is perhaps not coincidentally the year after the production of *Lo Specchio di Virtù*, the last opera performed at court until the end of the war. Perhaps Jesuit theater was viewed as a viable alternative to opera, a way in which Ferdinand could be associated with grand theatrical spectacles without needing to bear the brunt of the exorbitant production costs. The shift from the patronage of secular spectacle to pious Jesuit drama could have also been a calculated effort to aid in the transition of the Emperor's image from victorious warrior to pious, protective father.

Unlike court operas, Jesuit dramas do not generally seem to have been scheduled to coincide with special occasions; the only times at which dramas seem to have been regularly performed for the Emperor were New Year's Day and the important feast of Corpus Christi.[50] Nevertheless, the dates of some performances were very well timed. Some works, for instance, were clearly intended as hopeful responses to recent events in the war. Avancini's *Fiducia in Deum sive Bethulia liberata*, performed in 1643 as the Swedes ravaged Moravia after the Second Battle of Breitenfeld, relates the story of Judith decapitating Holofernes and liberating the town of Bethulia from his army. In June 1645, the play *Arma Austriaca Eucharistica*, which tells the story of David and Goliath, was performed shortly after the most crushing military defeat of the Thirty Years' War, when Vienna was under the threat of a Swedish siege.[51] An obvious relationship between Jesuit theater and recent political events can be seen in the title alone of Avancini's 1650 drama, *Pax Imperii*; the connection between the recently declared peace and the Old Testament story of Joseph reconciling with his brothers is made explicit in a prologue (not included in Avancini's later edition) in which Mars mentions the German blood that had been shed during the previous years.[52] The revival of Avancini's *Theodosius* in 1654, moreover, was clearly planned as a response to the Diet of Regensburg.[53] Telling the story of the fourth-century Roman Emperor Theodosius, who

---

[50] There is some evidence that dramas were also performed at the end of the academic year, during which awards were distributed (see, for instance, A-Wn, Cod. 13244); members of the imperial family do not seem to have attended these events.

[51] This drama is discussed in Chapter 6.

[52] The Prologue is described in the German scenario, a modern edn of which is in Jean-Marie Valentin, "Programme von Avancinis Stücken," *Literaturwissenschaftliches Jahrbuch der Görres-Gesellschaft*, N.F. 12 (1971): pp. 7–14.

[53] This work is discussed in Elida Maria Szarota, *Geschichte, Politik und Gesellschaft im Drama des 17. Jahrhunderts* (Bern and Munich, 1976), pp. 45–7.

through great difficulty defeated the pagan usurper Eugenius and declared his son his rightful successor, this work served as an obvious allegory of the end of the Thirty Years' War and Ferdinand IV's coronation as King of the Romans; its performance in Vienna helped give the local populace a taste of the Regensburg festivities. It is no accident that most of these libretti were by Avancini (1611–85), a famous writer who since 1642 had been Professor of Philosophy and Theology at the University of Vienna; Avancini had close ties to the imperial family, and in the first volume of his collected works (published in 1675), he remarked that his plays were occasionally commissioned by the Habsburgs.[54]

Until 1650, all of the dramatic productions by the Jesuits were held in a theater in the Jesuit profess house *am Hof* that had been built in 1620; after that year, productions were also held in a new 3,000-seat theater that Ferdinand III built in the new university buildings near the *Jesuitenkirche*.[55] This new theater featured the latest, most cutting-edge developments in Italian theatrical design, with not only machinery of the type expected in an opera house but also cleverly designed sets that made the stage appear larger than the auditorium.[56] The auditorium itself was adorned with beautiful architectural details, expert carpentry, and many paintings. Although we have no evidence of the seating arrangements, we can be sure that when the Emperor was present he was given a place of prominence and that his entrance was most likely announced with a regal fanfare.

Unlike court operas, seen by only an exclusive selection of the most important nobles, Jesuit dramas were open to the entire Viennese public, free of charge. Thus, these productions were an important opportunity for Ferdinand III's image to be presented to a broad populace. Scenarii were sometimes even distributed in German as well as Latin, to help those not fluent in Latin follow the plot and glean the important messages. Even those people who could not understand Latin (or read German) would have been impressed by the music, the dancing, and the spectacular stage effects that rivaled the court operas.[57]

---

[54] Avancini, *Poesis dramatica*, vol. 1, sig. *3v: "Per annos complures in Viennensi Universitate versatus jussus sum vel Principibus Austriacis, vel Academicis quandoque Scenam instruere." For a discussion of Avancini's plays, see Valentin, *Les jésuites et le théâtre*, pp. 601–87 and *Theatrum Catholicum: Les jésuites et la scène en Allemagne au XVIe et au XVIIe siècles; Die Jesuiten und die Bühne im Deutschland des 16.–17. Jahrhunderts* (Nancy, 1990), pp. 349–78.

[55] Valentin, *Les jésuites et le théâtre*, pp. 602–3; Adel, pp. 82–3.

[56] See the description of the theater from a contemporaneous report quoted in Duhr, vol. 2, p. 662 and Flemming, pp. 118–19.

[57] A letter from the Viennese College to Rome describing the first drama produced in 1555 (quoted in McCabe, p. 38) makes clear the effect that these productions could have on

Figure 3.3   Peter Paul van Mildert and Jacob Bruynel, scene from the 1654 production of *Theodosius*, engraving from the libretto, 1654

Although the surviving libretti from Ferdinand III's reign contain few stage directions or other scenic descriptions, the remarkably lavish and detailed libretto for the revival of *Theodosius*, which includes seven engravings of the stage, makes clear the extent to which Jesuit dramas could be just as spectacular as any opera produced at court.[58] From the proscenium alone, no audience member could have missed that this was a work glorifying the house of Habsburg (see Figure 3.3). Flanking the stage were two large statues of a knight on a rearing horse, crowned with laurel and holding the command baton. On the cornice were portrait busts of the three imperial family members present in the theater: Ferdinand III in the center, his third wife Eleonora Gonzaga on the left, and Ferdinand IV on the right. On both ends of the cornice were double-headed eagles holding swords and carrying banners in the their mouths; the banner on

---

the common people.

[58]   [Nicholas Avancini], *Theodosius Magnus Justus et Pius Imperator* (Vienna, 1654).

the left displayed Ferdinand III's motto (reinforced by the crucifix and scales in the eagle's left foot), and the banner on the right displayed the theme of the drama, "pro Deo et populo." The libretto contains frequent stage directions, as well as descriptions of stage machinery and specific scenes, among which were such spectacular visual feasts as a maritime scene, two scenes of Hell, and a lengthy incantation scene in which a sorcerer calls upon the black arts. The final scene of the drama is a grand coronation (pictured in Figure 3.3), which essentially recreated the Regensburg coronation for the Viennese audience. The coronation was followed by a ballet, during which the four parts of the world entered the stage on elaborate machines and paid homage to Theodosius and his son. As the chorus sang the Emperor's praises, two globes appeared, above which soared a pair of eagles.[59] The imperial imagery could not have been more obvious.

The Plots

As with court operas, it was the libretto that most clearly allowed for an identification of the drama with Ferdinand III. In at least nine plays, the connection is strengthened through the use of characters representing Piety and Justice, who always appear together in praise of the Emperor.[60] Two dramas, *Fortuna Eucharistico-Austriaca* and *Felix Annus 1644*, make the praise of the house of Habsburg explicit by including characters representing all of the former Habsburg emperors, from Rudolph I to Ferdinand II, and one is based on an event in the life of Emperor Maximilian I.[61] In other cases, it was left to the spectators to infer that the protagonist represented the Emperor, though they were undoubtedly helped in this regard by scenic elements such as those in *Theodosius*.

Also as in court operas, the sources of the plots varied widely. Over half of the works narrate a well-known story, with the tales drawn from

---

[59] Ibid., pp. 78–82. The description of the final ballet begins on p. 81: "Prodeunt quatuor Orbis partes, Europa equis, Africa Gryphibus, Asia Elephantis, America Camelis sub iuga missis vectae: plauditur choreis. Ex Arcubus inter saltum duo Orbes formantur. Advolant desuper geminae Aquilae, singula singulo Orbi insidet, una Arcadii, altera Honorii Genium, tertia media inter utramque Genium Theodosii vehit."

[60] The plays that we know included these characters are the undated *Fortuna Eucharstico-Austriaca* (A-Wn, Cod. 13341), the unnamed drama from 1643 (A-Wn, Cod. 13347), *Felix Annus 1644* (A-Wn, Cod. 13242), *Arma Austriaca Eucharistica* from 1645 (A-Wn, Cod. 13923), Avancini's *Clodoaldus* of 1647 and *Pax Imperii* of 1650, *Phlebotomia languentis Jesu* and *Liga Pietatis Austriacae cum Consilio et Industria* of 1652 (A-Wn, Cod. 13258), and *Regiae Virtutes* of 1656. The last two plays on this list also includes characters representing Consilium and Industria.

[61] A-Wn, Cod. 13275. This work is discussed in Chapter 6.

the Old Testament, world history and legends, and events in the lives of saints. Other works present freely written plots based upon a specific biblical passage; in these cases, the sole *argomento* provided in the scenario or libretto is the Bible passage. These dramas could also draw upon additional sources to enhance their explication of the biblical text. *Fortuna Eucharistico-Austriaco*, for instance, is based on three passages from the Old Testament, but it also draws upon the history of the House of Austria. *Zelus Ignatianus*, while celebrating St Ignatius, is not based upon any specific events in the saint's life but upon Psalm 8:3.

Finally, three dramas served solely as explicit encomiums to the house of Austria. *Felix Annus 1644* comments upon recent events through an allegorical tale featuring Year (*Annus*), the former Habsburg emperors, the four seasons, Mars, Austrian Happiness (*Felicitas Austriaca*), Victory, Glory, and of course, Piety and Justice. *Phlebotomia languentis Jesu* also tells an allegorical story, this one including such characters as Divine Love, Piety and Justice, Austria, Mantua (in honor of Eleonora Gonzaga), Majesty, Glory, Power (*Potentia*), Opulence, and Providence. *Liga Pietatis Austriacae* celebrates Ferdinand III and Ferdinand IV through an allegorical plot in which the military alliance of Piety and "Consilio et Industria" defeats Envy. Joining these main characters are Mars, Vulcan, Orpheus, Hercules, and characters representing the imperial provinces. This drama is an example of a work intended to stress the similarities between father and son, thereby emphasizing the continuity of the Habsburg dynasty while also laying out for Ferdinand IV the expectations people had of him as his father's successor.

Liturgy

Much more frequent than theatrical productions at court or the Jesuit college were the public liturgical ceremonies that Ferdinand III attended almost every day. With the exception of such special, one-time events as coronations, weddings, and funerals, scholars have not generally studied liturgical occasions as contributions to a monarch's representation. Nevertheless, these offer a valuable opportunity for examining Ferdinand's public image, especially as it morphed from the victorious warrior of the 1630s into the pious, protective father of the 1640s. Unlike theatrical productions, of which the Emperor was merely a witness, in liturgical services he often became an active participant (for example, in the sacrament of communion or in processions into the church), thereby expressing through his very actions important aspects of his character.[62] Not only did these regular events feature the physical presence of the Emperor himself, but they also included the music of his imperial chapel and were accompanied by the sensory accoutrements provided by the Catholic Church.[63]

Even without stage machinery and miraculous scene changes, the observance of the Catholic liturgy was a spectacle nonetheless, bombarding the participant with a wealth of aural, visual, and even olfactory sensations—from the sculptures, paintings, altars, monstrance, reliquaries, candlesticks, and other decorative items in the church to the vestments, incense, and music specific to each liturgical season and feast. Combining all of these sensations into a unified whole was ritual, an aspect of the early modern religious experience whose significance is impossible to exaggerate.[64] Ritual bound people together in common actions for a common purpose, fostering a sense of community and solidarity even when one might not actually exist.[65] Religious ritual provided an experience that was both comfortable and familiar yet at the same time infused with miraculous symbolism and the promise of a better future. And, especially important in the age of confessionalization, ritual helped define identities and distinguish Christian denominations from each other; a common citizen may never understand the difference between transubstantiation and consubstantiation, but he will certainly take notice if something in his weekly church service changes.

As Edward Muir has argued, the Catholic Church enriched and enhanced the ritual aspects of the liturgy in response to the simplifications introduced by Lutherans and Calvinists.[66] In a similar vein, Friedhelm Jürgensmeier has pointed out that as the line between Catholicism and Protestantism became more firmly drawn in the early modern era, Catholic piety became distinguished above all by an *active* devotion, stressing the "good works" downplayed by the Lutheran tenet of justification; this active devotion manifested itself in a variety of ways, including processions,

---

[62] Aerke, p. 34, also makes this distinction between the sponsor as observer in an opera but participant in other types of public occasions.

[63] Referring to Louis XIV, Edward Muir has stressed that the physical presence of the king provided a more powerful and effective message than visual representations; *Ritual in Early Modern Europe*, 2nd edn (Cambridge, 2005), p. 298.

[64] Ibid. The importance of ritual in expressions of Absolutism is explored in Ehalt, pp. 114–32. The significance of ritual to the Habsburgs in the seventeenth century is also discussed in John P. Spielman, *The City and the Crown: Vienna and the Imperial Court, 1600–1740* (West Lafayette, 1993), pp. 102–7.

[65] Muir, pp. 169–71.

[66] Ibid., p. 225.

pilgrimages, and especially liturgical rituals.[67] In light of these points, Ferdinand's active participation in the liturgy takes on a deep significance for his public image. Every time the Emperor attended a public worship service, he provided a concrete demonstration of his active Catholic piety. His mere presence at liturgical services thus became a representation of his immense piety, sending a more immediate and powerful message than anything that could be conveyed on stage or in a painting.[68] To this image of a deeply pious man could then be added other, more specific messages provided by the sermons, visual images, and music that formed an integral part of every service.

The Occasions

Ferdinand III participated in a number of different types of religious observations throughout the year, ranging from events specifically tailored for the Habsburgs to those in which all Catholics participated but that could nevertheless become identified with the Emperor and his family. The occasions most closely associated with the dynasty were those that also served a specific political function: royal elections, coronations, weddings, and funerals.[69] Performed within the context of a Mass, these services were infused with unique Habsburg symbols, including rich decorations adorning the church, elaborate regalia, and insignia such as scepters, globes, swords, and crowns, priceless artifacts that dated back hundreds of years. These artifacts did more than merely add opulence or tailor the event to the Habsburgs; they also stressed the longevity of the house of Habsburg, emphasizing the dynasty's continuous reign upon the Hungarian, Bohemian, and imperial thrones.[70] This was an especially important point for the Habsburgs, whose claim to two of their three crowns was not hereditary (and whose hereditary claim to the Bohemian crown had been only recently instituted by Ferdinand II). By emphasizing that the house of Habsburg remained constant regardless of whichever specific individual

---

[67] Friedhelm Jürgensmeier, "'Multa ad pietatem composita': Continuity and Change in Catholic Piety, 1555–1648," in Klaus Bussmann and Heinz Schilling (eds), *1648: War and Peace in Europe* (3 vols, [Münster], 1998), vol. 1, pp. 237–43.

[68] Duindam, p. 137, also comments on the representative nature of the ruler's public devotions. See also James Van Horn Melton, "From Image to Word: Cultural Reform and the Rise of Literate Culture in Eighteenth-Century Austria," *Journal of Modern History*, 58 (1986): pp. 97–9.

[69] On Habsburg weddings, see Seifert, *Sig-prangende*; on Habsburg funerals, see Magdalena Hawlick-van de Water, *Der schöne Tod: Zeremonialstrukturen des Wiener Hofes bei Tod und Begräbnis zwischen 1640 und 1740* (Vienna, 1989).

[70] This idea was also conveyed by the unchanging nature of the rituals across the centuries.

sat on the throne, these ceremonies created a sense of permanence and stability in the face of political uncertainty. The fact that these services occurred in a liturgical context, moreover, helped communicate the point, very important to the Habsburgs, that the longevity of their dynasty was a sign of God's grace and favor.

A number of other liturgical and non-liturgical religious occasions throughout the church year also hearkened back to long-standing dynastic traditions while providing opportunities for Ferdinand III to tailor the occasions to himself and recent events. Foremost among these were processions, by far the most public of any court event; these popular occasions presented—in addition to the music of the imperial chapel—the Emperor, the imperial family, and important secular and ecclesiastical authorities parading in full view of the throngs of common people who crowded the streets. Probably the most important of all such events were the annual Corpus Christi processions (held on the feast day itself in addition to the octave and Sunday within the octave), which celebrated the most uniquely Catholic of all Christian symbols and also stressed an important element of the *Pietas Austriaca* extending back to Rudolph I (see Chapter 6). Other processions that reflected long-standing dynastic traditions included annual processions on Monday, Tuesday, and Wednesday during the week of the Ascension (known in Vienna as *heilige Creuzwoche* and elsewhere in Europe as the "rogation days");[71] an annual Lenten procession featuring a musical performance of the penitential psalm *Miserere mei Deus* (Psalm 50);[72] and special penitential processions during Holy Week exhibiting items from the Passion.[73]

While these processions were annual events that reflected dynastic tradition, the court never hesitated to organize additional special processions to commemorate a wide variety of occasions, such as military victories, the ends of plagues, recoveries from illnesses, and even to pray for good weather.[74] Through careful selection of the prayers, orations, musical works, and visual artworks associated with the procession, the court could emphasize specific elements of the Emperor's image and also relate the image to current events, both good and bad; a superb example

---

[71] These processions are reported in the *Ordentliche Zeittungen*, May 16, 1626; May 23, 1626; May 8, 1627; June 3, 1628; May 26, 1629; May 11, 1630; May 31, 1631; May 27, 1634.

[72] Ibid., March 17, 1629; March 16, 1630.

[73] Ibid., April 11, 1626; April 3, 1627; April 22, 1628; March 30, 1630.

[74] Ibid., May 9, 1626; November 27, 1627; September 23, 1634; September 30, 1634, May 8, 1638; June 25, 1639 (military victories); August 2, 1625; September 21, 1630 (plague); May 6, 1628; October 28, 1628; March 17, 1629 (emperor's health); July 29, 1628 (weather).

is provided by the Marian processions organized by Ferdinand III in 1645 and 1647 in response to events during the Thirty Years' War (see Chapter 7). Another important type of ceremonial procession, which was common throughout Europe and which existed solely for the glorification of the ruler, was the joyous entry.[75] These occasions included the same music and pageantry encountered at other processions but also often featured grand temporary architectural structures such as triumphal arches and fireworks. The most significant joyous entries during Ferdinand III's reign occurred after the war, in conjunction with the Diet of Regensburg in the 1650s, and are discussed in the Epilogue.

Another public ritual event in which the Emperor frequently participated was the pilgrimage.[76] The Emperor participated in a number of different pilgrimages throughout his reign. As with processions, some of these looked back to Habsburg traditions, the most significant being the pilgrimage to Mariazell in Styria, a site of Marian miracles that had been connected to the Habsburg dynasty since the fourteenth century; so significant was this location that in 1642 Ferdinand III donated generous funds for the enlargement of the small gothic church, and Habsburg emperors continued to make the pilgrimage throughout the eighteenth century.[77] Despite the fact that the pilgrimage to Mariazell reflected dynastic tradition, it could also be linked to recent events. In 1642, for instance, Ferdinand III embarked on the pilgrimage to thank the Virgin for protecting the imperial army during this particularly difficult year of the war, and Archduke Leopold Wilhelm journeyed there in 1645 for the same reason.[78]

The Emperor could also institute new pilgrimages, as Ferdinand III did in 1639 with a pilgrimage to the formerly Protestant church of Hernals. Undertaken in honor of the Passion (an important element of Habsburg piety) and incorporating the Stations of the Cross, this pilgrimage became an annual tradition on the Tuesday of Holy Week, a custom that continued through the reign of Charles VI. The establishment of this new pilgrimage route was commemorated with a number of artworks, including a large medal issued in 1639 and a small duodecimo handbook published by the

---

[75] On entries elsewhere in Europe, see Strong, pp. 7–11, 44–50; Muir, pp. 262–71; Lawrence M. Bryant, *Ritual, Ceremony and the Changing Monarchy in France, 1350–1789* (Farnham, 2010).

[76] Howard Louthan discusses the importance of the pilgrimage in Central European Catholicism in his *Converting Bohemia: Force and Persuasion in the Catholic Reformation* (Cambridge, 2009), pp. 245–76.

[77] Laura Kinsey, "The Habsburgs at Mariazell: Piety, Patronage, and Statecraft" (Ph.D. diss., University of California, Los Angeles, 2000).

[78] Ibid., pp. 204–5.

Jesuit Carolus Musart in 1642, which served as both a chronicle of the first pilgrimage and as a step-by-step instruction manual for devout citizens who wished to make the trip on their own.[79]

As significant as special occasions such as these were for projecting the Emperor's public image, equally important were the many public liturgical services that he attended every week. As the Venetian ambassadors reported in 1638, the Emperor heard Mass at least once and usually twice every day; however, many of these were private Masses spoken by his personal clerics and did not involve the imperial chapel or many other spectators.[80] The musicians were required to perform at Mass on all Sundays and feast days; from this we can infer that these were the public ceremonies at which large numbers of people would have been present.[81] The Emperor also regularly attended Vespers; he did so every Sunday and possibly on many Saturdays, in addition to Second Vespers on the evening of all feasts and First Vespers on the vigil of especially significant feasts. He also attended Compline regularly during Lent, and enough musical settings of this office in a variety of musical styles survive from Ferdinand III's reign to suggest that he celebrated it during other times of the year as well. Although all of these liturgical celebrations were standard events governed by the universal Catholic liturgy, they nevertheless allowed ample room for the glorification of the Emperor through such elements as the visual decorations, sermons, and especially the music performed by the imperial chapel.

---

[79] The medal is KHM, Münzkabinett, #15086 1914/B. The handbook is Carolus Musart, *Nova Vienensium peregrinatio a templo Cathedrali S. Stephani per septem Christi patientis stationes ad s. sepulchrum in Hernals* ... (Vienna, 1642). On Hernals as an important pilgrimage location, see also Robert Douglas Chesler, "Crown, Lords, and God: The Establishment of Secular Authority and the Pacification in Lower Austria, 1618–1648" (Ph.D. diss., Princeton University, 1979), pp. 324–5 and Ernst Tomek, *Kirchengeschichte Österreichs* (3 vols, Innsbruck and Vienna, 1935–59), vol. 2, p. 647.

[80] Joseph Fiedler (ed.), *Die Relationen der Botschafter Venedigs über Deutschland und Österreich im 17. Jahrhundert* (2 vols, Vienna, 1866–67), vol. 1, p. 189: "È divotissimo, et religiosissimo, ascolta ogni giorno la messa, et molte volte due ...." Carlo Caraffa, the papal ambassador to the imperial court toward the end of Ferdinand II's reign, reported that every morning Ferdinand II had heard two private Masses. On feast days and Sundays the solemn sung Mass was performed by the chapel after these two private Masses; see Steven Saunders, "Sacred Music at the Hapsburg Court of Ferdinand II (1615–1637): The Latin Vocal Works of Giovanni Priuli and Giovanni Valentini" (2 vols, Ph.D. diss., University of Pittsburgh, 1990), vol. 1, pp. 91, 112. We have no solid evidence that Ferdinand III followed faithfully in his father's footsteps in this regard.

[81] For more details on the liturgical activities of the chapel discussed in this section, see Andrew H. Weaver, "Piety, Politics, and Patronage: Motets at the Habsburg Court in Vienna During the Reign of Ferdinand III (1637–1657)" (Ph.D. diss., Yale University, 2002), pp. 102–4, 114–18.

The Setting

As with any public appearance by the Emperor, Ferdinand's presence at religious services would have been accompanied by great pomp and the dictates of court ceremonial. Unfortunately there is very little surviving documentary evidence from the Baroque era recording the actions of the imperial family and other spectators during regular liturgical services.[82] However, it is reasonable to assume that, just as during an opera performance, the Emperor would have been prominently positioned during liturgical services and that the seating arrangement surrounding him would have been strictly regulated. Such was the practice at other European courts, especially the Spanish royal chapel.[83] We also have ample evidence that a strict protocol was followed at special liturgical occasions such as coronations. A report of Ferdinand III's 1636 coronation as King of the Romans, for instance, carefully notes the deliberate ceremonial positioning of over fifteen prestigious noblemen in attendance.[84] An engraving of the same coronation (Figure 3.2) labels the position of the electors in addition to eight other eminent attendees.

Attendees at services in the Hofburgkapelle, a small space that would have limited the congregation to only the most prominent members of the court, would have undoubtedly associated the service with the Emperor from the moment they walked into the chapel. Indeed, the Emperor was present even when not in attendance, for in 1639 Ferdinand remodeled the chapel and built private oratories that led directly from the imperial apartments and afforded a view into the chapel.[85] Because those in the

---

[82] The most detailed Viennese Baroque court ceremonial, the "Rubriche generali per le funzioni ecclesiastiche musicali di tutto l'anno" written by the imperial court musician Kilian Reinhart in 1727 (A-Wn, Suppl. mus. 2503), goes into great detail about the activities and music performed by the musicians during all important feasts, but Reinhart only recorded the activities of other people present if they were necessary as cues to the musicians. An examination of this source is Friedrich W. Riedel, *Kirchenmusik am Hofe Karls VI. (1711–1740): Untersuchungen zum Verhältnis von Zeremoniell und musikalsichen Stil im Barockzeitalter* (Munich and Salzburg, 1977). For a discussion of the few surviving ceremonial sources for the imperial court in the seventeenth century, see Weaver, "Piety, Politics, and Patronage," pp. 91–6.

[83] Antonio Álvarez-Ossorio, "The Ceremonial of Majesty and Aristocratic Protest: The Royal Chapel at the Court of Charles II," in Juan Josè Carreras and Bernardo García García (eds), *The Royal Chapel in the Time of the Habsburgs: Music and Ceremony in the Early Modern European Court*, trans. Yolanda Acker, English version ed. Tess Knighton, Studies in Medieval and Renaissance Music, vol. 3 (Woodbridge, 2005), pp. 246–99.

[84] *Le quattro Relazioni Seconda della Incoronatione dell'istessa Maestà li 30. Decembre 1636...*, sigs A2v–A3.

[85] Riedel, p. 33.

chapel could not be sure whether the Emperor was in the oratory or not, this created a permanent "invisible presence" at every service.[86]

It is reasonable to assume that a strict protocol was observed regardless of where the Emperor celebrated Mass and the divine office, whether in Vienna or any other city. Beginning in Ferdinand II's reign and continuing through the eighteenth century, the Habsburg emperors attended liturgical services not just in the Hofburg but throughout Vienna, regularly visiting many of the churches in the city and outlying areas.[87] Ferdinand III in fact followed a fixed schedule in terms of which churches he visited. He attended Mass on the most important days of the year (including Easter, Pentecost, Christmas, and the Immaculate Conception) at St Stephen's Cathedral, where he would sit under a grand canopy to the left of the altar as seen from the church.[88] He also often visited the church of a specific order (Augustinian, Franciscan, Dominican) on the feast day of its founder and on other feasts of special significance to them. Members of Ferdinand's court would travel with him to these liturgical services throughout the city, and he would also usually be accompanied by the imperial musicians, who would perform during the service.

The significance of the Emperor's stational worship services cannot be exaggerated. Unlike operas and services in the Hofburgkapelle, accessible only to an exclusive, elite audience, on these occasions the Emperor could be viewed by anybody who happened to be present at the service. (Even if Ferdinand attended a private observance with the monastic community of a collegiate church, his journey to the church was still visible to the people, and his attendance at the service was reported in the newspapers.) Moreover, the citizenry not only had the opportunity to be in the presence of their ruler, but they were also able to actively participate with him in a communal ritual (which was not true of Jesuit theater, another important opportunity the common people had to be in the presence of the Emperor). The pattern of stational worship was deemed so important that it continued even when the Emperor was not in Vienna, with other members of the imperial family, the court, and the chapel attending in his stead, thereby still creating the effect of Ferdinand's presence in the church. It was on these occasions that anybody present in church had the opportunity to experience musical performances by the imperial chapel, which perhaps

---

[86] On this concept of "invisible presence," see Treadwell, pp. 23–4, 43–4 and Sharpe, *Selling*, p. 37.

[87] On this phenomenon, see Weaver, "Piety, Politics, and Patronage," pp. 102–4, 115–18; Steven Saunders, *Cross, Sword and Lyre: Sacred Music at the Imperial Court of Ferdinand II of Habsburg (1619–1637)* (Oxford, 1995), pp. 33–7; Riedel.

[88] Duindam, p. 142. I am also grateful to Geraldine Rohling for providing me with evidence of this custom.

more than any other element of the service helped communicate important aspects of the Emperor's public image. It is to this music that we now turn.

Sound and Word in Imperial Sacred Music

Although, as argued above, the Catholic liturgy offered a multimedia spectacle, it was a different sort of spectacle from that of a theatrical event. Whereas at the opera everything was new—from the plot and music to the scenery and costumes—the liturgy was a familiar experience. It is only understandable that the congregation would eventually become accustomed to such things as the altarpiece and the smell of the incense. In light of such familiarity, those aspects of the liturgy that did change from service to service would have been pushed into the foreground. Music—a visceral sensory event (more so than the changing texts of prayers, homilies, and the proper of the Mass)—thus became one of the most important elements of a Catholic worship service and, for Ferdinand III, the medium through which he could most effectively communicate with the congregation. The remainder of this chapter discusses how listeners could glean meaning from sacred music, regardless of the other sensory effects of liturgical ritual. Although the focus remains the construction of meaning in light of monarchical representation, many of my observations will offer more general interpretations that would have taken on a specific representational function only in light of the larger performance context.

A single performance of a piece of sacred vocal music had the ability to speak to different people in a number of ways. There were three main cognitive levels at which music communicated with listeners, separated not by hard and fast lines but by a fluid continuum of possibilities. On the broadest level, music could exist as pure sound, communicating a variety of messages regardless of whatever words were sung.[89] It was in this way that the common people would have experienced the music of the imperial chapel. On the opposite end of the spectrum, to an educated listener who understood Latin, a musical performance could function as a heightened oration, with the music emphasizing specific messages in the text and sometimes adding meanings not present in the words alone. This was undoubtedly how the Emperor expected his primary audience, the nobles who comprised his court (as well as his peers at foreign courts), to experience the music. Between these two poles was a middle ground, in which the music existed primarily as pure sound but with significant words—those that even an illiterate commoner would recognize from a lifetime of attending Mass—highlighted by the music. In this way, the

---

[89] On the superfluity of text in performance, see also Treadwell, pp. 3–6.

sensory impression created by the music could be made more specific, for example by emphasizing specific aspects of Ferdinand's piety with words such as "Jesu," "Virgo," "Maria," and the names of Saints.

Music as Pure Sound

Music has long been thought to serve a number of different functions during a religious service: an offering to God by the congregants, an expression of the Lord's power, mercy, forgiveness, and the like, a means to draw the listener's thoughts away from this world and toward the contemplation of heavenly matters, to name just a few. If, however, the Emperor (or even just his retinue) were present in the church, then the music—written and performed by musicians known to be employed by him—also became capable of communicating messages about him. Like his mere presence in the sanctuary, the music filled the space with glory, with expressions of his piety, majesty, and magnificence. This was especially true when the Emperor visited churches throughout the city. The members of the congregation who attended the church on a regular basis would undoubtedly notice that the music was different whenever the Emperor was present. The music thus became identified with Ferdinand III, serving as a representation of him in the most literal sense by indicating his presence and drawing the congregation's attention toward his participation in the liturgy. The harmonious sounds of the musicians thus became more than a mere gift to God, but a gift to God *from the Emperor*, more than an expression of God's majesty, but an expression of *the Emperor's* majesty in the presence of God.

A crucial means by which listeners would have perceived aspects of the Emperor's image was the style of the music. Listeners respond to different styles in different ways; a good piece of music affects listeners viscerally on an affective, emotional level, something on which the court surely counted to help convey messages. To provide just one example, pompous, majestic, large-scale music is of course most appropriate for grand celebrations, but if the same type of music were performed at a time when there might actually be more to lament than to celebrate, the music would communicate a message of confidence in the face of seeming uncertainty. It is thus important to briefly survey the various styles of sacred music composed and performed at the imperial court during Ferdinand III's reign. The Emperor's musicians were well versed in all of the musical styles common in mid-seventeenth-century Italy; although there may have been no unique Viennese style, imperial composers nevertheless knew how best to take advantage of the compositional conventions of the day in order to effectively communicate with listeners.

While the Emperor enthusiastically supported all the latest musical styles, newly composed works in the most modern, fashionable styles comprised only a portion of the imperial chapel's repertoire. Alongside these works, the musicians performed a large body of plainchant and venerable compositions by sixteenth-century composers (including Palestrina) preserved in a group of well-used court manuscripts, many of which were recopied during Ferdinand III's reign.[90] Imperial composers also occasionally composed unaccompanied works following the strict rules of the *prima prattica*; many of these pieces became fixed repertoire performed every year, including a series of polyphonic introits and Vespers antiphons for every feast of the year by Sances and Antonio Bertali and offertories by Sances for penitential seasons.[91] Such works in older styles carried many potential associations for listeners, including penitence, austerity, and timelessness. More important in light of sacred music as monarchical representation is that these works also highlighted imperial traditions, emphasizing the continuity of the Habsburg dynasty. Composers could also bring these connotations into otherwise modern works with such allusions to the *stile antico* as traditional contrapuntal points of imitation and full polyphonic or homophonic textures in which the basso continuo merely doubles the lowest voice. Such older styles in newly composed works were generally labeled with the designation "da cappella," inferring that they were intended to be sung by the full ensemble rather than solo voices.[92]

In terms of modern Italianate styles, by far the most powerful and majestic was the one that has come to be known as the "Colossal Baroque."[93] Written for multiple choirs (usually four or more), this style consists entirely of large masses of sound. From what we can tell from the surviving musical scores, on the page it does not look particularly compelling. Much of it is actually in the *stile antico*, with each choir consisting primarily of homophonic blocks of sound that are either passed from choir to choir or combined to form large contrapuntal textures with each choir acting as a single voice. What made this music exciting was the manner of performance: each choir would be positioned in different

---

[90] On this repertoire, see Weaver, "Piety, Politics, and Patronage," pp. 132–65.

[91] Ibid., pp. 145–6, 162–3. See also Tassilo Erhardt, "A Longevous Cycle of Introits from the Viennese Court," in Tassilo Erhardt (ed.), *Sakralmusik im Habsburgerreich 1570–1770* (Vienna, 2011), pp. 147–68.

[92] On the definition of "da cappella," see Jerome Roche, "Monteverdi and the *Prima Prattica*," in Denis Arnold and Nigel Fortune (eds), *The New Monteverdi Companion* (London and Boston, 1985), p. 161.

[93] Graham Dixon, "The Origins of the Roman 'Colossal Baroque,'" *Proceedings of the Royal Musical Association*, 106 (1979–80): pp. 115–28.

areas of the church, often on elevated choir lofts located quite a distance from each other and encircling the congregation. The focus during the performance was therefore on sheer drama, on the powerful, magnificent effect of being bombarded by sound from all sides.

There is little evidence of performances of Colossal Baroque music at Ferdinand III's court. Although we have many written descriptions of performances by the chapel, very few explicitly mention multiple choirs, let alone special spatial effects. There is, however, some evidence that music of this type was performed at the imperial court. In 1621, for instance, Giovanni Valentini published a collection of sacred music for seven choirs,[94] and Ferdinand II also owned a set of manuscripts consisting of music for four choirs, which he had brought with him from Graz.[95] In 1648 the non-court musician Andreas Rauch published in Vienna a collection of motets for up to fourteen voices divided into three, four, and five choirs, which was dedicated to (and most likely commissioned by) Ferdinand III.[96] There are also at least two descriptions of multi-choir music during Ferdinand III's reign. A report of the consecration of the Emperor's *Mariensäule* in 1647 (see Chapter 7) describes the singing of the Litany of Loreto by "many choruses of both voices and instruments,"[97] and in 1653 the famous castrato Atto Melani described in a letter the music performed for Ferdinand IV's election as King of the Romans, mentioning that it included a Te Deum and a mass "con molti chori."[98]

In stark contrast to pieces in the immense Colossal Baroque style are those written on the smallest scale, featuring only solo voices accompanied by basso continuo. Whereas in large-scale polychoral music the focus was on the ensemble as a whole, in small-scale music the focus lay on the beautiful voices of the individual performers, to which was also often

---

[94] Giovanni Valentini, *Messa, Magnificat et Iubilate Deo a sette chori concertati con le trombe* (Vienna, 1621). On this work, see Steven Saunders, "The Hapsburg Court of Ferdinand II and the *Messa, Magnificat et Iubilate Deo a sette chori concertati con le trombe* (1621) of Giovanni Valentini," *Journal of the American Musicological Society*, 44 (1991): pp. 359–403.

[95] Saunders, *Cross*, pp. 38–40.

[96] Andreas Rauch, *Currus triumphalis musici, Imperatorum Romanorum Tredecim ex Augustissima Archiducali Domo Austriaca* (Vienna, 1648). This print is discussed in Chapter 4 and the Epilogue.

[97] Vilem Slavata, *Maria virgo immaculate concepta: Publico voto Ferdinandi III. Rom. Imp. in Austriae patronam electa* (Vienna, 1648), sig. B3r. See the transcription of this passage on p. 243.

[98] Mantua, Archivio di Stato, Seria E.VI.3, busta 554, fasc. Atto Melani—1653: "Per la nuova dell'elettione del Rè de Romani, si cantò Giovedì mattina nella Chiesa di S. Francesco il Tedeu~ [Te Deum] et una messa con molti chori di musica in rendim:to di gratie …." I am grateful to Roger Freitas for bringing this letter to my attention.

added an obbligato accompaniment by solo instruments. Small-scale music was capable of no less drama and magnificence than the Colossal Baroque. The most obvious means through which music for solo voices could astound listeners was through virtuosic passages and the addition of melodic ornamentation. Just as important, however, is that an individual singer was capable of shading his performance with emotional nuances in a way that was not possible with large blocks of sound; from weeping and anger to uncontainable joy, soloists could easily and directly communicate the emotional content of Ferdinand III's message, even if the words themselves were lost on the listeners.

It was not necessary, however, for composers to limit themselves to only one of these two contrasting styles in a single piece of music. Much more common was for imperial composers to combine both massed forces and solo voices in the concertato style. This was a style defined by its very variety: solo voices in various combinations contrasted with full chorus (sometimes divided into more than one choir), to which could also be added obbligato instruments (both soloists and tutti ensembles). This style allowed composers to have it all: the majestic power of large groups of performers and the virtuosity and emotional nuances of individual voices, joined together in constantly varied, unpredictable combinations that created a thrilling sensory experience in its own right.[99] Even the works in Rauch's above-mentioned 1648 publication make use of solo voices within an otherwise Colossal Baroque context.

A final way that sacred music could communicate with listeners through sound alone was by introducing timbres and compositional devices that would have carried specific associations. For instance, people may have responded in different ways to specific voice types; one that seems to have held special significance at the imperial court was the solo bass, which was featured frequently in imperial sacred music, sometimes (as argued in later chapters) seeming to represent Ferdinand III himself. Compositional devices that would have carried conventional associations for many listeners include unusual chromatic harmonies, which could evoke sorrow, tribulation, or other tortured affects, as well as the basso ostinato figures popular in the mid-seventeenth century, such as the passacaglia (descending tetrachord), which symbolized lament in its minor-mode form and love in the major mode, and the chaconne, used to express joyful affects. Specific instruments were also capable of bringing to mind certain

---

[99] For discussions of the concertato style in Italian sacred repertoires, see Jerome Roche, *North Italian Church Music in the Age of Monteverdi* (Oxford, 1984) and Graham Dixon, "*Concertato all romana* and Polychoral Music in Rome," in Francesco Luisi et al. (eds), *La scuola policorale romana del sei-settecento: Atti del Convegno internazionale di studi in memoria di Laurence Feininger* (Trent, 1997), pp. 129–34.

associations, many of which were universally understood: recorders and other soft woodwinds, for example, could evoke a pastoral atmosphere, while viols were often used to emphasize sorrow.

In this regard, no instrument was more powerful than the trumpet. Long used in non-musical contexts to herald the arrival of the monarch, trumpets had a long-established association with royalty, and the appearance of these instruments in a piece of sacred music created an unmistakably grand effect. Reports of any ceremonial occasions—from coronations to processions—invariably mention the presence of trumpets accompanying the imperial chapel, even if the reports say nothing else about music.[100] Trumpets could carry a wealth of different associations; in general religious contexts they could convey the Church triumphant (especially in a Counter-Reformation context), but in the Emperor's presence they might signal his power and majesty or allude to the military battlefield, especially if accompanied by *battaglia* figures or the *stile concitato*. Even if the actual instruments were not available, the sound of trumpets could be easily evoked through the use of such musical devices as triadic figures, many reiterations of the same pitch, dactylic rhythms, and repetitions of short motives with a limited melodic range.[101]

Ferdinand III seems to have been keenly aware of the value that trumpets added to the sacred music he composed. His Christmas hymn *Jesu Redemptor omnium*, for instance, begins in an appropriately pastoral manner, with solo voices accompanied by three recorders.[102] At bar 202, however, the mood suddenly shifts with the unexpected entrance of three trumpets, adding a majestic air that is perfectly appropriate for the celebration of the birth of the Lord. The Emperor's hymn for the Ascension, *Humanae salutis sator*, also shows him cleverly employing

---

[100] For examples, see Weaver, "Piety, Politics, and Patronage," pp. 31–4 and Saunders, *Cross*, p. 107.

[101] The styles of seventeenth-century trumpet fanfares and sonatas are recorded in such works as Girolamo Fantini, *Modo per imparare a sonare di tromba, tanto di guerra quanto musicalmente in organo, con tromba sordina, col cimbalo, e ogn'altro istrumento* (Frankfurt, 1638); facsimile in *Collezione di trattati e musiche antiche edite in fac-simile* (Milan, 1934); trans. Edward H. Tarr as *Method for Learning to Play the Trumpet in a Warlike Way* (Nashville, 1975) and Cesare Bendinelli, *Tutta l'arte della trombetta* (1614); facsimile ed. Edward H. Tarr, Documenta Musicologica, vol. 2:5 (Kassel, 1975); trans. Edward H. Tarr, *The Entire Art of Trumpet Playing* (Nashville, 1975). See also Georg Schünemann (ed.), *Trompeterfanfaren, Sonaten und Feldstücke, nach Aufzeichnungen deutscher Hoftrompeter des 16./17. Jahrhunderts* (Kassel, 1936).

[102] This hymn survives in two sources, D-Lr, Mus. ant. pract. K.N. 28 (a seventeenth-century source stemming from the imperial court) and A-Wn, Mus. Hs. 16042 (parts copied at the imperial court in the eighteenth century). Modern edns are in Andrew H. Weaver (ed.), *Motets by Emperor Ferdinand III and Other Musicians from the Habsburg Court*, Collegium Musicum: Yale University, second series (Middleton, in press) and Adler, vol. 1, pp. 17–30.

Example 3.1   Ferdinand III, *Humanae salutis sator*, bars 101–10

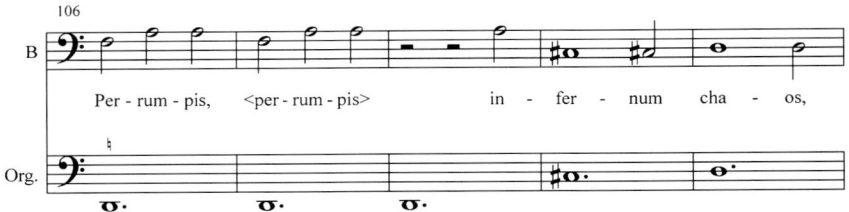

trumpet-like idioms.[103] The work is scored for four voices plus a large instrumental ensemble, the main melodic instruments of which are two violins and two cornetti. For the first hundred bars, the violins dominate, initiating melodic ideas that the cornetti simply echo back. In bar 101, however, a solo bass singer enters with triadic music clearly evoking a militant trumpet call (Example 3.1); the repetitive lines and short phrases create a markedly different effect than the lilting, long-breathed melodies heard thus far in the work. This section is followed in bar 132 by a triadic, harmonically static sonata in which the overall effect is one of trumpet rather than string music (Example 3.2).

Ferdinand III's motet *Deus misereatur nostri*—although a rather pedestrian compositional attempt (breathing the air of a student compositional exercise)—showcases perhaps better than any other work the extent to which the Emperor was aware of the power of different musical styles, textures, and timbres.[104] Scored for six voices and continuo, the work features a wide range of contrasting musical devices, all of which speak to listeners regardless of whether they know the words. It begins as an experiment in different combinations of massed sounds, overwhelming the listener with textural variety: full tutti in the first bar, homophonic blocks passed between groups of three voices in bars 2–5, a layered imitative effect in bars 6–17, and motives passed between constantly varied groups of voices in bars 18–36. In bars 34–6 Ferdinand suddenly introduces a

---

[103] D-Lr, Mus. ant. pract. K.N. 28; modern edn in Weaver, *Motets*.
[104] D-Lr, Mus. ant. pract. K.N. 206; modern edn in Weaver, *Motets*.

Example 3.2   Ferdinand III, *Humanae salutis sator*, bars 132–9

striking shift in mood: the predominant rhythmic values shift from quarter and eighth notes to half notes, creating the effect of a slower tempo, and an unusual chromatic chord progression (G–d–E–c–D) imparts a troubled, almost tortured mood. The music for the final section then shifts gears entirely. Completely disregarding a coherent presentation of the last line of text, Ferdinand instead divides it into three discrete verbal units, each of which consists of a single musical idea: the first ("in omnibus") consists

Example 3.3   Ferdinand III, *Deus misereatur nostri*, bars 48–51

of single pitch held to long note values, the second ("gentibus") of a simple repeating one-bar triadic figure with a dactylic rhythm, and the third ("salutare tuum") of a slower moving triadic figure. After stating each of these ideas individually (bars 37–47), Ferdinand presents all of them simultaneously, creating the unmistakable effect of a festive trumpet ensemble (Example 3.3). Within this single short work, then, the Emperor has presented a wealth of musical effects to which all listeners can respond regardless of whether they understand the words: after overwhelming concertato variety, the affective dissonance evokes tribulation, which is soon triumphantly overcome by the splendor of imperial trumpets.

Music as Pure Sound Highlighted by Important Words

As powerful as music could be as an affective expression of the Emperor's piety and majesty, a work could communicate an even stronger message if the listener understood the words. After all, in most pieces stylistic shifts and other compositional devices are motivated by the text and serve as a musical response to the words. This is certainly true of Ferdinand III's *Jesu Redemptor omnium* and *Humanae salutis sator*; in the former work, the trumpets enter immediately before the final stanza which praises Jesus' glory, while in the latter, the text of the militant bass section describes Jesus as a noble victor who breaks infernal chaos and frees prisoners from their chains (only in *Deus misereatur nostri* do the Emperor's compositional decisions seem unrelated to the text). While composers could not count on listeners' ability to understand every word of a composition, they knew well how to highlight specific words and make them easily audible. The frequent appearance of some words in the liturgy, moreover, would undoubtedly have made them familiar to even the most illiterate commoner; by carefully selecting important, recognizable key words for emphasis, a composer could emphasize the subject matter of a composition and help lead listeners' minds in specific directions.

There were many possible ways in which a composer could emphasize words. In the concertato style, for example, an important word could be given to a soloist (whose diction would be clearer than the full ensemble), or a word could be declaimed with homophonic clarity within a polyphonic context. Emphasis could also be created with shifts in harmony or musical style. In Example 3.4, for instance, the important word "miserere"—the central request of the work and a word that would most likely be recognizable from its use in every Mass—is strikingly highlighted by a shift from C-major to C-minor within the first syllable. In Example 3.5, the word "Mater" is emphasized in bar 76 by a sparse texture consisting of long note values, which stands in stark contrast to the florid vocal writing in the surrounding measures. The listeners, astounded by the singer's vocal agility during the long melismas, would recognize the words describing the Virgin Mary in the midst of the music (a similar treatment is given to the word "Virgo" shortly before) and would know to associate the wondrous singing with the blessed Virgin. Example 3.6 uses both textural and harmonic means to highlight the name of the saint for whom the motet is sung. As in Example 3.5, the word is highlighted by a sudden sparseness in the texture that interrupts the preceding phrase and leads to a contrasting section marked with a new tempo indication. The E-major triad over which the saint's name is sung, moreover, lies at the far edge of the *cantus mollis*; its incongruity is heightened by the fact that it appears a mere two beats after a B-flat triad, whose root is a tritone away from E. An

Example 3.4   Sances, O bone Jesu (1642), bars 21–3

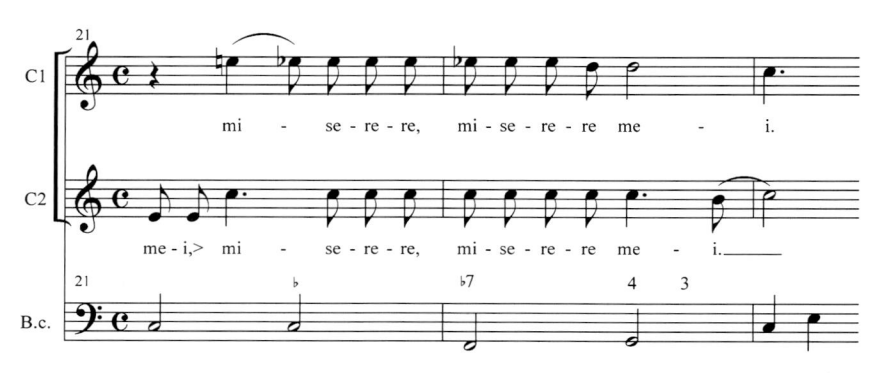

Example 3.5   Sances, O vos omnes (1638), bars 72–9

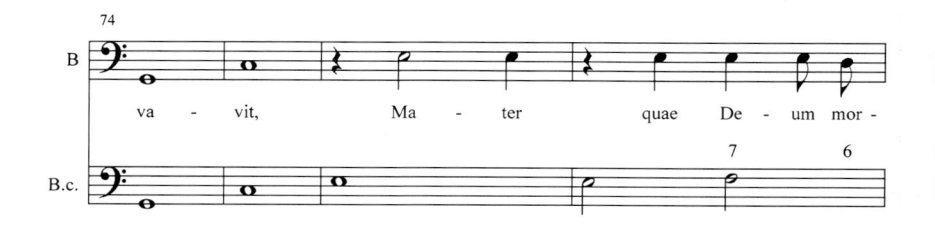

Example 3.6 Bertali, *Exultate et cantate* (1649), bars 47–51

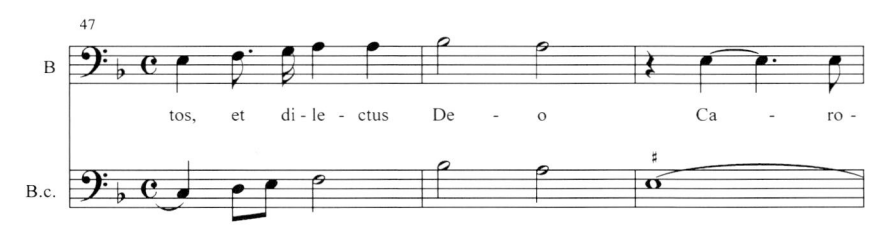

important word could also be emphasized through frequent repetition. In Giovanni Valentini's *O felix Maria*, scored for a solo soprano alternating with a four-part choir, the soprano's opening words (recognizable to any listener through the use of the Virgin's name) are repeated throughout the work by the choir as a refrain.[105] By continually repeating the opening words and music, the choir reminds the listeners of the subject matter, helping them associate the soprano soloist's beautiful voice with the Virgin.

Valentini's *Missa non erit finis*, which was most likely composed for a Habsburg coronation, is a superb example of a work that uses sheer sound not only to emphasize the Emperor's majesty but also to communicate an important message, one not present in the standard liturgical text alone.[106] Scored for a large ensemble including two four-voice choirs, two violins, and four violas, the work also features the participation of two clarini and two trumpets. The brass instruments, however, do not appear until the Credo, where they appear for the first time in an instrumental sonata that begins in bar 136. At 33 bars, this is the longest instrumental passage

---

[105] D-Lr, Mus. ant. pract. K.N. 28; modern edns in Weaver, *Motets* and ed. Konrad Ruhland, Musica pretiosa, vol. 14 (Niederaltaich, 1997).

[106] A-KR, ser. C, fas. 15, no. 715. For more on this work, see Steven Saunders, "Der Kaiser als Künstler: Ferdinand III and the Politicization of Sacred Music at the Hapsburg Court," in Max Reinhart (ed.), *Infinite Boundaries: Order, Disorder, and Reorder in Early Modern German Culture*, Sixteenth-Century Essays and Studies, vol. 40 (Kirksville, 1998), p. 197; Elisabeth Urbanek, "Giovanni Valentini als Messenkomponist" (Ph.D. diss., University of Vienna, 1974), pp. 34–5, 137–41, 213, 232–3.

in Valentini's entire surviving mass *œuvre,* and it consists primarily of chordal textures and triadic melodies ornamented with decorative flourishes typical of brass music. This sonata introduces the clause "cuius regni non erit finis,"[107] the setting of which lasts a full 84 bars. Valentini's highlighting of this clause is significant for a number of reasons. On one hand, the introduction of trumpets helps draw a parallel between Christ's eternal glory and the Emperor, emphasizing both the monarch's piety and the fact that the Habsburgs' claim to the throne stems from God himself. Even more important is the fact that by stressing Christ's endless reign, Valentini also emphasizes the same sense of permanence created by the coronation ritual itself, highlighting the continuity of the house of Austria and their eternal claim to their elected thrones.[108]

Music as Oration

If music could communicate by emphasizing only a few key words or phrases, then it could do so on an even larger scale for listeners who understood Latin and were able to follow the entire text during the performance. Such people comprised Ferdinand III's main target audience: the court dignitaries, ambassadors, visiting royalty, and other members of the nobility who would have been present at religious services. For these listeners, a musical performance became a true oration, an affective delivery of a text heightened by a wealth of musical devices adding new intensity to the rhetorical impact of the words. Many of these compositional tools have already been discussed in the preceding sections: the same stylistic variety, symbolic use of instruments, changes in texture, and harmonic shifts that catch the attention of people without a knowledge of Latin would have had an even stronger impact on those who could connect these compositional devices to specific ideas in the text.

A number of compositional devices depend on an understanding of the words for their full effectiveness. The most important of these are the contrasting styles of recitative and aria. With the former, a composer was able to provide a passionate, affective delivery of the text through speech-like, declamatory singing over a slow-moving bass line. In contrast, the aria style heightened the emotional impact of the words through a beautiful melody consisting of balanced phrases over an active bass.

---

[107] "Whose reign shall have no end."

[108] Another work by Valentini that makes excellent use of musical style to reinforce a dynastic message is his motet *Cantate gentes,* written for Ferdinand IV's 1647 coronation as King of Hungary. A modern edn of this work is ed. Andrew H. Weaver, Web Library of Seventeenth-Century Music, vol. 9 (December 2007); http://sscm-wlscm.org

A final way that a composer could enhance the delivery of a text was to employ large-scale structural devices that emphasized important passages over the entire span of the composition. Again, we have already discussed many of these structural strategies on a limited scale. As in Valentini's *Missa non erit finis*, for instance, a significant passage could be highlighted through extensive immediate text repetition, thereby lengthening the amount of time in which the words are heard (sometimes even transforming one short clause into a substantial musical section). An important passage could also be repeated throughout the work as a refrain, as in Valentini's *O felix Maria*. The specific ways in which imperial composers heightened the rhetorical effectiveness of the texts they set were diverse, imaginative, and ingenious and are explored in detail in Part III.

CHAPTER 4

The Politics of Printing: The Print Program of Giovanni Felice Sances

Most pieces of music—even in our electronic age—lead two parallel lives. The first is that discussed in the preceding chapter, the performance: powerful, immediate, affective, but ultimately ephemeral and doomed to survive only in the memories of listeners and performers.[1] The second is the life music leads as notation on the page. Although by necessity always lacking important aspects of the performance—the distinctive sound of specific voices, details of interpretation, improvisatory elements such as ornamentation and continuo realization, to name just a few—musical notation nevertheless grants this ephemeral art a sense of permanence, allowing the musical work to live on through re-creations by anyone able to decipher the notation (even if the re-creation occurs only in the reader's imagination).

The existence of music as written notation can assume many forms, from hastily written manuscripts intended for a single performance to sumptuous presentation copies given as gifts and never intended to be used for performance. The notated score can sometimes even take on a life of its own, becoming an independent work that possesses artistic value beyond that of the graphic representation of sound. For this reason, many scores can impart messages even to people unable to read music. Decorative elements such as illuminated initials and frontispieces, the sheer size of a score for many performing forces, the bewildering array of notes for a virtuosic solo work; these and other features can have as immediate an effect on the reader as the sound of the music itself. An example from Ferdinand III's court is a lament for the Emperor's son Ferdinand IV by Johann Jakob Froberger, which ends with an ascending scale that is commonly interpreted as Ferdinand's ascent to heaven; the composer's illuminated autograph confirms this interpretation with an illustration of the heavenly hosts at the end of the scale.[2] Also significant are verbal texts that appear on the page in conjunction with notation, including

---

[1] This is true even of recordings; although the performance is infinitely repeatable, the music still exists only as moments in time.

[2] A-Wn, Mus. Hs. 18707, fol. 113r; facsimile in *Vienna, Österreichische Nationalbibliothek, Musiksammlung, Mus. Hs. 18707 (Froberger Autographs)*, ed. Robert Hill, Seventeenth-Century Keyboard Music, vol. 3 (New York, 1988).

the words of a piece of vocal music as well as what modern scholars call paratexts—dedications, title pages, prefaces, rubrics, and the like—which often impart important information that may be completely absent (or easily overlooked) during the performance itself.[3]

The musical score serves another valuable function beyond that of the permanence it gives to a performance, a function that was especially important in helping music serve as a means of monarchical representation in the early modern era: it allows for the easy dissemination of the musical work. Performances by the imperial chapel were naturally dependent on the presence of the musicians themselves; paper copies of musical works, however, could easily and quickly travel throughout Europe, bringing the music of Ferdinand's chapel to a much wider audience than would have ever been able to attend a performance. Certainly there were some scores, such as those for operas and especially grand large-scale works, that the Emperor would have jealously guarded, to ensure that the splendor of his performances would not be duplicated elsewhere, but in many cases he was eager to take advantage of the opportunity to spread his image via the dissemination of scores. Although this posed some risks, such as the chance that the music would be degraded by a bad performance or that the audience would be unaware of the connection between the music and the Emperor, the original message would still have been clear to the people who owned or looked at the score, who in many cases would have comprised the Emperor's primary target audience of nobles, other rulers (including those of the Austrian estates and other principalities within the Empire), and important officials. This chapter focuses on the most common means of dissemination for the music of Ferdinand's chapel, the commercial print.

Music, the Printed Page, and Monarchical Representation

The printing press revolutionized the process by which early modern monarchs represented themselves.[4] So great were the conveniences

---

[3] On paratexts in early music prints, see Mary S. Lewis, "Introduction: The Dedication as Paratext," in Ignace Bossuyt et al. (eds), *"Cui dono lepidum novum libellum?": Dedicating Latin Works and Motets in the Sixteenth Century*, Supplementa Humanistica Lovaniensia, vol. 23 (Leuven, 2008), pp. 1–11.

[4] Kevin Sharpe discusses the benefits and dangers of print as a means of representation in *Selling the Tudor Monarchary: Authority and Image in Sixteenth-Century England* (New Haven and London, 2009), pp. 33–4 and "Sacralization and Demystification: The Publicization of Monarchy in Early Modern England," in Jeroen Deploige and Gita Deneckere (eds), *Mystifying the Monarch: Studies on Discourse, Power, and History* (Amsterdam, 2006), pp. 106–11.

offered by the medium of print—a much larger number of copies could be produced more efficiently and with huge savings of time, manpower, and money—that rulers were often willing to sacrifice the high quality and uniqueness of individually crafted, handmade documents and artworks. We have already encountered a variety of printed sources in the previous chapters: panegyrics, engraved portraits, descriptions of court events, as well as opera libretti and pictures of stage sets. Musical publications were another important medium through which representations of noble patrons could be disseminated in print. By considering the musical print as motivated by the patron rather than the composer, this section offers a new perspective on seventeenth-century music publishing, as scholars have tended to privilege the roles of the composer, printer, and bookseller as independent agents.[5]

As with many other printed sources, one of the main methods through which a book of music could contribute to the representation of a monarch was through its textual materials, especially those that have come to be known as paratexts—the verbal elements that frame the main body of the work, condition how the reader interprets it, and yet nevertheless exist outside the main text.[6] One of the most important types of paratext, and the one that has received the most attention from musicologists, is the dedication. By dedicating a book of music to somebody, a composer made an explicit connection between his music and the patron. Some have argued that the music essentially became the property of the dedicatee; through the gift of his music, the composer bolstered the dedicatee's prestige in the eyes of the buying public as an esteemed patron of the arts, while the dedicatee simultaneously helped raise the fame of the composer (often in a practical sense by providing the monetary resources to fund the print run).[7] The text of the dedication not only makes this relationship explicit but also

---

[5] See, for instance, Jane A. Bernstein, *Print Culture and Music in Sixteenth-Century Venice* (Oxford, 2001); Bernstein, "Publish or Perish? Palestrina and Print Culture in 16th-Century Italy," *Early Music*, 35 (2007): pp. 225–35; Susan Lewis Hammond, *Editing Music in Early Modern Germany* (Aldershot, 2007); Stephen Rose, "The Mechanisms of the Music Trade in Central Germany, 1600–40," *Journal of the Royal Musical Association*, 130 (2005): pp. 11–37; and three essays in Tim Carter, *Music, Patronage and Printing in Late Renaissance Florence* (Aldershot, 2000): "The Music Trade in Late Sixteenth-Century Florence" (Ch. X), "Music-Printing in Late Sixteenth- and Early Seventeenth-Century Florence: Giorgio Marescotti and Zanobi Pignoni" (Ch. XI), and "Music Selling in Late Sixteenth-Century Florence: The Bookshop of Piero di Giuliano Morosi" (Ch. XII).

[6] The term "paratext" was introduced by the literary scholar Gérard Genette in his *Seuils* (Paris, 1987); trans. Jane E. Lewis as *Paratexts: Thresholds of Interpretation* (Cambridge, 1997).

[7] For an excellent discussion of the "triangle formed by composer, patron/dedicatee and buying public," see Nele Gabriëls, "Reading (Between) the Lines: What Dedications Can Tell Us," in *"Cui dono lepidum,"* pp. 73–5.

often provides other valuable information about the dedicatee, thereby contributing directly to his image. Just as important as the dedication is the title page. As the first part of the print that the reader sees, the title page imparts the contents of the book and establishes its larger context. It seems clear that in many cases great attention was paid to the design of title pages, in a calculated effort to convey the most important information as efficiently as possible to anyone browsing titles in the bookshop. Other important paratexts in music prints include prefaces, letters to the reader, and rubrics placed before individual works. Rubrics were especially useful tools in helping a print function as representation, for they could impart specific information about individual works, contextualizing them and making explicit the ways in which the music served the patron.

Also included under the umbrella of the paratext are visual elements of the print, which can also provide important information and affect how the reader interprets the music. Large, elaborately engraved initials at the beginning of the musical works, for instance, add a level of sumptuousness to mass-produced books, enhancing the image of the patron to whom the book is dedicated. More important are engraved frontispieces; although these are rather rare in seventeenth-century music prints, when present they can impart valuable information about the music and its context. Frontispieces sometimes feature a portrait of the dedicatee, thereby contributing to his representation in the most literal sense, as does, for instance, the frontispiece of Andreas Rauch's *Currus triumphalis musici* of 1648 (see Figure 2.3).

As significant as paratexts are in framing a music print and helping to contribute to the dedicatee's representation, equally important are the actual texts in a collection of vocal music, namely the words to be sung by the singers. Indeed, most users probably would have looked at the table of contents and read the texts of the compositions before sounding any of the notes, and in this respect, a collection of vocal music could be read like a book by somebody unable to read music. Of the various types of seventeenth-century sacred publications, motet books allowed composers the greatest scope for turning a collection of music into a form of representation, as these publications not only gave them the freedom to include freely written texts that could be tailored to the dedicatee but also allowed them to arrange the texts in any order. For many composers, the arrangement of pieces in a music print was by no means haphazard; by far the most important positions were the first and last, but ordering principles can often be discerned in other sections of a print, with the result that the interpretation of a work may very well be conditioned by the pieces surrounding it.[8] Even compositions with standard liturgical texts can be viewed in a new light when placed in prominent positions or arranged into carefully planned groups. This is especially true in prints that contain primarily liturgical works, such as collections of Vespers psalms or Marian antiphons. The compositions in these common types of prints (the contents of which are usually ordered according to generic conventions) can take on new meanings if the composer also includes anomalous works setting texts of a different type (and places these works in a prominent position).

One factor that potentially rendered impractical the ability of a user to easily read the text of a printed musical work is that most seventeenth-century music prints were issued as partbooks. While this is not a problem with solo music, for larger-scale compositions there are often gaps in the presentation of a text when individual voices drop out of the texture. Partbooks can also obscure the ordering principles of a publication if all of the voice parts do not participate in every composition. Nevertheless, in the hands of a skilled composer, the partbook format could actually be an advantage. For example, ordering principles might be devised for each individual partbook (for instance, by placing a different significant work at the beginning of each one), which can then create an even more powerful message when all of the partbooks are considered as an aggregate. Within a musical work, a composer can also be sure to include especially important textual passages in all of the voices (even if not simultaneously); if someone were then to read all of the parts for a single composition in succession, this passage will be sure to stand out.

Finally, we cannot overlook the role that the visual appearance of the music itself could have played in helping represent a composer's patron, to both musically literate and illiterate readers. A printed collection of large-scale music for many voice parts, consisting as it does of a large number of partbooks, could have just as immediate and powerful an impression on someone as the sound of the music itself, communicating both the impressive size of the musical establishment of the person for whom it was

---

[8] One composer about whom scholars have had much to say regarding the ordering of pieces in his prints is Monteverdi. See, for instance, Massimo Ossi, *Divining the Oracle: Monteverdi's "Seconda Prattica"* (Chicago, 2003), pp. 58–110 (on the Fourth and Fifth Books of Madrigals); Jeffrey Kurtzman, *The Monteverdi Vespers of 1610: Music, Context, Performance* (Oxford, 1999), pp. 23–5, 35–6, 56–78, and 106–10 and John Whenham, *Monteverdi: Vespers (1610)* (Cambridge, 1997), pp. 19–22 (on the 1610 Vespers); Gary Tomlinson, *Monteverdi and the End of the Renaissance* (Berkeley, 1987), p. 156 (on the Sixth, Seventh, and Eighth Books of Madrigals); Linda Maria Koldau, *Die venezianische Kirchenmusik von Claudio Monteverdi* (Kassel, 2001), pp. 116–34 and Andrew H. Weaver, "Divine Wisdom and Dolorous Mysteries: Habsburg Marian Devotion in Two Motets From Monteverdi's *Selva morale et spirituale*," *Journal of Musicology*, 24 (2007): pp. 237–71 (on the *Selva morale et spirituale*).

composed as well as the wealth of the dedicatee who was able to fund the printing of so much music. Small-scale music could attempt to capture the wondrous sound of individual voices through the meticulous preservation of ornamental figures, especially extended cascades of virtuosic melismas, which can bewilder the eye as much as the ear. More importantly, almost all of the musical devices discussed in Chapter 3 as techniques that emphasize specific words can be just as effective in writing as in performance. Readers will be sure to notice if a word is suddenly given a long, virtuosic melisma in a non-virtuosic context, just as they will likely take note of a word placed underneath longer note values amid many eighth- and sixteenth-notes. The sudden appearance of accidentals in the music can alert the reader to a harmonic shift heightening a significant passage of text. Even distinctive musical styles can be visually apparent. A shift from duple into triple meter can signal for the reader the heightened emotionality of the aria style, and the repetitive triadic style of trumpet music often looks as striking as it sounds.

All of these ways in which notated music could represent hold just as true for handwritten manuscripts as for printed music. There were nevertheless several distinct benefits—aside from the obvious savings of time and money—that a patron could enjoy by relying on the printing press rather than his scriptorium to present his image through notated music. One such benefit was the fact that print allowed for the dissemination of just one "authentic" copy, free from the inevitable errors of hand copying, thus creating the impression that the patron wielded control over his representation (even if the large number of errors in early modern music prints belie the truth of this assumption). Another significant advantage is the fact that the printing press made one single work available to a wider potential audience than that for which even an army of scribes could provide copies. For a manuscript to reach someone, the patron needed to have a copy created specifically for that person; that is, he needed to have a specific audience in mind at the moment of creation, and the work would be delivered only to that audience. With the printing press, however, the work could reach audience members whom the patron did not even know, even possibly those with whom he did not have good diplomatic ties.

In Ferdinand III's case, for instance, it is entirely conceivable that a Lutheran Kapellmeister would want his chapel to perform the latest Latin sacred music by famous Italian composers employed at the imperial court (the presence of such works in seventeenth-century Lutheran anthologies attests to this).[9] This might very well lead him to purchase a collection of

---

[9] Note, for example, the large number of Italian Catholic sacred works—including works by Giovanni Felice Sances—in the motet anthologies published by the Lutheran publisher Ambrosius Profe in the 1640s; see Kristin M. Sponheim, "The Anthologies of

music by an imperial musician, in which case his employer would receive a representation of the Emperor that would have never come to him from the imperial court directly. Even if nobody else at the Lutheran court knew that the music was connected to the Habsburgs, those who saw the print would potentially connect the music to the Emperor every time they heard it. In fact, through the medium of print, local nobles could appropriate Ferdinand III's image for their own purposes while still receiving the imperial message. In these cases, the noble ends up modeling himself on the Emperor and passing the image along to his constituents.

The distribution of printed music to a wide, anonymous audience did not mean that the patron could not honor a specific individual with the gift of a musical publication, in which case the printed copy could be embellished with additional handmade decorations. Although we know that composers sometimes sent gifts of their music prints,[10] we unfortunately have no evidence that Ferdinand III actively sent prints to other nobles. We do know, however, that Leopold I frequently sent out opera libretti after a performance,[11] so it is conceivable that his father would have done the same with the printed music that served as an important vehicle for his representation.

The benefits of the printing press did not come without some disadvantages. The most obvious of these was the inevitable loss of quality, for even the most elaborate and beautifully engraved print could not match the potential beauty of a meticulously created, handwritten, original piece of calligraphic art. This was especially true for music, as the single-impression printing method always created unseemly gaps in the staff, and rarely could the syllables of the text be lined up perfectly underneath the note heads. Such defects could at least be partially assuaged through the use of decorative elements such as illuminated initials.

A more serious downside to the use of the printing press was that, even when the print run was subsidized by the patron, the finished product was nevertheless dependent on the commercial market for its successful dissemination. If the patron wanted it to reach the widest possible audience, the print had to meet the demands of the anonymous mass market. In addition, the print embodied not only the wishes of the patron but also those of the composer—for whom the print served as a career

---

Ambrosius Profe (1589–1661) and the Transmission of Italian Music in Germany" (Ph.D. diss., Yale University, 1995). Mary E. Frandsen discusses the popularity of Italian music at the Protestant Dresden court in *Crossing Confessional Boundaries: The Patronage of Italian Sacred Music in Seventeenth-Century Dresden* (Oxford, 2006).

[10] Bernstein, *Print Culture*, pp. 106–7.

[11] Maria Goloubeva, *The Glorification of Emperor Leopold I in Image, Spectacle, and Text* (Mainz, 2000), p. 48.

builder, spreading his own fame just as much as that of the dedicatee—and especially of the printer, whose ultimate aim was to make money.

Commercial demands meant that the musical works had to be usable by a wide range of people in a variety of institutional settings. In terms of the music, this often meant focusing on small performing forces, omitting especially difficult virtuosic passages, and leaving out details of instrumentation (even possibly entire instrumental parts). In this regard, prints that flaunt such commercial demands take on an especially strong significance; one striking example from the Habsburg court is Giovanni Valentini's 1621 publication of "Colossal Baroque" sacred music for seven choirs with written-out trumpet parts, a print that would have never sold enough copies to make a profit and that served instead as a powerful assertion of Ferdinand II's power in the early years of his reign.[12] In terms of the texts included in a sacred music print, the commercial market demanded the omission or alteration of explicit references to specific events or people, even the names of saints (who are typically identified with "n" for *nomen*). Composers and printers would also have wanted to ensure that the print included settings of popular "crowd-pleasing" texts, works such as psalms, litanies, and Marian antiphons that served many functions and would have been performed frequently throughout the year. For all of these reasons, many modern readers may not even realize at first glance that a music print served a specific political purpose, and it is only through a careful analysis of the entire print—taking into account the paratexts, the organization, subtle textual details, and musical devices that offer idiosyncratic readings of the texts—that we today can unlock the messages that may very well have been obvious to seventeenth-century readers.

The Prints of Giovanni Felice Sances, 1638–1648

In early 1638, just over a year after joining the imperial chapel as a tenor, Giovanni Felice Sances (ca. 1600–1679) published his *Motetti a una, due, tre, e quattro voci*, dedicated to Ferdinand III.[13] Over the next ten years, Sances proved to be the most prolific composer at the Habsburg court (at least in terms of publications), issuing a total of seven books of sacred music, all of which he dedicated to members of the Emperor's immediate

---

[12] Steven Saunders, "The Hapsburg Court of Ferdinand II and the *Messa, Magnificat et Iubilate Deo a sette chori concertati con le trombe* (1621) of Giovanni Valentini," *Journal of the American Musicological Society*, 44 (1991): pp. 359–403.

[13] Giovanni Felice Sances, *Motetti a una, due, tre, e quattro voci* (Venice, 1638); modern edn by Steven Saunders, RRMBE, vol. 126 (Middleton, 2003).

family or other important political figures.[14] This remarkable collection of prints is the result of what must have been a conscious effort to represent the Emperor during the crucial first decade of his reign, a true "program" through which we can discern the strategies employed by court artists as they revised Ferdinand's image from invincible warrior to wise, pious, protective father. The existence of Sances's large body of printed music makes him the focus of much of the musical discussions in this book. This should not be taken as evidence that he was the only court composer who actively represented Ferdinand III; it is merely the necessary circumstance of the surviving musical sources.

Sances's Early Career and Employment at the Imperial Court

As much as Sances's print program served the Emperor, it also served Sances himself, providing him with the means to ingratiate himself to his employer and rise through the ranks of the imperial chapel while also maintaining widespread fame. Thus, before turning to the prints, it is crucial that we examine the composer's life and his possible motivations for the project. Born in Rome to a musical family (his father Orazio was a singer, and his brother Lorenzo would become a famous opera virtuoso), Sances received his earliest musical training as a choirboy at the Jesuit *Collegio Germanico* in Rome, where he matriculated in November 1609.[15] This early training proved crucial for his later career at the Habsburg court, not only because it connected him with the religious order that enjoyed the greatest influence at court but also because it provided him with a rich education in Classical rhetoric, upon which he would draw to create musical works of strong persuasive and emotional power.[16] Within five years of his matriculation he had grown into a star pupil; a document from 1614 praises his progress

---

[14] Giovanni Felice Sances, *Motetti a voce sola* (Venice, 1638); *Antifone e litanie della Beatissima Vergine a più voci* (Venice, 1640); *Motetti a 2. 3. 4. e cinque voci* (Venice, 1642); *Salmi a 8 voci concertati, con la comodità de suoi ripieni per chi li desiderasse* (Venice, 1643); *Salmi brevi a 4 voci concertate* (Venice, 1647); *Antiphonare Sacrae B.M.V. per totum annum una voce decantandae* (Venice, 1648).

[15] The best biography of Sances is in Saunders's introduction to the composer's *Motetti*, pp. ix–xii, to which this discussion is much indebted. See also Peter Webhofer, *Giovanni Felice Sances (ca. 1600–1679): Biographische-bibliographische Untersuchung und Studie über sein Motettenwerk* (Rome, 1964).

[16] For details of Sances's rhetorical education at the German College and some examples of rhetoric applied to his sacred music, see Andrew H. Weaver, "The Rhetoric of Interruption in Giovanni Felice Sances's *Motetti a voce sola* (1638)," *Schütz-Jahrbuch*, 32 (2010): pp. 127–47.

in Latin studies, his excellent singing, and his skill at composing.[17] He was also beginning to receive recognition outside of the College; in February of the same year he sang in the opera *Amor pudico*, produced by the famous Roman patron Cardinal Alessandro Montalto.

Sances's participation in a musical production outside the German College must have encouraged him (or at least his father) to pursue a career as a star singer, for in April 1614 Orazio was sent to jail for withdrawing Felice prematurely from the College. Although we have no evidence, it seems likely that the young Sances returned to the school, for our next documentary trace of him is a cordial letter that he wrote to the rector of the College in December 1618, in which he asks after the health of his father and brother. At this time he had definitely left the school and was in Padua, traveling with an unnamed patron who treated him "as an equal of anyone else in the house."[18] This patron may have been the Paduan Marquis Pio Enea degli Obizzi, who seems to have played an important role in helping Sances establish a career in northern Italy. Sances honored the Marquis with the dedications of his earliest surviving publications, a pair of cantata collections printed in Venice in 1633,[19] and the Marquis also commissioned the composer's first opera, *Ermiona*, performed in Padua on April 11, 1636. This work is of singular importance in the history of opera, for the professional troupe that produced it would in the following year mount the first production of a public opera in Venice.[20]

We know precious little about Sances's career in northern Italy during the 1620s and '30s. Our only concrete information is that he worked in Venice in the service of Nicolò Sagredo, future ambassador to the imperial court, but we do not know the dates of his service.[21] Nevertheless, it seems clear that his star was quickly rising, even before *Ermiona*. In addition to the 1633 prints, he had by 1636 published at least three other books of

---

[17] An English translation of the document is in Thomas D. Culley, *Jesuits and Music, vol. 1, A Study of the Musicians Connected With the German College in Rome During the Seventeenth Century and of Their Activities in Northern Europe* (Rome and St Louis, 1970), p. 143; the original Latin is on p. 310.

[18] The full text of the letter is in ibid., pp. 143 (English translation) and 327–8 (original Italian).

[19] Giovanni Felice Sances, *Cantade ... a voce sola ... libro secondo, parte prima* (Venice, 1633) and *Cantade ... a doi voci ... libro secondo, parte seconda* (Venice, 1633).

[20] Ellen Rosand, *Opera in Seventeenth-Century Venice: The Creation of a Genre* (Berkeley, 1991), pp. 67–70.

[21] Sances mentions this service in the dedication to Sagredo of his *Capricci poetici* (Venice, 1649), in which he mentions "quall'antica servitù, ch'in Venetia già molti anni sono le consecrai."

secular music, only one of which survives.[22] The surviving prints show him to be on the cutting edge of compositional practices of his day; he was, for instance, among the earliest composers to make extensive use of ostinato bass patterns in vocal works. There are also a number of striking similarities between Sances's secular works of the 1630s and contemporaneous works by Monteverdi, suggesting that the two composers knew each other and perhaps even engaged in a compositional rivalry.[23]

Sances joined the imperial court in December 1636 (shortly after the production of *Ermiona*); his employment thus began not in Vienna but in Regensburg, where he would have performed during the lavish festivities celebrating Ferdinand III's election and coronation as King of the Romans. Steven Saunders has suggested that Sances was hired specifically to augment the chapel at the Regensburg electoral meeting and has speculated that he was the "virtuosissimo Musico" who played the role of the Empire in the ballet discussed in Chapter 1.[24] It is only reasonable that, upon becoming a permanent member of the imperial chapel under the new Emperor, Sances would have wanted to maintain his reputation as a leading figure of the Italian musical world; this helps account for his continued relationship with his Venetian publisher Bartolomeo Magni. His abrupt switch from secular to sacred publications, however, can only be understood within the context of his new position. As someone who had been well connected to nobility throughout his early career, Sances clearly knew how to play the game for increased recognition and wealth; in order for him to rise in status at the imperial court, he had to ensure that his new publications would be seen to serve his employer.

That Sances's sacred prints were part of a conscious effort to elevate his prestige over that of his colleagues is confirmed by his other activities in the early years of his imperial service. He received his court lodgings already in May 1637, through the rather unusual intervention of chapel master Valentini, and less than a month later he received the first of a number of pay raises.[25] By 1638 he was making additional money as a teacher, even stealing some of the better students from other members of

---

[22] Giovanni Felice Sances, *Il quarto libro delle cantate, et arie a voce sola* (Venice, 1636).

[23] On the artistic connections between Sances and Monteverdi, see Weaver, "Divine Wisdom"; Sances, *Motetti*, ed. Saunders, pp. ix–x; Silke Leopold, *Al modo d'Orfeo: Dichtung und Musik im italienischen Sologesang des frühen 17. Jahrhunderts*, Analecta Musicologica, vol. 29 (Laaber, 1995), pp. 270–78.

[24] Sances, *Motetti*, ed. Saunders, p. x.

[25] This and the following information is from Sances, *Motetti*, ed. Saunders, pp. x–xi.

the chapel.[26] By 1639, Sances's salary had more than doubled, from an initial 720 florins per year to 1,561 florins, a salary higher than that earned by even the star castrati and only 439 florins less than Valentini's.

Sances did ultimately realize the ambitions embodied in his print program. He received the commission for *I Trionfi d'Amore*, the aborted 1648 opera for Ferdinand III's second wedding that marked the return of secular spectacle to the imperial court. More significantly, upon Valentini's death the following year, Sances rose to the position of vice chapel master (the coveted post of chapel master went to Antonio Bertali, who had more than ten years seniority over Sances). Sances continued to serve the imperial court until his death in 1679, being promoted to chapel master by Leopold I in 1669 and receiving a patent of nobility from the Emperor in the same year.

The Prints

Sances explicitly announced the intentions of his print program right from the first sentence of the dedicatory text to the Emperor of his *Motetti a una, due, tre, e quattro voci*: "Previously I devotedly dedicated to you my voice; today I reverently dedicate to you my pen, with the sentiment of making known to the world in these little notes my current service, in which I take pride."[27] Sances's motets, then, exist as evidence of his devoted service to Ferdinand III and, by extension, as representative examples of the music of the imperial chapel. And since (as detailed in the previous chapter) the music of the chapel contributed to the public image of the Emperor, the print thus served as a concrete representation of Ferdinand III himself.

Sances's devotion to the Habsburgs—and the function of his print program as a contribution to the Emperor's public image—is clear from his carefully planned series of dedications to members of Ferdinand III's immediate family, which he organized according to a strict hierarchy based on their rank and prestige at court. He dedicated his *Motetti a voce sola*, published in the same year as the *Motetti a una, due, tre, e quattro voci* (but with the dedication signed seven months later), to the person at court second in prestige and seniority to Ferdinand III, the dowager Empress Eleonora Gonzaga,[28] and two years later he dedicated a book of Marian antiphons and litanies to the current Empress, Maria of Spain. His

---

[26] See the letter from the imperial musician Domenico Rodomonte to the German College in Culley, pp. 212–14 (original Italian on pp. 329–30).

[27] The full Italian (or Latin) texts and English translations of all of the dedications discussed in this chapter are in the Appendix.

[28] A facsimile edn of this print is available in Anne Schnoebelen (ed.), *Solo Motets from the Seventeenth Century: Facsimiles of Prints from the Italian Baroque* (10 vols, London,

next Habsburg dedications appear in two books of Vespers psalms; the first, published in 1643, is dedicated to Ferdinand III's brother Archduke Leopold Wilhelm, while the second, from 1647, is dedicated to the Emperor's eldest son Ferdinand IV. That the Emperor actively supported Sances's publication efforts is apparent from the fact that on December 17, 1637 (within a month of Sances's signing the dedication of the first book of *Motetti*) Ferdinand awarded the composer 100 Reichsthaler for "Ihr May: praesentierter gewisser Composition."[29] Although there is no evidence for further gifts of this kind (perhaps because they were paid from different accounts), it is inconceivable that Sances would have continued honoring his employers with dedications had he not continued receiving similar financial compensation.

Sances made a point in the texts of his dedications to tailor them to the dedicatee. His dedication to the dowager Empress pays homage to her Gonzaga heritage, first with a pun in the first sentence on the word "MANTO" (a variant spelling of "Mantua") and then with an explicit declaration of devotion to the house of Gonzaga, in which he references the fact that his brother Lorenzo was at that time employed by the Mantuan court. The dedication to Empress Maria takes care to point out that the Empress shares the same name with the Blessed Virgin. The dedications to Leopold Wilhelm and Ferdinand IV allude to their careers. In writing to the Archduke in 1643, less than a year after the disastrous Second Battle of Breitenfeld, Sances ends the dedication by wishing for him "prosperity and most fortunate events"; although this is a common enough sentiment, when spoken to the General of the imperial army, "fortunate events" could easily be interpreted as victorious battles. The dedication to Ferdinand IV begins with a clear didactic statement, expressing the important anti-Machiavellian sentiment that rulers serve as mirrors of God and should therefore seek to imitate the Lord in their virtue and deeds. Ferdinand IV had only recently received his first two crowns—Bohemia in 1646 and Hungary in 1647 (the same year Sances published the print)—so this dedication serves as a "mirror of princes," instructing the young King of his duties as a Habsburg ruler.[30]

Despite these passages tailored to each dedicatee, the texts also contain general sentiments that explicate the books' functions as representations of the Habsburg dynasty generally and of the Emperor specifically. All of them, for instance, explicitly beseech the dedicatee for protection.

1987–88), vol. 8. The dedication of Sances's first motet book is dated November 21, 1637, that of the solo motets June 1, 1638.

[29] "Certain compositions presented to His Majesty" (Webhofer, pp. 7, 169).

[30] Sances did not date the dedication, so we cannot know whether it was timed to coincide with the Hungarian election and coronation in June.

Although this is a common trope in most dedications (the author relies on the magnanimity of the patron to add prestige to his work and protect it from the criticism of detractors), it takes on a deeper meaning within the context of the Thirty Years' War, especially in light of the Emperor's image as paternal protector of his people. References to the difficulties of the war years seem especially explicit in the dedication of Sances's 1642 motet book, signed just one day before the Second Battle of Breitenfeld.[31] Sances opens this dedication with the general statement that a dedication to a great man can protect a work from "the voracity of time and the malice of age"; although a platitude, the harsh language would have resonated strongly with those suffering through the difficult years of the early 1640s. Also striking is the language in the dedication to Eleonora Gonzaga, when Sances states his hope that she will protect his works "from the hail of persecution" and "the thunder and lightning of slander from others." Saunders has interpreted these words from a personal perspective, as evidence that Sances's self-serving actions were creating tension between him and his fellow chapel members.[32] Without discounting that interpretation, I propose a broader meaning in the context of the Counter-Reformation: Sances may be relying on the Catholic ruler to protect his sacred music from the persecution and slander of heretical Protestants.

Sances also makes frequent references to the dedicatee's strong piety, thereby contributing directly to the Habsburg public image. In the 1642 and 1643 dedications, for instance, he makes a point of stating that his sacred music is perfectly suited for the dedicatee's pious soul. Even more explicit are those dedications in which he draws direct comparisons between the Habsburgs and the divine. In his dedication to Empress Maria, he mentions not only that she shares a name with the Blessed Virgin but also that she imitates the Virgin "in the customs of life." The dedication to Leopold Wilhelm makes a direct (if oblique) comparison between the Archduke and Jesus with a reference to the story of the Samaritan woman at the well from John 4. We have already seen the explicit comparison between the Habsburg dynasty and God in the *Fürstenspiegel* text of the dedication to Ferdinand IV. That Sances intended his prints as messages to a broad public and not just as private transactions between him and his employer is made clear in his dedication to the Empress, when he explicitly states that he intends his print "to demonstrate to so many others ... the communal benefit of the praises of the Most Sacred Mother." With this statement, he draws the anonymous readers into the conversation, elucidating the Counter-Reformation purpose of the print.

---

[31] Modern edn in Giovanni Felice Sances, *Motetti a 2, 3, 4, e cinque voci (1642)*, ed. Andrew H. Weaver, RRMBE, vol. 148 (Middleton, 2008).

[32] Sances, *Motetti*, ed. Saunders, p. xi.

It seems clear that with his prints Sances sought to represent not only the specific dedicatee but also the Habsburg dynasty as a whole. By honoring the dynasty, he was also implicitly honoring the Emperor himself, something that is emphasized on the title pages, which all users of the volumes would have seen before reading the dedication. Indeed, the title pages of all of Sances's prints are carefully designed to highlight not the dedicatee but Ferdinand III. Most of them identify Sances as a musician of the Holy Roman Emperor; because of this, Ferdinand III's name always appears on the title page, before the name of the dedicatee. The typographical design of some pages actually draws more attention to Ferdinand III than the actual dedicatee. On the title page of the 1638 solo motets, for instance, both the names "FERDINANDO III" and "ELEONORA" are in the same large typeface; however, because Ferdinand's name is placed in almost the exact center of the page, it occupies a prime location that cannot help but catch the eye. The name of the (non-Habsburg) dedicatee is entirely absent from the title page of the 1648 print, but the Emperor's name is present. Especially significant is the title page of the 1642 motet book (Figure 4.1). Although not dedicated to a member of the imperial family, this title page draws a clear connection between the print and the Emperor. The largest word on the page is "MOTETTI," and the words in the next largest typeface are "DI FERDINANDO III"; although these lines are separated by four lines of smaller text, at first glance the title page nevertheless seems to read, "Motetti di Ferdinando III."[33] Thus, before even reading the dedication, the readers of any of these prints would have known that the music was written originally for the Emperor, which would undoubtedly have colored their interpretation of the dedicatory text and the musical works.

As significant as dedications to members of the Habsburg dynasty were, just as important were Sances's dedications to non-Habsburgs, for with these the composer was able to make explicit political statements. The 1642 dedication is particularly striking, especially considering that it interrupts Sances's otherwise clearly planned "dedication program" to the imperial family. The dedicatee is Count Vilem Slavata, Grand Chancellor of Bohemia and member of the Emperor's Privy Council, a shrewd choice that placed Sances's print directly into the context of the Thirty Years' War and the Habsburgs' Counter-Reformation program. As a former Protestant who had become one of the most ardent Bohemian supporters of the Catholic Church (and of Habsburg authority), Slavata served as a shining example of the Habsburgs' re-Catholicization efforts

---

[33] This can scarcely be an accident, as there is no reason why the word "di" needed to be placed on the same line as the Emperor's name. The 1643 title page puts "Musico della S.C. Maestà di" on one line and "Ferdinando Terzo" on the next.

Figure 4.1 Title page of Giovanni Felice Sances, *Motetti a 2, 3, 4, e cinque voci*, 1642

at work.[34] For contemporary readers, this choice of dedicatee would have

---

[34] On Slavata, see Henry Frederick Schwarz, *The Imperial Privy Council in the Seventeenth Century* (Cambridge, MA, 1943), pp. 343–7 and Howard Louthan, *Converting Bohemia: Force and Persuasion in the Catholic Reformation* (Cambridge, 2009), pp. 51–74.

made two positive references to a war that was now entering its darkest hour. On one hand, Sances's dedication to a prominent Bohemian noble would have recalled recent fortunate events, as Bohemia had only recently been relieved of the threat of Swedish occupation. On the other hand, this dedication simultaneously referenced glorious memories from earlier in the war: Slavata was one of the men who had miraculously survived being hurled out of an upper-story window at the Defenestration of Prague in 1618. The dedication to Slavata may also have been an attempt to market Sances's print to a Bohemian audience, in an attempt to keep the Bohemian citizens loyal to the imperial crown in the aftermath of the ruthless plundering by the Swedes. Sances's dedication of his 1648 print to Abbot Antonio Spindler also made an important political statement, which is discussed in Chapter 7.

Sances's prints also contributed to the Emperor's representation through the careful selection of the music included in each volume. It is not surprising that his first two prints focus on works for one to four voices, considering the greater marketability of small-scale music over that for many performing forces. It seems significant, however, that as the Habsburgs' situation in the war grew increasingly dire, the scale of Sances's published works actually grew larger, in strong contrast to the practice of other composers working in locales adversely affected by the war, most famously Heinrich Schütz.[35] Sances's 1642 motet book, for instance, avoids solo works entirely, presenting instead pieces for two to up to six voices, and in the very next year he published a book of concertato psalms for eight voices divided into two four-voice choirs, with explicit indications that the music was intended for eight soloists plus a full ripieno choir.[36] Although his next book, issued four years later, reduces the number of voices to four, these "salmi brevi" are not austere *da cappella* settings but elaborate concertato works for full choir, with "solo" and "tutti" indications throughout the partbooks. Sances thus seems to have consciously published larger-scale works during the 1640s, in order to present a sumptuous image of the imperial musical establishment during the leanest years of the war.

Sances's prints most directly contribute to Ferdinand III's representation through the selection and organization of texts. Throughout the prints, the

---

[35] As is well known, Schütz published his volumes of *Kleine geistliche Konzerte* in 1636 and 1639 as a direct response to the fact that the Dresden musical establishment had dramatically decreased in size; see the text of the dedication of the second volume in Heinrich Schütz, *Gesammelte Briefe und Schriften*, ed. E.H. Müller von Aslow (Regensburg, 1931; reprint, New York, 1976), p. 139.

[36] Throughout the print, Sances uses the letters "S" and "R" to indicate which sections are meant to be sung by soloists and which could be reinforced by the ripieno. He explains the labels in a letter to the readers at the beginning of the volume (included in the Appendix).

composer took special care to highlight the pillars of the *Pietas Austriaca*; although the individual texts are by and large typical for Italian sacred prints (which is to be expected considering the demands of the commercial marketplace), the prints are nevertheless striking for their high concentration of Habsburg-specific themes and the deliberate organizational principles that highlight them. In Sances's three motet books, for instance, Marian works account for by far the greatest percentage of the contents, followed closely by works celebrating the Christological aspects of Habsburg piety and works for saints (who, unfortunately, are never identified with specific names).[37] Two of Sances's prints consist entirely of works celebrating the Blessed Virgin Mary, and two Marian works (*Regina caeli* and *Stabat Mater*) are included in his eight-voice psalms of 1643. Specific works with direct relevance to the Habsburg situation of the late 1630s and '40s are discussed in Part III.

Careful ordering principles are especially apparent in the two motet books from 1638. The first of these opens with *Ardet cor meum* for solo soprano, a work in praise of the religious symbol of greatest importance to Ferdinand III, the Blessed Virgin of the Immaculate Conception (see Chapter 7). The entire print, in fact, makes it unmistakable to the reader how important the Blessed Virgin is to the Emperor: each of the four vocal partbooks opens with a different Marian solo motet, and because the print ends with a four-voice *Salve Regina*, each partbook features a distinct Marian frame. Sances's second motet book opens with *Audite me divini fructus*, a work that celebrates the Most Holy Rosary, a religious symbol that Eleonora Gonzaga held especially dear.[38] This publication also ends with a Marian work, *Pianto della Madonna* for solo soprano, which sets the *Stabat Mater* sequence as an affective, operatic lament over the minor descending tetrachord. The partbooks are again framed by works with Marian associations; this could perhaps even be considered a "rosary frame," as the dramatic lament would have been well-suited for the Lenten celebration of the Fifteen Mysteries, a service unique to Vienna that Eleonora instituted in 1637.[39] The organization of the partbooks of

---

[37] Sances's first motet print contains nine Marian, seven Christological, and four saint motets out of a total 27; the second book contains six Marian and five Christological motets (none for saints) out of a total 17; the 1642 publication features 11 Marian, seven Christological, and three saint motets out of a total 25.

[38] The text of this motet comes from Ecclesiasticus 39:17–19, portions of which were said at both the offertory and communion at Mass on the feast of the Most Holy Rosary. On the importance of the rosary to Eleonora Gonzaga, see Sances, *Motetti*, ed. Saunders, p. xiv and Weaver, "Divine Wisdom," p. 262.

[39] On the celebration of the Fifteen Mysteries and the suitability of the *Pianto della Madonna* for this service, see Weaver, "Divine Wisdom," pp. 262–8.

the *Motetti a voce sola* draws special attention to the framing works.[40] The structure of the print is eminently logical, with four discrete groups of four motets each, scored respectively for soprano, alto, tenor, and bass; the *Pianto*, however, is notably "out of place," occurring outside this four-by-four structure and appearing far removed from the other works for soprano.

Even before hearing a note of Sances's music, then, the representational function of his prints would have been apparent to a seventeenth-century reader. Their political significance as encomiums to the Habsburgs would have been clear from the dedications and title pages, even in the two books not dedicated to members of the imperial family. By highlighting the Emperor through the design of the title pages and through the careful selection and prominent positioning of works directly related to his personal devotional preferences, the books announce to readers that the music belonged ultimately to Ferdinand III, inviting them to interpret the works not just as general religious statements but as connected to the Emperor, his court, and the political situation of the final decade of the war.

Reception

Although we can assume from Sances's important commissions and promotions beginning in 1648 that his print program fulfilled his personal goal of furthering his career, it is not as immediately apparent whether the publications actually succeeded in presenting Ferdinand III's image to a large audience. While the reception of the Emperor's representation is not my primary concern in this book, it is nevertheless important to ascertain that Sances's prints circulated in the Empire, especially since their publication in Venice (which, as suggested above, presumably happened because the composer wanted to maintain his fame in Italy) does not automatically guarantee that they were disseminated north of the Alps. In this regard, only Sances's first motet book seems to have been an unqualified success in achieving widespread dissemination. Not only did Magni reissue it in 1641, but the Lutheran musician Ambrosius Profe included four of the motets in very popular anthologies published in Leipzig in 1641 and 1649.[41] Manuscript copies of several of the works—

---

[40] The print was issued in only two partbooks: one containing all of the vocal music, and one for basso continuo, which contains the vocal line (and text) in score.

[41] The motets included in Profe's anthologies are *Conditor Caeli*, in *Erster Theil geistlicher Concerten und Harmonien* (Leipzig, 1641); *Ardet cor meum* (refitted with a Christological text) and *Laetamini in Domino*, in *Ander Theil geistlicher Concerten*

and of the entire print—circulated as far abroad as England,[42] and the print also appears (along with a number of Sances's earlier secular prints) in the 1639 catalogue of the London bookseller Robert Martin.[43]

Evidence for the widespread circulation of Sances's other six sacred prints is much sparser. These prints appear neither in the catalogues of the northern European book fairs nor in a large sampling of seventeenth- and eighteenth-century library inventories (from both Catholic and Lutheran institutions), and no known manuscript copies of works from them exist.[44] There is nevertheless some evidence that these prints circulated north of the Alps, thereby validating my argument that they were intended to represent Ferdinand III to his citizens. Four of them (along with the 1641 reprint of the 1638 *Motetti*) are currently held in the university library of Wrocław (Breslau),[45] and two of them survive in the cathedral archives of

---

und Harmonien (Leipzig, 1641), and *Plagae tuae, Domine*, in *Corollarium geistlicher Collectaneorum* (Leipzig, 1649).

[42] Many of the British manuscripts still exist at the British Library and other English libraries; see Jonathan P. Wainwright, *Musical Patronage in Seventeenth-Century England: Christopher, First Baron Hatton (1605–1670)* (Aldershot, 1997), pp. 202–3. Manuscript copies of *Ardet cor meum* and *Laetamini in Domino* (most likely copied from Profe's anthology) are recorded in a catalogue of the City Church of St Magni in Braunschweig (Werner Greve, *Braunschweiger Stadtmusikanten: Geschichte eines Berufstandes 1227–1828* [Braunschweig, 1991], p. 268), *Plagae tuae Domine* (also likely copied from Profe) appears in an inventory in Rothenberg ob der Tauber (Ernst Schmidt, *Die Geschichte des evangelischen Gesangbuches der ehemaligen freien Reichsstadt Rothenburg ob der Tauber* [Rothenburg ob der Tauber, 1928], p. 273), and all four of the motets published by Profe appear in an inventory of the Royal and University Library in Königsberg (Joseph Müller, *Die musikalischen Schätze der Königlichen- und Universitäts-Bibliothek zu Königsberg in Preußen* [Bonn, 1870; reprint, Hildesheim, 1971]).

[43] The secular prints by Sances that appear in Martin's catalogues are both volumes of the 1633 cantatas (in the 1635, 1639, and 1640 catalogues) and his lost third book of cantatas (in the 1639 and 1640 catalogues); see D.W. Krummel, "Venetian Baroque Music in a London Bookshop: The Robert Martin Catalogues, 1633–50," in Oliver Neighbor (ed.), *Music and Bibliography: Essays in Honor of Alec Hyatt King* (New York, 1980), p. 24.

[44] Sances's prints appear nowhere in Albert Göhler, *Verzeichnis der in den Frankfurter und Leipziger Messkatalogen der Jahre 1564 bis 1759 angezeigten Musikalien* (Leipzig, 1902; reprint, Hilversum, 1965). Sances's prints (or copies of individual works from them) also do not appear in the inventories (of both lost and existing collections) listed in the Appendix of this chapter. I am grateful to Alexander Fisher, Mary Frandsen, and Tassilo Erhardt for sharing with me information from unpublished inventories.

[45] The prints are the 1638 *Motetti a voce sola* and the 1640, 1643, and 1648 publications. They have been in Wrocław since at least the nineteenth century; see Emil Bohn, *Bibliographie der Musik-Druckwerke bis 1700 welche in der Stadtbibliothek, der Bibliothek des Academischen Instituts für Kirchenmusik und der Königlichen und Universitäts-Bibliothek zu Breslau aufbewahrt werden: Ein Beitrag zur Geschichte der Musik im XV., XVI., und XVII. Jahrhundert* (Berlin, 1883; reprint, Hildesheim, 1969), pp. 374–5.

Koper, Slovenia.[46] (The absence of the prints from other Central European libraries by no means proves that they were never there, especially as the volatile political situation in recent centuries has increased the chance that obscure music prints would have been destroyed. It is telling that none of the prints discussed in this chapter are currently held in the Österreichische Nationalbibliothek, although the Habsburgs certainly owned them.) In addition, an inventory of the Cathedral of St Martin's in Bratislava (Preßburg), drawn up in 1700, lists an "Opus impressum Motettarum. Auth: Sances" as well as a manuscript "Vesperae. a 4 Voc. Auth: Felice Sances," which could very well be a copy of his 1647 *Salmi brevi*.[47] Another possible manuscript copy of the 1647 *Salmi* is an "Integrae Vesp. Brev." by Sances that appears in a Regensburg inventory from 1674.[48] Manuscripts of individual works that may have been copied from Sances's prints include a setting of *Ave maris stella* attributed to "Sancii" in an early-eighteenth-century Moravian inventory from the Benedictine Monastery Church of Sts Peter and Paul in Rajhrad (near Brno),[49] as well as an unattributed "Si criminum immanitate â 2. Sopran:" in a 1689 inventory of a monastery in Maria Luggau, Austria, which on account of the rarity of settings of this particular text was likely copied from Sances's 1642 *Motetti*.[50] Finally, 11 of the Marian antiphons from Sances's 1648 print (all fitted with Christological texts) appear in a singing treatise published by Georg Falck in Nuremberg in 1688.[51]

Additional inventories may yet provide more evidence of the dissemination of Sances's prints in the Empire, but even these few sources

---

[46] These are the first motet print from 1638 and the 1642 *Motetti*. One partbook of the 1642 *Motetti* also survives in the British Library in London.

[47] Jana Kalinayová, *Musikinventare und das Repertoire der mehrstimmigen Musik in der Slowakei im 16. und 17. Jahrhundert* (Bratislava, 1995), pp. 158–9.

[48] Johann Georg Metteleiter, *Musikgeschichte der Stadt Regensburg: Aus Archivalien und sonstigen Quellen bearbeitet* (Regensburg, 1866), p. 132.

[49] Theodora Straková, "Rajhradský hudební inventář z roku 1725: Příspěvek k poznání hudební kultury na Moravě v 1. pol. 18. století," *Časopis Moravského Musea. Acta Musei Moraviae*, 58 (1973): p. 241.

[50] Franz M. Weiß, "Das Musikalien- und Instrumenteninventar des Servitenklosters Maria Luggau in Oberkärnten aus dem Jahre 1689," *Kirchenmusikalisches Jahrbuch*, 82 (1998): p. 112. The work is listed under the rubric "Motettae Maiores De B.ma Semper Virg.c Maria."

[51] Georg Falck, *Idea boni cantoris* … (Nuremberg, 1688). The existence of Sances's "de-Marianized" antiphons is discussed in Mary E. Frandsen, "*Salve Regina/Salve Rex Christi*: The Lutheran Appropriation of the Marian Antiphons in the Era of New Piety (*neue Frommigkeit*)," paper presented at the 75th Annual Meeting of the American Musicological Society, Philadelphia, November 15, 2009. The treatise is translated in Ralph McDowell Taylor, Jr., "Georg Falck's *Idea boni cantoris* …: Translation and Commentary" (Ph.D. diss., The Louisiana State University and Agricultural and Mechanical College, 1971).

attest to the fact that the prints circulated north of the Alps, and the frequent presence of additional unpublished works by Sances in inventories affirms that there was indeed a market for them. We can thus confidently assume that the court did intend imperial citizens to receive the prints. Indeed, perhaps a main reason why Sances signed some of the dedications in Venice was so that he could hand carry a supply of prints back to Vienna. All the same, even if the dissemination of these prints was not as widespread as the Emperor (or composer) would have liked, this does not lessen their value for our understanding of Ferdinand III's representation. Regardless of the actual readership—and even regardless of the effect that the books had on the population—the intent to communicate is clear, making these books valuable cultural artifacts through which we can perceive the strategies through which Ferdinand's representation was transformed during the 1640s.

Foreign Publications and Ferdinand's Public Image

Sances's publications were the central vehicle through which Ferdinand III's image was disseminated to a wider audience through the medium of printed music during the 1640s. They were not, however, the only one, for the same decade also saw a number of other music publications that contributed directly or indirectly to the Emperor's representation. These prints were all initiated outside of Ferdinand's direct influence; in some cases he still seems to have had a hand in their contents, but in others he may have not even been aware of the work until the finished product reached his hands. As discussed in Chapter 1, such foreign contributions to his image would have been especially welcome, as they could demonstrate to audiences the widespread esteem in which the Emperor was held, supplementing and reinforcing the "official" image being promulgated in Sances's publications.[52]

Venice: Giovanni Antonio Rigatti, Claudio Monteverdi—and Bartolomeo Magni?

In 1640 and 1641, Sances's publisher Magni issued two of the largest and grandest sacred prints of the seventeenth century, both bearing dedications to the Viennese court: Giovanni Antonio Rigatti's *Messa e salmi, parte concertati* (published in 1640 with a dedication to the Emperor) and Monteverdi's *Selva morale et spirituale* (published in 1641 with a

---

[52] This section does not examine all of the musical publications dedicated to the Emperor, only the ones that overtly served as representation.

dedication to Eleonora Gonzaga).[53] On the surface, the two prints follow a popular generic model: they are "messa e salmi" collections featuring a polyphonic mass and a selection of Vespers psalms, a type of publication most familiar to modern audiences from Monteverdi's celebrated Vespers of 1610.[54] Both prints, however, go far beyond the expectations for the genre, in both the immense performing forces (each print contains works for up to eight principal voices plus obbligato instruments) and also in that they contain multiple settings of the same psalms, as well as additional works.[55] Rigatti's print features two Marian antiphons (the last of which, a setting of *Ave Regina caelorum*, is headed with a rubric explaining that it is dedicated to Empress Maria), while Monteverdi's print contains concertato mass movements, seven hymns, three Marian antiphons, four solo motets, and five Italian madrigals.

These two prints contributed to Ferdinand III's public image in the most general sense, by elevating his prestige as an important patron of sacred music and by highlighting the grandeur of his chapel through their large, non-commercial scope. Monteverdi's print goes a step further by including anomalous works that point to important aspects of the *Pietas Austriaca*.[56] The print falls into two large sections, one devoted to the Mass and one to the Vespers settings; this division is reinforced by the gathering structure and pagination of the partbooks.[57] Monteverdi further highlighted this bipartite division by concluding each section with a solo motet that stands out from the rest of the music in the print.[58] In a publication consisting primarily of music that is liturgically appropriate for the feasts of male saints, the first motet (*Ab aeterno ordinata sum*) sets

---

[53] Giovanni Antonio Rigatti, *Messa e salmi, parte concertati* (Venice, 1640); modern edn by Linda Maria Koldau, RRMBE, vols 128–30 (Middleton, 2003). Claudio Monteverdi, *Selva morale et spirituale* (Venice, 1641); facsimile and modern edn in Monteverdi, *Opera Omnia: Edizione nazionale*, vol. 15, ed. Denis Stevens (Cremona, 1998). Koldau compares the two prints in Rigatti, *Messa e salmi*, pp. vii–xi.

[54] The best overview of the 1610 Vespers, as well as of *messa e salmi* collections of the seicento, is Kurtzman.

[55] The *Selva morale* also includes one psalm for ten voices plus instruments. For a schematic overview of the contents of both prints, see Rigatti, *Messa e salmi*, ed. Koldau, pp. viii and x.

[56] For a more detailed discussion of the relationship of the *Selva morale* to the Habsburg court, see Weaver, "Divine Wisdom."

[57] In every partbook signature B begins with the first psalm setting, at which point the pagination returns to one.

[58] Monteverdi's Sixth and Eighth Madrigal books are similarly organized. As Tomlinson, p. 156, has commented, "Monteverdi's strengthened urge to schematic clarity … is evident as well in the internal organization of the Sixth, Seventh, and Eighth Books. The *Sesto libro de madrigali* of 1614 falls into two sections, articulated by a series of lengthy madrigals that act as structural pillars."

an utterance by Divine Wisdom from the Old Testament book of Proverbs (8:23–31), and the second (*Pianto della Madonna*) is a Latin contrafactum of the composer's celebrated *Lamento d'Arianna*. Monteverdi seems to have consciously chosen these motets to honor Ferdinand III and Eleonora Gonzaga respectively: the first sets a passage that in the seventeenth century was widely understood as a prefiguration of the Immaculate Conception, while the second would have been perfectly suited (like the *Pianto della Madonna* that closes Sances's 1638 print dedicated to Eleonora) for the Fifteen Mysteries Devotion. That both Monteverdi's and Sances's prints conclude with a work titled *Pianto della Madonna* could scarcely be a coincidence. Not only was it rare for seventeenth-century sacred prints to conclude with Marian laments, but Sances's print also includes a setting of the same Proverbs passage set by Monteverdi; very few other settings of this text by seventeenth-century composers survive.[59] Monteverdi may even have used Sances's Proverbs setting as a compositional model; both are virtuosic works for solo bass, a style rare in Monteverdi's *œuvre* but very popular at the Viennese court.[60]

What could have inspired Rigatti and Monteverdi to dedicate such similar publications to the imperial court within the space of a year? In the younger composer's case, the dedication seems to have been motivated primarily by career aspirations. Although by 1640 Rigatti had started making a name for himself with music prints (he had published a collection of motets for two to four voices in 1634 and a madrigal book, also for two to four voices, in 1636) and had held a series of positions as *maestro* of minor chapels (at the Udine Cathedral, 1635–37, and then at the Venetian *Ospedale dei Mendicanti*), the young composer (b. 1613) had yet to receive the "big job" to which seventeenth-century musicians aspired for a lifetime of security.[61] The dedication of an impressive collection of

---

[59] Sances's motet is titled differently (*Dominus possedit me*) because it sets one additional Bible verse at the beginning and end. I have located only one other surviving setting of this passage, a motet by the obscure composer Giovanni Battista Treviso published in an anthology from 1645: *Motetti a voce sola de diversi Eccelentissimi Autori* (Venice, 1645); facsimile edn in Schnoebelen, *Solo Motets*, vol. 3. Significantly, the text was also apparently set by Antonio Bertali; a motet by him entitled *Ab aeterno ordinata* is listed in a catalogue of Leopold I's music library (A-Wn, Cod. suppl. mus. 2451, fol. 18r).

[60] For a detailed comparison of Monteverdi's and Sances's Proverbs settings, see Weaver, "Divine Wisdom," pp. 255–8. There are only two known extended solo bass works by Monteverdi: this motet and the long second section of the madrigal *Ogni amante è guerrier* from his Eighth Book. On Monteverdi's solo bass music, see Werner Braun, "Monteverdis große Baßmonodien," in Ludwig Finscher (ed.), *Claudio Monteverdi: Festschrift Reinhold Hammerstein zum 70. Geburtstag* (Laaber, 1986), pp. 123–39. It is undoubtedly significant that the other solo bass work appears not only in a madrigal book dedicated to Ferdinand III but in a work that names the Emperor.

[61] Rigatti, *Messa e salmi*, ed. Koldau, p. vii.

sacred music to the imperial court in 1640 thus seems to have served as a job application, introducing him to a potential employer to whom he had no other known contact. In contrast, Monteverdi's print, coming at the end of a long, successful career, seems to have served primarily as an homage and gift of thanks. On one hand, the dedication can be viewed as a bow to the family that had given him his first important job and had helped make him famous, as Eleonora was the daughter of his first patron Vincenzo Gonzaga.[62] On the other hand, Monteverdi had enjoyed a profitable association with the Habsburgs since the turn of the century, through whose intervention he had received a benefice in Cremona in 1633.[63] That he intended the dedication as an homage to the Habsburgs and not just the Gonzagas is strengthened by the fact that it forms a pair with his immediately preceding publication, the *Madrigali guerreri, et amorosi* dedicated to Ferdinand III in 1638 (see Chapter 1).

Linda Maria Koldau has suggested another compelling possibility for the appearance of these two publications: that they were the result not just of the composers' personal motives but of the active intervention of the publisher.[64] Indeed, just as Monteverdi's *Selva morale* seems to form a dedicatory pair with his Eighth Book of Madrigals, so too do Monteverdi's and Rigatti's prints seem to form a similar pair with each other. Koldau's hypothesis that "it is conceivable that Magni was under great pressure to issue these representative church music collections at a certain point in time" leads her to a convincing explanation for one of the most frustrating features of both prints: the huge number of typographical errors throughout the partbooks, indicating that neither print was very carefully proofread.[65] It is certainly conceivable that it was Magni himself who instigated both prints. After all, he already had a solid working relationship with Sances, and it may even have been the publisher who suggested to Monteverdi that he use Sances's *Motetti a voce sola* as a model for the *Selva*. Although we have no concrete evidence as to why Magni would have wanted to honor the Habsburgs in this way, it is possible that he was still suffering financially from the lag in publications brought on by the devastating Venetian plague of 1629–31 and was therefore hoping to secure substantial financial support from the imperial court as a means of helping him get

---

[62] This is reinforced by the text of Monteverdi's dedication (given in the Appendix).

[63] Ferdinand II wrote a letter of recommendation for the composer in support of the benefice after receiving a gift of musical works; see Steven Saunders, "New Light on the Genesis of Monteverdi's Eighth Book of Madrigals," *Music & Letters*, 77 (1996): pp. 183–93. For more details on Monteverdi's relationship with the Habsburgs, see Weaver, "Divine Wisdom," pp. 244–5.

[64] Rigatti, *Messa e salmi*, ed. Koldau, p. ix.

[65] Ibid., pp. x–xi.

back on his feet. (Magni's desire to honor the Habsburgs may be another reason why Sances's prints were published in Venice instead of within the Empire.) Regardless of the specific motivations that led to the publication of these two remarkable prints, they nevertheless stand as important artifacts celebrating Ferdinand III's image in the early 1640s; while the representation is undoubtedly magnificent, it is perhaps significant that the focus has shifted from the secular music of Monteverdi's Book Eight to sacred music.

Milan: Giorgio Rolla

In 1649, the Milanese printer and composer Giorgio Rolla published the *Teatro musicale de concerti ecclesiastici*, an anthology of 42 motets for two to four voices by a wide selection of Italian composers (plus a mass and litany by Rolla himself).[66] As Jerome Roche has pointed out, this print is markedly different from the Milanese anthologies issued earlier in the century (between 1608 and 1626, some from Rolla's own presses).[67] Whereas the earlier publications feature only composers from Milan, in the *Teatro* Rolla published works by 11 local composers alongside pieces by some of the most prominent composers of the day, including Rigatti and Giovanni Rovetta in Venice; Orazio Benevoli, Francesco Foggia, and Giacomo Carissimi in Rome; as well as the two most famous Italian composers working at the imperial court, Bertali and Sances. Many of the local works—and some of the others (including the works by Bertali and Sances)—appear in no other printed sources than this anthology, which led Roche to conclude that Rolla may have taken an active role in commissioning some of the contributions.[68] It seems clear that Rolla's motivation in assembling this collection was to place the works of local composers on the same level as the other "diversi celebri ... autori," thereby both elevating the prestige of the Milanese composers and also perhaps raising Rolla's own prestige and drumming up sales. What Rolla may not have realized, however, was that by commissioning works from two prestigious composers from the Viennese court, he also ended up contributing to Ferdinand III's representation.

---

[66] *Teatro musicale de concerti ecclesiastici a due, tre, e quattro voci di diversi celebri, e nomati autori* (Milan, 1649).

[67] Jerome Roche, "Cross-Currents in Milanese Church Music in the 1640s: Giorgio Rolla's Anthology *Teatro Musicale* (1649)," in Alberto Colzani et al. (eds), *La musica sacra in Lombardia nella prima metà del Seicento: Atti del convegno internazionale di studi Como, 31 Maggio–2 Giugno 1985* (Como, 1987), pp. 13–29.

[68] Ibid., pp. 17–18, 21. Bertali's motet is in fact the only of the composer's works published during his lifetime.

At first glance, the three imperial motets—Bertali's *Exultate et cantate* and Sances's *Miserere servorum tuorum* and *Excita furorem*—do not seem different from the other works in the anthology. Their paraliturgical texts are primarily freely written but with various phrases selected from (or freely based upon) the Bible, and as one would expect from a commercial print, they express general religious themes that would have been welcome throughout the Catholic world. At the same time, however, the texts of all three works are directly relevant to Ferdinand III's situation at the end of the Thirty Years' War. When taken as a whole, the three works reflect the most important pillars of the *Pietas Austriaca*: *Excita furorem* extols general praise of Christ, while *Miserere* addresses the Virgin Mary and *Exultate* a named saint.[69] Even more significant is the fact that all three works reference war, explicitly calling out for protection from enemies. As will be discussed in Chapter 5, textual and musical details in the motets present veritable portraits of Ferdinand III, delivering prayers for the sake of his subjects.

Although such Habsburg-specific meanings could have easily become lost when the motets were published alongside the music of many other Italian composers, for one of the works great care was taken to ensure that readers would associate the music with the Emperor. A rubric placed before Sances's *Excita furorem* in the tenor partbook announces that "Le Parole di questo Motetto, furono messe insieme da S.M. Cesarea."[70] This rubric explicitly connects the work to Ferdinand III, not only by reminding the reader of Sances's connection to the court but also by drawing the Emperor into the creative process. Although we have no evidence for Ferdinand's further participation in the creation of these three motets, it seems fair to speculate that upon learning that two of his composers had received commissions for a Milanese anthology, he would have used his influence to ensure that Bertali's and Sances's motets served his political and religious goals, even to the point of providing a text and insisting that his contribution be acknowledged in the print.

An interpretation of this print as a contribution to Ferdinand III's public image during the final years of the war hits one snag: the fact that the anthology did not appear until at least July 12, 1649 (the date of the dedication), whereas the Peace of Westphalia was signed on October 24, 1648. While this would have certainly affected the *reception* of the motets, it nevertheless has no bearing on their *inception* as works intended to contribute to Ferdinand's public image. After all, by 1648 the Westphalian

---

[69] The print provides both the generic "N" as well as the name "Carolus"; while this could very well have been a specifically Milanese addition by Rolla, the Counter-Reformer St Charles Borromeo was an important figure in Habsburg piety.

[70] "The words of this motet were put together by His Imperial Majesty."

peace talks had been dragging on for more than five years; no one could have foreseen—even as late as May 1648—that the treaty would be ready to be signed in October.[71] There is also evidence from the print itself that Rolla had much of the publication ready to go before October 1648. The opening pages of each partbook include a list of contributors with brief biographies for each one, in which Rigatti is listed as "Maestro di Capella in Venetia." What this entry does not indicate is that Rigatti had died in October 1648; because Rolla did not make the effort to indicate that the composer was deceased, we can assume that at least this page was prepared before Rigatti's death and that Rolla had started gathering the works for the print long before the Peace of Westphalia was signed.

Although it seems unlikely that Rolla had Ferdinand III's representation in mind when he solicited motets from Bertali and Sances, paratextual details in the anthology seem to indicate that once he began to put the print together he made a concerted effort to honor the imperial court. That Rolla would have wanted to honor the Habsburgs is not surprising considering that Milan was under the control of the Spanish crown and therefore intimately connected to the imperial dynasty; this also would have been an important potential audience for Ferdinand III. One detail is the list of contributors mentioned above, in which Sances and Bertali are given pride of place at the end of the list (followed only by Rolla himself). The imperial composers are the only people on the list for whom Rolla provided superlative, fawning descriptions. Whereas the biographies of the other musicians list merely their current position and place of employment, the imperial musicians are listed as "Musico di Camera di Sua Maestà Cesarea" followed by additional information; Sances is described as "gratiosissimo Tenorista" and Bertali as "celeberrimo Violinista." Another telling detail is the dedication of the print to Cardinal Francesco Peretti di Montalto, nephew of Cardinal Alessandro Montalto (mentioned above as the sponsor of *Amor pudico*, in which the young Sances performed). While on the surface this dedication does not seem connected to the Habsburgs, it takes on new significance in light of the fact that Montalto was a member of the party who accompanied Ferdinand III's daughter Maria Anna on her travels from Vienna to Spain to marry King Philip IV. Maria Anna arrived in Milan on May 30, 1649, and the city gave her a joyous entry on June 17, less than a month before Rolla signed the dedication of his anthology.[72] The text of Rolla's dedication

---

[71] On the final years of the peace negotiations, see Geoffrey Parker (ed.), *The Thirty Years' War*, 2nd edn (London and New York, 1997), pp. 160–69.

[72] I am grateful to Claudio Bernardi for informing me of Montalto's participation in Maria Anna's journey. Montalto's presence in her entourage is mentioned in C. Cantú, "La Pompa della solenne entrata fatta nella città di Milano dalla Serenissima Maria Anna

makes frequent references to the Queen's joyous entry and Montalto's participation in it (see the Appendix).

The *Teatro musicale*, then, offers a curious example of how a sacred print can come to contribute to a monarch's representation. The initial instigation for the publication surely came from outside of the court, most likely without any intent to contribute to the Emperor's image. Although Ferdinand III probably did not have a hand in initiating the print, he nevertheless does seem to have played an active role in making sure that his musicians' contributions represented him. In response to this, the publisher may have then consciously added additional paratexts to solidify the relationship between the print and the Habsburg dynasty, thereby confirming the function of the print as a contribution to the Emperor's image.

Hungary: Andreas Rauch

By far the most magnificent and most explicit representation of Ferdinand III produced by a non-court musician is the *Currus triumphalis musici* published in 1648 by Andreas Rauch (1592–1656), an Austrian musician living in the Hungarian town of Sopron (Ödenburg).[73] This "triumphal musical chariot" dedicated to Ferdinand III features 13 sacred works in an unmistakably "Colossal Baroque" style, scored for three to five choirs and obbligato instruments with indications for the insertion of trumpet fanfares. The paratextual material could not make the connection to Ferdinand III any more explicit: in addition to the elaborate frontispiece that pictures the Emperor riding majestically in an imperial chariot overtop a magnificent illustration of his chapel (Figure 2.3) and a dedicatory text that celebrates both the Peace of Westphalia and Ferdinand's recent marriage to Maria Leopoldine, the print also contains an index specifying that each work is dedicated to one of the 13 Habsburg emperors throughout history (Figure 4.2). This print marked the first important peacetime representation of

---

Austriaca," *Archivio storico lombardo*, 14 (1887): p. 345. For more information on Maria Anna's joyous entry, see Elena Cenzato, "La festa barocca: La real solenne entrata di Maria Anna d'Austria a Milano nel 1649," *Archivio storico lombardo*, 112 (1987): pp. 47–100 and Cenzato and Luisa Rovaris, "'Comparvero finalmente gl'aspettati soli dell'Austriaco cielo': Ingressi solenni per nozze reali," in Annamaria Cascetta (ed.), *Aspetti della teatralità a Milano nell'età barocca*, Comunicazioni sociali, vol. 16 (Milan, 1994), pp. 71–112.

[73] Andreas Rauch, *Currus triumphalis musici, Imperatorum Romanorum Tredecim ex Augustissima Archiducali Domo Austriaca* (Vienna, 1648). On Rauch, see Josef Pausz, *Andreas Rauch: Ein evangelischer Musiker, 1592 bis 1656* ([Vienna], 1992), which contains facsimiles of the front matter of the *Currus triumphalis* as well as all of the motet texts (pp. 109–18).

INDEX ET ORDO

Tredecim Auſtriaco-Romanorum Imperatorum Nominum, cum ſingulis ſibi appropriatis Cantionibus'.

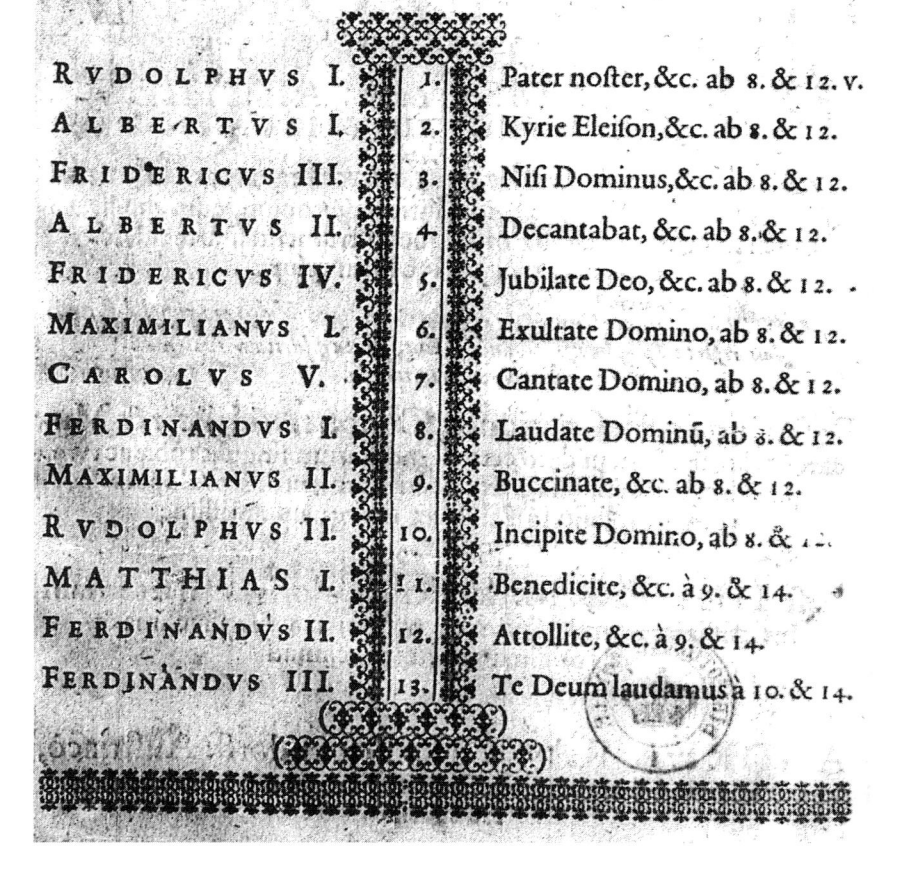

RVDOLPHVS I.	1.	Pater noſter, &c. ab 8. & 12. v.
ALBERTVS I.	2.	Kyrie Eleiſon, &c. ab 8. & 12.
FRIDERICVS III.	3.	Niſi Dominus, &c. ab 8. & 12.
ALBERTVS II.	4.	Decantabat, &c. ab 8. & 12.
FRIDERICVS IV.	5.	Jubilate Deo, &c. ab 8. & 12.
MAXIMILIANVS I.	6.	Exultate Domino, ab 8. & 12.
CAROLVS V.	7.	Cantate Domino, ab 8. & 12.
FERDINANDVS I.	8.	Laudate Dominū, ab 8. & 12.
MAXIMILIANVS II.	9.	Buccinate, &c. ab 8. & 12.
RVDOLPHVS II.	10.	Incipite Domino, ab 8. & 12.
MATTHIAS I.	11.	Benedicite, &c. à 9. & 14.
FERDINANDVS II.	12.	Attollite, &c. à 9. & 14.
FERDINANDVS III.	13.	Te Deum laudamus à 10. & 14.

Figure 4.2 Table of contents of Andreas Rauch, *Currus triumphalis musici*, 1648 (Bibliothèque nationale de France)

Ferdinand III, setting the tone for a second revision of the Emperor's image in the post-war years.

That this magnificent image of Ferdinand III should come from a non-court musician is not necessarily surprising, for people throughout Europe were thankful for the end of the war, and formerly dissenting towns within the Empire would have been eager to re-establish good relations with the Emperor. It is nevertheless curious that it was Rauch who produced this sumptuous print for Ferdinand III's benefit. A devout Lutheran throughout his life, Rauch had been exiled from his native Lower Austria by Ferdinand II's edicts of September 1627 and April 1628 purging Protestants from the realm; Rauch settled in Sopron, where the mayor guaranteed religious freedom, and never returned to his homeland.[74] Why would this Lutheran musician, who had personally suffered the consequences of the Habsburgs' Counter-Reformation program, produce such a significant (and decidedly non-commercial) print in honor of the imperial dynasty?

Although we have no solid evidence, the most obvious answer is that Ferdinand III likely commissioned the *Currus triumphalis musici* directly from Rauch. The Emperor would have been well aware of Rauch's compositional ability in the Colossal Baroque style, for the town of Sopron had earlier commissioned Rauch to compose a motet, *Attollite portas*, in honor of Ferdinand II's entry into the town for a diet that opened on December 18, 1634. The work, the text of which praises Ferdinand by name, was published in Vienna in 1635, and Rauch included it (with a reduced scoring) in the *Currus triumphalis* as the work dedicated to Ferdinand II.[75] It is reasonable that, upon the conclusion of the war, Ferdinand III would have wanted to take charge in the dissemination of a new celebratory image, and by commissioning it from a non-court musician, he not only received the honor of a foreign dedication but was also able to distance himself somewhat from a peace treaty that was unfavorable to his Counter-Reformation cause. Rauch, as a musician who had already displayed a willingness to celebrate the Habsburg dynasty with magnificent large-scale music, may have seemed the most obvious candidate for the commission. That the print was produced at the instigation of the Emperor is suggested by the fact that it was printed in Vienna, and the title page states in large type that it was published "Cum Privilegio Sacratissimae Caesareae Majestatis."

---

[74] Pausz, pp. 20–26.

[75] Andreas Rauch, *Concentus votivus ... ad Comitia Semproniana ingressum solemnem et auspicatissimum, incliti senatus eiusdem loci, jussu et voluntate decantatus, anno MDCXXXIV, die 18. Decembris* (Vienna, 1635); facsimile of the front matter (including the text of the motet) in Pausz, pp. 99–100.

Conclusion

These examples illustrate three different ways that printed musical representations by non-court musicians could come into being. In the case of the prints issued by Magni in the early 1640s, Ferdinand III quite likely had nothing to do with the preparation of the prints, but the dedications may have stemmed in part from the fact that Magni had already established a working relationship with one of the Emperor's musicians. In contrast, Rauch's seemingly non-court publication was most likely instigated by the Emperor directly, for there are no other obvious explanations as to why the composer would publish such grand, non-commercial music in Vienna for the Emperor's benefit. Rolla's print, moreover, seems to have resulted from a variety of motivations, including the publisher's bid for increased prestige and the Emperor's desire to take advantage of his musicians' recent commission. These webs of motivations—together with the various motivations that resulted in Sances's extended print program in honor of the Emperor—resulted in a remarkable group of publications that have not only preserved for posterity the music of Ferdinand's chapel but that also provide the most valuable medium through which we can study the Emperor's representation during the most critical years of his reign.

Appendix
Sources Consulted for Evidence of the Dissemination of Sances's Prints (in which the Prints do not Appear)

Aber, Adolf, *Die Pflege der Musik unter den Wettinern und wettinischen Ernestinern von den Anfängen bis zur Auflösung der Weimarer Hofkapelle 1662* (Bückenburg and Leipzig: C.F.W. Siegel, 1921).
Benedikt, Erich, "Ein altes Noteninventar (kurz nach 1700) der Klosterkirche der Barmherzigen Brüder in Wien," *Studien zur Musikwissenschaft*, 47 (1999): 35–52.
Bohn, Emil, *Die musikalischen Handschriften des XVI. und XVII. Jahrhunderts in Stadtbibliothek zu Breslau: Ein Beitrag zur Geschichte der Musik im XVI. und XVII. Jahrhundert* (Breslau, 1890; reprint, Hildesheim: Georg Olms, 1970).
Braun, Werner, "Musik in deutschen Gelehrtenbibliotheken des 17. und 18. Jahrhunderts," *Die Musikforschung*, 10 (1957): 241–50.
Fellerer, Karl Gustav, "Ein Musikalien-Inventar des fürstbischöflichen Hofes in Freising aus dem 17. Jahrhundert," *Archiv für Musikwissenschaft*, 6 (1924): 471–83.
Fidlerová, Alena et al. (eds), *Repertorium rukopisů 17. a 18. století z muzejních sbírek v Čechách* (2 vols to date, Prague: Karolinum, 2003–).
Hintermaier, Ernst, "Musikpflege und Musizierpraxis an Kollegiatstiften des Erzbistums Salzburg im 17., 18. und 19. Jahrhundert," in Ladislav Kačic (ed.), *Musik der geistlichen Orden in Mitteleuropa zwischen Tridentinum und Josephinismus* (Bratislava: Slavistický kabinet SAV, 1997), pp. 67–79.
Jung, Hans Rudolf, "Zur Pflege der Figuralmusik in Goldbach bei Gotha im 17. und 18. Jahrhundert," in Reinhard Szeskus (ed.), *Johann Sebastian Bachs Traditionsraum*, Bach-Studien, vol. 9 (Leipzig: Breitkopf & Härtel, 1986), pp. 111–41.
Kim-Szacsvai, Katalin, "Dokumente über das Musikleben der Jesuiten: Instrumenten- und Musikalienverzeichnisse zur Zeit der Auflösungen," *Studia musicologica Academiae Scientiarum Hungaricae*, 39 (1998): 283–366.
Kolbuszewska, Aniela, *Katalog zbiorów muzycznych legnickiej biblioteki księcia Jerzego Rudolfa 'Bibliotheca Rudolphina'* (Legnica: Legnickie Towarzystwo Muzyczne, 1992).
Krummacher, Friedhelm, *Die Überlieferung der Choralarbeitungen in der frühen evangelischen Kantate: Untersuchungen zum Handschriftenrepertoire evangelischer Figuralmusik im späten 17. und beginnenden 18. Jahrhundert* (Berlin: Merseburger, 1965).

Mikanová, Eva, "Hudební kultura v České Lípě a okolí v 17. století: Příspěvek k dějinám hudby v severních Čechách," in Marie Vojtíšková (ed.), *Sborník příspěvků k době poddanského povstání roku 1680 v severních Čechách* (Prague: Tisková, edicní a propagační služba místního hospodářství, 1980), pp. 194–229.

Möller, Eberhard, "Die Weimarer Noteninventare von 1662 und ihre Bedeutung als Schütz-Quellen," *Schütz-Jahrbuch*, 10 (1988): 62–85.

Müller, Joseph, *Die musikalischen Schätze der Königlichen- und Universitäts-Bibliothek zu Königsberg in Preußen* (Bonn, 1870; reprint, Hildesheim: Georg Olms, 1971).

Neubacher, Jürgen, *Die Musikbibliothek des Hamburger Kantors und Musikdirektors Thomas Selle (1599–1663): Rekonstruktion des ursprünglichen und Beschreibung des erhaltenen, überwiegend in der Staats- und Universitätsbibliothek Hamburg Carl von Ossietzky aufbewahrten Bestandes* (Neuhauen-Stuttgart: Hänssler, 1997).

Pass, Walter, "Die Bregrenzer Musikalieninventare von 1609 und 1638," in Elmar Vonbank (ed.), *Musik im Bodenseeraum um 1600: Katalog der Ausstellung* (Bregrenz: Vorarlberger Landesmuseum, 1974), pp. 23–7.

Renton, Barbara Ann, "The Musical Culture of Eighteenth-Century Bohemia, with Special Emphasis on the Music Inventories of Osek and the Knights of the Cross" (Ph.D. diss., City University of New York, 1990).

Sandberger, Adolf (ed.), *J.K. Kerll: Ausgewählte Werke, Erster Teil*, Denkmäler der Tonkunst in Bayern, vol. 2/2 (Leipzig: Breitkopf & Härtel, [1901]), pp. lxxxiii–lxxxv.

Schaal, Richard (ed.), *Die Musikhandschriften des Ansbacher Inventars von 1686* (Wilhelmshaven: Heinrichshofen, 1966).

Schering, Arnold, "Die alte Chorbibliothek der Thomasschule in Leipzig," *Archiv für Musikwissenschaft*, 1 (1918–19): 275–88.

Sehnal, Jiří and Jitřenka Pešková (eds), *Caroli de Liechtenstein-Castelcorno Episcopi Olomucensis operum artis musicae collectio Cremsirii reservata*, Artis Musicae Antiquioris Catalogorum, vol. 5 (2 vols, Prague: Biblioteca Nationalis Rei Publicae Bohemicae Editio Supraphon Praha, 1998).

Sehnal, Jiří and Svatava Přibánová, *Průvodce po archívních fondech: Ústavu dějin hudby Moravského musea v Brně* (Brno: Moravského musea Brně, 1971).

Seifert, Herbert, "Ein Gumpoldskirchner Musikalieninventar aus dem Jahr 1640," *Studien zur Musikwissenschaft*, 39 (1988): 55–61.

Seiffert, Max. "Die Chorbibliothek der St. Michaelisschule in Lüneburg zu Seb. Bach's Zeit," *Sammelbände der Internationalen Musik-Gesellschaft*, 9 (1907–1908): 593–621.

Steude, Wolfram (ed.), *Die Musiksammelhandschriften des 16. und 17. Jahrhunderts in der Sächsischen Landesbibliothek zu Dresden*, Quellenkataloge zur Musikgeschichte, vol. 6 (Wilhelmshaven: Heinrichshofen, 1974).

Waldner, Franz, "Zwei Inventarien aus dem XVI. und XVII. Jahrhundert über hinterlassene Musikinstrumente und Musikalien am Innsbrucker Hofe," *Studien zur Musikwissenschaft*, 4 (1916): 128–47.

Walter, Rudolf, "Kirchenmusik-Inventar einer schlesischen Gebirgsstadt," in Axel Beer, Kristina Pfarr, and Wolfgang Ruf (eds), *Festschrift Christoph-Hellmut Mahling zum 65. Geburtstag* (Tutzing: Hans Schneider, 1997), pp. 1509–29.

Welter, Friedrich, *Katalog der Musikalien der Ratsbücherei Lüneburg* (Lippstadt: Kistner & Siegel, 1950).

Werner, Arno, "Die alte Musikbibliothek und die Instrumentensammlung an St Wenzel in Naumburg a. d. S.," *Archiv für Musikwissenschaft*, 8 (1927): 390–415.

Zirnbauer, Heinz, *Der Notenbestand der Reichsstädtisch Nürnbergischen Ratsmusik: Eine bibliographische Rekonstruktion* (Nuremberg: Fränkische Verlagsanstalt, 1959).

Zulauf, Ernst, *Beiträge zur Geschichte der Landgräftlich-Hessischen Hofkapelle zu Cassel bis auf die Zeit Moritz des Gelehrten* (Kassel: Döll, 1902).

PART III
Music as Representation

CHAPTER 5

Musical Portraiture: Representations of the Emperor in Sound

How does a piece of Baroque music paint a portrait? An instrumental work could be named after a specific person and attempt to capture that person's personality through the predominant affect, as in François Couperin's famous character sketches for solo keyboard.[1] Or a composer might set to music a text that provides a detailed physical description of an individual, as in Barbara Strozzi's cantata *Cieli, stelle, deitadi*, an explicit musical portrait of Sophie, Duchess of Brunswick-Lüneberg.[2] Beyond such obvious examples, scholars have generally overlooked the representational potential of much Baroque music. Nevertheless, even a work with a seemingly neutral text can paint a portrait through such means as multivalent texts that allude to somebody, evocative musical settings that add layers of meaning, and the context in which the work appeared.

With sacred music the issue is more complex, for how could a composer create a work that represents a specific person and yet at the same time is suitable for religious services? One solution was the specific context for which the work was intended, be it during a service at which the honoree was present or in a print with paratextual material connecting the music to the individual. The composer could also take advantage of the same multivalence in text and music possible in secular works, though in many cases a careful negotiation between sacred and secular was necessary in order to avoid charges of blasphemy. Skillfully done, however, the interaction of a religious text with an overlaid representational message could potentially craft a more powerful portrait than anything possible with paint and canvas.

---

[1] Jane Clark, "Les folies françoises," *Early Music*, 8 (1980): pp. 163–9.
[2] This cantata is the opening work of Strozzi's *Arie … Opera Ottava* (Venice, 1664), which is dedicated to Sophie; facsimile edn in Barbara Strozzi, *Cantatas*, ed. Ellen Rosand, The Italian Cantata in the Seventeenth Century, vol. 5 (New York, 1986).

Representations of Ferdinand III in Sances's 1638 *Motetti*

"Judge me, God, and distinguish my cause from that of the unholy nation; deliver me from the unjust and deceitful man." These words, the first verse of Psalm 42 and the opening line of a motet in Sances's *Motetti a una, due, tre, e quattro voci*, exemplify one of the primary methods through which Sances represented his employer in his 1638 prints.[3] For listeners who knew that this text served as the introit for Passion Sunday, the motet could offer a Christological message, an emotional response to the events of Holy Week. Others could have recognized the plea for deliverance from enemies as a common trope in seventeenth-century motets and interpreted it as a prayer for the expiation of sin or for deliverance from enemies of the Church. At the same time, however, the plea for deliverance from an unjust adversary resonates strongly with the historical moment during which the motet was published; in fact, the reference to an "unholy nation" could be understood as applying directly to the Thirty Years' War, in which the Habsburgs were battling heretical Christians. Also significant is the first-person singular voice. The text presents a private conversation, a personal utterance by an individual directed only to God, which invites speculation as to who is speaking. In a Christological reading, this could be understood as the voice of Jesus, though many listeners would also probably have recognized their own situation in the text and inserted themselves in the place of the speaker. In the politicized context of Sances's print dedicated to Ferdinand III—or when sung by imperial musicians in the presence of the Emperor—the voice could also be transformed into that of the Emperor himself. In this way the motet paints a portrait of Ferdinand kneeling before God, seeking the strength to win the war. This image is only enhanced by the ambiguity of the speaking voice: the Christological reading emphasizes the Emperor's piety, showing him imitating Christ and implying that his current tribulations will end in triumph, and Ferdinand joins in solidarity with those listeners who identify the speaking voice as their own, thereby forging a community based on a shared religious belief.

The fact that the motet text is drawn from the book of Psalms adds even more potential meaning. The psalms had a long-established exegetical tradition, which many elite Catholics would have known from published handbooks that provide commentary on the psalms for lay readers. Upon hearing a musical setting of a psalm, educated listeners (such as the nobles who constituted Ferdinand III's target audience) would have brought to it associations coloring their reading of the work. Helping us understand how seventeenth-century imperial listeners would have interpreted the

---

[3] Modern edn of the motet in Giovanni Felice Sances, *Motetti a una, due, tre, e quattro voci (1638)*, ed. Steven Saunders, RRMBE, vol. 126 (Middleton, 2003), pp. 40–46.

psalms are two books that are known to have been held in the library of the Viennese court: Martin Sebald's *Novum Romanum breviarum* (1622) and Dominicus Ruzola's *Argumenta Psalmorum* (1623).[4] Both of these books describe Psalm 42 as a song of hope in times of tribulation.[5] In addition, the book of Psalms adds another possible speaking voice to the work, that of the traditionally understood author of the poems, King David. Thus, a motet that creates the image of Ferdinand III speaking a psalm text places him in the position of David, thereby presenting a portrait of the Emperor modeled upon the revered warrior King of the Old Testament, a common trope in many early modern royal portraits.[6]

It takes more than just the text alone, however, to clarify the representational message of a psalm, and indeed, Sances's musical setting highlights the most important passages and also imparts a specific mood that guides the listener's interpretation of the work. The motet text consists of the first three verses of the psalm (the entire text of the Passion Sunday introit), but Sances manipulated the original text by repeating the opening clause at the beginning of verses two and three:

---

[4] Martin Sebald, *Novum Romanum breviarum* (Mainz, 1622) and Dominicus Ruzola [Dominicus a Jesu Maria], *Argumenta psalmorum ad utiliorem divini officii recitationem* (Rome, 1623). Both works are listed in a posthumous catalogue of Ferdinand II's library copied in 1638 (A-Wn, Cod. ser. n. 4450, fols 14v and 15r), and the latter is listed in a catalogue of Ferdinand III's library copied in 1652 (A-Wn, Cod 13556, fol. 434r).

[5] Sebald's description of the psalm is "De spe habenda in Deo tempore tribulationis" (*Novum Romanum breviarum*, p. 269), and Ruzola's wording is practically identical: "De spe in Domino habenda in tempore tribulationis" (*Argumenta psalmorum*, p. 42).

[6] See for instance John N. King, "Henry VIII as David: The King's Image and Reformation Politics," in Peter C. Herman (ed.), *Rethinking the Henrician Era: Essays on Early Tudor Texts and Contexts* (Urbana, 1994), pp. 78–92. Maximilian I had also represented himself as David; Larry Silver, *Marketing Maximilian: The Visual Ideology of a Holy Roman Emperor* (Princeton, 2008), pp. 122–6.

[1] **Judica me, Deus,**
et discerne causam meam
de gente non sancta;
ab homine iniquo et doloso erue me.

Judica me, Deus,
[2] quia tu es Deus fortitudo mea;
quare me repulisti,
et quare tristis incedo
dum affligit me inimicus?

Judica me, Deus,
et discerne causam meam
de gente non sancta.
[3] Emitte lucem tuam et veritatem tuam;
ipsa me deduxerunt
et adduxerunt in montem sanctum tuum
et in tabernacula tua.
Alleluia.

Judge me, God,
and distinguish my cause
from that of the unholy nation;
deliver me from the unjust and deceitful man.

Judge me, God,
for you are God my strength;
why have you cast me off,
and why do I go sorrowful
while my enemy afflicts me?

Judge me, God,
and distinguish my cause
from that of the unholy nation.
Emit your light and your truth;
they have led me
and have brought me to your holy hill
and into your tabernacles.
Alleluia.

Example 5.1   Sances, *Judica me Deus*, bars 1–8

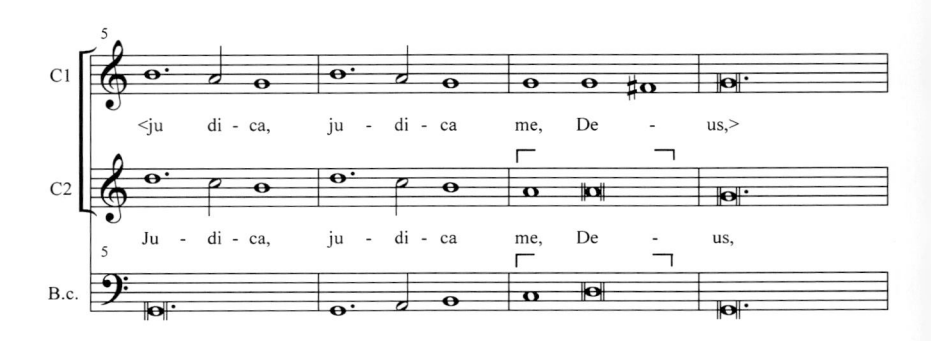

Example 5.2   Sances, *Judica me Deus*, bars 19–26

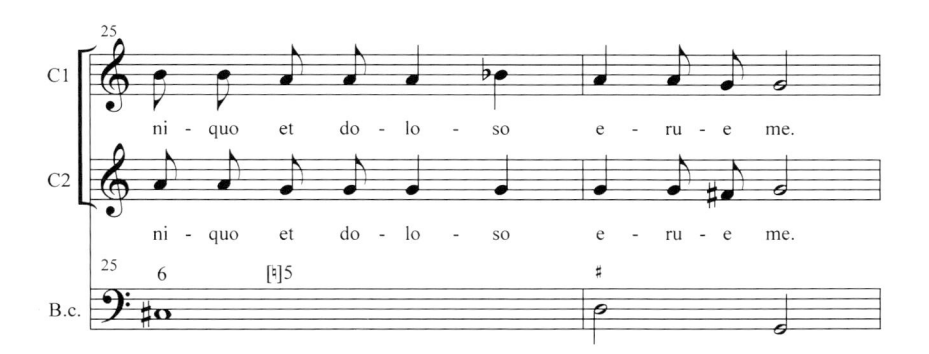

By reiterating this passage, the work stresses the very text that refers explicitly to the concept of a holy war, strengthening the topical meaning of the work over a more neutral reading. The musical style also plays an important role in interpreting the text. On first glance (and especially when interpreted from a Christological perspective) the first two verses are not positive in tone; in fact, the call for judgment seems almost anguished, especially as it is followed by a plea for deliverance and then by grating, almost spiteful rhetorical questions. Many composers might have chosen to set the first two verses with music of a plaintive character. Sances, however, set the opening sentence in a joyous triple-meter aria style (Example 5.1), with the same music recurring for each later reiteration of the text. This creates an undeniably optimistic tone for the work: there is never any doubt that God's judgment shall be in the speaker's favor.

This joyous mood is perfectly appropriate for the opening years of Ferdinand III's reign, when his representations in other media still stressed his image as a mighty warrior whose protection by divine providence assured his victory. The optimism is nevertheless tempered by the musical setting of the remaining sentences in the first two verses, which are in a contrasting duple-meter style. The setting of the rest of verse 1 (Example 5.2), for instance, eschews melodic elegance in favor of monotone recitation that is intensified with such harsh, brutal dissonances as the tritone between the bass and singing voice in the first half of bar 20 and last half of bar 22, and especially the grating parallel seconds between the two voices in bars 24–6. Although the motet as a whole is dominated by the triple-meter aria style in the recurring opening section and in the long concluding section (in which God's light elevates the speaker to almost divine status), these duple-meter sections cannot be easily swept aside. While the music of the second section could possibly be understood as portraying the sinful man described by the text in comparison to the uplifting, positive speaker, the earnestness of the duple-meter sections could also be interpreted as adding a new facet to Ferdinand's image, hinting that all is not as rosy as indicated by his powerful militant representations. Thus already in 1638 we can sense the beginning of a shift in the Emperor's public image, presaging the more radical revision that will occur just a few years later.

Other psalm settings in Sances's 1638 motet books also feature the representational strategy seen in *Judica me Deus*. An especially significant example is *Laetamini in Domino*, the second work in the *Motetti a una, due, tre, e quattro voci*.[7] As Steven Saunders has pointed out, the text of this motet, which combines passages from four different psalms with freely composed text couched in the language of that book, is decidedly disjointed:

---

[7] Modern edn in Sances, *Motetti*, ed. Saunders, pp. 9–14.

MUSICAL PORTRAITURE

Laetamini in Domino, qui diligitis eum,	Rejoice in the Lord, you who love him,
exultate in eo omnes recti corde.[a]	exalt in him, all you of a righteous heart.
Sumite psalmum et date timpanum	Offer psalms and start the timpani,
psalterium jucundum cum cithara;[b]	sing joyfully with the harp;
jubilate et exultate, psallite illi.	be jubilant and be glad, sing psalms to him.
Quoniam suavis est Dominus,[c]	**Because the Lord is sweet,**
misericors miserator et justus.	**merciful, compassionate, and just.**
Tu Domine, salvum me fac,	**O Lord, make me safe**
et ab inimicis meis eripe me,	**and deliver me from my enemies,**
et non confundar,	**and I shall not be confounded,**
quoniam speravi in te.[d]	**for I have hoped in you.**
Laetamini in Domino, qui diligitis eum,	Rejoice in the Lord, you who love him,
exultate in eo omnes recti corde.	exalt in him, all you of a righteous heart.
Alleluia.	Alleluia.

Example 5.3   Sances, *Laetamini in Domino*, bars 64–75

A repeated passage exhorting the righteous to rejoice in the Lord frames verses calling upon the listener to celebrate with music-making and a central section in the first person singular (given in bold) calling out to God for protection from enemies. The allusion to the Te Deum at the conclusion of the central section may have carried clear political overtones in light of the frequent performance of that work in celebration of military victories.[8] Saunders has further argued that this unusual combination of texts offers "a virtual thumbnail biographical tribute" to Ferdinand III, combining references to his much publicized piety and his well-known love of music with a text relevant to the current political situation.[9] This portrait once again draws parallels between the Emperor and King David, who was as famous for his musical ability as he was for his military might.

The music of *Laetamini in Domino* reinforces the general affect of each section of text. The first two passages are set in a celebratory, buoyant triple-meter aria style, similar to that in the opening section of *Judica me Deus*, whereas the central section is in highly contrasting duple-meter recitative (Example 5.3). A serious tone for the duple section is signaled in the opening measures by the slower-seeming tempo (created by long note values) and by the emphasis on the words "misericors miserator" (bars 69–73), with the latter word emphasized by the unusual interval of a descending diminished fourth. The recitative section highlights the most important passages of text, through the repetition of lines and virtuosic melismas on the most significant words: "salvum me fac" (bar 83), "eripe me" (bars 86–7 and 91–2), "et non confundar" (bars 95–6, 98–9, 100–101, 103–5), and "speravi" (bars 107–8 and 110–11). The overall effect of *Laetamini in Domino* is thus identical to that of *Judica me Deus*. Because the opening music is repeated verbatim for the return of the first line of text, the motet begins and ends in a joyous mood, mirroring the confident, victorious spirit of Ferdinand III's representations of the 1630s. The joy is colored, however, by the utter seriousness of the musical setting of the passage that can be understood as a prayer delivered by the Emperor to God. Although the text of this central section declares confidence in the Lord's protection, the musical affect nevertheless injects an important new expressive quality into Ferdinand III's victorious public image.

The similar message of *Laetamini in Domino* and *Judica me Deus* would have been especially apparent for those people who became acquainted with the music by reading Sances's print, for the composer placed the two works adjacent to each other in the soprano partbook. In addition, they follow a motet that illustrates the Emperor's personal devotion to the Blessed Virgin of the Immaculate Conception (and that contains the

---

[8] I am grateful to Rachel Barham for suggesting this to me.
[9] Sances, *Motetti*, ed. Saunders, p. xv.

same allusion to the Te Deum as in the central section of *Laetamini*).[10] The proximity of these three works helps bind them together and reinforces their function as representations of Sances's employer. *Judica me Deus*, moreover, is followed by two additional psalm settings, each of which echoes one of the dominant themes of the preceding works. The first, *Domine ne memineris* (Psalm 78:8–9), beseeches God for liberation (from sins, not enemies), while the second, *Psallite Domino* (which paraphrases Psalms 9:12 and 99:3), joyfully exhorts the listener to sing praises to the Lord. Although neither of these serves an explicit representational function when considered individually (both of them, for instance, use the first person plural instead of singular), when viewed in the larger context of the complex of works opening Sances's soprano partbook, they help emphasize the function of the print as a representation of Ferdinand III.

Another significant feature of *Laetamini in Domino* in light of its function as a portrait of the Emperor is its address in the opening section to those "of a righteous heart" (*recti corde*) who love the Lord (*qui diligitis eum*), which in the imperial context stresses important anti-Machiavellian virtues that were necessary in an effective ruler. Another motet in the same print, *Laudemus viros gloriosos*, is a virtual compendium of the virtues required of a Catholic prince:[11]

---

[10] This work, *Ardet cor meum*, is discussed in detail in Chapter 7. The motet contains the words "et non confundar" and also mentions hope ("quia spes tua in ipsa est").

[11] Modern edn in Sances, *Motetti*, ed. Saunders, pp. 92–8.

Laudemus viros gloriosos	Let us praise glorious men
et parentes nostros in generatione sua.	and our fathers in their generation.
Multa gloria fecit Dominus	The Lord created great glory
magnificentia sua a seculo	in his magnificence from the beginning
dominantes in potestatibus suis,	for those ruling in their dominions,
hominis magni virtute	men of great virtue
et prudentia sua praediti,	and gifted in their wisdom,
nunciantes in profetis	giving prophesy
dignitatem profetarum,	with the dignity of prophets,
et imperantes in presenti populo,	and ruling over the present people,
et virtute prudentiae	and with the strength of wisdom
populis sanctissima verba.[e]	instructing people with holiest words.
Benedictionem omnium gentium dedit illi Dominus,	The Lord gave him the blessing of all nations,
et testamentum confirmavit super caput Jacob.[f]	and confirmed his covenant upon the head of Jacob.
Corpora ipsorum in pace sepulta sunt,	Their bodies are buried in peace,
et nomen eorum vivit in aeternum.[g]	and their name lives in eternity.
Alleluia.	Alleluia.

While one can read this Biblical text as a general celebration of God's saints, in a Habsburg context it is nearly impossible not to interpret it as a tribute to the long line of Habsburg rulers leading up to Ferdinand III ("their bodies are buried in peace, and their name lives in eternity") and as a portrait of the recently deceased Ferdinand II. After the opening triple-meter exordium inviting us to praise glorious men, a long duple-meter section paints the portrait of an ideal Catholic ruler: a man "of great virtue and gifted in wisdom" who displays "the dignity of prophets" and rules "with the strength of wisdom." It is on account of these virtues, moreover, that God glorified the ruler ("The Lord created great glory in his magnificence") and bestowed temporal power upon him ("The Lord gave him the blessing of all nations"). No motet speaks more eloquently to the foundation upon which Ferdinand III asserted his imperial authority at the beginning of his reign.

Another psalm setting that presents the same image as *Laetamini in Domino* and *Judica me Deus*, albeit in a slightly different way, is *Domine quid multiplicati sunt* from Sances's *Motetti a voce sola*.[12] Like *Judica me*, this text (drawn from Psalm 3:2–6) carries clear Christological resonances with its reference to "arising again":

---

[12] Facsimile edn in Anne Schnoebelen (ed.), *Solo Motets from the Seventeenth Century: Facsimiles of Prints from the Italian Baroque* (10 vols, London, 1987–88), vol. 8.

Domine, quid multiplicati	Lord, how increased
sunt qui tribulant me.	are they who trouble me!
Multi insurgent adversum me.	Many rise up against me!
Multi dicunt animae meae,	Many say of my soul,
non est salus ipsi in Deo eius.	"there is no hope for him in his God."
Tu autem, Domine, susceptor meus es.	But you, Lord, are my supporter.
Voce mea ad Dominum clamavi,	My voice cried out to the Lord,
et exaudivit me de monte sancto suo.	and he heard me from his holy hill.
Ego dormivi et soporatus sum,	I slept and dreamed,
et exurexi, quia Dominus suscepit me.	and I arose again, for the Lord sustains me.

Indeed, both Sebald and Ruzola describe the psalm as a prefiguration of the Passion and resurrection of Christ.[13] Sebald, however, also glosses the psalm as a celebration of victory over one's enemies,[14] which draws a clear connection to Ferdinand III's political situation, as does the speaker's description of the "many" opponents who "rise up against" him and scorn his faith in God (thus the same "unholy nation" described in *Judica me*). Once again we are presented with a portrait of the pious Emperor who imitates Christ by trusting in the Lord during times of tribulation, always confident of his impending salvation (and again the Emperor joins in solidarity with listeners who put themselves in the position of the speaker). Unlike *Judica* and *Laetamini*, this motet foregrounds the serious, troubling aspect of Ferdinand's military image. Although the second half is optimistic in its description of God as a source of support, the music maintains a somber tone throughout, remaining almost entirely in duple meter and ending without "alleluia."[15] The only decoration comes from virtuosic melismas that highlight important words, including two especially long melismas on the significant word "suscepit" ("sustained," bars 87–9 and 100–7).

Sances also transformed motets into representations of the Emperor by infusing them with royal imagery. An excellent example is *Conditor caeli*, the second work in the tenor partbook of the *Motetti a una, due, tre, e quattro voci*.[16] This motet sets not a psalm text but excerpts from a well-known prayer found in early modern Catholic prayer books:[17]

---

[13] Sebald, *Novum Romanum breviarum*, p. 17; Ruzola, *Argumenta psalmorum*, p. 5.

[14] Sebald, *Novum Romanum breviarum*, p. 17: "de Victoria de hostibus reportata praedixit."

[15] The only triple-meter passage in the work occurs early in the piece (bars 15–26), where it adds dramatic intensity to the phrase "multi insurgunt adversum me."

[16] Modern edn in Sances, *Motetti*, ed. Saunders, pp. 26–30.

[17] On the source of the text, see ibid., p. xxvi. The prayer was known as the "Oratio praeparatoria ad confessionem sacramentalem."

Conditor caeli et terrae,	**Creator of heaven and earth,**
Rex regum et Dominus dominantium,	**King of kings and Lord of lords,**
qui me de nihilo fecisti	who made me out of nothing
ad imaginem et similitudinem tuam,	in your image and likeness,
et me proprio tuo sanguine redemisti.	and who redeemed me by your own blood.
Conditor caeli et terrae,	**Creator of heaven and earth,**
Rex regum et Dominus dominantium.	**King of kings and Lord of lords.**
Tu es Creator meus,	You are my Creator,
Tu es Redemptor meus,	You are my Redeemer,
Dominus meus et Salvator meus,	my Lord and my Savior,
Rex meus, et Deus meus.	my King and my God.
Tu es spes mea et fiducia mea,	You are my hope and my trust,
gubernatio mea et auxiliatio mea,	my guide and my aid,
consolatio mea et fortitudo mea.	my comfort and my strength.
Tu es defensio mea, liberatio mea,	You are my defense, my liberation,
vita mea, salus mea et resurrectio mea,	my life, my salvation and my resurrection,
lumen meum et desiderium meum,	my light and my desire,
adjutorium meum et patrocinium meum.	my help and my protection.
Conditor caeli et terrae,	**Creator of heaven and earth,**
Rex regum et Dominus dominantium.	**King of kings and Lord of lords.**
Te deprecor et rogo,	I pray and entreat you:
adjuva me et salvus ero.	help me, and I shall be safe.

Although the original purpose of the prayer was to prepare the individual for confession, the final request for safety resonates with the similar plea in *Laetamini in Domino*. Thus, in the imperial context this work can be understood as an utterance by Ferdinand III praying for help with the war; this interpretation is strengthened by the sentences referring to God as the speaker's hope (*spes*), strength (*fortitudo*), defense (*defensio*), liberation (*liberatio*), help (*adjutorium*), and protection (*patrocinium*). A reading of the work as a presentation of the Emperor's voice is reinforced by the opening passage describing God as "King of kings and Lord of lords." Sances emphasizes this passage by repeating it two times in the course of the work as a refrain; he also draws attention to the words "Rex regem" by decorating them with melismas. Neither the wholesale repetition nor the emphasis on these words makes much sense were the work intended as an utterance by the typical lay person preparing for confession. The highlighting of this text thus emphasizes the Emperor as speaker while also calling attention to his privileged relationship with God, reminding listeners that Ferdinand III's kingly power was derived from the Lord's divine authority.[18]

---

[18] Saunders also makes this point in ibid., p. xv.

Because the request for safety comes only at the very end of the long motet, much of the work comes across as a conventional song of praise that paints the Emperor as a confident, faithful, strong ruler. Significant in this regard is the fact that, of the words mentioned above, only "fortitudo" is stated more than once, and five times at that (bars 82–95). Only after this portrait has been sharply drawn are we presented with the more humble image of the Emperor kneeling before God for aid; such a double image, in which the individual's vulnerabilities are revealed only after his strength and power have been established, is not easily possible in a single painting or sculpture.

Through a variety of means, then, Sances's two motet books of 1638 served as an important contribution to Ferdinand III's powerful, militant image explored in Chapter 1. The combination of text and music in these prints, however, offers a more nuanced interpretation of this image than that found in the artworks examined above. Whereas in those works Ferdinand's faith in God was lauded primarily as the source of his military victories, in many of Sances's motets the Emperor's piety is construed largely as a source of protection and deliverance from invading enemies (that is, from a defensive rather than offensive perspective). Although the overall message is still one of steadfast confidence in God's providence, this shift in focus, which was more in line with the political reality of the late 1630s, helped pave the way for the more drastic revision of the Emperor's image during the 1640s.

Ferdinand III's Revised Image in Motets of the 1640s

The first surviving artwork that presents the new image of Ferdinand III as a wise, protective father is Sances's *Motetti a 2, 3, 4, e cinque voci*, published in 1642.[19] This print, whose paratexts draw an explicit connection to the Thirty Years' War, is strikingly different from Sances's motet books of just four years earlier.[20] This is especially apparent if the contents of the print are considered as a whole, in which case the publication takes on a remarkably uniform tone, an unusual feature for seventeenth-century prints that do not announce a specific overarching theme on the title page. Over half of the works in the print (15 out of 25) contain direct pleas to the Lord or the Blessed Virgin Mary for assistance, while only seven are

---

[19] Giovanni Felice Sances, *Motetti a 2, 3, 4, e cinque voci (1642)*, ed. Andrew H. Weaver, RRMBE, vol. 148 (Middleton, 2008).

[20] The paratexts are discussed in Chapter 4.

general songs of praise.[21] The overall tone of the book is thus decidedly one of devout yearning and supplication, which reflects the troubled times during which Sances assembled the volume. This tone is apparent in even the most conventional texts in the print. Although Sances included four settings of Marian antiphons, he set only the penitential *Salve Regina* and *Alma Redemptoris Mater*, completely avoiding the celebratory *Ave Regina caelorum* and *Regina caeli*. The print concludes, moreover, with the Litany of Loreto; although this is a common work to find at the end of seventeenth-century sacred prints, the supplicatory litany nevertheless contributes to the overall tone. Also telling are the specific themes found among the motets, the two most common of which are steadfast faith in the Lord and Blessed Virgin (explicitly expressed in seven works) and ardent repentance of sins (found in 12 works). Both of these themes would have held great significance for Ferdinand III in the early 1640s, the first because it broadcasted a confident message and assured the Emperor's subjects that God had not forsaken them, and the second because it provided a model for imperial citizens, an example of something they should do to ensure that they could emerge successfully from this difficult time.

One work in particular showcases well the strategies through which Sances offered a new image of the Emperor to the public. This motet is *Audi Domine* for four voices, the text of which would have been immediately relevant to the Habsburgs' situation in the early 1640s:[22]

---

[21] For a detailed examination of the contents as a whole, see Sances, *Motetti*, ed. Weaver, p. xi.

[22] Modern edn in ibid., pp. 139–45.

Audi Domine,	Hear, O Lord,
audi hymnum et orationem	hear the hymn and prayer
quam servus tuus orat coram te hodie.	that your servant prays in your presence today.
Domine, Domine,	O Lord, O Lord,
si conversus fuerit populus tuus	if your people repent and return to you
et oraverit ad santuarium tuum,	and pray in your sanctuary,
tu exaudies de caelo Domine,	you shall hear them from heaven, O Lord,
et liberabis eum	and shall liberate them
de manibus inimicorum suorum.	from the hands of their enemies.
Audi Domine,	Hear, O Lord,
audi hymnum et orationem	hear the hymn and prayer
quam servus tuus orat coram te hodie,	that your servant prays in your presence today,
ut sint oculi tui aperti	so that your eyes are open
et aures tuae intentae.	and your ears are attentive.
Domine, Domine,	O Lord, O Lord,
si peccaverit in te populus tuus	If your people sin against you
et confessus egerit penitentiam	and having confessed, do penance
veniensque oraverit in isto loco,	and coming to this place, pray,
tu exaudies de caelo Domine,	you shall hear them from heaven, O Lord,
et liberabis eum	and shall liberate them
de manibus inimicorum suorum.	from the hands of their enemies.

The work opens with a refrain sung by the upper three voices, which beseeches the Lord to hear the hymn and prayer being offered "today" by his servant. Following the two statements of the refrain are the actual prayers, sung by a solo bass, each of which is given in the form of a conditional statement. Provided that the Lord's people repent their sins and pray to him, then he shall act in their favor, granting a request that was surely on many lips during the early 1640s: he "shall liberate them from the hands of their enemies."

As obviously relevant to the Habsburgs' situation as this seems, such an interpretation does not necessarily follow from the original source of the text. Adapted from the Old Testament book of III Kings (I Kings in the modern Bible), the text does not appear in a warlike or even penitential context; rather, it is the public prayer spoken by King Solomon at the consecration of the temple he built to house the Ark of the Covenant. Devout Catholics would have been aware of this original context, for Sances's entire text appears in the Catholic liturgy as a responsory during Matins for the dedication of a church. A number of prominent earlier composers, including Hans Leo Hassler and Giovanni Gabrieli, wrote settings of this text (often only the refrain), which circulated in early-seventeenth-century printed anthologies.[23] Sances's music, however, completely reinterprets this standard liturgical and biblical text, even to the point of transforming the prayer into a miniature drama.

On the surface, the musical structure of the motet is entirely predictable, as Sances mirrors the repetitive structure of the text with recurring music: the three-voice refrain is sung, as expected, to identical music on both occasions, and although the two solo bass prayers contain different music, each one opens with the same figure on the repeated invocation "Domine." Even within this predictable framework, Sances is able to create much musical interest. Note, for instance, the extreme stylistic contrast between the refrain and the prayers (Example 5.4). The former is in an austere, homophonic *da cappella* style; the music is plodding and regular, with cadences punctuating every line. The solo sections, however, feature an intense, affective recitative style. In stark contrast to the refrain, these sections feature phrase structures, rhythms, and harmonies that are extremely irregular, disjointed, almost incoherent. There are very few authentic cadences, and the cadential moments that do occur are fleeting. The harmonies, in fact, only add to the dramatic intensity; at the end of the first prayer (bars 21–6), the rising melodic line is enhanced by the introduction of sharps that push beyond the controlling *mollis* harmonies, increasing the tension until the *durus* move is crushed in bar 24 by the sudden appearance of B-flat.

The solo bass sections vividly depict the mind of the anguished soul, of someone who can barely think clearly enough to form coherent thoughts. In essence, Sances has transformed the bass into an "actor," who is introduced by—and sings on behalf of—the other voices; note how the text of the refrain draws attention to an individual "servant," who then provides a communal prayer for the Lord's "people." (Significantly, the text avoids the ambiguous first person singular. In contrast to the 1638 motets, few listeners would have been tempted to put themselves in the place of the speaker; the bass soloist is clearly singing for them.) This has important implications for an interpretation of the motet: whom does this actor represent? If the motet were performed in a neutral religious context for listeners with no knowledge of the composer or his patron, one might say that the soloist represents an officiating priest singing on behalf of his congregation. With knowledge of the biblical source of the text, we could also surmise that the bass embodies King Solomon. Bearing in mind the politicized context of Sances's motet book (as well as the mention of

---

[23] Gabrieli's motet was published in *Promptuarii musici, sacras harmonias sive motetus V. VI. VII. et VIII. vocum .. pars altera* (Strasbourg, 1612); Hassler's was published in *Reliquiae sacrorum concentum Giovan Gabrielis, Johan-Leonis Hasleri, utriusque praestantissimi musici* (Nuremberg, 1615).

Example 5.4   Sances, *Audi Domine*, bars 1–27

Example 5.4   *continued*

Example 5.4   *concluded*

enemies in the final clause of the motet), we cannot, however, overlook the possibility that the bass represents Ferdinand III himself, a devout "servant" before God whose special relationship to the Lord (on account of his "holy" crown) gives him the authority to present this prayer for his people. It is significant that the "servant" comes across as rather blameless in the situation, and that his prayers are in essence directed not to the Lord but to the people, who are instructed that their repentance and prayers (not to mention, we might add, their conversion from Protestantism to Catholicism) are necessary before they can be saved. Indeed, when we listen to this work with a full sense of its immediate historical context, we are hearing the Emperor's voice as he offers a public prayer—and an important imperative—for his suffering people. Because the bass soloist is dramatically set apart from the other voices, the identification of the singer with the Emperor is both stronger and more emotionally affective than in the 1638 motets.

Although Sances's music distances the work from its biblical source and offers this new interpretation, the origin of the text adds an important layer of meaning. The work may present the voice of Ferdinand III, but an educated listener would still have been aware that the words stemmed originally from King Solomon. Like the psalm settings of the 1638 prints, *Audi Domine* conflates Ferdinand III and the sage Old Testament King, embodying multiple voices into the single figure of the bass soloist. In doing so, Sances has painted a portrait of the Emperor modeled upon the revered, wise, and just Old Testament monarch. The shift from King David in the 1638 motets to David's son Solomon in 1642 is a small but telling detail. David, after all, was the model of the just warrior, who battled infidels in the name of the Lord. Solomon, in contrast, was not associated with war; rather, his dominant image was that of the just, pious, and wise king who settled conflicts peacefully. Whereas David served well as a model for Ferdinand III's militant image, Solomon was better suited as a model for someone seeking to successfully conclude peace negotiations.[24]

Other artworks from later in Ferdinand's reign confirm that this identification with King Solomon became an important part of his image. In 1656, for instance, a Jesuit drama presented in Vienna before Ferdinand III, his third wife Eleonora Gonzaga, Leopold I, as well as the Duke and

---

[24] That Ferdinand's image as David was not entirely abandoned is indicated by a Jesuit drama performed in the face of the Swedish siege in 1645 that tells the story of David and Goliath, equating the Emperor with the biblical King (see Chapter 6). Solomon and David (especially the former) were also appropriated for the image of Emperor Charles VI; Franz Matsche, *Die Kunst im Dienst der Staatsidee Kaiser Karls VI.: Ikonographie, Ikonologie und Programmatik des "Kaistertils,"* (2 vols, Berlin and New York, 1981), vol. 1, pp. 283–91.

Duchess of Bavaria presented events from the life of King Solomon.[25] The title makes explicit the connection between Solomon and the Habsburgs in that it incorporates both Ferdinand III's and Leopold I's personal mottos, which in turn form the basis of the play's structure. Each of the five acts presents a different vignette from the early years of Solomon's reign, exemplifying a specific virtue. The first act portrays wisdom, with Solomon praying to God for wisdom at the beginning of his reign (III Kings 3:3–15), while the other four acts are organized around the words in the mottos: Justice (Solomon's confrontation with Joab, III Kings 2:28–34), Piety (the consecration of the temple, III Kings 8), Good Counsel (Solomon's judgment in the dispute over the baby, III Kings 3:17–27), and Industry (the visit from the Queen of Sheba, III Kings 10). An identification of Ferdinand III with Solomon also appeared on a triumphal arch erected by the citizens of Regensburg for the Emperor's joyous entry into that city in December 1652 for an imperial Diet.[26] One section of the arch (Figure 5.1) provides an image of the Emperor seated upon the "imperial throne." The lions flanking the throne draw an immediately recognizable comparison with the throne of Solomon; this is confirmed by a poetic description of the arch published in 1653.[27] A thesis title page published shortly after Ferdinand IV's coronation as King of the Romans transfers the Solomon image to the new King, with the younger Ferdinand seated upon a throne flanked by lions.[28] Significantly, these later representations all originated outside the court, demonstrating that by the 1650s Ferdinand's image as Solomon was sufficiently well known to be imitated in non-court artworks.[29]

---

[25] *Regiae Virtutes, seu Initia Regni Salomonis Pietate & Justitia, Consilio & Industria, Duce Sapientia semper felicia* (Vienna, 1656), performed on February 20. Only a bilingual (Latin and German) scenario survives, a facsimile edn of which is in Elida Maria Szarota (ed.), *Das Jesuitendrama im deutschen Sprachgebiet: Eine Periochen-Edition*, vol. 2, *Tugend- und Sündensystem* (2 vols, Munich, 1980), vol. 1, pp. 51–62, with commentary in vol. 2, pp. 2, 167.

[26] This arch is discussed in detail in the Epilogue.

[27] Christian Adolph Balduin, *Poetische Entdeckung der Ehren-Pforte* (Regensburg, 1653), sig. Av: "Das auff der Seiten steht, das ist **des Keysers Thron**, / Auff den der Keyser sitzt als König Salomon, // Mit Löwen umb und umb."

[28] For a reproduction and discussion of this image, see Werner Telesko, "Barocke Thesenblätter in der Sammlung von Prof. Adolf Karl Bodingbauer, Steyr, II. Teil," *Jahrbuch des Oberösterreichischen Musealvereines*, 147 (2002): pp. 205–7.

[29] Another artwork that equates Ferdinand III with Solomon is an undated engraving issued at some point after the war: A-Wn, Bildarchiv, Pg 149 137/3 in Ptf 123: I (34). Underneath a full-length portrait of the Emperor in armor and wearing a laurel crown is an inscription reading, "Per Me tot discors Bellis *Europa* quievit. Quod fuerim SALOMON, PAX satis ista probat [Through me fully discordant Europe was quieted of so many Wars. Even if I were SOLOMON, this PEACE is sufficient]."

Figure 5.1   Wolfgang Kilian, triumphal arch erected in Regensburg for Ferdinand III (detail), engraving, 1653

Audi Domine does more, however, than simply identify Ferdinand III with King Solomon, for not only does the motet offer a prayer, but it also proclaims another important message from the Emperor to his subjects, essentially providing an answer to his prayer. In bars 58–9, at the end of the second solo bass petition, the important recurring phrase "tu exaudies de caelo Domine" is sung to exactly the same motive heard earlier in bars 19–21 (Example 5.5). As before, the phrase ends on an E-major triad; however, instead of pushing ahead into the intense rising line of the previous solo section, it cadences smoothly with a falling fifth to A, the first authentic cadence to A in the entire motet.[30] The harmonies

---

[30] Previous cadences to A have been either phrygian cadences, approached from a B-flat in the bass (as in the figure on "Domine, Domine"), or tenor cadences, approached

MUSICAL PORTRAITURE 181

Example 5.5   Sances, *Audi Domine*, bars 53–60

have again pushed in the sharp direction; in fact, with this cadence the harmonic framework of the motet shifts entirely, from the *cantus mollis* to the *cantus durus*. This harmonic shift is amplified by other musical changes. Upon reaching this cadence, all four voices join together for the first tutti texture in the motet. The overall style also changes: from here to the end of the work the melodies are organized into coherent, rhythmically active phrases articulated by imitative repetitions of recognizable motives, a style completely unlike anything heard thus far in the work.

By the end of the second solo bass section, the dolorous mood that has completely dominated the motet has been successfully expunged, allowing the work to conclude in a positive vein. Despite the entirely supplicatory text, the music ends with a sense of confidence; the conditional future

---

from a B-natural in the bass (as in bar 54).

tense has been fully transformed *by the music alone* into a positive vision of the future. It is surely significant that one of the phrases that stands out the strongest in the concluding four-voice texture is "et liberabis eum" ("and you shall liberate them"). In bars 66–7, these words are sung by the upper two voices in homophony while the other two voices rest, and two bars later the homophonic figure is repeated by the alto and tenor over a long held note in the bass.

Within this single work (which in a neutral context could easily be heard as just a universal message of comfort during difficult times), Sances has masterfully provided an effective representation of his employer. Not only does it enhance Ferdinand III's reputation by identifying him with King Solomon, but it also allowed Ferdinand to speak directly to his subjects, offering a prayer for their salvation and instructing them on the importance of penance while simultaneously delivering an optimistic message of comfort, hope, and unwavering faith in God. This reading of the work could have been gleaned both by readers of Sances's print (who in examining the partbooks could have noticed such musical features as the solo–tutti alternation and the change in style at the end of the work) and by those who experienced a live performance in the Emperor's presence. Even listeners not fluent in Latin may have been able to glean the basic thrust of the message: the style of the refrain would have evoked conventional sacred genres such as the litany, and the intensely personal style of the solo bass sections would have expressed the yearning, uncertain mood (listeners who understood the word "Domine" may have also realized that they were hearing prayers to the Lord). The optimistic message of the conclusion of the work would also have likely been apparent on an emotional, affective level. If, as suggested in Chapter 4, Sances's print was marketed specifically to a Bohemian audience, this message would have been especially relevant during the years following the Swedish army's ravaging of the Bohemian countryside. The motet would also have been especially powerful in its prescribed liturgical context for the dedication of a church, particularly if sung during the re-dedication of one of the many formerly Protestant churches that Ferdinand restored back to the Catholic Church. On these occasions, the motet would have reinforced yet another important element of the Emperor's image, that of the devout Counter-Reformer defending and restoring the one true Church.

The strategies apparent in *Audi Domine*—modeling Ferdinand's image upon a revered religious figure, offering prayers for imperial subjects, and delivering a confident message of faith in God—also appear in other motets of the 1640s. Another example from Sances's 1642 print is *Honestum fecit*.[31] The text of this work, drawn primarily from the apocryphal Book

---

[31] Modern edn in Sances, *Motetti*, ed. Weaver, pp. 27–32.

of Wisdom (10:11–14), extols the theme of the Lord's steadfast protection, describing a number of ways in which God safeguarded an unnamed honest man and delivered him from enemies:

Honestum fecit illum Dominus,	The Lord made him honest,
et custodivit eum ab inimicis,	and protected him from his enemies,
et a seductoribus tutavit illum,	and guarded him from seducers,
et dedit illi claritatem eternam,	and gave him eternal fame.
descenditque cum illo in foveam,	He descended to him in the pit
et in vinculis non dereliquit eum.[h]	and did not leave him in chains.
Stola jucunditatis induit eum Dominus,	The Lord clothed him with the stole of delight
et coronam pulchritudinis posuit	and placed the crown of beauty
super caput eius.[i]	upon his head.
Alleluia.	Alleluia.

Again the references to enemies would have resonated with recent political events, drawing a parallel between the "honest man" and Ferdinand III, and the work would have proclaimed an important message of hope, assuring listeners that the Lord had not deserted the Emperor. Especially significant are the clauses appended to the end, drawn from the liturgy of saints: "The Lord clothed him with the stole of delight and placed the crown of beauty upon his head." The coronation imagery is unmistakable and would have evoked royalty (thereby discouraging most listeners from identifying themselves as the honest man); regal connotations are strengthened by the musical setting of the first clause (Example 5.6), which consists primarily of a single pitch followed by a simple descending figure, an allusion to a trumpet fanfare for a monarch's entrance.[32] As in *Laetamini in Domino*, the combination of texts in this work is unusual and disjointed; while the motet could have been performed in honor of a saint, it also paints a portrait of Ferdinand III that lauds God's protection of the Emperor and depicts the Lord bestowing worldly power upon him. This work would have assured listeners that, despite present tribulations, God was still on the Emperor's side, while also powerfully reminding them of his political sovereignty, granted by God himself.

The fact that the concluding passage is drawn from the liturgy of saints adds an explicitly sacral element to the portrait, conflating the Emperor's image with that of a specific martyred saint. Due to the commercial nature of the print, we cannot know whether Sances had a specific saint in mind when he composed the work, but the saint's identity would have been

---

[32] See, for instance, the "Entrada Imperiale per sonare in concerto" in Girolamo Fantini, *Modo per imparare a sonare di tromba* (Frankfurt, 1638); facsimile edn, *Collezione di trattati e musiche antiche edite in fac-simile* (Milan, 1936), pp. 17–21.

Example 5.6 Sances, *Honestum fecit*, bars 56–62

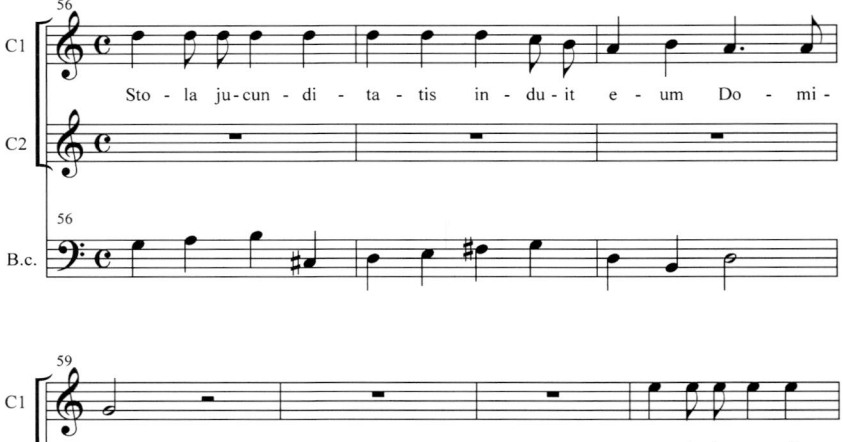

clear for listeners from the liturgical or devotional context in which the motet was performed. Here again a presumed Bohemian audience for Sances's print adds further meaning, for two martyred saints held special significance for the Bohemian people: St Wenceslaus (the patron saint of Bohemia) and St John Nepomuk (Bohemia's "home-grown" saint, who though not canonized until 1729 had already taken on a cult following by the end of the sixteenth century).[33] Conflating Ferdinand III with two of the most popular saints in Bohemia would have given his image the added luster of popular appeal and may have perhaps even helped ingratiate the Emperor to a nation that still looked upon Habsburg political authority with some suspicion.

These strategies are also apparent in the three imperial motets published in Giorgio Rolla's *Teatro musicale* of 1649.[34] As mentioned in

---

[33] On the importance of Nepomuk for Bohemia, see Howard Louthan, *Converting Bohemia: Force and Persuasion in the Catholic Reformation* (Cambridge, 2009), pp. 280–300.

[34] See Chapter 4 for a discussion of this anthology and its relationship to the imperial court. Modern edns of the three works are in Andrew H. Weaver, ed., *Motets by Emperor*

Chapter 4, the texts of all three works ask for protection from enemies (see Table 5.1): Sances's *Excita furorem* begins with a call to the Lord to "remember war" and "hurl rage" upon enemies, his *Miserere servorum tuorum* pleads for the Virgin to "judge our cause" and "liberate us from those who rise up against us," and Bertali's *Exultate et cantate* beseeches St Charles Borromeo to "defend us, save us, and liberate us from insidious enemies." Like the other works discussed in this chapter, these motets are immediately relevant to the Habsburgs' situation in the 1640s. The texts nevertheless differ significantly from the 1638 motets: whereas the earlier works presented a portrait of the Emperor through texts in the first person singular, the 1649 works all use the first person *plural*, thereby drawing Ferdinand's subjects together in a communal prayer uttered (as in *Audi Domine*) by the Emperor himself.

The function of these works as representations of Ferdinand III delivering prayers for his people is especially apparent in the opening lines of *Miserere servorum tuorum*. By asking mercy for "the servants upon whom your name is invoked," the text makes it clear that this is a work uttered not *by* the community but rather *for* the community, by someone with the authority to invoke the Virgin's name on the people's behalf. Further distinguishing the person praying from those for whom the prayer is said is the fact that the very next clause refers to the people in the third person: "do not let them be anguished." Significantly, after 15 measures of a full three-voice texture, these words are sung by a solo bass (bars 16–20). Coming from the same composer as *Audi Domine*, this could very well be another instance in which the solo bass represents the Emperor's voice.

Although the text of *Miserere servorum tuorum* refers primarily to personal tribulations and sorrows (thereby making it a work of broad appeal for all audiences), Sances subtly implies a connection to the Thirty Years' War with the paraphrase of Psalm 73:22 in the third section.[35] Other verses of this psalm describe the sufferings inflicted by impious enemies; Sebald's commentary describes the psalm as a work celebrating the liberation of captives, while Ruzola describes its meaning as the protection and defense of the Church.[36] Sances's motet presents these words in recitative by each of the three voices in turn, which highlights the passage aurally and ensures not only that the listener can understand the words but also that the reader of any of the partbooks will notice the

Ferdinand III and Other Musicians from the Habsburg Court, Collegium Musicum: Yale University, second series (Middleton, in press).

[35] The actual biblical text is "Exsurge, Deus, judica causam tuam."
[36] Sebald, *Novum Romanum breviarum*, p. 339 ("De Judaeorum captivitate a qua liberari precantur"); Ruzola, *Argumenta psalmorum*, p. 12 ("De Judaeorum desolatione, et Ecclesiae protectione, et defensione").

Table 5.1 Texts of the three imperial motets in Rolla's *Teatro musicale*

Bertali, *Exultate et cantate*
Exultate et cantate, jubilate et plaudite.
Sumite psalmum et date timpanum,
psalterium jucundum cum cithara.[j]

Haec est enim illa dies toti orbi
jucundissima, In qua stella confessorum,
gemma fulgens inter sanctos,
et dilectus Deo N. [Carolus]
evolavit ad regna caelorum.

Exultate et cantate … cum cithara.
Haec est enim … regna caelorum.

Hunc precemur, hunc rogemus
ut pro nobis intercedat
apud filium unigenitum.
O dulcis N. [Carole],
o amabilis, o dilecte Deo et hominibus,
defende nos, salva nos,
et libera nos ab insidiis inimici
nunc et semper.

Sances, *Miserere servorum tuorum*
Miserere servorum tuorum
super quibus invocatum est nomen tuum,
et ne sinas angustiari eos
in tentationibus suis.

Aufer tribulationes nostras,
dulcifica languores nostros.

Trahe nos post te vinculis misericordiae,
et fomentis gratiae et pietatis tuae,
sana dolores nostros.

Exurge Domina,
et judica causam nostram,[k]
et ab insurgentibus in nos,
libera nos.

Recordare nostri Domina,
et non appraehendent nos mala.

Succurre nobis in fine,
et inveniemus vitam aeternam.

Exalt and sing, jubilate and applaud.
Offer psalms and start the timpani,
sing joyfully with the harp.

This is indeed the most joyful day of all,
in which the star of confessors,
the gleaming gem among saints,
and the delight of God, N. [Charles],
soared to the kingdom of Heaven.

Exalt and sing … with the harp.
This is indeed … kingdom of Heaven.

Now let us pray, now let us request
that you intercede on our behalf
in the place of the only son.
O sweet N. [Charles],
O beloved, O delight of God and men,
defend us, save us,
and liberate us from insidious enemies
now and always.

Have mercy upon your servants
upon whom your name is invoked,
and do not let them be anguished
when they suffer temptations.

Take away our tribulations,
sweeten our sorrows.

Attract us to you with your bond of mercy,
and with the remedy of grace and piety,
relieve our sorrows.

Rise up, Lady,
and judge our cause,
and from those who rise up against us,
liberate us.

Remember us, Lady,
and evil shall not seize us.

Help us in the end,
and we shall find eternal life.

Sances, *Excita furorem*

Excita furorem, et memento belli,	Rouse fury and remember war,
et super hostes nostros effunde iram tuam.[l]	and upon our enemies hurl your rage.
Tu enim salus nostra in Domino,[m]	For you are our safety in the Lord,
quae morti adjudicatos liberasti.	who liberated us who were destined to die.
Hauriemus aquas cum gaudio de rivulo,[n]	We joyfully draw waters from the river,
et semper invocabimus nomen tuum.	and we shall continually invoke your name.
Opervit enim Coelos gloria tua,	For your glory has filled the heavens,
et misericordia tua plena est terra.	and the earth is full of your mercy.
Repleatur os nostrum laude tua;	Let our mouths be filled with your praises;
decantemus tota die magnificentiam tuam.[o]	let us sing of your magnificence all day.
Amor enim tui expellit peccatum a corde,	For love of you expels sin from the heart,
et gratia tua expiat conscientiam peccatoris.	and your grace atones the conscience of the sinner.

text. To the knowledgeable listener or reader who recognizes the allusion to the psalm, the work could thus be understood as an explicit plea for protection from enemies during a religious war. Also significant may be the final clause, which asks the Virgin for aid "in the end." Although this obviously refers to the end of life (or the apocalypse), Sances highlights the words "in fine" in an exaggerated manner that seems unwarranted by anything else in the motet: within a "presto" triple-meter passage, two iterations of these words occur over a phrygian cadence in an "adagio" tempo (Example 5.7). For those who understood the work as referring to the Thirty Years' War, these passages could very well be interpreted as a prayer for the end of the long, disastrous conflict.

In contrast to the penitential, supplicatory *Miserere servorum tuorum*, Bertali's *Exultate et cantate* exudes confidence and celebration; the motet opens with long joyful passages (one in triple-meter aria style, the other in duple meter decorated with virtuosic melismas) exhorting the listeners to "exalt and sing" on this "most joyful day." The triple-meter sections feature a quotation from Psalm 80:3, the same passage in *Laetamini in Domino* inviting the listeners to make music, which Ruzola interprets as celebrating the liberation of the just and Sebald as a song of gratitude for divine aid.[37] Both the triple- and duple-meter sections are stated two times in their entirety, with differences in voicing and ornamentation in the repeat of the duple section. Because of this heavy emphasis on celebration, the work implies that, despite the need to request protection from

---

[37] Ruzola, *Argumenta psalmorum*, p. 13 ("Hortatur ad Dei laudem pro bonorum liberatione, et malorum reprobatione"); Sebald, *Novum Romanum breviarum*, p. 381 ("De Judaeorum in gratitudine post divina beneficia suscepta, ad quae recolenda inuitabatur").

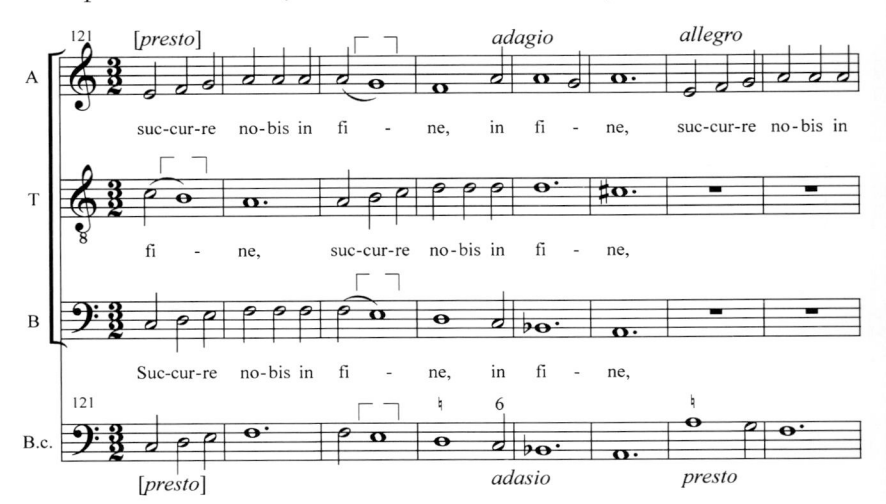

Example 5.7　　Sances, *Miserere servorum tuorum*, bars 121–8

"insidious enemies," the Emperor and his people can still celebrate the fact that God and his saints have not deserted them. Just as in Wassenberg's 1647 panegyric discussed in Chapter 1, which does not entirely relinquish the image of the Emperor as a powerful warrior, so too does this work complement the other two imperial motets in the anthology by maintaining a connection to the image presented in Sances's 1638 prints.

The most explicit reference to war comes in the motet whose text, according to the rubric in the tenor partbook, was written by the Emperor himself.[38] Unlike the other texts discussed in this chapter, which beseech the Lord for defense and protection, this motet goes on the offensive, calling upon God to attack the enemy: "Rouse fury and remember war, and upon our enemies hurl your rage." This aggressive stance is heightened by Sances's musical setting, which features a simple, repetitive, almost banal scalar and triadic melody passed among the voices before being sung by all four together (Example 5.8). This simple melodic material—especially coming from such a skilled melodist as Sances—is striking, and it is most certainly intended to evoke the sound of trumpets on the field of battle, perhaps echoing to each other across the range.[39] Because the passage

---

[38] See p. 147 for the text of the rubric.

[39] A very similar figure to Sances's opening measure appears in the "Seconda chiamata, che và sonata avanti la Battaglia" in Fantini, p. 14. It is also very similar to the clarino passages in Cesare Bendinelli, *Tutta l'arte della trombetta* (1614); facsimile ed. Edward H. Tarr, Documenta Musicologica, vol. 2:5 (Kassel, 1975), pp. 55–6.

Example 5.8 Sances, *Excita furorem*, bars 1–8

appears in all four voices, the reader of any of the four vocal partbooks will be sure to notice it. This aggressively militant imagery at the start of the motet demonstrates (as does Wassenberg's panegyric) that by the mid- to late-1640s Ferdinand III had not entirely relinquished his warrior image of the 1630s.

After the first passage, however, the text and music of the motet shift gears entirely, never returning to the warlike imagery of the opening measures.[40] The combination of freely-written text and allusions to miscellaneous Bible verses once again creates an unusual, disjointed text, inviting us to read the work as a personal message from the Emperor to a broad audience. It is surely significant that immediately following the militant battle cry is a passage expressing the very sentiments emphasized in the other imperial motets that reference war: the Lord as a source of safety and liberation. These sentiments are expressed using a paraphrase of a verse from Psalm 123, which Sebald interprets as the thanks of the faithful for liberation from danger through God's aid.[41] At the same time, Ferdinand's text deliberately tempers the blatantly militaristic opening (which carries by far the most obviously political connotations of any of the passages discussed in this chapter) by emphasizing a Christological reading that focuses on the expiation of sin (which, as the fourth line clarifies, is the true enemy from which we need protection). The Emperor thus seems to have been acutely aware of the need for multivalent texts when using sacred music as a means of representation. Without the opening passage, any listener would interpret this motet as a conventional song of praise to Christ. However, the knowledge that the Emperor himself wrote the text and opened it with words directly relevant to his political situation cannot help but color one's understanding of the motet, painting a portrait of the Emperor that compares him to Christ and demonstrates that, like any good Catholic ruler, Ferdinand imitates the Lord.

In the next three sentences, a celebration of Jesus' glory and mercy is framed by passages in which the people joyously express their intent to praise Him. The riparian imagery at the start of this section seems to evoke the sacrament of baptism, which clarifies the Christological reading while simultaneously adding a subtle reference to an important aspect of Ferdinand's character. In a political reading, the allusion to baptism seems to draw attention to the conversion of Protestants to Catholicism, thereby infusing the motet with a triumphant Counter-Reformation message: the people are impelled to continually praise Jesus not just for his atonement of sins but also on account of the cleansing baptismal waters upon their joyful return to the one true Church. The last sentence continues this Counter-Reformation message with a lesson for the listeners, instructing them on the importance of loving Christ in order to be absolved of their

---

[40] Jerome Roche has pointed to this as an unusual feature of the work that distinguishes it from the other two "battle motets" in the anthology, by Carissimi and Foggia; "Cross-Currents in Milanese Church Music in the 1640s: Giorgio Rolla's Anthology *Teatro Musicale* (1649)," in Alberto Colzani et al. (eds), *La musica sacra in Lombardia nella prima metà del Seicento: Atti del convegno internazionale di studi Como, 31 Maggio–2 Giugno 1985* (Como, 1987), p. 20.

[41] Sebald, *Novum Romanum breviarum*, p. 517 ("Gratiarum actio fidelis liberati a periculis per Dei auxilium. Sancti suam liberationem Deo attribuunt").

sins. This final sentence can also be interpreted as an anti-Machiavellian description of the person who wrote the text: Ferdinand III loves the Lord to such an extent that sin has been expelled from his heart, making him the ideal Christian monarch. Sances's setting emphasizes this final sentence by devoting to it a full 92 bars, nearly half of the 190-bar motet.

As a whole, *Excita furorem* transforms an otherwise conventional Christological text into an important prayer spoken by the Emperor for the sake of his people; its expression of complete confidence in Christ's protection and mercy would have assured listeners that His grace would see them through the difficult war. At the same time, it can also be interpreted as a composite self-portrait of Ferdinand III. It opens with a reference to the Emperor's valiant military image of the 1630s, but the warrior soon gives way to the protective father who turns to the Lord as a source of safety and liberation. The Emperor then subtly alludes to his role as a triumphant Counter-Reformer before ending with a description of the immense piety that validates his rule. In the final sentence Ferdinand presents himself as a model for his subjects, encouraging them to imitate his immense love for Christ (in the same manner that he himself follows Jesus' call). He also reminds them that his magnificence is ultimately due to his strong piety, thereby illustrating important tenets of his anti-Machiavellian political policy.

The three imperial motets in Rolla's *Teatro musicale* thus seem to have been carefully prepared in order to present all of the facets of Ferdinand III's public image. Sances's *Miserere servorum tuorum* and Bertali's *Exultate et cantate* form a complementary pair that present the Emperor from a supplicatory and celebratory perspective respectively. Sances's *Excita furorem*, the text of which was provided by the Emperor himself (so the print tells us), goes a step further, presenting not only a confident prayer but also a veritable portrait of Ferdinand III, one that could be comprehended by anybody who looked at the page and realized the Emperor's personal involvement in the creation of the motet. Although the three works do not appear adjacent to each other in the anthology, that was a decision made by the publisher, over which the imperial contributors likely had no say; Bertali and Sances may have actually intended *Miserere servorum tuorum* and *Exultate et cantate* to appear next to each other, since both are written for the same number of voices. The fact that Rolla's anthology was not offered to the public until 1649, a year after the signing of the Peace of Westphalia, does not diminish its value as a cultural artifact that provides valuable insights into the strategies through which Ferdinand III was represented during the most difficult years of the Thirty Years' War.

Indeed, it is only through the music of Ferdinand III's chapel that we can witness the shift in the Emperor's image discussed in Chapter 1. Whereas the 1638 motets present portraits of a confident, David-like warrior celebrating victory over his enemies, during the 1640s this image morphed into that of a wise ruler praying for protection and liberation, a Solomon praying not just for himself but for his people. One thing, however, remains constant throughout all of the works discussed in this chapter: dominating all of them is an avowed certainty in the Lord's goodness and mercy, a total confidence that, despite present difficulties, God's divine hand will protect the Empire. It is important to acknowledge that the music discussed in this chapter is surely only a small fraction of the entire body of similar works performed by the imperial chapel; moreover, on account of their dissemination in print, these pieces omit explicit references that may very well have been included in other musical works not destined for publication. Even this necessarily incomplete sample, however, highlights the strategies through which sacred music painted Ferdinand III's portrait during the critical years of his reign, emphasizing his roles as wise leader, devout Counter-Reformer, and protective father watching over his people.

Notes to Motet Texts

a Paraphrase of Psalm 31:11.
b Psalm 80:3.
c Psalm 33:9.
d Psalm 24:20. These two clauses are also reminiscent of the last line of the Te Deum.
e Ecclesiasticus 44:1–4.
f Ecclesiasticus 44:25.
g Ecclesiasticus 44:14.
h Wisdom 10:11–14.
i Liturgical text found in several places in the Common of One Martyr.
j Psalm 80:3.
k Paraphrase of Psalm 73:22.
l Paraphrase of Ecclesiasticus 36:8.
m Allusion to Psalm 123:8.
n Paraphrase of Isaiah 12:3.
o Paraphrase of Psalm 70:8.

CHAPTER 6

Mirrors and Models: Piety and Spirituality in the Service of the Crown

Like generations of Habsburg rulers before him, Ferdinand III relied on the *Pietas Austriaca* to enhance his reputation as the ideal Catholic monarch. Two of the most fundamental components of the *Pietas* were those centered on the adoration of Jesus: devotion for the Eucharist and the cross. Although neither of these was unique to the imperial family, they nevertheless became such central elements of the Habsburg public image that they came to be defining characteristics of not only the ruler's piety but also Austrian and Bohemian culture. A citizen's acknowledgement of devotion to these important Christian symbols was considered tantamount to joining with the Emperor and affirming one's status as a loyal subject of both the Catholic Church and the Holy Roman Empire.

There was nevertheless a distinction between these two forms of Christological devotion as they were practiced at Ferdinand III's court. The Emperor's veneration of the Eucharist was a display of public piety geared toward the widest possible audience, from the wealthiest noble to the most common peasant, and as such it impacted both elite and popular religious culture. Cross devotion, in contrast, was an aspect of Ferdinand's inner spirituality that manifested itself not in public celebrations but in individual prayer and private devotional services. As such, it was directed to a much more limited audience of elite nobles able to comprehend complex theological concepts. And yet these two different sides of the *Pietas Austriaca* had the same two functions: they provided a highly visible mirror of the Emperor's pious soul while simultaneously serving as a model for imperial subjects (just as Christ was a model for the Emperor), inviting them to imitate Ferdinand III in their own lives. They also had in common their reliance on music as a valuable means through which the Emperor's pious image was promulgated to the public. This chapter will examine these two facets of Habsburg Christological devotion, focusing in each case on the ways that music helped incorporate these elements of the *Pietas Austriaca* into Ferdinand III's representations.

Public Piety: Habsburg Eucharistic Devotion

The Eucharist was long recognized as one of the most powerful Counter-Reformation weapons in the Catholic Church's arsenal, not only because of the theological distinctions made by the various confessions regarding the nature of communion, but also for the ritual differences between the denominations, which was something even common people could grasp. It makes sense that the Habsburgs would rely on the Eucharist to help solidify their image as Catholic rulers, but in doing so they faced an obstacle. Unlike other popular religious symbols such as the Blessed Virgin and saints, who could be claimed as patrons and invoked at any extra-liturgical occasion (even in the absence of clergy), the Eucharist, one of the central sacraments of the Catholic Church, could not be altered or "personalized" for the imperial family without raising charges of heresy. The consecrated host, moreover, could only be handled by a priest. The Habsburgs nevertheless claimed a unique relationship with the Eucharist, so much so that they considered themselves the most Catholic of all European rulers and shaped their identity around this important sacrament. How were they able to do this?

The imperial dynasty secured their claim to the Eucharist by promulgating centuries-old tales about important members of the family. The first and most well-known of these legends is a simple story about the Habsburg founding father Rudolph I: one day as Rudolph was riding through his countryside he encountered a priest on foot carrying the Eucharist; immediately Rudolph leapt off his horse and offered his animal to the priest.[1] Later generations instilled this straightforward tale with great importance. For instance, the event was said to have occurred in 1264, the same year in which Pope Urban IV instituted the feast of Corpus Christi. This allowed historians to stress that Rudolph's intense reverence for the Eucharist was directly connected to the establishment of the feast, giving the Habsburgs a personal claim on this important religious symbol; God gave the Eucharist to the universal Church while establishing the divine right for Rudolph and his successors to rule the Empire.[2] Other writers, drawing parallels between Rudolph and St Eustachius, claimed that the Habsburg ruler's humble act was the result of following God's

---

[1] On this legend and its earliest sources (as well as the other information in this paragraph), see Anna Coreth, *Pietas Austriaca*, trans. William D. Bowman and Anna Maria Leitgeb (West Lafayette, 2004), pp. 14–18.

[2] This claim was first made in the introduction to Gualterius Paullus, *Affectus Eucharistici Pietati Ferdinandi Tertii Imperatoris* (Vienna, 1640), sig. A6 and elaborated upon in Wenceslaus Adalbert Czerwenka, *Annales et acta pietatis augustissimae ac serenissimae Domus Habspurgo-Austriacae* (Prague, 1694), pp. 10–11, 461–4.

call, which is what led to his temporal power over a vast realm.[3] Thus was the Habsburgs' political authority rooted at its very foundation in their Eucharistic devotion, cementing their unique relationship to the sacrament. Another important Eucharistic legend concerned Maximilian I (r. 1493–1519), the ruler responsible for the marriage alliance with Spain that established the Habsburgs as a true world power in the sixteenth century. According to the story, Maximilian's devotion to the Eucharist saved his life after he got lost on the dangerous mountain cliff known as the Martinswand;[4] thus, the Eucharist served for the Habsburgs as not just the foundation of their worldly power but also as an important source of aid in times of tribulation.

An important reason why these legends served as such powerful representations of the Habsburgs' Eucharistic piety was their visual nature. Not only did they lend themselves to representation in paintings,[5] but the Rudolphine tale also lent itself to physical imitation by later rulers. Stories abound reporting that Ferdinand II, Ferdinand III, and other Habsburg emperors would kneel bareheaded on a public street in front of a priest bearing the Eucharist before offering the royal carriage to the clergy, all in full view of the citizenry.[6] In such instances, Rudolph served as a model for the current emperor, while the emperor simultaneously served as a model for his subjects; nothing could speak more strongly to the divine source of worldly power and to the importance of Catholic piety in one's daily life than the image of the powerful ruler engaged in a humble act of reverence for the Eucharist. In addition to their importance as a double model for both emperor and citizenry, such reenactments of the Rudolphine tale also served as a reflection of Habsburg piety; the seemingly simple pious act reinforced the legendary source of their power and divine right to rule. Even the public nature of the ritual of communion within the Catholic liturgy, during which Ferdinand III was reported to have knelt in reverence at the altar for extended periods of time, served as both a mirror of the Emperor's pious soul and a model for his subjects, inviting them to participate with him in this important Catholic rite, thus endorsing

---

[3] The comparison to St. Eustachius was first made in Paullus, *Affectus Eucharistici* and expanded upon in Didacus Lequille, *Pietas Austriaca, secundo sibi Fortuna, ac suae fortunata Posteritati in Matrimonialium Foederum ingenuitate* (Innsbruck, 1656), pp. 181–202.

[4] The story is related in (among other places) Lequille, *Pietas Austriaca*, p. 194.

[5] See, for instance, the Florentine fresco cycle painted in the 1620s by Matteo Rosselli, which includes a picture of Rudolph leading the priest: Adam Wandruszka, "Ein Freskenzyklus der 'Pietas Austriaca' in Florenz," *Mitteilungen des Österreichischen Staatsarchivs*, 15 (1962): pp. 495–9. Another example is a landscape painting by the Flemish artist Josse de Momper the younger (1564–1635) held at the *Schottenstift* in Vienna, which pictures Rudolph and the priest in the lower left corner.

[6] Coreth, pp. 16–17.

the dictates of the Council of Trent encouraging regular observances of communion.[7] In this way, Habsburg Eucharistic piety extended far beyond the devotional practices of a single family and was transformed into a public cult for the entire realm.

The promotion of the Eucharistic cult to the broad public was achieved not only through the Emperor's actions, but also through a variety of public artworks. A number of examples date to Ferdinand III's reign and became an integral part of his public image. Significantly, the earliest books that connect the Rudolphine tale to the establishment of the feast of Corpus Christi and draw comparisons with St Eustachius date from 1640 and 1656; these stand in addition to other historical narratives of Habsburg Eucharistic devotion published during Ferdinand III's reign.[8] Another literary work celebrating the Emperor's Eucharistic devotion is a handbook published by the Jesuit priest Carolus Musart shortly after Ferdinand III's ascension, which describes the mysteries of the Eucharist and provides prayers, meditations, and litanies; appended to the end is an appendix that relates the history of the Habsburgs' public devotion to the Eucharist, followed by a lengthy apostrophe to Ferdinand III that congratulates him on his recent coronation and urges him to continue his family's strong veneration.[9] A set of three anagrams on the word "EVCHARISTIA," all of which include the word "Austria," also circulated widely in print.[10] The Eucharist was also the subject of an Italian oratorio (with a printed libretto) by Giovanni Valentini, which was performed in the Hofburg during Holy Week 1642. This *Ragionamento sovra il Santissimo* glosses a number of liturgical texts from the feast of Corpus Christi, and its entire large-scale structure is based on the Magnificat antiphon for Second Vespers of that feast, *O sacrum convivium*.[11]

---

[7] Ibid., p. 18. On p. 28, Coreth provides figures attesting to the dramatic increase in the number of communicants in Vienna's Jesuit churches from 1638 to 1649.

[8] Paullus, *Affectus Eucharistici* and Lequille, *Pietas Austriaca*. Other works include Nikolaus Vernulz, *Virtutum augustissimae gentis Austriacae libri tres* (Louvain, 1640), Ch. 3 and Johann Peter Lotichius, *Austrias Parva: id est, gloriae Austriacae, et belli nuper Germanici, sub divo Matthia, Ferdinandis II. et III. Impp. gesti, compendaria* (Frankfurt, 1653), which relates the tale about Rudolph I on p. 4.

[9] Carolus Musart, *Sunamitis Christiana, sive affectus pii, quibus exemplo mulieris sunamitidis Elisaeum Hospitio recipientis, Anima disponitur ad rite, et magno cum fructu suscipiendum Christum, in Venerabili Eucharistia …* (Vienna, 1637), pp. 302–45.

[10] The anagrams are in Coreth, pp. 23 (in English), 33–4 (in Latin). They appeared in (among other places) Lequille, *Pietas Austriaca*, pp. 184–5. A similar unpublished collection of 100 anagrams on the word "SACRAMENTVM" was written in 1651 and dedicated to Ferdinand IV by Francesco Valentini, son of the former *maestro di cappella* Giovanni Valentini (A-Wn, Cod. 9894).

[11] Giovanni Valentini, *Ragionamento sovra il Santissimo* (Vienna, 1642). For more information on this work, see Theophil Antonicek, "Musik und italienische Poesie am Hofe

These literary commemorations of Ferdinand III's Eucharistic piety were geared toward an elite audience, those who could afford to purchase books and read Latin or Italian (or were fortunate enough to be invited to a performance at the Hofburg). A broader audience was addressed through public events that promoted the Emperor's piety, many of which were sponsored by churches, confraternities, and religious orders but still patronized by the imperial family. One such occasion was the Forty Hours Devotion, during which the consecrated host would be publicly displayed in a church for three days, housed in an elaborate monstrance placed in front of a sumptuous painting.[12] This devotion was held frequently in Viennese churches, often with members of the imperial family present.[13] One regular occurrence of the Forty Hours Devotion, in which the Emperor and his family always participated, was held every year since 1609 in the Jesuit church *am Hof* from Sunday to Tuesday before Ash Wednesday, ending with a solemn procession through the city displaying the host.[14] Another regular event drawing a large audience were the Jesuit dramas performed in Vienna within the octave of Corpus Christi. Nine dramas celebrating the Eucharist are known to have been performed in the imperial city during Ferdinand III's reign, five of which the Emperor (or at least members of his family) can be documented as attending (see Table 3.2). Three plays, moreover, explicitly praise the Emperor's Eucharistic piety and draw upon the themes of the *Pietas Austriaca*. *Fortuna Eucharistico-Austriaca Pietati et Justitiae* proclaims the power and good

---

Kaiser Ferdinands III.," *Mitteilungen der Kommission für Musikforschung*, 42 (1990): pp. 8–10 and Steven Saunders, "The Antecedents of the Viennese Sepolcro," in Alberto Colzani et al. (eds), *Relazioni musicali tra Italia e Germania nell'età barocca: Atti del VI convegno internazionale sulla muisca italiana nei secoli XVII-XVIII* (Como, 1997), pp. 66–8.

[12] On the Forty Hours Devotion in Vienna, see Gernot Gruber, *Das Wiener Sepolcro und Johann Joseph Fux, 1. Teil* (Graz, 1972), pp. 17–18. On the service in general, see also Howard E. Smither, "The Function of Music in the Forty Hours Devotion of Seventeenth- and Eighteenth-Century Italy," in Carmelo P. Comberiati and Matthew C. Steel (eds), *Music from the Middle Ages through the Twentieth Century: Essays in Honor of Gwynn McPeek* (New York, 1988), pp. 149–74 and Mark S. Weil, "The Devotion of the Forty Hours and Roman Baroque Illusions," *Journal of the Warburg and Courtauld Institutes*, 37 (1974): pp. 218–48.

[13] Viennese newspapers report that the celebration occurred in 1626 during Holy Week in the Capuchin Cloister, in 1627 and 1629 during Advent in St Stephen's Cathedral, and in 1631 two weeks after Easter in the Augustinian church (*Ordentliche Zeitungen*, April 11, 1626; December 25, 1627; November 24, 1629; May 10, 1631). Ferdinand III occasionally mentioned the Forty Hours Devotion in letters to Archduke Leopold Wilhelm; on August 16, 1642 he wrote that his wife was currently at the devotion, and he wrote about it in early January 1643 (HHStA, Familienarchiv, Familienkorrespondenz A, Karton 11, fols 148, 245).

[14] This annual occurrence is reported in the *Ordentliche Zeitungen* on February 28, 1626; February 20, 1627; March 11, 1628; March 18, 1628; February 16, 1630; March 8, 1631; February 9, 1636.

fortune that Habsburg Eucharistic devotion has bestowed on the entire imperial dynasty (with actors portraying each previous emperor) as well as on Ferdinand III himself (who is represented by Justice and Piety), all in the context of celebrating the Peace of Westphalia.[15]

The other two dramas, both performed during the darkest years of the war, draw upon the topos of the Eucharist as a source of aid in times of tribulation. The first of the plays, performed in 1644, enacts the legend of Maximilian I's rescue from the Martinswand, and the second, performed in 1645 as the Swedish army besieged Vienna, presents the story of David and Goliath, thereby casting Ferdinand III as the young David whose faith in the Lord gives him strength over his stronger enemy.[16] The latter play is framed with proclamations of Habsburg Eucharistic piety, which cements the identification of David with Ferdinand III and also ensures that spectators know that divine aid comes specifically from reverence for the sacrament. At the conclusion of the drama, characters representing each of the Habsburgs' realms join together with Piety and Justice in a final chorus with the recurring refrain, "O ardor Eucharistice! O Austriae calores!"[17]

By far the grandest of all public celebrations of Habsburg Eucharistic piety were the religious ceremonies that could be attended by any Viennese citizen. In a way, almost any Mass attended by Ferdinand III would have showcased the Eucharist, for the elevation of the Host would undoubtedly have been accompanied by magnificent music, likely for instruments alone. The most highly publicized veneration of the Eucharist, however, was the feast of Corpus Christi, whose lavish celebrations lasted an entire week and were surely among the most exciting and festive times of the liturgical year. Solemn Mass was observed daily throughout the octave of this feast, and crowds of people filled the streets to witness the many Corpus Christi processions, which in addition to displaying the consecrated host, sumptuous religious regalia, and the splendor of magnificent music and trumpets also featured the Emperor processing humbly on foot with his head uncovered (which again brought to mind Rudolph I and helped emphasize that the Habsburgs' magnificence stemmed from pious humility).[18] A document from 1648 lists the participants in the Corpus Christi procession in the following order: the Emperor, the King of the Romans, the Princesses, the Papal ambassador, Cardinal von Harrach, the Venetian ambassador, members of the court, members of the *Stadtrat*, the *Dom-Herren*, priests,

---

[15] A-Wn, Cod. 13341.
[16] A-Wn, Cod. 13275 and 13923.
[17] A-Wn, Cod. 13923, fols 6v–7v.
[18] Coreth, pp. 18–22.

singers, trumpeters, and "sonsten antern Personen."[19] On both the feast day and its octave these processions originated at St Stephen's Cathedral, and on Sunday within the octave the imperial family together with the entire court marched in two processions, one starting at the Jesuit church *am Hof* and the other at the Dominican church.[20] These processions were so important that when the Emperor was out of town the imperial retinue continued to observe them in Vienna, with participation by family and chapel members left behind. The Emperor also celebrated Corpus Christi processions in whichever city he was in at the time. An extraordinary report from 1653 mentions the Emperor's participation in a Corpus Christi procession in Regensburg featuring 40 trumpeters and timpani.[21]

For the common citizen, the music of Ferdinand III's chapel would have been a primary feature of Eucharistic celebrations, both during Corpus Christi and throughout the liturgical year, wondrously enhancing the miraculously transformed body of Christ. Ferdinand III himself composed a setting of the Corpus Christi hymn *Pange lingua*, for a large ensemble consisting of four soloists, five instruments, and ripieno choir.[22] Table 6.1 lists all surviving Eucharistic motets written by composers employed by Ferdinand III (though those by Bertali and Schmelzer were likely composed after his reign), and Table 6.2 lists lost works itemized in two inventories compiled after Ferdinand's death (and therefore not necessarily composed for him). It should come as no surprise that most of these works either do not survive or survive only in manuscript, for such grand, large-scale compositions intended to impress listeners would have been unsuitable for publication. Nor would the Emperor necessarily have wanted the music to circulate; by reserving the splendid performances solely for his own musical establishment he was able to preserve the music solely for his own representation.

---

[19] WSLA, Hs. A 41/16, Kirchenmeisteramtsrechunungsbuch, Jg. 1648, fols 63v–64r. I am grateful to Steven Saunders for bringing this document to my attention.

[20] The newspapers reported these processions every year without fail. Surviving accounts are in *Ordentliche Zeittungen*, May 31, 1625; June 7, 1625; June 13, 1626; June 20, 1626; June 5, 1627; June 12, 1627; June 24, 1628; June 8, 1630; June 21, 1631; May 24, 1636; May 31, 1636; June 5, 1638; June 25, 1639. The second Sunday procession from the Dominican church seems to have been instituted only during Ferdinand III's reign.

[21] *Extra-Ordinari Mittwochs Postzeittungen*, June 16, 1653; Johann Christian Lünig, *Theatrum Ceremoniale historico-politicum*, vol. 2 (Leipzig, 1720), p. 312.

[22] For an analysis of this work, see Andrew H. Weaver, "Piety, Politics, and Patronage: Motets from the Habsburg Court in Vienna During the Reign of Ferdinand III (1637–1657)" (Ph.D. diss., Yale University, 2002), pp. 315–16. A modern edn is in Weaver (ed.), *Motets by Emperor Ferdinand III and Other Musicians from the Habsburg Court*, Collegium Musicum: Yale University, second series (Middleton, in press).

Table 6.1   Surviving Eucharistic motets by composers employed by Ferdinand III

Title	Composer	Performing Forces (plus basso continuo)	Source
Caro mea	Giovanni Felice Sances	4 voices (CCTB)	*Motetti a 2, 3, 4, e cinque voci* (Venice, 1642)
Inquietum est cor meum	Heinrich Schmelzer	4 voices (CATB), violin, 3 violas, ripieno	CS-KRa, II-56 (A230)
Jesu dulcis amor meus	Antonio Bertali	5 concertato voices (CCATB), ripieno	S-Skma, Musik rar (incomplete set of parts)
Lauda Sion Salvatorem	Giovanni Felice Sances	2 voices (AT)	*Motetti a 2, 3, 4, e cinque voci* (Venice, 1642)
Mensa sacra	Giovanni Valentini	8 voices (CCAATTBB), 2 violins, ripieno	A-Kr, L14
Pange lingua	Ferdinand III	4 voices (CATB), 5 strings, ripieno	D-Lr, K.N. 28
Quis loquetur potentias Domini	Antonio Bertali	6 concertato voices, 6 instruments, ripieno	S-Skma, Musik rar (continuo part only)
Sileat misericordiam tuam	Heinrich Schmelzer	4 voices (CATB), violin, 3 violas, ripieno	CS-KRa, II-64 (A236)

Table 6.2   Lost Eucharistic motets by composers employed by Ferdinand III

Title	Composer	Performing Forces (plus basso continuo)
Works listed in A-Wn, Suppl. mus. 2451		
Anima surge	Antonio Bertali	6 concertato voices, ripieno
Hic est panis	Antonio Bertali	8 concertato voices, 6 violas, ripieno
O admirabile convivium	Antonio Bertali	6 concertato voices, ripieno
O Domine Jesu Christe	Giovanni Felice Sances	5 voices (CCATB)
O quam dellectabile	Giovanni Felice Sances	solo voice (B), 4 violas
Sospiro pro te [a]	Antonio Bertali	6 concertato voices, ripieno
Untitled motet "de Sanctissimo Sacramento"	Giovanni Felice Sances	4 voices, 4 violas
Untitled motet "de Sanctissimo Sacramento"	Giovanni Felice Sances	5 voices, 5 violas, ripieno
Untitled motet "de Sanctissimo Sacramento"	Giovanni Felice Sances	6 voices, 6 violas, ripieno

Title	Composer	Performing Forces (plus basso continuo)
Untitled motet "de Venerabile"	Giovanni Felice Sances	2 voices (CC)
Untitled motet "de Venerabile Sacramento"	Heinrich Schmelzer	4 voices, 5 violas, ripieno
Works listed in HKA, NÖHA, W61/A/32, fols. 2-11		
Ave in aevum	anonymous	4 voices, 4 instruments
O Jesu mi dulcissime	anonymous	5 voices
O quantum dilexissi hominem	anonymous	5 voices
O sacrum convivium	anonymous	5 voices, 5 instruments
Pange lingua	anonymous	5 voices, ripieno
Untitled motet "de Corpore Christi"	anonymous	8 concertato voices, unspecified number of instruments
Untitled motet "de Corpore Christi"	anonymous	5 voices, 2 violins

[a] This may be the same work listed as "Suspiro pro te" in a 1686 inventory from Ansbach; see Richard Schaal (ed.), *Die Musikhandschriften des Ansbacher Inventars von 1686* (Wilhelmshaven, 1966).

Only one other large-scale Eucharistic work can be securely dated to Ferdinand's reign, a setting of *Mensa sacra* by Giovanni Valentini that was copied in the 1640s in the Benedictine abbey of Kremsmünster.[23] Written for a large ensemble of eight concertato voices, two violins, and ripieno choir, this work uses its vast resources to provide a kaleidoscope of shifting textures blatantly intended to overwhelm the listener. The very simple text emphasizes key words for Eucharistic devotion without making any claim to literary sophistication, clearly in an attempt to reach as many listeners as possible. A large portion of the work, for instance, consists of a homophonic triple-meter refrain (sung variously by pairs of soloists and the full ensemble) that emphasizes the transubstantiation through a series of simple, easy-to-remember rhyming phrases: "Jesus cibus, Jesus potus, solus Jesus, Jesus totus" (Example 6.1).[24] The refrain catches the listener's attention with an unconventional harmonic progression marked by jarring cross relations (for instance, F-sharp–F-natural in bars 22–3 and B-natural–B-flat in bars 26–7).

Music, in cooperation with the other arts as well as liturgy and ritual, presented a triumphant image of Ferdinand III as a powerful, righteous ruler whose strength—not to mention his protection during the dark years

---

[23] A-KR, L14, fols 363–7. The manuscript was copied 1645–49 by Benedikt Lechler, the choirmaster of the abbey; see Altman Kellner, *Musikgeschichte des Stiftes Kremsmünster: Nach den Quellen dargestellt* (Kassel, 1956), pp. 202, 207–8, 217–19.

[24] "Jesus [is] food, Jesus [is] drink, only Jesus, entirely Jesus."

Example 6.1   Valentini, *Mensa sacra*, bars 21–9

of the 1640s—stemmed from his immense reverence for the uniquely Catholic symbol of the Eucharist. By presenting this image on grand public occasions accessible to even the common folk, the Emperor drew his subjects together in communal celebrations of Eucharistic piety, thereby creating a public cult that not only sought to strengthen the people's loyalty to the Catholic Church and encourage their active piety but that also stamped this brand of popular Catholic culture with a distinctly Habsburg image.

There was nevertheless nothing in this Habsburg image that was unique to Ferdinand III. As the chroniclers and artists continually stressed through their insistent reiteration of the roots of this piety in Rudolph and Maximilian I, Ferdinand was participating in a larger tradition that stretched far beyond the scope of just a single ruler; one could almost say that the magnificence of Habsburg Eucharistic piety was too great for any individual family member. This idea was also stressed by the annual nature of the rituals and processions in which Ferdinand III participated; just as his father before him had observed the same occasions, so too would his son and his son's sons after him. Much of the strictly liturgical music that the imperial chapel performed during Corpus Christi, in fact, consisted of venerable *stile antico* settings preserved in large manuscript choirbooks that had been recopied during Ferdinand III's reign and show signs of much use;[25] the timeless nature of this music, performed year after year, emphasized the dynastic tradition of which the Emperor was a part. Through the fostering of a popular Catholic cult centered on Eucharistic devotion, Ferdinand III both affirmed his place in one of the leading ruling dynasties of Europe and assured the world of its continuity while also securing his own reputation as a pious Catholic ruler, using his fervent piety as a means of asserting his authority over his people.

Private Spirituality Made Public: Mystical Theology in Motets for Ferdinand III

In contrast to the public ostentation of Ferdinand III's Eucharistic piety, his adoration of the cross was more private, a reflection of his inner spiritual life that revealed itself primarily through prayer and intimate devotional

---

[25] A-Wn, Cod. 16202 and 16207. On these manuscripts, see Friedrich W. Riedel, *Kirchenmusik am Hofe Karls VI. (1711-1740): Untersuchungen zum Verhältnis von Zeremoniell und musikalischem Stil im Barockzeitalter* (Munich and Salzburg, 1977), pp. 96–100 and Steven Saunders, "Sacred Music at the Hapsburg Court of Ferdinand II (1615–1637): The Latin Vocal Works of Giovanni Priuli and Giovanni Valentini" (2 vols, Ph.D. diss., University of Pittsburgh, 1990), vol. 1, pp. 146–8, 157–9.

services, not grand artworks and public ceremonies for the entire populace. The dearth of public displays of cross piety during Ferdinand's reign may at first seem surprising, since this pillar of the *Pietas Austriaca* was closely linked to war; a long tradition beginning with Rudolph I claimed that the Habsburgs' cross devotion ensured their victories against heretics and infidels on the battlefield, even when the Emperor (like Christ himself) had to suffer tribulations.[26] Even the early victories of the Thirty Years' War had been attributed to Ferdinand II's prayers to the crucifix and to a monk who had carried a cross-shaped icon into the Battle of White Mountain.[27]

Ferdinand III's eschewing of public celebrations along these lines nevertheless accords perfectly with his shifting fortunes in the war and his need to revise his image. With victories on the battlefield and a triumphant conclusion to the war no longer a feasible reality in the 1640s, Ferdinand recognized that to continue to flaunt his cross devotion as a source of certain victory would invite only laughter and scorn and highlight what could be interpreted as his abandonment by divine providence. It is telling that Ferdinand's only major public observance of cross devotion came in 1639 (before the war had taken a decisive turn for the worse), with the institution of the pilgrimage to Hernals discussed in Chapter 3; the transformation of a formerly Protestant church into the destination of an imperial *Kreuzweg* pointedly proclaimed that Christ's Passion assured victory over heretics.[28]

In light of the state of the war in the 1640s, Ferdinand III opted instead to turn his cross devotion inward, transforming it into a personal source of comfort and hope during difficult times. An important aspect of the Emperor's cross devotion was veneration of the five wounds of the crucified Christ, in which respect he followed the example of his father before him.[29] Ferdinand III also followed his father in that his personal brand of devotion to the wounds was infused with mystical theology. Unlike Ferdinand II, however, for whom the wounds served as the focal point of his cross devotion, Ferdinand III's adoration of the wounds was but one element of a more general mystical veneration of Christ. Although Ferdinand III's adherence to mystical theology seems on the surface to have served no obvious political or public function, it nevertheless contributed to his shifting public image and to his larger goals at the end of the Thirty Years' War. This is especially apparent when one compares the mystical motets written for him with those for Ferdinand II.

[26] Coreth, pp. 37–42.
[27] Ibid., pp. 39, 41 and Steven Saunders, *Cross, Sword and Lyre: Sacred Music at the Imperial Court of Ferdinand II of Habsburg (1619–1637)* (Oxford, 1995), pp. 203–4.
[28] Coreth, p. 41.
[29] On Ferdinand II's adoration of the wounds, see Saunders, *Cross*, pp. 203–22.

Central to all strains of mystical theology is the longing for ecstasy, the union of the mortal soul with God in this lifetime.[30] As the ultimate embodiment of the union of God and man, Jesus served as the focal point of mystical devotion; in addition to prayer and the confession of sins, important steps in the process of achieving spiritual ecstasy were imitating Christ and meditating intensely on aspects of his life, especially those that made him the most human: his sufferings on the cross. As emphasized in the influential writings of the medieval mystic St Bonaventure, concentrating on Christ's death leads to our own spiritual "love death," what Bernard McGinn calls "dying into love." McGinn continues:

> The "ecstatic anointings and totally enflamed affections" (*excessivis unctionibus et ardentissimis affectionibus*) that carry us over into God are enkindled by Christ "in the heat of his totally enflamed passion." Our love for his death leads us to our sharing in his archetypal *mors mystica*: "Let us die and enter into the darkness ... ; with Christ crucified let us pass out of this world to the Father."[31]

As a corollary to this notion of the "love death," an important mystical symbol was the *vulnus amoris*, the mutual wounding of two hearts though love, which then dissolve together into a perfect union.[32] For St John of the Cross (1542–91, canonized 1726), the *vulnus amoris* produces a love so great and beyond our comprehension that it leads to a total *transcendence*, *dissolution*, even *negation* of the bodily senses, a concept that Margaret Murata has explicated in several small-scale motets by Monteverdi.[33] A number of books by or about St Bonaventure, St John of the Cross, and that other extremely influential sixteenth-century mystic

---

[30] On mysticism in general I have found especially useful Bernard McGinn, *The Presence of God: A History of Western Christian Mysticism* (4 vols to date, New York, 1991–) and Joseph B. Dallett, "The Mystical Quest for God," in Gerhart Hoffmeister (ed.), *German Baroque Literature: The European Perspective* (New York, 1983), pp. 270–91. An examination of mysticism in seventeenth-century Italian motets is Margaret Murata, "'Quia amore langueo' or Interpreting 'Affetti sacri e spirituale,'" in Paola Besutti et al. (eds), *Claudio Monteverdi: Studi e prospettive* (Florence, 1998), pp. 89–94; see also the excellent examination of mystical motet texts (in a Lutheran context) in Mary E. Frandsen, *Crossing Confessional Boundaries: The Patronage of Italian Sacred Music in Seventeenth-Century Dresden* (Oxford and New York, 2006), pp. 117–41.

[31] McGinn, vol. 3, *The Flowering of Mysticism: Men and Women in the New Mysticism, 1200–1350*, p. 110.

[32] Ibid., p. 274.

[33] Murata, "'Quia amore langueo,'" pp. 92–3.

St Teresa of Avila (1515–82, canonized 1622) are listed in catalogues of Ferdinand III's library.[34]

Mystical Theology in Motets for Ferdinand II

A crucial book for understanding Ferdinand II's mystical devotion to Christ's wounds is *Fascetto di mirra, overo considerationi varie sopra le piaghe di Christo* by Vincenzo Carafa, an eminent Neapolitan Jesuit who went on to be elected Superior General of the Society of Jesus in 1646.[35] For Carafa, Christ's wounds are the outward manifestation of the *vulnus amoris*, the miraculous portal through which the mystical union between the soul and God occurs. As such, the reader is instructed to meditate frequently upon the wounds in order to best imitate Christ and experience the wounds himself, which is what makes the mystical union possible.[36] In order most effectively to focus the mind upon the wounds, the book is overflowing with powerful sensory descriptions of Christ's physical pain, often going into graphic, even grisly detail. The main tenet that runs through the work, in fact, is the antithesis of mortal suffering and transcendent rapture, of harshness and sweetness, that coexists in Christ's wounds, which Carafa describes with the term "dolcissime piaghe" (sweetest wounds). A specifically Viennese audience for the book is implied not only by the fact that was it published in Vienna but also by Carafa's dedication to the Congregation of the Immaculate Conception at the Viennese Jesuit church. Although not published until 1638, after Ferdinand II's death, it nevertheless reflects the spiritual life of the court in the 1620s and '30s and holds the key to understanding cross motets written for the elder Ferdinand.

Two musical works that illustrate well Ferdinand II's devotion to Christ's wounds are Giovanni Valentini's *Salve tremendum* and *Deus qui*

---

[34] A-Wn, Cod. 13556 (from 1652), fols 240v ("Operum S. Teresae pars 2.da Colon: 1627"), 372v ("Stimulus divini Amoris S. Bonaventurae Brixiae. 1599"), 384 ("Historia et miracula et revelationes Virg. Joa. de Cruce. ord S. Francisci. Antonii Dacae. Leridae. 1613"), 388 ("Vita SS. Matris Theresiae hispanice Salamancae 1590"), 415 ("Libri S.ta Teraesiae Salamanca. 1588"), 416 ("Vita S. Teresiae Italice translata a Francisco Bordini Venetiis 1611"), 434v ("Psalterium à S. Bonaventurae compilatum in honore B. Virginis. Valentiae. 1570"); A-Wn, Cod. Ser. n. 4450 (a posthumous catalogue of Ferdinand II's library compiled in 1638), fol. 15 ("Racolta Di alcuni Brevissima ma utiliss. trattati spirituali composit da la gloriosa Verg.e Madre S. Teresa di Jiesu").

[35] Vincenzo Carafa, *Fascetto di mirra, overo considerationi sopra le piaghe di Christo* (Vienna, 1638). This book is listed in the 1652 catalogue of Ferdinand III's library (A-Wn, Cod. 13556, fol. 392v). On Carafa, see Robert Bireley, *The Jesuits and the Thirty Years War: Kings, Courts, and Confessors* (Cambridge, 2003), pp. 232–3.

[36] Carafa, *Fascetto di mirra*, pp. 188–9. For a more detailed discussion of Carafa's text, see Saunders, *Cross*, pp. 218–20.

pro redemptione mundi, part of a set of five cross motets in dialogue style published in 1625.[37] The texts of both works (Tables 6.3 and 6.4) offer meditations on the Passion, *Salve tremendum* by contemplating Christ's body and *Deus qui pro redemptione mundi* by dwelling on the events of the crucifixion. As Steven Saunders has pointed out, both texts are rich in allusions to literary and liturgical genres, which help inform our understanding of the pieces just as much as Carafa's book, yet the overall topos nevertheless falls directly in line with Carafa's brand of spirituality.[38] As in *Fascetto di mirra*, there is a distinct emphasis in both motets on the intense physicality of Christ's suffering; *Salve tremendum*, moreover, exemplifies the *dolcissime piaghe* through its juxtaposition of superlative descriptions of the sweetness of Christ's body parts with graphic, detailed accounts of the tortures inflicted upon them.

---

[37] Giovanni Valentini, *Sacri concerti a due, tre, quattro et cinque voci* (Venice, 1625). The other three works are *O vos omnes*, *O Domine Jesu Christi*, and *Popule meus*; modern edns of *Salve tremendum*, *Deus qui pro redemptione mundi*, and *O vos omnes* are in Saunders, *Cross*, pp. 307–31 and Saunders (ed.), *Fourteen Motets from the Court of Ferdinand II of Hapsburg*, RRMBE, vol. 75 (Madison, 1995), pp. 47–68.

[38] See the superb discussion of all five cross motets in Saunders, *Cross*, pp. 204–22.

Table 6.3 Valentini, *Salve tremendum*

Tenor	Salve, tremendum	Hail, terrible
	cunctis potestatibus	in all its majesty,
	caput Domini Jesu Christi	the head of Lord Jesus Christ
	Salvatoris nostri,	our Savior,
	pro nobis spinis coronatum	for us crowned with thorns
	et arudine percussum.	and flogged with a whip.
Canto 2	Salve, spetiosissima	Hail, most handsome
	Salvatoris nostri Jesu Christi facies,	face of our Savior Jesus Christ,
	pro nobis sputis et alapis caesa.	for us struck with spit and blows.
Canto 1	Salvete, benignissimi Domini nostri	Hail, most kind eyes of our Lord
	Jesu Christi Salvatoris nostri oculi,	Jesus Christ our Savior,
	pro nobis lacrymis perfusi.	for us filled with tears.
Tenor	Salve, mellifluum os	Hail, honey-sweet mouth
	gutturque sauvissimum	and most sweet throat
	Domini nostri Jesu Christi,	of our Lord Jesus Christ,
	pro nobis felle et aceto potatum.	for us having drunk gall and vinegar.
Canto 2	Salvete, aures nobilissimae	Hail, most noble ears
	Domini Jesu Christi	of our Lord Jesus Christ
	Salvatoris nostri,	our Savior,
	pro nobis contumeliis	for us affected by insults
	et opprobriis affectae.	and reproaches.
Canto 1	Salve, collum humile Jesu Christi,	Hail, humble neck of Jesus Christ,
	pro nobis colaphizatum	for us beaten,
	dorsumque sanctissimum	and most holy back
	pro nobis flagellatum.	for us flagellated.
Tenor	Salvete, venerabiles manus,	Hail, venerable hands,
Canto 2	pectus mitissimum,	most mild breast,
Canto 1	latus gloriosum,	glorious side,
Tenor	sacra genua,	sacred knees,
Canto 2	pedes adorandi,	venerable feet,
Canto 1	sanguis praetiosissime,	most precious blood,
Tenor	anima sanctissima.	most sacred soul.
Tutti [Adagio]	Salve, totum corpus Jesu Christi, pro nobis in cruce suspensum, vulneratum, mortuum, et sepultum.	Hail, entire body of Jesus Christ, for us hung on the cross, wounded, dead, and buried.

Source: adapted from Saunders, *Cross, Sword and Lyre*, pp. 204–5.

Table 6.4 Valentini, *Deus qui pro redemptione mundi*

Canto 1	Deus, qui pro redemptione mundi voluisti nasci, circumcidi, a Judaeis reprobari, a Juda traditore osculo tradi, libera me a poenis inferni.	God, who for the redemption of the world was willing to be born, circumcised, condemned by the Jews, betrayed by Judas with a kiss, liberate me from the pains of Hell.
Canto 2	Deus, qui pro redemptione mundi voluisti vinculis alligari, sicut agnus innocens ad victimam duci, atque conspectibus Annae, Caiphe, Pilati et Herodis indecenter offeri, libera me a poenis inferni.	God, who for the redemption of the world was willing to be bound in chains, led as an innocent lamb to the sacrifice, and in the sight of Anna, Caiaphas, Pilate, and Herod indecently offered, liberate me from the pains of Hell.
Canto 1	Deus, qui pro redemptione mundi voluisti a falsis testibus accusari, flagellis et opprobriis vexari, sputis conspui, spinis coronari, libera me a poenis inferni.	God, who for the redemption of the world was willing to be accused by liars, to be plagued with whips and taunts, to be spit upon, crowned with thorns, liberate me from the pains of Hell.
Canto 2	Deus, qui pro redemptione mundi voluisti colaphis caede, arundine percuti, libera me a penis inferni.	God, who for the redemption of the world was willing to be struck with blows, to be beaten with whips, free me from the pains of Hell.
Tutti C1 C2 C1 C2 Tutti	Deus, qui pro redemptione mundi voluisti cruci clavis affigi, voluisti in cruce levari, voluisti inter latronis deputari, voluisti felle et aceto potari, voluisti lancea vulnerari, libera me a poenis inferni;	God, who for the redemption of the world was willing to be nailed to the cross, was willing to be lifted on the cross, was willing to considered a thief, was willing to drink gall and vinegar, was willing to be speared, free me from the pains of Hell;
Tutti	et perducere digneris quo perduxisti latronem tecum crucifixum.	and by your merits, lead me to where you led the thief crucified with you.

Source: adapted from Saunders, *Cross, Sword and Lyre*, pp. 209–10.

Example 6.2   Valentini, *Salve tremendum*, bars 16–22

Especially significant for one's perception of the motets in performance is the highly schematic nature of both texts, which Valentini mirrors with his disposition of the voices (illustrated in Tables 6.3 and 6.4); the first six sentences of *Salve tremendum* and the first four of *Deus qui pro redemptione mundi* are sung by solo voices, which rotate in regularly repeating and predictable patterns. Saunders has stressed the expressive impact of the final sections of both works, in which the acceleration of the vocal rotation and the joining together of the voices create a crescendo that coincides with the most important words.[39] Just as significant, however, are the long expanses of solo singing that precede these final sections. In both works, each sentence is set in a static recitative style featuring many repetitions of the same pitch in roughly equal note values over an extremely slow-moving bass, punctuated by jarring unexpected dissonances and unusual harmonic juxtapositions that highlight the harshness of the graphic descriptions (see

---

[39] Ibid., pp. 208–9, 212.

Example 6.2 for one example). While no verse is set to exactly the same music as another, the overall effect is nevertheless one of repetition, almost redundancy. Valentini has stripped the motets of music's most appealing qualities—melodic interest, goal-directed harmonic movement—resulting in pieces that are difficult, almost painful to listen to; the pain is only intensified by the brutal dissonances accompanying the grisly descriptions. Far from a defect, this difficulty actually seems to be the point: Valentini's music creates an atmosphere in which the listener has no choice but to pay close attention to the words and meditate intensely on the gory details of the Passion. The music invites us to immerse ourselves in the text and give ourselves over to contemplation of the mystical wounds, just as Ferdinand II is reported to have done every day of his life.

Mystical Theology in Motets for Ferdinand III

The slightly different brand of mystical theology that Ferdinand III observed is best exemplified by a meditation on the wounds published in 1649 by the Belgian Jesuit Guillaume de Wael.[40] Like Carafa's book, this text regards the wounds as signs of the *vulnus amoris* through which the mystical union can be achieved; however, graphic descriptions of the wounds do not play a significant role. Rather, Wael describes the wounds with abstract metaphors such as "magnes animarum," "domicilium animarum," and "testes amoris."[41] Similar symbolic language was common in the writings of Sts Teresa and John of the Cross,[42] and in fact, Wael's decreased emphasis on the sensory quality of the wounds corresponds to St John's vision of the dissolution of the bodily senses during the mystical ecstasy.

Sances's first motet book from 1638 contains a discrete set of three cross motets that exhibit Wael's brand of mystical theology: *Plagae tuae Domine*, *O Crux benedicta*, and *O Domine guttae tui sanguinis*.[43] The composer seems to have intended users of the print to consider these works a set; not only do they appear next to each other as the first works for three

---

[40] Guillaume de Wael, *Corona Sacratissimorum Jesu Christi Vulnerum XXXV. Considerationibus* (Antwerp, 1649). This work is listed in the 1652 catalogue of Ferdinand III's library (A-Wn, Cod. 13556, fol. 383v), as well as in a catalogue of Leopold I's library compiled in 1666 (A-Wn, Cod. 12590, fol. 8).

[41] "Magnet of the soul," "home of the soul," "witness of love"; Wael, *Corona Sacratissimorum*, pp. 185–205.

[42] Massimo Marcocchi, "Spirituality in the Sixteenth and Seventeenth Centuries," in John W. O'Malley (ed.), *Catholicism in Early Modern History: A Guide to Research* (St Louis, 1988), pp. 169, 173.

[43] Modern edn in Giovanni Felice Sances, *Motetti a una, due, tre, e quattro voci (1638)*, ed. Steven Saunders, RRMBE, vol. 126 (Middleton, 2003), pp. 99–128.

voices, but they are also written for the same combination of alto, tenor, and bass. This binds the works together despite the fact that they could be used in a variety of liturgical and devotional contexts; only the first one, in fact, makes an explicit reference to the wounds. The other two are more general in their celebration of the cross, with less overt mystical overtones: *O Crux* sets a standard liturgical text,[44] and *O Domine* concludes with a pre-existing prayer in the first person plural.

The opening of *O Domine guttae tui sanguinis* nevertheless corresponds closely to Wael's meditations. It begins in a similar manner as Valentini's *Domine qui pro redemptione mundi*, with a literary anaphora consisting of four sentences that begin with exactly the same words before providing different descriptions of Christ's blood. Instead of the graphic physical descriptions in Valentini's works, however, the text extols the wounds through metaphors similar to those in Wael's book:

O Domine, guttae tui sanguinis sunt amoris insigna.	O Lord, the drops of your blood are signs of love.
O Domine, guttae tui sanguinis sunt salutis vulnera.	O Lord, the drops of your blood are wounds of healing.
O Domine, guttae tui sanguinis sunt pietatis ubera.	O Lord, the drops of your blood are breasts of holiness.
O Domine, guttae tui sanguinis sunt caelorum ostia.	O Lord, the drops of your blood are the gates of Heaven.
Sanguine nostro redemisti et eripuisti animas nostras de manu inimici.	By your blood have you redeemed and delivered our souls from the hand of the enemy.
Exaudi Domine, supplicum preces et confitentium tibi parce peccatis, ut pariter nobis indulgentiam tribuas benignus et pacem.	Hear, Lord, hear our prayers and pardon our sins as we confess them to you, that you might grant us in your kindness both indulgence and peace.

Significantly, the second section of the work praises Christ's blood as a source of protection from enemies, which calls to mind the current political situation and the Habsburg tradition of cross devotion as a source of victory in time of war. Mystical theology appears in *O Crux benedicta* through a recurring refrain that celebrates the crucifixion through Carafa's antithesis of sweetness and harshness, but without the grisly detail: "Dulce lignum, dulces clavos, dulcia ferens pondera!"[45] The most explicitly mystical of the three works is the first one:

---

[44] The entire text is the Magnificat antiphon for the feasts of the Exultation and Finding of the Cross.

[45] "How sweet the wood, how sweet the nails, bearing such sweet weights!"

Plagae tuae, Domine, meum cor non mortali vulnere sed divino sauciarunt amore.	Your wounds, O Lord, have wounded my heart, not with mortal wounds but with divine love.
In te igitur, amantissime Jesu, spiro in te, in te respiro.	In you, therefore, O most loving Jesus, in you I live and breathe.
Miserere rogo mihi peccatori.	I beseech you, have mercy on me, a sinner.
Transfige obsecro medullas et viscera animae mea, ut possim te diu ac nocte laudare, te perfrui, tibi servire.	I implore you, pierce the marrow and heart of my soul, so that day and night I may praise you, delight in you, and serve you.
Et sic divina saucius caritate misericordiam Domini in aeternum cantabo.	And thus, wounded by divine charity, of the Lord's mercy I shall sing forever.

Not only does this text open with an explanation of the *vulnus amoris*, but the fourth section paraphrases a popular Catholic prayer attributed to St Bonaventure (the "Oratio Sancti Boneventurae") as the speaker beseeches Christ to "pierce the marrow and heart of my soul."[46]

Even with the mention of Christ's wounds at the beginning of *Plagae tuae*, the devotion expressed in this work encompasses more than just this one aspect of the Passion. By eschewing graphic descriptions of the crucifixion, the motet transforms the wounds into a synecdoche for the entire redemptive body of Christ: "in *you* therefore, O most loving Jesus, I live and breathe [emphasis mine]."[47] This is symptomatic of Ferdinand III's mystical devotion in general, which extends well beyond the wounds and even the cross. Indeed, two additional motets from Sances's *Motetti a una, due, tre, e quattro voci* invoke the mystical love-death without mentioning the Passion at all (see Table 6.5): *O Jesu mi* uses a paraphrase of the "Oratio Sancti Boneventurae" to express the desire to dissolve and become one with the Lord, while *Dulcis Amor Jesu* explicitly alludes to the *vulnus amoris* by requesting Christ to "pierce me with your arrows, that I may die through you."[48]

---

[46] The "Oratio Sancti Boneventurae" opens with "Transfige, dulcissime Domine Jesu, medullas et viscera animae meae suavissimo ac saluberrimo amoris tui vulnere." The text was known at the Habsburg court through such publications as Jacob Merlo (ed.), *Paradisus animae christianae* (Cologne, 1644), where it appears on p. 458.

[47] For an examination of devotion to the body of Christ, see James Clifton (ed.), *The Body of Christ in the Art of Europe and New Spain, 1150–1800* (Munich and New York, 1997), especially the essay by David Nirenberg, "The Historical Body of Christ," pp. 17–25.

[48] Modern edns of the works are in Sances, *Motetti*, ed. Saunders, pp. 37–9, 136–43.

Table 6.5   Texts of two mystical motets from Sances's *Motetti a una, due, tre, e quattro voci*

Dulcis amor Jesu,	Jesus, sweet love,
dulce bonum, dilecte mi.	sweet goodness, my delight.
Rogo te sagittis tuis confige me	I beseech you, pierce me with your arrows
moriar pro te.	that I may die through you.
Ah mi Jesu,	Ah, my Jesus,
trahe me rogo post te;	I pray, draw me toward you;
inter flores pone me,	place me among the flowers,
quia langueo pro te,	for I languish for you,
tu lux, tu spes, tu vita,	you light, you hope, you life,
tu bonitas infinita.	you infinite good.
O Jesu mi, dulcis amor meus, vita vitalis,	O my Jesus, my sweet love, abundant life,
vita sine qua morior,	life without which I would die,
quando ad te veniam?	when shall I approach you?
Cupio dissolvi et esse tecum,[a]	I long to dissolve and be one with you,
amor mi Jesu.	Jesus, my love.
O amantissime Jesu	O most loving Jesus,
veni et intra in animam meam,	come and enter into my heart,
ut omnia desideria mea	so that all my desires
in te quiescant.	might repose in you.

[a] Paraphrase of the "Oratio Sancti Boneventurae." The original text reads "cupiat dissolvi et esse tecum."

The veneration of the body of Christ as the medium through which mystical union is achieved provides an important point of contact with the Habsburgs' Eucharistic piety, demonstrating that even this most public of religious symbols was an important component of Ferdinand III's private spiritual life. All of these issues converge, in fact, on the sacrament of communion, during which the consecrated body (the miraculously transformed host) and blood (poured from the sacred wounds) are intimately internalized;[49] the passage from the "Oratio Sancti Boneventurae" included in *Plagae tuae* appears in many Catholic prayer books in the section for communion.[50] It is thus not surprising that a

---

[49] Dallet, "Mystical Quest for God," p. 272; Nirenberg, "Historical Body of Christ," pp. 18–19.

[50] This is true of Merlo's *Paradisus animae* cited above; while the entire prayer is given on p. 458, just the "transfige" text appears on pp. 622–3 under the rubric, "post communionem."

number of the lost Eucharistic works in Table 6.2 bear titles that betray the deeply personal nature of mystical spirituality.[51] A surviving example of a work of this type is *Caro mea* from Sances's 1642 motet book.[52] This work opens with a recitative passage for solo bass setting John 6:56–7, the words of institution uttered by Christ as he offered the bread and wine to his disciples during the Last Supper. The rest of the text, however, consists of six stanzas from St Bernard of Clairvaux's well-known hymn *Jesu dulcis memoria*, a text used frequently in seventeenth-century sacred music as an expression of yearning for mystical ecstasy.[53] Even more explicit is Bertali's *Jesu dulcis amor meus*, the penultimate section of which opens with the words "Pro Amore langueo, vulnus Amoris sentio."[54]

The texts of Sances's mystical motets are thus notably different from Valentini's, expressing explicit desires to merge with Christ's body but in a variety of devotional contexts and without graphic contemplation of the wounds. Sances's music is also different, employing all of music's sensuous pleasures to create appealing settings that aim to delight the listener. Compare, for instance, the request for Christ to pierce the soul in *Dulcis Amor Jesu* (Example 6.3)—with its affective chromatic half-step ascent on "rogo" and rhythmically complex, highly ornamented monody—to the stark declamatory melody in Valentini's *Salve tremendum*. Sances also makes liberal use of the tuneful triple-meter aria style, as for instance in the recurring refrain of *O Crux benedicta* (Example 6.4). In addition, although he matches the literary anaphora at the start of *O Domine guttae tui sanguinis* with musical anaphora, with every phrase sung to essentially the same melody by a solo voice (similar to Valentini's approach in both of his motets), Sances avoids the static redundancy of Valentini's music through a graceful initial ascending melodic figure and a virtuosic melisma at the end of the phrase (Example 6.5). These musical differences are the natural result of the fact that Valentini and Sances belonged to different generations; whereas the older composer followed an aesthetic that focuses on individual words, crafting music that emphasizes their meaning through striking musical devices, Sances responded more to the overall affect of the text, representing the general mood through conventional

---

[51] Examples include Bertali's *Sospiro pro te*, catalogued under the rubric "per il SS.mo Sacramento" (A-Wn, Cod. suppl. mus. 2451, fol. 17v), and the anonymous *O Jesu mi dulcissime* listed under a similar rubric in HKA, NÖHA, W61/A/32, fol. 3.

[52] Modern edn in Giovanni Felice Sances, *Motetti a 2, 3, 4, e cinque voci (1642)*, ed. Andrew H. Weaver, RRMBE, vol. 148 (Middleton, 2008), pp. 131–9.

[53] Frandsen, pp. 125–41.

[54] "I languish for Love, I experience the wound of Love."

Example 6.3   Sances, *Dulcis Amor Jesu*, bars 19–27

musical materials.⁵⁵ At the same time, however, it is precisely Sances's musical aesthetic that helped these intensely personal motets serve a public representational function.

The representational potential of Sances's mystical motets is most apparent in the two-voice motet *O Domine Jesu*, which receives pride of place as the opening work of his 1642 motet book.⁵⁶ Although the text does not explicitly mention the cross, the Eucharist, or even the *vulnus amoris*, its veneration of the body of Christ as the locus of the mystical union is unmistakable:

---

⁵⁵ On these aesthetic differences, see Tim Carter, "Resemblance and Representation: Towards a New Aesthetic in the Music of Monteverdi," in Iain Fenlon and Tim Carter (eds), *Con che soavità: Studies in Italian Opera, Song, and Dance* (Oxford, 1995), pp. 118–34.

⁵⁶ Modern edn in Sances, *Motetti*, ed. Weaver, pp. 3–7.

Example 6.4 Sances, *O Crux benedicta*, bars 23–32

Example 6.5 Sances, *O Domine guttae tui sanguinis*, bars 1–7

O Domine Jesu,	O Lord Jesus,
quando tibi per omina placebo?	when shall I please you in all things?
O Domine Jesu,	O Lord Jesus,
quando totus ero tuus?	when shall I be entirely yours?
O Domine Jesu,	O Lord Jesus,
quando ardentissime diligam te?	when shall I love you ardently?
Quando nihil praeter	When shall nothing except
gratissimam voluntatem tuam	your most gracious will,
nihil praeter te vivet in me?	nothing except you live in me?
Quid faciam Domine Jesu	What must I do, Lord Jesus,
ut placeam tibi?	to be pleasing to you?
Usque hodie totus sum abominabilis	Even today I am entirely abominable
et plenus iniquitate.	and full of iniquities.
Eia unice cordis mei digneris	Yet in my heart you think it fit
hoc citius perficere	to bring this swiftly to perfection
quia te desidero, ad te anhelo,	because I desire you, I sigh for you,
et tui amore langueo.	and I languish for your love.

The work opens with a series of five questions directed toward Christ, each expressing an increasingly intense yearning to be one with the Lord. Following a penitential section in which the soul confesses its sins, the

MIRRORS AND MODELS 219

Example 6.6   Sances, *O Domine Jesu*, bars 26–33

Example 6.7   Sances, *O Domine Jesu*, bars 96–101

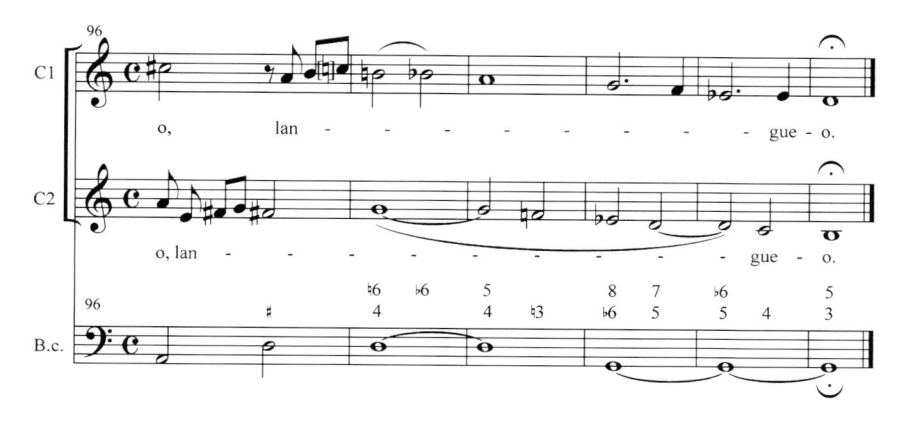

motet concludes with sensual, erotic language, an allusion to the Song of Songs that served as a common mystical strain: "I languish for your love."

Musically, *O Domine Jesu* is a marvel of dramatic pacing, in which the very process of the soul uniting with Christ seems to take place before our very ears. Although it begins in a rather static fashion, with the first three questions sung to essentially the same musical phrase (another instance of anaphora), Sances quickly begins to build intensity with the fourth question (bar 19), first by omitting the opening address "O Domine Jesu" and then by following this in bars 26–36 with increased rhythmic variety and downbeat rests that propel into the second beat of each phrase (Example 6.6). The tension continues to build with many repetitions of the last question in close succession, pushing directly into a climatic section, marked "presto" in the score, in which the voices seemingly scream out to the Lord, confessing their sins in sequential repetitions of a single figure sung in close imitation by both voices. With a repeated cadential figure, sung back at an "adagio" tempo, the soul seems to have purged its sins, after which it can look forward to its merging with Christ. Sances thus concludes the work by lavishing attention on the final clause, "et tui amore langueo": the two voices first alternate singing this phrase over a constantly descending stepwise bass (bars 84–92), and they then rhapsodize on the single word "langueo" for four bars. Upon reaching a second-inversion G triad in bar 97, Sances concludes the motet with one of the most remarkable harmonic progressions in his entire *oeuvre* (Example 6.7): a very gradual descent of the voices by half and whole steps through the space of a sixth to a root position triad on G. Throughout this extended five-bar process each voice moves independently, creating a string of extraordinary sonorities along the way; because the half note governs the harmonic rhythm, we experience each chord for a full two beats. Although it was conventional to set texts of this sort with drooping, chromatic suspensions, in this passage Sances stretches that convention to its very limits, providing an astonishingly graphic portrayal of the dissolution of the soul into Christ.

Herein lies the crucial distinction between this motet and Valentini's cross motets from the *Sacri concerti*: whereas Valentini's works provide a static image, the material to be contemplated in a musical setting that invites us to meditate upon the words, Sances's motet creates an *experience*, taking us into the soul of a pious individual and offering a glimpse of the bliss of mystical ecstasy. Put another way, Valentini's motets provide the means to achieve the mystical union (which would presumably occur after the music is over), while Sances's creates a staged scene in which the listeners vicariously experience the union, thereby encouraging them to bring mystical spirituality into their own lives so that they can achieve something even more blissful in the future. And because this music comes from Ferdinand III's chapel, the soul represented in O Domine Jesu can be interpreted not just as the listener's own but also as that of the Emperor himself, turning the motet into a mirror of his private spiritual life as well as a model for his subjects to imitate in their own lives.

Despite the personal, intimate nature of Ferdinand III's mystical devotion, it thus served exactly the same function as his Eucharistic piety: both were integral aspects of his public image, enhancing his reputation by reflecting his reverent soul and inviting others to model themselves on him. The crucial difference lies in the intended audience and mode of dissemination. As a public cult in which all imperial subjects were invited to participate, the Emperor's Eucharistic piety was celebrated in grand public fashion, complete with sumptuous large-scale music for many performers. To ensure that the music would be performed by his chapel alone, the Emperor did not permit the manuscript copies to be published. Ferdinand's mystical adoration of the body of Christ, in contrast, was geared toward a much smaller audience of elite intellectuals due to its private character and the esoteric nature of mystical theology, which required an ability to understand Latin and knowledge of complex theological concepts. Musical performances by the imperial chapel at devotional services served an important function in enhancing the Emperor's reputation, but these intimate events would have been presented to a very limited audience consisting primarily of the inner circle at court. More important is the fact that Sances's mystical motets were distributed to a broad audience via print; it was primarily through the printed page that Ferdinand's spirituality became embedded in his public image.[57] In contrast to his attitude about the dissemination of the Eucharistic works, Ferdinand *wanted* other musical institutions to perform Sances's motets. Even if the majority of listeners to these performances did not know that the music was connected to the Emperor, those who knew the prints from which the works came would have received a vivid image of Ferdinand III as a deeply pious ruler with an ardent devotion to Christ, to whom he turned as a source of comfort, solace, and protection during the final decade of the Thirty Years' War.

---

[57] Kevin Sharpe discusses the publicizing of the private, interior life as a means of monarchical representation in *Selling the Tudor Monarchy: Authority and Image in Sixteenth-Century England* (New Haven and London, 2009), p. 11.

CHAPTER 7

Maria Patrona Ferdinandi (et Austriae): Ferdinand III's Marian Devotion as Public Image

On March 6, 1645 the imperial troops suffered a devastating defeat at the hands of the Swedish army at the Battle of Jankov in Bohemia.[1] This prolonged and painful skirmish was without doubt one of the most significant events of the war, laying bare the Emperor's weaknesses in military matters. To make matters worse, five months later the Bavarian army (Ferdinand III's most important ally) suffered an equally devastating defeat to the French at the Battle of Allerheim on August 3.[2] As Geoffrey Parker has aptly put it, "After Jankov and Allerheim, there was no longer any Catholic field army able to withstand the Swedes and their allies; and everyone knew it."[3] For Ferdinand III and his allies, the war was essentially over; the question was no longer whether it could be won, just whether the Emperor could extricate himself from it without losing too much. Indeed, before the end of the year Count Maximilian von Trautmannsdorf, Ferdinand's most trusted political advisor and chief negotiator, arrived at the Westphalian peace talks with instructions to make whatever concessions necessary to achieve peace.

By the end of March the Swedes had overtaken the city of Krems, less than fifty miles from Vienna, and it was clear that a siege of the imperial capital was imminent. Immediately Ferdinand III sent his family to Graz for their protection, and by April 10 the enemy was camped at the *Neutor* on the northern end of Vienna. The Emperor would soon join his family in the safe haven of Graz, but before fleeing the besieged city he orchestrated

---

[1] On the battle, see Geoffrey Parker, *The Thirty Years' War*, 2nd edn (London and Boston, 1997), pp. 156–8; William P. Guthrie, *The Later Thirty Years War: From the Battle of Wittstock to the Treaty of Westphalia* (Westport, 2003), pp. 128–44; Karsten Ruppert, *Die kaiserliche Politik auf dem Westfälischen Friedenskongreß (1643–1648)* (Münster, 1979), pp. 72–85. For a detailed discussion of this *annus horribilis*, see Thomas Winkelbauer, "Finanznot und Friedenssehnsucht: Der Kaiserhof im Jahre 1645," in Lorenz Mikoletzky et al. (eds), *"Wir aber aus unsern vorhero sehr erschöpfften camergeföllen nicht hernemben khönnen …": Beiträge zur Österreichischen Wirtschafts- und Finanzgeschichte vom 17. bis zum 20. Jahrhundert* (Vienna, 1997), pp. 1–15.
[2] Guthrie, *Later*, pp. 214–24.
[3] Parker, p. 158.

one of the most brilliant acts of his career: an official, public declaration of devotion to the symbol of the *Pietas Austriaca* that was most important to him, the Blessed Virgin of the Immaculate Conception.

The Immaculate Conception as Personal Devotion in the 1630s

Unlike the Emperor's Eucharistic piety, which reflected long-standing dynastic tradition, Ferdinand III's devotion to the Blessed Virgin of the Immaculate Conception was a more recent and more personal addition to the *Pietas Austriaca*.[4] Although legends about Rudolph I's Marian devotion circulated in the seventeenth century, these stories were not nearly as popular as those concerning his devotion to the Eucharist, nor did they concern the Immaculate Conception.[5] Despite the fact that the Immaculate Conception had played an important role in Spanish Habsburg devotions since the reign of Charles V,[6] the doctrine was not elevated to a significant level within Austrian Habsburg piety until the reign of Ferdinand III's father Ferdinand II. Influenced by his Jesuit education and by his mother Mary of Bavaria's strong Marian devotion, the elder Ferdinand espoused a fervent devotion to the Immaculate Conception even before assuming the imperial crown.[7] Already in 1598 Ferdinand (then Archduke of Styria) embarked on a pilgrimage to the Holy House of Loreto in order to pledge to the Immaculata his intention to expel Protestants from Inner Austria,

---

[4] Telling evidence for the recent nature of Habsburg Marian piety comes from a catalogue of Ferdinand III's library prepared in 1652 (A-Wn, Cod. 13556), which contains a section devoted to books on the life and Passion of Christ (fols 402–4v) and another devoted to books on the Virgin Mary (fols 408–9v). Whereas most of the books in the former section date from before Ferdinand III's reign (many from the sixteenth century), the books in the latter section are much more recent; most of them date from the seventeenth century, many from the 1640s and '50s.

[5] The two most important Rudolphine Marian legends are that he never began a major undertaking without invoking Mary's aid and that the foul air of the swamp Todtmoos miraculously cleared after he established a Marian shrine there in 1270. Both tales are in Wenceslaus Adalbert Czerwenka, *Annales et acta pietatis augustissimae ac serenissimae Domus Habspurgo-Austriacae* (Prague, 1694), Book 1, pp. 28–9. See also Anna Coreth, *Pietas Austriaca*, trans. William D. Bowman and Anna Maria Leitgeb (West Lafayette, 2004), pp. 47–8.

[6] Steven N. Orso, *Art and Death at the Spanish Habsburg Court: The Royal Exequies for Philip IV* (Columbia, 1989), pp. 92–3; Suzanne L. Stratton, *The Immaculate Conception in Spanish Art* (Cambridge, 1994). It was under the patronage of the Spanish King that the first systematic defense of the Immaculate Conception was published: Lukas Wadding, *De definienda controversia Immaculatae Conceptionis B. Virginis Mariae* (Louvain, 1624).

[7] The information on Ferdinand II's Marian devotion in this paragraph is drawn from Coreth, pp. 50–52.

and he took a similar pilgrimage to Mariazell in 1621 for divine support in the re-Catholicization of Bohemia after the Battle of White Mountain. Throughout the 1620s he lobbied tirelessly for official papal recognition of the Immaculate Conception, even submitting unsuccessful petitions to the Pope requesting that the doctrine be declared a dogma of the Catholic faith. Despite papal rejection, Ferdinand II continued to seek official status for the devotion in his own realm, and in 1629 the feast of the Immaculate Conception on December 8 was declared binding in the diocese of Vienna.[8]

By the early modern era, belief in Mary's Immaculate Conception—that she had been conceived by human parents without acquiring any touch of original sin—had acquired a long and troubled pedigree.[9] This is one of the few doctrines of the Catholic faith for which there is no direct biblical evidence, which—together with the fact that the doctrine bestows special status on Mary's human (as opposed to Jesus' divine) conception—sparked strong opposition almost from the inception of the belief. As early as the twelfth century, the arguments about its validity were becoming passionate and even violent.[10] Nor had the controversy subsided by the seventeenth century. The clashes over the Immaculate Conception remained so heated, in fact, that Popes Paul V and Gregory XV issued decrees in 1617 and again in 1622 that banned any public statements denying the truth of the doctrine. Although these decrees implicitly upheld the Immaculata, papal support was uneven throughout the century, especially during Ferdinand III's reign. In 1642, for instance, Pope Urban VIII issued the bull *Universa per orbem*, which catalogued the universally required Catholic feasts and conspicuously omitted the Immaculate Conception; two years later he dealt a further blow to official acceptance of the doctrine with a decree forbidding any writer from using the adjective "immaculate" to modify "conception."[11] The controversy surrounding this doctrine persisted well beyond the seventeenth century; not until 1854 did it become dogma of the Catholic Church and receive an official liturgy.

---

[8] Ibid., pp. 53–4 and Steven Saunders, "Sacred Music at the Hapsburg Court of Ferdinand II (1615–1637): The Latin Vocal Works of Giovanni Priuli and Giovanni Valentini" (2 vols, Ph.D. dissertation, University of Pittsburgh, 1990), vol. 1, p. 99 and vol. 2, p. 880 (Document 51).

[9] Marina Warner, *Alone of All Her Sex: The Myth and Cult of the Virgin Mary* (New York, 1976), pp. 236–54; Stratton.

[10] Nancy Mayberry, "The Controversy over the Immaculate Conception in Medieval and Renaissance Art, Literature, and Society," *Journal of Medieval and Renaissance Studies*, 21 (1991): pp. 207–24; Wenceslaus Sebastian, "The Controversy over the Immaculate Conception from after Scotus to the End of the Eighteenth Century," in Edward Dennis O'Connor (ed.), *The Dogma of the Immaculate Conception: History and Significance* (Notre Dame, 1958), pp. 228–41.

[11] Stratton, pp. 98, 101.

The controversial history of the Immaculate Conception was a large part of why it was important to the Habsburgs. Widely publicized adherence to this non-standard doctrine did much to personalize their Catholic image and differentiate their devotion from the widespread Marian cult that had long prevailed throughout Christendom, including at the Bavarian court. In addition, the contentious nature of the Immaculata required its adherents to embrace the doctrine with fervor, thereby granting the Habsburgs the perfect opportunity to display how deeply felt and impassioned was their Catholic piety. From the perspective of confessionalization, moreover, if they could cement their citizens' faith in this controversial and decidedly non-Protestant doctrine, then they were practically assured of the people's full adherence to the Catholic Church (and, by extension, to the crown).[12]

If Ferdinand II elevated the Immaculate Conception within Habsburg devotions, his son raised it to the pinnacle of importance, making it an absolutely integral and central aspect of his Catholic piety.[13] The significance of the Immaculata to the new ruler had been signaled already in 1625 with Ferdinand III's coronation as King of Hungary, which occurred on the feast day of the Immaculate Conception. Another important expression of his devotion to the Immaculata came in 1642, when he refused to publish the bull that excluded the feast of the Immaculate Conception from the official Catholic calendar, thereby asserting the importance of his own beliefs over the Pope's mandates.[14] Despite these public demonstrations, until the mid-1640s most manifestations of Ferdinand III's Marian devotion came in more personal (if not entirely private) forms. For instance, the Emperor explored the theme of the Immaculata in his own Italian poetry; the first stanza of one of his many poems exalting the Virgin Mary reads

---

[12] This last point was voiced in the 1640s in a letter from Prince-Bishop Breuner (Bishop of Vienna) to Ferdinand III; see Coreth, p. 53 and Josef Kurz, *Zur Geschichte der Mariensäule am Hof und der Andachten vor derselben* (Vienna, 1904), p. 8.

[13] On Ferdinand III's adherence to the Immaculate Conception, see Andrew H. Weaver, "Music in the Service of Counter-Reformation Politics: The Immaculate Conception at the Habsburg Court of Ferdinand III (1637–1657)," *Music & Letters*, 87 (2006): pp. 361–78; Coreth, pp. 55–7; and Steven Saunders, "Der Kaiser als Künstler: Ferdinand III and the Politicization of Sacred Music at the Hapsburg Court," in Max Reinhart (ed.), *Infinite Boundaries: Order, Disorder, and Reorder in Early Modern German Culture*, Sixteenth-Century Essays and Studies, vol. 40 (Kirksville, 1998), pp. 200–7.

[14] In 1641 Ferdinand had declared that all papal bulls needed to receive his *placet* before being published in his realms; Robert Bireley, "Confessional Absolutism in the Habsburg Lands in the Seventeenth Century," in Charles W. Ingrao (ed.), *State and Society in Early Modern Austria* (West Lafayette, 1994), p. 45.

Vergine Pia, e Santa, e Immaculata,	Pious Virgin, both Holy and Immaculate,
Che Cinthia tieni sotto i piedi tuoi.	you hold the Moon under your feet.
Ti cinge Phebo ognor' con raggi suoi,	The Sun constantly surrounds you with its rays,
E il capo calchi alla serpe dannata.	and you crush the head of the infernal serpent.

(*Poesie diverse*, sig. B7r)

The personal nature of Ferdinand's devotion to the Immaculata is also evident in the motet books issued by Sances during the early years of the Emperor's reign.

This is especially apparent in Sances's *Motetti a una, due, tre, e quattro voci*, the print dedicated to Ferdinand III himself. We have already noted in Chapter 4 how the partbooks highlight the Emperor's Marian devotion, both through the large number of Marian works and also through the placement of such motets at the beginning and end of each book. Also significant is the fact that many of the Marian works specifically honor the Immaculate Conception, and all of them that do so are of an intensely personal nature.

Three motets, for instance, use imagery from the Song of Songs to express a deep, ardent love for the Blessed Virgin of the Immaculate Conception: *O quam speciosa*, *Tota pulchra es*, and *Vulnerasti cor meum*.[15] The passionate, often erotic celebration of connubial bliss in the Song of Songs had long made it one of the most popular books of the Bible, and during the Counter-Reformation theologians were eager to capitalize on this popularity to draw people back to the Catholic Church. By the seventeenth century, a solid exegetical tradition had been established in which the book was understood as a representation of the relationship between Christ and either the Christian soul, the Church, the Blessed Virgin, or Mary Magdalene.[16] In fact, the Jesuit theologian Cornelius a Lapide (1567–1637), whose immensely popular Bible commentaries were considered the most authoritative works of the day (even by some Protestants), organized every chapter of his *Commentarii in Canticum Canticorum* into three parts, one each for the soul, the Church, and the Virgin.[17] Despite this multi-faceted interpretation, one passage—Songs 4:7—had long been interpreted as a reference only to the Immaculate Conception: "Tota pulchra es amica mea et macula non est in te [You are wholly beautiful, my love, and there is no stain in you]." In fact, when

---

[15] Modern edns in Giovanni Felice Sances, *Motetti a una, due, tre, e quattro voci (1638)*, ed. Steven Saunders, RRMBE, vol. 126 (Middleton, 2003), pp. 15–18, 59–64, 71–8.

[16] Robert L. Kendrick, "'Sonet vox tua in auribus meis': Song of Songs Exegesis and the Seventeenth-Century Motet," *Schütz-Jahrbuch*, 16 (1994): pp. 102–5.

[17] Cornelius a Lapide, *Commentarii in Canticum Canticorum* (Antwerp, 1638; reprint, Antwerp, 1657).

discussing this verse, Lapide argued that it could be applied only to the Virgin Mary, supporting his claim with eight venerable sources.[18]

The wholly beautiful, stainless Virgin of Songs 4:7, or the "Virgin *tota pulchra*," had by the seventeenth century assumed canonical status in the iconography of the Immaculate Conception.[19] The earliest known representations of this image appeared in books of hours published in Paris in the first decade of the sixteenth century, and by the seventeenth century it had undergone very little change.[20] In fact, when the Spanish artist Francisco Pacheco painstakingly described the proper method of depicting the Immaculate Conception in his 1649 treatise *El arte de la pintura*, his rules could almost be applied to the earliest images.[21] The Virgin is always shown as a young, beautiful woman without the Christ child, and she is almost always surrounded by a number of images, many of which are drawn from other verses of the Song of Songs. One of the most common of these passages is Songs 6:9, from which are derived the popular images of the Virgin *tota pulchra* as "electa ut sol" and "pulchra ut luna."[22] These references to the sun and moon provide a connection between the Old Testament *sponsa* and another Biblical image commonly used to represent the Immaculata, the Apocalyptic woman (clothed in the sun with the moon under her feet and crowned with twelve stars) from Revelations 12:1.[23] These passages, along with others from the books of Ecclesiasticus and Wisdom in praise of Divine Wisdom (another Biblical figure interpreted in the seventeenth century as a prefiguration of the Immaculata), provided writers, artists, and musicians with a rich tapestry of images with which to portray the Immaculate Conception.[24]

---

[18] Ibid., p. 192: "Unde haec verba Cantici: *Tota pulchra es, et macula non est in te*, B. Virgini soli appropriant ...."

[19] Stratton, pp. 39–66.

[20] For illustrations of this image, see ibid., pp. 41, 45, 49.

[21] The relevant excerpt from Pacheco's treatise is in Robert Enggass and Jonathan Brown, *Italy and Spain, 1600–1750: Sources and Documents* (Englewood Cliffs, 1970), pp. 165–7.

[22] "Bright as the sun," "beautiful as the moon."

[23] On the Apocalyptic woman as a representation of the Immaculata, see Bonnie J. Blackburn, "The Virgin in the Sun: Music and Image for a Prayer Attributed to Sixtus IV," *Journal of the Royal Musical Association*, 124 (1999): pp. 157–95.

[24] For comprehensive lists of Immaculata references, see Maurice Vloberg, "The Iconography of the Immaculate Conception," in *Dogma of the Immaculate Conception*, p. 476, fn. 39 and Stephan Beissel, *Geschichte der Verehrung Marias im 16. und 17. Jahrhundert* (Freiburg, 1910; reprint, Nieuwkoop, 1970), pp. 249–50. On the exegetical tradition that interpreted Divine Wisdom as a prefiguration of the Immaculate Conception, see Andrew H. Weaver, "Divine Wisdom and Dolorous Mysteries: Habsburg Marian Devotion in Two Motets from Monteverdi's *Selva morale et spirituale*," *Journal of Musicology*, 24 (2007): pp. 250–55.

The most explicitly Immaculist Song of Songs motet from Sances's *Motetti* is a duet for alto and tenor that begins with the very "tota pulchra" verse itself.[25] Another motet, *O quam speciosa*—the opening work in the alto partbook—is the perfect expression of the Virgin *tota pulchra*, even though its text is not drawn verbatim from the Bible:

O quam speciosa, o quam suavis, o quam jucunda es, filia Sion.	O how beautiful, O how sweet, O how happy you are, daughter of Zion.
Stella fulgens, placida ut columba,[a] electa ut sol,[b] nive candidissima.	Shining star, gentle as a dove, bright as the sun, most dazzling white cloud.
O quam speciosa … filia Sion.	O how beautiful … daughter of Zion.
Ecce anima mea in deliciis tuis gaudet, et in venustate tua exultat.	Behold, my soul rejoices in your delights, and exults in your beauty.
O quam speciosa … filia Sion.	O how beautiful … daughter of Zion.
Cantabo tibi, et psalam nomini tuo ex hoc nunc et usque in saeculum. Alleluia.	I shall sing to you and praise your name from now on and in eternity. Alleluia.

After an opening triple-meter refrain that praises the Virgin with adjectives redolent of the Song of Songs, the second section (bars 16–26) provides a string of popular attributes of the Immaculate Virgin: shining star, gentle dove, dazzling white cloud, and bright sun. This last attribute is described using the quote from Songs 6:9 discussed above; Sances dwells on it extensively, stating it five times in the space of eight measures.

That Sances included Song of Songs texts in his motet book is not in itself remarkable, as this Biblical book had long been one of the most popular sources for motet texts among European composers, and Sances's musical settings are not strikingly different from Songs motets by his Italian contemporaries. The significance of these works lies rather in that they eloquently express the personal nature of the Emperor's devotion to the Immaculate Conception; like the psalm motets discussed in the first section of Chapter 5 and the mystical motets discussed in Chapter 6, these works are spoken in the first person singular, thereby painting portraits of Ferdinand III communicating directly with the Blessed Virgin (while simultaneously inviting listeners to forge their own intimate relationship with Mary). This is especially true of *Vulnerasti cor meum*, a passionate

---

[25] The full text of *Tota pulchra es* is Songs 4:7, 4:9, 2:10, and 2:14.

love duet for soprano and tenor that sets Songs 4:8–10 and culminates in an extended passage over the major descending tetrachord ostinato, a conventional musical symbol for romantic love.[26]

Although the works do not appear as a single group in the partbooks, Sances may very well have intended users of the print to understand them as a set, for they share musical features: they all have a modal final of F, they feature many harmonic shifts between the one-flat and two-flat hexachords, and they even share melodic similarities.[27] Sances did, moreover, place the works in close proximity in individual partbooks. *Vulnerasti cor meum* and *Tota pulchra es* appear adjacent to each other as the third and fourth works in the tenor partbook. In the soprano partbook, *Vulnerasti cor meum* appears immediately after the complex of four psalm settings discussed in Chapter 5, while *Tota pulchra es* appears in the alto partbook in the same location after this complex of psalms.

A more significant expression of Ferdinand III's personal devotion to the Immaculate Conception is provided by *Ardet cor meum*, the work that receives pride of place as the first piece in the soprano partbook.[28] The text opens with an intensely passionate declaration of love featuring such highly charged words as "ardet" and "languet," echoing the mystical yearning of the Christological motets discussed in Chapter 6 and making explicit the very personal nature of the work:

---

[26] In its compositional structure in which each voice sings a phrase in turn before the two voices sing it together in homophony, the work also partakes of the conventions of the love duet from the Venetian operatic stage; see Ellen Rosand, *Opera in Seventeenth-Century Venice: The Creation of a Genre* (Berkeley, 1991), pp. 335–8.

[27] I have argued elsewhere that these works form a "family" of imperial Song of Songs motets, which also includes a motet by Giovanni Giacomo Arrigoni; see Andrew H. Weaver, "Piety, Politics, and Patronage: Motets at the Habsburg Court in Vienna During the Reign of Ferdinand III (1637–1657)," (Ph.D. diss., Yale University, 2002), pp. 369–83.

[28] Modern edn in Sances, *Motetti*, ed. Saunders, pp. 3–8.

Ardet cor meum,[c]	My heart burns,
et anima mea languet in te.	and my soul languishes for you.
Tu succurre illi, dulcissima Mater.	Come to its aid, most sweet Mother.
O quam pulcra es, amica mea,	O how beautiful you are, my love,
et macula non est in te.[d]	and there is no stain in you.
Intende mihi et exaudi me,[e]	Pay heed to me and hear me;
exaudi orationem meam.	hear my prayer.
Tibi Virgo dulcissima,	To you, most sweet Virgin,
Tibi laus et gloria.	To you belongs praise and glory.
Respice in me, et miserere mei,[f]	Look upon me, and have mercy on me,
et non confundar.[g]	and I shall not be confounded.
Laetare cor meum et gaude,	Rejoice, my heart, and be glad
quia spes tua in ipsa est.	because your hope is in her.
Alleluia.	Alleluia.

The remainder of the text portrays Mary in her most important roles at the Habsburg court, as protector, comforter, and source of hope during troubled times. Several of the lines are redolent of the psalms and are echoed in the next motet in the print, *Laetamini in Domino*, which was interpreted in Chapter 5 as a portrait of the Emperor;[29] this similarity in adjacent works helps connect them to each other as representations of Ferdinand III. The text of *Ardet cor meum* is nevertheless entirely conventional, alternating general pleas for aid with stock expressions of praise. The language after the first section is generic and almost clichéd, and the work ends with the typical closing conceit of an affirmative statement plus "alleluia." Sances nevertheless set these words to music of powerful emotional intensity, moving beyond convention and imbuing the text with new meaning.

The motet opens with intense declamatory singing punctuated with powerful chromatic shifts to enharmonic neighbor notes (Example 7.1). This strikingly affective recitative style recurs for each of the imploring passages of text, alternating with sections in triple meter that differ in almost every way from the duple-meter sections (see Example 7.2). The music of these contrasting passages conforms to the standard triple-meter aria style, with regular, balanced phrases of flowing, melodious lines and conventional harmonies that emphasize different tonal areas from the recitative passages. The harmonic contrast is most striking in the first two sections: the opening duple-meter section emphasizes *durus* harmonies (including B-major and E-major chords), and the contrasting triple-meter

---

[29] The lines in *Letamini in Domino* are "et ab inimicis eripe me, et non confundar, quoniam speravi in te."

Example 7.1   Sances, *Ardet cor meum*, bars 1–12

passage dwells almost entirely on *mollis* sonorities (such as B-flat and F). This *durus–mollis* contrast holds a symbolic significance. It is consistently the portions of the music that portray human uncertainty and pleas for divine assistance that Sances accompanies with "harsh" *durus* harmonies, while the laudatory passages in praise of the Virgin are set to *mollis* harmonies with their connotations of softness and mildness. This use of *mollis* harmonies by Ferdinand III's musicians became a harmonic symbol for the Immaculate Conception; recall, for instance, that all of the Song of Songs works discussed above are centered on the one-flat and two-flat hexachords.[30] By differentiating the human and the divine through strikingly contrasting harmonic palettes, Sances was able to create a clear and instantly recognizable musical reference to the Virgin *tota pulchra*.

---

[30] In Sances's *Tota pulchra es*, the first move from the 1-flat to the 2-flat hexachord occurs in bars 21–40, on the first statement of the phrase "et macula non est in te." The Immaculata symbolism of *mollis* sonorities in music from Ferdinand III's court was first discussed in Saunders, "Kaiser als Künstler," pp. 203–7.

Example 7.2   Sances, *Ardet cor meum*, bars 25–34

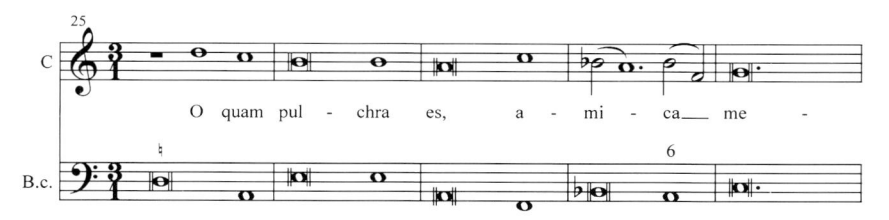

On a general level, the through-composed structure of *Ardet cor meum*, created by eight contrasting sections that alternate duple-meter recitative and triple-meter aria, is entirely standard for the small-scale motet in the middle of the century. A closer examination of the motet, however, reveals a more nuanced, large-scale bipartite structure in which the concluding positive statement is expanded and receives as much attention as the sections preceding it, thus emphasizing a crucial change from despair to triumph under the Virgin's protection.

This two-part division is most apparent if we examine in detail the fifth section of the motet (bars 84–101), one of the duple-meter sections and the one that enacts the pivotal shift from imploring to rejoicing (Example 7.3). The text here contains the very crux of the motet's meaning, for the singer finally pleads for the Virgin's intercession. Still in this same section, Mary's good will is anticipated with the declaration that the singer "shall not be confounded." Sances has depicted these contrasting ideas both melodically and harmonically, the only time in the entire work when such contrasts occur within a single section. Bars 84–91 conform to the other duple-meter sections of the motet: the declamatory melody features primarily stepwise melodic motion and many consecutive repetitions of a single pitch. *Durus* sonorities are signaled by the transposition of the first measure up a whole step, juxtaposing G- and E-major triads with a corresponding shift from G to G-sharp in the voice. Until bar 91 the harmonies remain entirely on the sharp side of the natural hexachord, with chords on D, A, and E. In bar 92, on the text "et non confundar," sudden and striking changes occur: the continuo becomes considerably

Example 7.3   Sances, *Ardet cor meum*, bars 84–103

Example 7.3   *concluded*

more rhythmically animated, the vocal line becomes more disjunct, and the formerly discursive melody is now organized into repetitions of small modules. The harmonies also flirt briefly with the flat side of the natural hexachord at the precise moment of change, with triads on F and C in bars 93–4. Bars 98–101 then introduce material unlike anything heard so far in the work: the text "et non confundar" is stated for the sixth and final time, now sung to the longest rhythmic values of the motet. These curious four bars seem to signal that a major change is about to occur, and indeed, this is the critical juncture before the second large-scale section begins.

The motet as a whole thus falls into two large sections (the first consisting of five smaller subsections and the second of three), each of which is articulated with an opening invocation to "my heart." When considered independently, both sections display a roughly symmetrical chiastic structure. The first large section begins and ends with duple-meter passages (of 24 and 18 bars respectively), with another central 19-bar duple-meter subsection flanked by two shorter triple-meter passages. The second large section, in contrast, features two long triple-meter passages (of 36 and 28 bars respectively) surrounding a considerably shorter 11-bar subsection in duple meter. Sances created these three subsections by splitting up the final affirmative statement: the first subsection consists of many repetitions of the words "laetare cor meum et gaude," the second sets the words "quia spes tua in ipsa est," and the final subsection uses a substantial setting of "alleluia" to balance out the triple-meter "laetare."

The predominant character of the first large section comes from the duple portions, with their extremely affective *durus* harmonies, declamatory melodies, and irregular phrase structures. The two triple-meter passages give a foretaste of what is to come; they provide antidotes to the excruciating harshness of the duple music and yet are so terse that they cannot be considered independent, closed forms in their own right. The second large section is then dominated by the aria style and *mollis* sonorities, providing a full expression of the earlier triple-meter interpolations and, one could say, acting as the culmination of the entire work. Even the central duple subsection (bars 138–48) borrows the regularity and stability of its framing passages, exhibiting a balanced duple-meter aria style that had been only hinted at in the repeating modules and "walking bass" at the end of the fifth subsection. The very stable second large section successfully balances and even overcomes the jarring, volatile opening of the motet, firmly establishing a confident, jubilant mood.

This triumphant conclusion is highly significant: despite present uncertainties, the motet expresses total faith in Mary's divine aid. Even without direct references to enemies or war, this work acts as a powerful representation of Ferdinand III during a pivotal time of the Thirty Years' War, expressing his personal devotion to the Blessed Virgin of the Immaculate Conception and celebrating the joy and comfort she offers during times of tribulation. Like the mystical motets discussed in Chapter 6, *Ardet cor meum* served as both a mirror of the Emperor's soul and a model for others to imitate, directed toward an elite audience consisting of such people as courtiers attending intimate devotional services in the Hofburg and purchasers of Sances's print.

From Private to Public: Ferdinand III's *Mariensäule*

As the Thirty Years' War entered its darkest hour and Ferdinand III's image morphed from victorious warrior to protective father, the manifestations of the Emperor's Marian devotion shifted significantly from personal devotion to public piety of the kind seen in Habsburg veneration of the Eucharist. In March 1645, with the enemy rapidly approaching, Ferdinand III turned to the very source of comfort celebrated in *Ardet cor meum*. On March 29 the Emperor and his entire court participated in a grand, solemn procession, illustrated in Figure 7.1.[31] The procession began with all of the religious orders of the city, followed by the Bishop of Vienna and the papal ambassadors. The centerpiece of the procession was a revered wooden statue of the Blessed Virgin usually housed in the

---

[31] Albertina, Vienna, Historische Blätter Wien 1. This engraving was made well after the actual procession, for it includes a picture of the *Mariensäule am Hof*, which was not erected until two years after the procession.

Figure 7.1 Procession from the *Schottenkirche* to St Stephen's Cathedral on March 29, 1645, anonymous engraving

Schottenkirche, immediately behind which followed Ferdinand III and his wife. Beginning at the *Schottenkirche*, the procession wound through the city and concluded at St Stephen's Cathedral, where the Marian statue was prominently displayed and would continue to be honored for a week. Once at the cathedral, the Emperor prayed publicly for the Immaculata to watch over and protect his city, promising that if the city were saved, he would declare the feast of the Immaculate Conception binding in his entire realm and not just in the diocese of Vienna. Moreover, he swore that he would erect a public statue to the Virgin as a permanent symbol of his devotion, where litanies and prayers could be offered.[32] By acting as an intercessor between his troubled people and the Virgin, Ferdinand put himself in the place of a saint, putting into practice the image presented in Sances's motets discussed in Chapter 5.[33]

Two years later these promises became a reality, and on May 18, 1647 Ferdinand's new *Mariensäule* (Marian column) on the *Platz am Hof* in front of the Jesuit church was consecrated in a grand ceremony. A detailed published report of the events of this day, the frontispiece of which features an engraving of the column, was issued the following year by Vilem Slavata, Chancellor of Bohemia (and dedicatee of Sances's 1642 motet book).[34] Johann Christian Lünig also included a description of the ceremony in his *Theatrum Ceremoniale* published nearly a hundred years later, in 1720.[35] At 8:00 that morning, an immense crowd gathered at the Augustinian church near the Hofburg; among them were the Emperor with his entire family and court; ambassadors representing the Pope, Spain, and Venice; prominent members of religious orders; all the aristocrats of the city; and a huge throng of the common citizens. The crowd processed to the Jesuit church *am Hof*, where the Emperor's Jesuit confessor Johann

---

[32] On these events and the resulting Marian column, see Ludwig Donin, *Die marianische Austria*, 3rd edn (Vienna, 1884), pp. 80–87; Kurz, pp. 7–11, 21–5; Coreth, pp. 52–5; Herma Piesch, "Domina Austriae," in Josef Stummvoll (ed.), *Die Österreichische Nationalbibliothek Festschrift: Herausgegeben zum 25 jährigen Dienstjubiläum des Generaldirektors Uni.-Prof. Dr. Josef Bick* (Vienna, 1943), pp. 523–33; and Susan Tipton, "'Super aspidem et basiliscum ambulabis ...': Zur Entstehung der Mariensäulen im 17. Jahrhundert," in Dieter Breuer et al. (eds), *Religion und Religiosität im Zeitalter des Barock* (2 vols, Wiesbaden, 1995), vol. 1, pp. 375–98.

[33] In putting himself in the place of a saint, Ferdinand III was following a dynastic tradition, one that would be continued by Leopold I: Maria Goloubeva, *The Glorification of Emperor Leopold I in Image, Spectacle and Text* (Mainz, 2000), pp. 196–9.

[34] Vilem Slavata, *Maria virgo immaculate concepta: Publico voto Ferdinandi III. Rom. Imp. in Austriae patronam electa* (Vienna, 1648). On Slavata, see pp. 135–7. The engraved frontispiece is reproduced in Piesch, "Domina Austriae," p. 529 and Weaver, "Music in the Service," p. 371.

[35] Johann Christian Lünig, *Theatrum Ceremoniale historico-politicum*, vol. 2 (Leipzig, 1720), pp. 311–12.

Gans gave a sermon in praise of the Immaculata, followed by a solemn Mass officiated by the Bishop of Vienna. During communion Ferdinand III approached the altar, and as the Eucharist was elevated he knelt and recited in a loud clear voice the oath that is now inscribed on two sides of the Marian column. In this oath he officially placed all of his realms under the protection and patronage of the Immaculata and solemnly swore that her feast day of December 8 and its octave would be celebrated every year throughout his lands.[36] Henceforth, the Litany of Loreto would be sung in front of the *Mariensäule* every Saturday and on every Marian feast; the Emperor established an endowment to ensure that this new tradition would continue after his reign.[37]

The *Mariensäule* still stands in Vienna's *Platz am Hof*; in 1667 Leopold I replaced his father's stone column with one made of bronze, but the design of the current statue is identical to the original.[38] The idea of a column topped with a statue of the Blessed Virgin was not original; Ferdinand borrowed the concept from a similar column that Duke Maximilian I of Bavaria had erected in Munich in 1638 under similar circumstances (and which in turn was modeled upon the Marian column that stands before the church of Santa Maria Maggiore in Rome).[39] As does the Bavarian column, Ferdinand's *Mariensäule* reminds the viewer of the Virgin's role as protector during a religious war through the four armed angels at the base of the column, each of which vanquishes a dragon representing heresy.[40] This aspect of the Viennese column is reinforced in an engraving of it included in a thesis submitted to the University of Vienna in 1650 (Figure 7.2), in which two soldiers stand at the base of the column while over their heads fly two angels, one holding a rosary and the other a sword.[41] Despite

---

[36] In addition to being inscribed on the column, the full text of the oath is reprinted in Slavata, *Maria virgo immaculate concepta*, sigs B2r–v; A-Wn, Cod. 11540, fols 28v–29r; Lünig, *Theatrum Ceremoniale*, pp. 311–12. Among modern sources, the text can be found in Weaver, "Piety, Politics, and Patronage," p. 416, Piesch, "Domina Austriae," p. 527, and in German translation in Donin, pp. 83–4.

[37] Kurz, p. 23 and Tipton, "'Super aspidem'," p. 382. The weekly Litany performances were still taking place in 1884, though in St Stephen's Cathedral instead of outside by the column (Donin, p. 82).

[38] The original column now stands in the Austrian town of Wernstein am Inn; a photo of the original column in its new location is in Tipton, "'Super aspidem'," p. 395. When Leopold I replaced the column, he substituted "III" for "TertIVs" in the inscription on the base, thereby altering the chronogram to an incorrect date.

[39] For more information on the Bavarian column, including seventeenth-century engravings of it, see ibid., pp. 376–9, 385–92.

[40] On the iconographical significance of the angels on both columns, see ibid., pp. 385–90.

[41] Matthias Bastianschiz, *Oliva Pacis, sive Virgo sine macula concepta* (Vienna, 1650). The engraving appears on an unpaginated folio inserted after p. 14.

Figure 7.2 Sebastian Jenet, engraving of the *Mariensäule* from Matthias Bastianschiz, *Oliva Pacis*, 1650

the similarities to the Bavarian column, there is one significant difference between the two monuments. Unlike the Munich column, which is topped by the traditional image of the Virgin holding the baby Jesus, Ferdinand III's *Mariensäule* was the first such monument on which the figure of Mary was clearly a depiction of the Immaculate Conception: an amalgamation of the woman crushing the head of the serpent from Genesis 3:15 and the apocalyptic woman crowned with stars from Revelations 12:1 (the same image described in his poem).

Another important feature of the column is the fact that it played a significant role in the development of Viennese Baroque sculpture; Gerhardt Kapner has argued that it was the first major example of the Habsburgs' public support of a saint with a visual image as had been decreed by the Council of Trent.[42] Indeed, it set an important precedent, for following its consecration in 1647, similar Immaculata columns began to appear in other cities of the Habsburgs' realms, including one erected in 1650 in Prague's Old Town Square in direct imitation of the Viennese column.[43] No visitor to Vienna, furthermore, can miss the grandest monument inspired by Ferdinand's *Mariensäule*: the immense Baroque *Pestsäule* that Leopold I erected in the *Graben* in 1679.

The Emperor's public acts in honor of the Immaculate Conception did not end with the consecration of the column. Two years later, in May 1649, Ferdinand III issued a decree that required all faculty members and graduates of the University of Vienna to swear an oath of allegiance to the Immaculata. The entire university faculty was also henceforth required to participate in an annual procession from St Stephen's Cathedral to the *Platz am Hof* on December 8.[44] Attesting to this new tradition is a series of printed sermons in honor of the Immaculate Conception preserved in the Österreichische Nationalbibliothek, which bear dedications to Ferdinand

---

[42] Gerhardt Kapner, *Barocker Heiligenkult in Wien und seine Träger* (Vienna, 1978), p. 26.

[43] On the Prague column, see Tipton, "'Super aspidem'," pp. 380–81, 388–90, 393; Howard Louthan, *Converting Bohemia: Force and Persuasion in the Catholic Reformation* (Cambridge, 2009), pp. 160–62. Additional Marian columns were erected in the eighteenth century in both Vienna (in front of the Maria Treu Kirche) and Prague (in Hradcanske Square). Louthan, pp. 273–5, claims that by 1740 there were nearly 200 similar Marian columns in Bohemia and Moravia; Tipton offers a more modest estimate of "no fewer than" 162 Marian columns and 35 Trinity columns ("'Super aspidem,'" p. 375).

[44] The decree was printed in full in the introduction to a sermon by Johannes Ernestus Lindelauf, *Maria Virgo sine macula concepta, in rosa repraesentata* (Vienna, 1653), sigs A2r–A3r, and the oath is also given in A-Wn, Cod. 11540, fol. 27v. A transcription is in Weaver, "Piety, Politics, and Patronage," p. 417.

III.[45] The Emperor himself wrote a setting of the Marian hymn *Ave maris stella* that was most likely intended to accompany the inaugural procession in 1649.[46]

As Anna Coreth has pointed out, Ferdinand III's official acts of 1647 and 1649, in which he dedicated his entire realm to the Immaculate Conception rather than simply introducing the feast into the liturgical calendar, go far beyond the initial promise he had made in 1645.[47] By placing the Habsburg lands under the protection of the Immaculate Virgin, the 1647 ceremony in effect transferred Ferdinand's private devotion to his subjects, thereby transforming his personal beliefs into a civic cult that bound the community together under the patronage of the Immaculata.[48] The *Mariensäule*—and the annual processions and sermons instituted in 1649—served as an important locus for this public cult, which helped introduce in the Habsburg hereditary lands a new brand of Catholicism marked by processions, pilgrimages, public liturgies, and other popular elements that increasingly invited active participation by the common people.[49]

Because the Immaculata cult originated from the Emperor's personal beliefs, the column and its ceremonies also served a powerful representational function. Due to its role as a reminder of Ferdinand III's piety, it is perhaps not a stretch to interpret the *Mariensäule* as a statue *of the Emperor himself*. The column serves as a stand-in for Ferdinand III, reinforcing both his pious, protective image and his Counter-Reformation aims more powerfully than his own likeness ever would.[50] When similar

---

[45] Four sermons survive from the years 1649–51 and 1653: Cornelius Gentilotto, *Maria Virgo sine macula concepta Ferdinando III. Romanorum Imperatori in arcu coelesti repraesentata ipso die Immaculatae Conceptioni Sacro, dum primum Antiq. et Celeber. Universitate Viennensi solenniter hoc festum celebrante in Basilica D. Stephani, Sacra Maiestas Augustissimam sua praesentia reddidit solennitatem* (Vienna, 1649); *Maria Virgo sine macula concepta Ferdinando III. Romanorum Imperatori in columba repraesentata* (Vienna, 1650); Gotthulphus Khueffstain, *Maria Virgo sine macula concepta Ferdinando III. Romanorum Imperatori in speculo repraesentata* (Vienna: Cosmerovius, 1651); Lindelauf, *Maria Virgo sine macula concepta*.

[46] On this work, see Weaver, "Music in the Service," pp. 375–7 and Saunders, "Kaiser als Künstler," pp. 201–8. A modern edn is in Andrew H. Weaver (ed.), *Motets by Emperor Ferdinand III and Other Musicians from the Habsburg Court*, Collegium Musicum: Yale University, second series (Middleton, in press).

[47] Coreth, p. 52.

[48] On the importance of civic cults in the early modern era, see Edward Muir, *Ritual in Early Modern Europe*, 2nd edn (Cambridge, 2005), pp. 255–62.

[49] Louthan, p. 257, makes this point regarding Marian devotion in Bohemia.

[50] The representational function of Leopold I's *Pestsäule* is strengthened by the fact that an image of the Emperor appears at the base of the column. Leopold's appearance on the *Pestsäule* merely makes explicit the function of the monument on which it is modeled.

Marian columns went up in other Habsburg towns, Ferdinand III's image was thus being promulgated throughout his lands; that the columns were viewed as representations of the Habsburgs is powerfully expressed by the fact that the Czech people destroyed the *Mariensäule* in Prague's Old Town Square in 1918, in order to free the city from an oppressive symbol of Habsburg hegemony.[51]

Music for the Consecration of the *Mariensäule*

The communicative function of the 1647 ceremony as a representation of the Emperor was reinforced not only by the ritual itself but also by the music of Ferdinand III's chapel that inevitably accompanied it. That people associated music with the *Mariensäule* comes through in Figure 7.2, in which the clouds framing the Virgin contain a host of angels singing and playing instruments.

We can be sure that the imperial musicians would have performed during the Mass that occurred after the procession from the Augustinian church, even though this is not mentioned in the existing reports. These reports do, however, describe the chapel's participation in the events that occurred after the Mass. After the communion, the entire assembly exited in grand ceremonial fashion to the plaza in front of the church, where the Bishop formally consecrated the column. As the Emperor knelt upon a stage erected in the *Platz am Hof* just for the occasion, the imperial chapel, joined by "Symphoniacorum omnium e tota urbe collectorum, et in plures qua vocum, qua instrumentorum, ac etiam tubarum campestrium, ac tympanorum choros divisorum [all the choirs of the city, divided into many choruses of both voices and instruments, and even field trumpets and timpani]," performed the Litany of Loreto in a performance so moving that, according to Slavata, it "calidam in circumprostrato populo devotionem, certamque praesidii fiduciam excitarunt [excited in the pious people both passionate devotion and unwavering faith in the Virgin's providence]."[52] Following the performance, the crowds dispersed. At 7:00 that evening, however, Ferdinand returned to the *Mariensäule*, where

---

[51] Cynthia Paces, "The Fall and Rise of Prague's Marian Column," *Radical History Review*, 79 (2001): pp. 141–55.

[52] Slavata, *Maria virgo immaculate concepta*, sig. B3r: "Insecutus est Symphoniacorum omnium e tota urbe collectorum, et in plures qua vocum, qua instrumentorum, ac etiam tubarum campestrium, ac tympanorum choros divisorum plausus, qui cum Lauretanam elogiorum seriem Augustissimae Matri decantarent, calidam in circumprostrato populo devotionem, certamque praesidii fiduciam excitarunt." The report in Lünig's *Theatrum Ceremoniale* estimates (quite likely with considerable exaggeration) that the musicians numbered 300 (p. 311).

his musicians once again performed a litany with the accompaniment of trumpets and timpani. The music for these litanies has not survived, but we can get an idea of what they were like from descriptions of two litanies by Sances listed a catalogue of Leopold I's music library with the label "per l'Assunta alla Collonna."[53] Both works require the accompaniment of a full instrumental ensemble that includes violins, violas, cornetti, trombones, and clarini; one is composed for two distinct choirs, and the other includes a toccata for trumpets.

Although the litanies do not survive, we are fortunate to possess a music print that was undoubtedly published as a commemoration of the 1647 events: Sances's *Antiphonare Sacrae B.M.V. per totum annum una voce decantandae*, published in 1648 (the same year as Slavata's description).[54] Although on the surface this is merely a generic, utilitarian collection of the four Marian antiphons (featuring five solo settings of each one, four for soprano and one for bass), paratexts connect the print to the consecration of the *Mariensäule*. The first of these is the dedication to Antonio Spindler; as abbot of the *Schottenkirche*, Spindler would have reminded readers of the 1645 procession (centered upon that church's Marian statue) that served as the instigation for the building of the column.[55] Even more significant are two motets for solo bass that appear at the end of the print, O *Domina gloriae* and O *dulcis Virgo*.[56] According to rubrics above each work (and in the *tavola*), they were written especially for the court singer Carlo Benedetto Riccioni, who had been a member of the imperial chapel since at least 1646.[57] The print thus connects the works directly to the Emperor's chapel, implying that they were intended for imperial performance. The texts of both motets (Table 7.1), moreover, clearly relate to the circumstances surrounding the *Mariensäule*, expressing contrasting aspects of the column's function.

---

[53] A-Wn, Suppl. mus. 2451, fol. 65v.

[54] Giovanni Felice Sances, *Antiphonare Sacrae B.M.V. per totum annum una voce decantandae* (Venice, 1648).

[55] For more information on Spindler, see P. Cölestin Wolfsgruber (ed.), *Die Correspondenz des Schottenabtes Anton Spindler von Hofegg* (Vienna, 1893).

[56] Modern edns of both works are in Weaver, *Motets*.

[57] Each motet is labeled "Motetto Della Glo. B. V. Ad instanza del Sig. Carlo Benedetto Riccioni Musico di Sua Maestà Cesarea." On Riccioni's service in the imperial chapel, see Weaver, "Piety, Politics, and Patronage," p. 85.

Table 7.1   Texts of Sances's *O Domina gloriae* and *O dulcis Virgo*

O Domina gloriae, O Regina laetitiae, O fons pietatis, O vena misericordiae, O sanctitatis libertas, O jucunditatis amoenitas, O splendor caeli, O dulcedo paradisi, O Domina Angelorum, O Sanctorum laetitia, O Virginum gemma, O felix et beata tibi, Domina mea Virgo Maria. Hodie commendo totum corpus et animam meam, quinque sensus corporis mei et totam vitam meam, omnia facta mea, mortem meam, cum sis benedicta in aeternum. Amen.	O Lady of glory, O Queen of joy, O font of piety, O channel of compassion, O liberty of sanctity, O charm of delight, O splendor of the skies, O sweetness of paradise, O Lady of the Angels, O joy of the Saints, O jewel of Virgins, O fortunate and blessed are you, my Lady Virgin Mary. Today I commend to you my whole body and my soul, the five senses of my body and my entire life, all of my deeds, and my death, because you are blessed in eternity. Amen.
O dulcis Virgo Virginum, Quae genuisti Dominum, Triumfatorem zabuli, Reparatorem saeculi. Ego peccator nimium, A te peto remedium. Esto patrona misero, Salus atquae defensio. Incumbunt hostes undique Mortem quaerentes animae. O dulcis Virgo Virginum… Reparatorem saeculi. Imploro te piissima, Pro impetranda gratia, Ut mihi Christi passio Culparum sit remissio Virtutum augmentatio. Amen.	O sweet Virgin of Virgins, who gave birth to the Lord, vanquisher of the Devil, restorer of the ages. I, too much of a sinner, beseech from you a remedy. Be patron to my miserable self, my salvation and defense. Enemies close in from all sides seeking the death of my soul. O sweet Virgin of Virgins… restorer of the ages. I implore you, most pious one, that I may achieve grace, that the passion of Christ may absolve me of my sins and increase my virtue. Amen.

Example 7.4 Sances, *O dulcis Virgo*, bars 48–55

O dulcis Virgo is penitential in tone, beseeching the Virgin for aid and intercession. Sandwiched between two statements of a triple-meter refrain is a section in duple meter whose text relates directly to the events that led to the construction of the column: not only does it mention that "enemies close in from all sides," but the singer also entreats the Virgin to "be patron to my miserable self, my salvation and defense." This final statement is repeated three times in close succession, set to a distinctive figure over a phrygian cadence (Example 7.4). *O Domina gloriae*, in contrast, is fully celebratory, opening with a string of laudatory addresses to the Virgin. This long series of standard acclamations, many of which are drawn from well-known antiphons, transforms the motet into a monumental emblem comprised of liturgical mottos, thereby serving as a literary-musical analogue to the emblematic column itself. It also follows the structure of a litany (minus the intervening supplications), thereby carrying associations with the use of litanies in procession and the litanies sung at the *Mariensäule*. The centerpiece of the work is a section labeled "recitato" in the score (bars 74–85) in which the singer declares that "today" he is commending to the Blessed Virgin his body, soul, five senses, entire life, all of his deeds, and even his death (Example 7.5). The melodic line in this section cannot help but catch the listener's attention, with its gradual ascent through semitones accompanied by juxtaposed third-related chords in the bass (for instance, F–D in bar 78 and G–E in bars 79–80).

The use of the first person singular in both motets, together with the use of the solo bass, seems to present (as in works such as *Audi Domine*

Example 7.5   Sances, *O Domina gloriae*, bars 71–85

and *Miserere servorum tuorum*, discussed in Chapter 5) the voice of Ferdinand III as he participates in the consecration of the *Mariensäule*. Despite this personal connection to the Emperor, these works serve a significantly different communicative function from the Marian motets Sances had published ten years earlier. Instead of the deeply personal declarations of love and the mystical overtones of the 1638 works, the 1648 motets feature emotionally neutral prayers expressed largely through conventional language. By virtue of their dissemination via print (through which they could be performed by countless other individuals, perhaps in commemorations of the 1647 ceremony or even for the consecration of other Marian columns), these two motets enact the same shift from private to public embedded in the column itself: the individual "I" commending himself to the Virgin is transferred from Ferdinand III to the corporate identity of his subjects. The "I" of the motets simultaneously represents both the Emperor and his people; Ferdinand's voice becomes the voice of the community. These works thus serve as expressions of both personal devotion and public piety, as the individual partakes in the civic cult created by the consecration of the column. Like the *Mariensäule* itself, these motets serve as a powerful reminder both of the Emperor's immense piety and of the Virgin Mary's constant protection of imperial subjects, communicating even to the present day the most important aspect of Ferdinand's public image, one that—through its transformation into a popular state cult—long outlasted his reign.

Conclusion

Besieged by enemies and with little hope for success, Ferdinand III took quite a gamble in 1645 with his strong public declaration of allegiance to the Immaculate Conception. Yet in the end his gamble paid off handsomely. When the Swedes retreated from the imperial city in September 1645 without inflicting a single wound, no one in Vienna could have realized that this occurred primarily because Sweden was deprived of her Transylvanian allies on account of a skirmish with the Turks.[58] To the Viennese citizens cowering in fear within the city walls, the only explanation for this miracle was the divine intervention of the Blessed Virgin of the Immaculate Conception, who clearly had answered the Emperor's prayer. By demonstrating his deep piety in the face of certain defeat, a piety that had long been exposed to the Viennese people through the music that, more than any other art, promulgated his image as a wise protective father, Ferdinand III brilliantly turned the very lowest point of the war to his advantage. The Emperor could henceforth count on his people's full reverence for the Blessed Virgin and, correspondingly, on their allegiance to both the Catholic Church and his political authority; the central section of *O Domina gloriae* could just as well have been a declaration of allegiance to the Emperor as to the Virgin. In fact, by the 1650s the re-Catholicization of Ferdinand III's own lands, especially Austria and Bohemia, had proved remarkably successful, and Habsburg sovereignty in these realms had been firmly established. This was a tremendous victory for the Habsburg dynasty, a victory that even the forced concessions of the Peace of Westphalia could not diminish.

---

[58] Parker, p. 158; Guthrie, *Later*, pp. 143–4.

Notes to Motet Texts

a. Allusion to Songs 6:8.
b. Songs 6:9.
c. Allusion to the Mary Magdelene antiphon, "Ardens est cor meum."
d. Songs 4:7.
e. Psalm 54:3.
f. Psalm 24:16; Psalm 85:16.
g. Allusion to the last line of the Te Deum.

Epilogue
Ferdinand III's Image after the War

The end of the Thirty Years' War seems to have come rather quietly at the Habsburg court. The signing of the Peace of Westphalia was not, after all, the happiest of occasions for all parties. While the German Protestant states openly celebrated the political recognition of their religion, this very recognition was the final nail in the coffin for Catholic hegemony in the Empire, causing the Pope to publish an inevitable protest against the peace treaty.[1] The Emperor, too, had to face the many concessions he had made for the achievement of peace; not only had he essentially surrendered his sovereignty in the German states, but he had also reluctantly cut himself off from his Spanish cousins, leaving them to face defeat at the hands of the French army. The lack of any reports of grand public celebrations of the peace in Vienna should thus come as no surprise; the only indication that a commemoration of some sort may have happened is an entry in the catalogue of Leopold I's music library citing a "Te Deum della Pace" by Bertali for three concertato choirs, including trumpets.[2]

The only known public events in Vienna in honor of the peace treaty occurred in the Jesuit theater. Two plays, both of which praise Ferdinand III, were explicitly connected to the peace. One is the undated *Fortuna Eucharistico-Austriaca Pietati et Justitiae* discussed in Chapter 6, which lauds the Emperor together with the entire Habsburg line while celebrating the Eucharist as the foundation of their power.[3] The *argumentum* of the printed scenario cites two Bible verses as the source of the play: Psalm 71:7 ("Orietur in diebus ejus Iustitia, & abundantia Pacis, donec auferatur Luna") and Baruch 5:4 ("Pax Iustitiae & Honor Pietatis"), the latter of which incorporates both words of Ferdinand III's motto.[4] The fifth and final act also cites Isaiah 32:17 ("Et erit opus Iustitiae Pax").[5] The other play is Avancini's fittingly titled *Pax Imperii*, which tells the story

---

[1] Konrad Repgen, "Der päpstliche Protest gegen den Westfälischen Frieden und die Friedenspolitik Urbans VIII.," *Historisches Jahrbuch*, 75 (1955): pp. 94–122.

[2] A-Wn, Suppl. mus. 2451, fol. 32r.

[3] A-Wn, Cod. 13341.

[4] "There will rise in those days Justice and an abundance of Peace, until the moon is taken away"; "the Peace of Justice and the Honor of Piety." The printed scenario is sewn into the binding of the manuscript libretto.

[5] "And the work of Justice shall be Peace."

of Genesis 41–5, thereby casting Ferdinand III as Joseph, the youngest son of Jacob, who voluntarily reconciled with his brothers after they sold him into slavery.[6] Tellingly, Avancini's drama was not performed until September 1650, nearly two years after the signing of the peace treaty. Many imperial artworks in honor of the peace did not appear until at least 1650, suggesting that Ferdinand III perhaps needed some time to pass before he could fully claim responsibility for the treaty and embrace without reservation an image as a peacemaker.[7]

Only two artworks from 1648 explicitly paint the Emperor as the main agent through which the peace was achieved, but they nevertheless helped initiate a second revision of Ferdinand's public image, from protective father to father of peace. One is a medal that pictures on one side a profile bust of Ferdinand III surrounded by the German inscription, "Er schaefet deinen Graentzen Friede."[8] The other side (Figure E.1) shows a bareheaded Emperor kneeling before God (represented by the Hebrew word "Jehova") and praying for peace, while the Empire, France, and Sweden seal the peace treaty in Münster. The other work is the *Currus triumphalis musici*, a sumptuous music print by the Hungarian Protestant composer Andreas Rauch (discussed in Chapter 4).[9] This collection of 13 "Colossal Baroque" Latin sacred works, each dedicated to one of the Habsburg emperors from Rudolph I on (see Figure 4.2), is without doubt the first truly magnificent celebration of the peace treaty; significantly, the concluding work (bearing the dedication to Ferdinand III) is that traditional song of celebration, the Te Deum, in a grand setting for four choirs plus trumpets and timpani. Ferdinand's grandeur is unmistakably presented in the richly illustrated frontispiece (Figure 2.3), while the dedication (see the Appendix) praises him as "most invincible" and "peace-making" and celebrates his recent marriage to Maria Leopoldine (in July 1648) as "anticipating (with the help of Divine Providence) the most beautiful end of the war." The fact that this lavish commemoration of the peace came from a non-court composer is significant; the public demonstration of loyalty to Ferdinand III by a Protestant subject would have been an important display of the Emperor's authority at the end of the war, and Ferdinand was also able to

---

[6] A modern edn of a German scenario from the production is in Jean-Marie Valentin, "Programme von Avancinis Stücken," *Literaturwissenschaftliches Jahrbuch der Görres-Gesellschaft*, N.F. 12 (1971): pp. 7–14; Avancini published the entire text (minus the prologue) in Nicholas Avancini, *Poesis dramatica*, vol. 1 (Cologne: Friessem, 1675), pp. 409–96.

[7] For instance, two medals commemorating the peace were issued in 1650 (KHM, Münzkabinett, #b 974) and 1653 (KHM, Münzkabinett, #144419).

[8] "He makes peace for his lands" (KHM, Münzkabinett, #136796).

[9] Andreas Rauch, *Currus triumphalis musici, Imperatorum Romanorum Tredecim ex Augustissima Archiducali Domo Austriaca* (Vienna, 1648).

Figure E.1   Medal honoring the Peace of Westphalia (reverse), 4 cm, 1648

enjoy a glorification of himself as a peacemaker without personally having to take credit for a treaty that was not favorable to him. Even if, as argued in Chapter 4, Ferdinand III commissioned the print, to the general public it nevertheless came across as an unsolicited display of the Emperor's authority and as the first large-scale work to establish his new image as the father of peace.

When the Emperor himself began to promulgate this new image through theatrical court spectacles in 1651 and 1652, there was a simultaneous rehabilitation of his warrior image of the 1630s. Both of the operas produced in those years (in honor of Ferdinand III's birthday and the birth of the Spanish Infanta Margarita Teresa respectively) featured tournaments as their central spectacles, thereby bringing celebrations of war back into Habsburg courtly entertainments.[10] The most significant aspect of these staged enactments of war, however, is the fact that in both works the battle is ended through the intervention of Jove. In *La Gara* (the 1652 work), the identification of the peace-making Jove with Ferdinand III is made explicit by his majestic entrance on an eagle.[11] The Emperor's image as a peacemaker was also announced to those in attendance at *La Gara* (and to those reading the libretto) by the baldacchino over his throne, which was supported by statues representing Peace and Virtue (see Figure 3.1).[12] The glorification of Ferdinand III is even more explicit in the 1651 opera in that the main subject is the Emperor himself: the central tournament is a battle between Mars and Minerva, who are arguing about which of them best exemplifies Ferdinand III. This tournament has no winner; rather, Jove declares the battle a draw, for the Emperor is "egual in armi, e in senno" (thereby implying that the war ended only because of Ferdinand's wise governing, not because of any military weaknesses).[13] To this pronouncement, the now peaceful combatants joyfully respond with a ballet that ends with them in the shape of the letter "F."[14] The Emperor's reclaiming of his image as a triumphant warrior is made most explicit in the reissuing at some point in the late 1640s or 1650s of an engraving by Lucas Schnitzer celebrating the Battle of Nördlingen (Figure 1.5); the reprint is identical to the earlier version but with an older head superimposed on Ferdinand III's young body.[15]

The representation of the Emperor through the figure of Jove in *La Gara* and his association with Roman gods and goddesses in the 1651 opera point to another important aspect of Ferdinand III's post-war image, one drawing upon a dynastic tradition that had been present but not strongly emphasized in the Emperor's previous representations: the idea that there was an unbroken connection between the modern Holy Roman

---

[10] *Attione da rappresentarsi in musica nel giorno natalitio di S. Maestà Cesarea Ferdinando III. a 13. Luglio 1651* (Vienna, 1651); Alberto Vimina, *La Gara* (Vienna, 1652).

[11] Vimina, *La Gara*, sig. O; see p. 81.

[12] Ibid., sig. A2v.

[13] "Equal in arms and in judgment"; *Attione da rappresentarsi in musica*, sig. D2: "Ch'essendo AUGUSTO egual in armi, e in senno, / Da Marte, e da Bellona à un tempo denno, / Le lodi celebrarsi anche a vicenda."

[14] Ibid., sig. D4v: "Si formano alla conclusione del verso Viva, &c. un Viva in modo di due V V. da i Signori danzatori colla littera F. per esprimere colla figura, ciò, che viene augurato col canto."

[15] A-Wn, Bildarchiv, Pg 149 137/3 in Ptf 123: I (67). The new head is identical to one on an engraving issued by Elias Wideman in 1648: A-Wn, Bildarchiv, Pg 149 137/3 in Ptf 123: I (19).

Figure E.2   Franciscus van den Steen after a painting by Joachim von Sandrart, *The Triumph of Ferdinand III*, engraving, 1653

Emperor and ancient Rome.[16] This connection is made explicit in Rauch's *Currus triumphalis musici*, for the very idea of a "triumphal musical

---

[16] Marie Tanner, *The Last Descendant of Aeneas: The Hapsburgs and the Mythic Image of the Emperor* (New Haven and London, 1993). On Maximilian I's attempts to prove a genealogy extending back to ancient Rome, see Larry Silver, *Marketing Maximilian: The Visual Ideology of a Holy Roman Emperor* (Princeton and Oxford, 2008), pp. 41–76.

chariot" was an important trope in ancient Greek and Roman poetry.[17] The illustration of Ferdinand III in his chariot on the frontispiece thus explicitly paints him as an ancient Roman emperor in military triumph. Rauch further solidified the connections to antiquity in the dedication, which is rife with allusions to Classical poetry: to provide just one notable example, the mention of "tenues Musas" in the penultimate sentence is a common Greek and Latin poetic trope extending back to the ancient Greek Alexandrian poet Callimachus.[18] Perhaps the most explicitly "Classicizing" portrait of Ferdinand III is an engraving published in 1653 by Franciscus van den Steen (after a lost painting by Joachim von Sandrart) that portrays the Emperor's family as Olympian gods (Figure E.2).[19] Among those represented are Ferdinand III as Jove, Empress Eleonora Gonzaga as Juno, Archduke Leopold Wilhelm as Mars, Ferdinand IV as Apollo, and Leopold I as Cupid, while the inscription proclaims, "IoVI aVstrIaCo paCIfICoqVe, CharI CaeLItes, Deae DIIqVe sVI, gratI VenIVnt, LItantqVe [To the peace-making Austrian Jove, the loving gods in heaven, his Goddesses and Gods, come and offer thanks]." Considering that claims to ancient Roman heritage had always been a significant means through which all emperors asserted their God-given right to rule,[20] the increase in ancient Roman imagery in Ferdinand III's representations after the war helped reassert his legitimacy and power in the aftermath of an unfavorable peace settlement.

The early 1650s was a time of increasing optimism at the imperial court, as Ferdinand III gradually relinquished his reservations about the Peace of Westphalia and gloried instead in the triumphant image of a powerful, wise ruler who had helped bring peace to the world. Significantly, in 1651 Ferdinand initiated a substantial reform to the court ordinances, in a conscious effort to increase the dignity and magnificence of the imperial court after the dark years of the war.[21] With the re-Catholicization of his hereditary lands well solidified, the Emperor also seems to have felt a less pressing need to represent himself with sacred music, and he increasingly returned to such traditional modes of representation as paintings, Italian

---

[17] M.L. West, *Indo-European Poetry and Myth* (Oxford, 2007), pp. 41–3; Michael Simpson, "The Chariot and the Bow as Metaphors for Poetry in Pindar's Odes," *Transactions and Proceedings of the American Philological Association*, 100 (1969): pp. 437–73.

[18] Zane Udris, "Tenuis musa: The Response of Propertius and Ovid to the Literary Views of Callimachus" (Ph.D. diss., Yale University, 1976). I am grateful to Sarah Ferrario for pointing these allusions out to me.

[19] Albertina, Vienna, Ö.K. fol. 4–5, Nr. 5+6.

[20] Tanner.

[21] Jeroen Duindam, *Vienna and Versailles: The Courts of Europe's Dynastic Rivals, 1550–1780* (Cambridge, 2003), pp. 144, 194–5.

poetry and music, and grand theatrical and ritual spectacles. The pattern of Sances's publications is telling evidence, for after 1648 he did not issue a single print devoted to sacred music. Although his new position as vice chapel master beginning in 1649 was undoubtedly a major reason for this (since his new duties would have included commissions for grand occasional works unsuitable for publication), Sances nevertheless published two collections of music in the final decade of Ferdinand's reign, both containing only secular works.[22] The culmination of the optimistic spirit at court came in the biggest political event of the decade, the Diet of Regensburg of 1653–54, at which the Emperor achieved his most pressing goal: the election and coronation of his son Ferdinand IV as King of the Romans.[23]

The city greeted the imperial court in grand style with a traditional joyous entry on December 12, 1652, which featured a triumphal arch that merged all of the elements of Ferdinand III's new image as the triumphant father of peace (Figures E.3 and E.4).[24] Standing in glory under the central baldacchino on the front of the arch is Ferdinand III clad in full armor and crowned with laurel, thereby referencing his image as a victorious military leader. Above him is the Hebrew word "Jehovah," reminding viewers that it is above all through God's will that he rules, while directly above him is the word "PACEM." Taken together, these images and words create the sentence, "Hoc duce pacem Ferdinandus III Romano Imperio reduxit."[25] The images and words on the spires on both sides of the Emperor's image create two additional sentences that describe the anti-Machiavellian foundation of Ferdinand's good governance: on the left, "Ferdinandus III vigilando bono consilio thronum caesarum firmavit" (paired with the image discussed in Chapter 5 of the Emperor as King Solomon),[26] and on the right, "Ferdinandus III pugnando foedere libertatem statuum conservavit" (paired with an image of the council of electors).[27] Across the cornice and over the main arch appear the official welcoming statements

---

[22] Giovanni Felice Sances, *Capricci poetici* (Venice, 1649); *Trattenimenti musicali per camera* (Venice, 1657).

[23] On this Diet, see Konrad Repgen, "Ferdinand III., 1637-1657," in Anton Schindling and Walter Ziegler (eds), *Die Kaiser der Neuzeit, 1519-1918: Heiliges Römisches Reich, Österreich, Deutschland* (Munich, 1990), pp. 161–6.

[24] In addition to the two oversize engravings by Wolfgang Kilian of the front and back of the arch, the entire arch is described in Christian-Adolph Balduin, *Poetische Entdeckung der Ehren-Pforte* (Regensburg, 1653). The copy of Balduin's print at A-Wn has Kilian's engravings sewn into the back cover.

[25] "Through this leader [God], Ferdinand III restores peace to the Roman Empire."

[26] "Ferdinand III has strengthened the imperial throne through vigilance and good counsel."

[27] "Ferdinand III has in this time of war preserved the states' freedom with the treaty."

Figure E.3 Wolfgang Kilian, triumphal arch erected in Regensburg for Ferdinand III (front), engraving, 1653

Figure E.4 Wolfgang Kilian, triumphal arch erected in Regensburg for Ferdinand III (back), engraving, 1653

by the city of Regensburg, thanking the Emperor for bringing peace and offering him laurels (illustrated by the angel above the arch preparing the laurel wreath). On each corner above the central arch are portraits of the Ancient Roman Emperors Caesar Augustus and Trajan, thus contributing to the tradition of linking Ferdinand to the ancient Roman Empire; this link is confirmed with the words above the small portal to the right: "May you, our Augustus, be and always remain better than Trajan and more fortunate than Augustus."

On the back of the arch, standing in the location occupied on the other side by Ferdinand III is the Archangel Michael slaying a demon. This representation not only strengthens the Emperor's triumphant military image by putting him in the same spot as the victorious leader of God's army, but it also explicitly sacralizes his image, presenting Ferdinand's triumph as nothing less than God's triumph. The text once again reminds viewers of the importance of the Emperor's piety to his successful rule: "Firmamenta regnorum quibus hoc victore regna gubernantur."[28] The words and images on the side spires again describe important aspects of anti-Machiavellian political theory, this time with sentences that begin with the two virtues of Ferdinand III's motto: "Pietate majestate laus sapientiae regis crescit" (on the left, with an image of the Queen of Sheba's visit to King Solomon),[29] and "Justitia aequitate labor salusque populi florescit."[30] If the front of the arch had celebrated the Habsburgs' glorious lineage extending back to ancient Rome, this side honors Ferdinand III's more recent lineage, with small portraits of Ferdinand I and Ferdinand II over the main arch. The Emperor is explicitly praised as the father of his realm in the inscription that traces the curve of the arch: "May you enter as the peace-making Father of the Fatherland, and with you may there always be Justice, nourishing Health, and noble Virtue." Ferdinand's status as the father of his people is further reinforced in a portrait engraved by Jacob Sandrart and issued in Regensburg in 1653, in which underneath an image of Ferdinand III wearing his coronation mantle and crowned with laurel is the inscription, "HOC viget ALMA THEMIS, viget HOC CONCORDIA REGNI. OPTIMUS hinc PACIS, JUSTITIAEque PATER. HUNC magno IMPERII CIVES venerantur amore, et LAETI acclamant: VIVE PATER PATRIAE! [May this nourishing Themis [goddess of justice] flourish; may this peace of the realm flourish. Greatest father of this peace and justice. The citizens of the Empire venerate this father with great love, and happy they shout: Live, Father of the Fatherland!]"[31]

---

[28] "The foundations of his royal power and his reign are governed by this victor."
[29] "Through piety and majesty does the glory of the King's wisdom thrive."
[30] "Through justice and fairness do the people's work and health blossom."
[31] A-Wn, Bildarchiv, Pg 149 137/3 in Ptf 123: I (39a).

During the Diet, Ferdinand III lived up to the expectations of magnificence expressed by the triumphal arch, using all the pomp and splendor of the imperial court to present a mighty, powerful image to the citizens of Regensburg. This splendor came through in the sheer size of his retinue, which was publicized through such artifacts as an engraving of the immense parade of horses and wagons approaching the city as well as a pamphlet listing the names and titles of every member of the imperial entourage (including 43 chapel members and 11 trumpeters).[32] It was also apparent in the impressive festive events the court sponsored, both sacred and secular, such as a magnificent Corpus Christi procession featuring 40 trumpeters (mentioned in Chapter 6) and the full-fledged Venetian opera *L'Inganno d'Amore* (with libretto by Benedetto Ferrari and music by Bertali), given in two performances during Carnival 1653.[33]

The Emperor maintained this magnificence upon his return to Vienna in May 1654 with a sumptuous joyous entry into the city that included four triumphal arches (upon which musicians performed to the accompaniment of trumpets and timpani) and no fewer than 60 trumpeters, not including those stationed upon the arches.[34] As discussed in Chapter 3, the spectacular revival of Avancini's Jesuit drama *Theodosius Magnus Justus et Pius* shortly after the imperial family's return was also an important event commemorating the Regensburg festivities for the Viennese people (see Figure 3.3). On its first performance in 1644, this tale of the ancient Roman Emperor Theodosius' grueling defeat of the pagan usurper Eugenius and the coronation of his son as his successor was an optimistic prayer during the darkest years of the war, an expression by the Jesuits of their strong desire for an end to the Thirty Years' War and the banishment of heresy. Ten years later, with the war over and Ferdinand IV wearing the Roman crown, the same play now served as a metaphor for actual recent events, a fulfillment of the prophesy announced in the 1644 production.

---

[32] The engraving is by Melchior Küsel (Albertina, Vienna, Historische Blätter 5). The pamphlet is *Der Röm. Kayserl. Mayest. FERDINANDI III. Wie auch Der Röm. Königl. Mayest. FERDINANDI IV. Hoff-Stat: Wie sich derselbe in Jahren 1653. und 1654. uff dem Reichstag zu Regenspurg eingefunden* (Frankfurt, 1654), in which the members of the chapel and trumpeters appear on pp. 12–14.

[33] Bendetto Ferrari, *L'Inganno d'Amore* (Regensburg, 1653); the music is lost. On the Corpus Christi procession, see p. 199.

[34] The procession is described in *Eigentliche Beschreibung deß den 24. May Anno 1654 Ihrer Kayserlich und Königlicher Mayestätten zu Wienn beschehenen Einzugs* (Vienna, 1654). The trumpeters are itemized on sigs A4v–Bv, and the arches are discussed on sig. B2v: "auff allen disen Porten, Heerpaucken, Trompeten, und andere Musicen gewesen, welche sich bey Ihrer Kay: und Königlicher Mayestätten Durchzug lieblich hören lassen." The author promises that detailed descriptions of the arches will be provided in a separate pamphlet, which seems not to have survived.

Even the unspeakable tragedies that soon befell the imperial family—the unexpected death of Ferdinand IV from smallpox on July 9, 1654 (two months shy of his 21st birthday) and the death of the dowager Empress Eleonora Gonzaga on June 6, 1655—could not entirely quell the optimistic spirit of the decade. Already in July 1656 Ferdinand III's birthday was celebrated with a grand five-act opera with music by Bertali, *Theti*, a work that used Classical mythology to proclaim an anti-Machiavellian message about the imperial family.[35] The plot tells the story of Thetis, a shape-shifting sea goddess who is romantically pursued by Jove. When Thetis' father foresees that her son will one day be stronger than his father, he urges Jove to stop pursuing her, and after much tribulation she consents instead to marry the mortal Pelleus (who has wooed her unsuccessfully throughout the opera). Although it may initially seem odd to put the male Emperor in the place of the female protagonist, doing so produces a model of princely virtue: rather than overweening ambition (the desire to marry the king of the gods), the protagonist shows a virtuous restraint, and it is on account of this restraint that she will eventually (after the opera ends) give birth to one of the greatest Classical heroes, Achilles.[36] Tellingly, when Thetis' father urges Jove not to marry her, he uses as his main argument the fact that their son would upset the balance of Heaven, Hell, the sea, and the earth, leading to a "piú terribil guerra."[37] The final chorus of the opera sings praises to Ferdinand III during a ballet featuring the participation of the new heir to the throne and future Emperor Leopold I. As stressful as it must have been for Ferdinand III to scramble to have Leopold crowned King of Hungary and Bohemia in order to ensure the succession of the Habsburg line, the coronations in June 1655 and September 1656 were nevertheless grand occasions that could only have fostered a spirit of celebration.

By the final year of Ferdinand's reign, secular activities were dominating the cultural activities at court, though never at the expense of displays of piety and virtue. It was in that year, for instance, that the Emperor and his brother founded their literary academies.[38] The meetings of these academies were splendid events accompanied by music, for which Sances apparently

---

[35] Diamante Gabrielli, *Theti* (Vienna, 1656); Bertali's music has not survived.

[36] Irving Lavin has interpreted a similarly anti-Machiavellian lesson of restraint in Bernini's famous sculptures of Francesco I d'Este and Louis XIV; "Bernini's Image of the Ideal Christian Monarch," in John W. O'Malley et al. (eds), *The Jesuits: Cultures, Sciences, and the Arts, 1540–1773* (Toronto, 1999), pp. 442–79.

[37] Gabrielli, *Theti*, p. 15: "Che se Theti la bella / In nodo marital s'unisce à Giove, / Porsi vedremo ancora / Con piú terribil guerra / Sossopra il Ciel, l'Inferno, il Mar, la Terra."

[38] See p. 59.

provided works.[39] It was also around this time that both Ferdinand III and his brother published their books of Italian poetry; at least 47 poems in these books were set to music by Bertali and Sances.[40] Even upon Ferdinand III's death, the two most celebrated extra-liturgical musical responses are telling examples of a new spirit at court: a keyboard *tombeau* in the French manner by Johann Jakob Froberger and an instrumental work by Johann Heinrich Schmelzer for four strings.[41]

The increasingly secular spirit of the final decade of Ferdinand III's reign marked a new chapter in the history of the Habsburg monarchy, one that was to be developed at length in the long and celebrated reign of Leopold I. The Catholic religion as manifested in anti-Machiavellian political policy and the *Pietas Austriaca*—not to mention in the Emperor's patronage of sacred music—nevertheless continued to mold the dynasty and play an important role in court culture. Despite the fact that Leopold I's patronage of (and participation in) magnificent operas and other secular musical activities remains one of his most enduring legacies, the new Emperor nevertheless continued to follow and sometimes even strengthened the pious representational strategies pioneered by his father: the rebuilding and re-consecrating of the *Mariensäule* in 1667 (which was further monumentalized with a scale model in gold and precious stones),[42] the construction of the *Pestsäule* in 1679, the continued dedication of Habsburg lands to saints,[43] even public displays of resigned trust in God

---

[39] On Sances's participation in the meetings of Leopold Wilhelm's academy, see Herbert Seifert, "Akademien am Wiener Kaiserhof der Barockzeit," in Wolf Frobenius et al. (eds), *Akademie und Musik* (Saarbrücken, 1993), pp. 216–17.

[40] Ferdinand III, *Poesie diverse composte in hore rubate d'Academico Occupato* (n.p., n.d.) and Leopold Wilhelm, *Diporti del Crescente, divisi in rime morali, devote, heroiche, amorose* (Brussels, 1656). Ferdinand's collection dates to at least 1651, as it contains several love poems to his third wife. The catalogue of Leopold I's music library (A-Wn, Suppl. mus. 2451) lists eight works by Bertali that correspond to titles in Ferdinand III's book and 11 works by Bertali that correspond to titles in Leopold Wilhelm's book; it also lists one work by Sances that corresponds to a title by Ferdinand III and 25 the correspond to titles by the Archduke. There are also three anonymous works listed in the catalogue of Leopold Wilhelm's library that correspond to titles of Ferdinand III's poems (HKA, NÖHA, W61/A/32, fols 2–11).

[41] Johann Jakob Froberger, *Lamentation faite sur la mort tres douloureuse de Sa Majestè Imperiale, Ferdinand le troiseme; et se joue lentement avec discretion. An. 1657*; modern edn in *Orgel- und Clavierwerke 3*, ed. Guido Adler, Denkmäler der Tonkunst in Österreich, vol. 21 (Vienna, 1903), pp. 116–17. Johann Heinrich Schmelzer, *Lamento sopra la morte Ferdinani III*, ed. Wolfgang Gamerith (Graz, 1975).

[42] Philip Küsel, Replica of the Mariensäule, ca. 1675–78, KHM, Schatzkammer, Inv. Nr. KK 882.

[43] Leopold declared St Leopold the patron of Austria in 1663 and consecrated the Empire to St Joseph in 1675; Maria Goloubeva, *The Glorification of Emperor Leopold I in Image, Spectacle, and Text* (Mainz, 2000), p. 206.

during times of tribulation.[44] Nor were Ferdinand III's strategies limited to the Austrian dynasty; Peter Burke, for instance, has observed that during the later years of Louis XIV's reign, when the King was less successful on the battlefield, he turned to a "protective father" image in very much the same manner of Ferdinand III.[45]

Herein lies the ultimate test of the success of Ferdinand III's representations. We may never know the true impact that any of Sances's prints had on European consumers of sacred music, or whether performances by imperial musicians truly delivered the political messages argued in this book. We can, however, verify the resonances between Ferdinand's wartime music and Wassenberg's 1647 panegyric, the appearance of the Solomon image in an array of "unofficial" representations of the 1650s, and the perfect encapsulation of all aspects of Ferdinand III's image in a triumphal arch created in 1652 not by the court but by the citizens of Regensburg. More importantly, we can see Leopold I, the Emperor who led the Habsburgs victoriously out of the seventeenth century and reestablished their claims as a world power, following in his father's footsteps to great success. Leopold's success vindicates the troubled, almost forgotten reign of his father. Indeed, Leopold I's achievement would not have been possible without the strong foundation laid by Ferdinand III, a foundation that drew its greatest strength from the musical representations of the Emperor in the sacred repertoire of the imperial chapel.

---

[44] Ibid., pp. 198–201, 218.
[45] Peter Burke, *The Fabrication of Louis XIV* (New Haven, 1992), pp. 112–13.

Appendix
Dedicatory Texts of Music Prints Dedicated to the Emperor and Other Imperial Figures

Claudio Monteverdi, *Madrigali guerrieri, et amorosi* (1638)
Dedicated to Ferdinand III

SACRA CESAREA REAL MAESTA.
Presento a i piedi della Maestà Vostra, come à Nume tutelare della Virtù, queste mie compositioni Musicali.

    FERDINANDO, il gran Genitore della Maestà Vostra, degnandosi, per la sua innata bontà, di gradirle, & honorarle scritte, mi hà conceduto quasi un authorevole passaporto per fidarle alla Stampa.

Ed ecco, che arditamente io le publico consacrandole al riveritissimo Nome di Vostra Maestà, herede non meno de' Regni, e dell'Imperio, che del Valore, e benignità di lui.

    Questi nuovi, ma deboli germogli della mia penna, non farebbono degni di venir in quelle mani, dove riposa il peso dell'humana tranquillità, per interrompere i gloriosi effari di un Cesare, se la Musica non fusse privilegiata in Cielo dall'Istesso Dio, all'orecchie del quale incessantemente facendosi udire, non gli turba però la cura del sovrano maneggio.

    In questo i sommi Principi devono esser imitatori ancora di lui, che opera, & ascolta insieme i canti degli Angeli, e le suppliche de' Mortali.

    Aggrandirà questa picciola offerta del mio suiscenatissimo affetto l'eccesso della mia devota riverenza, con le quale inchinandomi al Cielo, prego alla Maestà vostra, & alla Augustiss Casa d'Austria la perpetuità di quelle glorie, che l'hanno sublimata sovra ogni terrena grandezza. Di Venetia il primo Settembre 1638.

Di Vostra Maestà,
Humillissimo, & Devotissimo Servitore
Claudio Monteverde.

TO THE SACRED IMPERIAL ROYAL MAJESTY.[1]
I lay at the feet of Your Majesty, as the tutelary Deity of Virtue, these musical compositions of mine.

FERDINAND, the great Father of Your Majesty, deigning with his inborn kindness to approve and honor them in manuscript, granted me, as it were, an authoritative passport for commending them to the Press.
And now I boldly publish them, dedicating them to the most reverend Name of Your Majesty, who is not less the heir of his Kingdoms and Empire than of his Valor and goodness.

These new but feeble offspring of my pen would not be worthy to come into those hands in which the burden of human tranquility rests, to interrupt the glorious doings of an Emperor, were it not that Music is authorized in Heaven by God Himself and, although ceaselessly resounding in His ears, does not prevent Him from managing the affairs of the universe.

In this, too, the mightiest Princes ought to be His imitators, since He acts and at the same time listens to the songs of the Angels and the prayers of the Mortals.

This small offering of my most sincere affection will be augmented by the excess of my devoted reverence, with which, bowing to Heaven, I pray that your Majesty and the most August House of Austria may enjoy in perpetuity those glories that have raised it above all earthly greatness. From Venice, the first of September 1638.
Your Majesty's
Most Humble and Most Devoted Servant,
Claudio Monteverdi.

---

[1] Translation from Claudio Monteverdi, *Madrigals, Book 8: Madrigali guerrieri et amorosi*, ed. Gian Francesco Malipiero and Stanley Appelbaum (New York, 1991), p. xii.

Giovanni Felice Sances, *Motetti a una, due, tre, e quattro voci* (1638)
Dedicated to Ferdinand III

SACRA CESAREA MAESTÀ

Già divoto dedicai la Voce; hoggi consacro riverente la penna, con sentimento di far noto al Mondo in queste poche Note l'attual servitù, di cui mi glorio, & alla Maestá Vostra l'ardente desiderio, che tengo di serrar gl'ochi nel Grembo dell' Augustissima Casa d'Austria, ne seno di sì Gran Mecenate. Esse alla vivacità de Vocali colori, perche maggiormente apparisse il rilevo, piacque alla Maestá Vostra avvicinar l'ombra, e l'oscuro del mio povero Talento; non deve recar maraviglia se hoggi l'ardita Penna procura so levarsi à volo, e di fermar l'ombra fugace de veloci passaggi all'ombra Augustissima dell' Imperial Alloro, dell' Austriaca Protettione. Sol questa desidero per gratia, e la Maestà Vostra suol concederla per propria natura; Con che le so profondissimo inchino.

Vienna li 21 Novembre 1637
D.V. Sacra Cesarea Maestà
Humilissimo, e divotissimo servo.
Gio. Felice Sances

TO YOUR SACRED IMPERIAL MAJESTY
Previously I devotedly dedicated to you my Voice; today I reverently dedicate to you my pen, with the sentiment of making known to the World through these meager Notes my current service, in which I take pride, and my ardent devotion towards Your Majesty, for I am embraced firmly in the Bosom [patronage] of the Most August House of Austria, no less a bosom than that of the Great Maecenas. This dedication is through the liveliness of Vocal colors, in that it would be a great relief, if it please Your Majesty, for me to bring near you the shadow and the humility of my poor talent. I do not have to produce marvels if today my ardent Pen manages to lift itself in flight and end the fleeting darkness of fast passages in the shadow of the Most August Imperial Laurel, under the Protection of Austria. I have only this wish for grace, and Your Majesty is accustomed to granting it on account of your nature; with which I most profoundly bow.
Vienna, the 21st of November, 1637
Your Sacred Imperial Majesty's
Most Humble and most devoted servant,
Giovanni Felice Sances

Giovanni Felice Sances, *Motetti a voce sola* (1638)
Dedicated to Eleonora Gonzaga

SACRA CESAREA MAESTA

Consacro alla Maesta V. questi musici componimenti; acciò coperti da Augustissimo MANTO[2] dall'Ombra di SACRA CESAREA MAESTA, venghino assicurati non meno dalle grandini delle persecutioni, che da tuoni e fulmini delle calunnie altrui. Ho sfuggito nella varietà de motetti la multiplicità delle voci; per additare al mondo, che io, benche esposto alla mutatione, difetto dell'humana natura; conservo nell unitá un istesso Tenore, cioé la divotione, e l'ossequio de miei Antenati, e di mio fratello in particolare verso la Serenissima Casa GONZAGA; nel cui Cielo, si come la Maestà V. vien riverita da tutti come unico & Augustissimo Sole, cosi anc'io le fó profondissimo inchino.

Vienna il Primo Giugno 1638.
Di V. Sacra Cesarea Maestà.
Humilissimo e divotissimo servo
Gio. Felice Sances.

---

[2] A variant spelling of "Mantua."

TO YOUR SACRED IMPERIAL MAJESTY
I dedicate to Your Majesty these musical compositions, so that covered by the Most August MANTLE of the Shadow of YOUR SACRED IMPERIAL MAJESTY, they might be protected no less from the hail of persecution than from the thunder and lightning of slander from others. I have avoided in the variety of motets the multiplication of voices, in order to point out to the world that although I am exposed to the changeable defects of human nature, I preserve in unity the same Tenor, that is, the devotion and deference of my Ancestors (and of my brother in particular) toward the Most Serene House of GONZAGA, under whose sky, in which Your Majesty is revered by all as a unique and Most August Sun, in this way I also profoundly bow.
Vienna, the First of June, 1638.
Your Sacred Imperial Majesty's
Most Humble and most devoted servant,
Giovanni Felice Sances

Giovanni Felice Sances, *Antifone e litanie della Beatissima Vergine a più voci* (1640)
Dedicated to Ferdinand III's first wife Maria of Spain

SACRA CESAREA MAIESTÀ
Dovendo mandar in luce questa mia opera sacra, ho preso ardire carcarli ricovero sotto l'ombra Augustissima del'Imperial protettione del la Maiestà Vostra, la cui singular divotione verso la Regina del Cielo m'ha indotto spender quel tempo che mi avanza dal servitio di S.M.C. mio Clementissimo Signore in lode & honore di MARIA Vergine di cui V.M. porta insieme il nome, & immita con la vita i costumi; Giovando, mi credere, che sia per agradite altr'e tanto, in veder publicare per benefitio commune le lodi della Santissima Madre quanto si compiace d'udirle con rinovata mente mentre si cantano con ogni devota attentione. Degnisi per tanto la M.V. come humilissimamente ne la suplico, non misurando dalla piciolezza del mio talento la mia divotione, accettar questo, per testimonio del'humilissima mia servitù, e dovuto riconoscimento de favori riceuti da S.M. mentre con farle profondissima riverenza le prego dal Cielo compita felicità.

Vienna il Primo Lugio 1640
Della Sacra Cesarea M.V.
Divotissimo servo
Gio. Felice Sances

TO YOUR SACRED IMPERIAL MAJESTY
Having to bring to light these sacred works of mine, I have dared to find shelter in the Most August shadow of Your Majesty's Imperial protection. Your singular devotion toward the Queen of Heaven has induced me to spend that time left over to me in the service of my Most Clement Lord, His Sacred Imperial Majesty, in the praise and honor of the Virgin MARY, with whom Your Majesty shares the same name and whom you imitate in the customs of life. Being that I believe it is useful to demonstrate to so many others in this publication the communal benefit of the praises of the Most Sacred Mother, it is so pleasing to hear them with a renewed mind while they are sung with all devoted attentions. Above all, I most humbly beseech Your most dignified Majesty that you accept, notwithstanding the smallness of my talents, this my devotion, for I testify to my most humble service and must acknowledge the favors received from Your Majesty while, making a most profound bow, I pray for you all happiness from Heaven.
Vienna, the First of July, 1640
Your Sacred Imperial Majesty's
Most Devoted servant,
Giovanni Felice Sances

Giovanni Felice Sances, *Motetti a 2, 3, 4, e cinque voci* (1642)
Dedicated to Vilém Slavata, Chancellor of Bohemia

ILL[USTRISSI]MO ET ECC[ELLENTISSI]MO SIG[NO]RE MIO SIG[NO]R ET PATRONE COLL[ENDISSI]MO
Chi procura alle proprie compositioni difesa de grandi, preserva le medesime e dalla voracitá del tempo, e dalla malignità del secolo. Queste doi cagioni ad ogni modo non mi servono di motivo per consacrare al glorioso nome dell' Ecc.V. i presenti Motteti, non comportando la mia antica, e ossequiosissima devotione, che qual si voglia mio interesse le sia preferito; Dedico per tanto all' E.V. con solo titolo d'ossequioso tributo questi sacri Componimenti, quali se per propria debolezza non riusciranno ben aggiustati alla grandezza del suo merito, saranno almeno ben addattati alla sempre pia, e Religiosissima sua intentione. Suplico dunque l' E.V. restar servita di gradire questa mia dimostratione, col solito della sua inemitabile benignitá, ch'io non cessatò[3] giamai per l'avvenire di moltiplicare gl'atti della mia humilissima osservanza, per corrispondere come posso, se non come son tenuto à gl'honori, che in tante occasioni ho riceuti dalla sua benignissima gratia, alla quale inchinandomi bramo all' E.V. ogni più vera, e più desiderata felicità: e me le inchino.

Di Venetia Di Primo Novembre 1642
Humilissimo e Devotissimo servitore
Gioan. Felice Sances.

---

[3] Spelled "cessarò" in canto and tenor partbooks.

TO THE MOST ILLUSTRIOUS AND MOST EXCELLENT LORD, MY MOST HONORED LORD AND PATRON

He who obtains for his own compositions the protection of the great preserves them from both the voracity of time and the malice of age. These two reasons in any case do not serve as my motive for consecrating the present Motets to Your Excellency's glorious name, leading my ancient and most obsequious devotion not to my own interests but to whatever would be preferred by you. Above all, it is for the sole reason of an obsequious tribute that I dedicate to Your Excellency these sacred Compositions, which if through their own weaknesses do not succeed in being worthy of the greatness of your merit will at least be well suited to your always pious and most religious intentions. I request, therefore, that Your Excellency remain willing to accept this, my demonstration, with your usual inimitable goodness, for which I shall in the future never cease to multiply the acts of my most humble observance, in order to match it as I am able to; if in doing this I have not held onto the honors that I received from your most benign grace on so many occasions, then prostrating myself I yearn for Your Excellency all that is good and for all desired happiness: and I bow down to you.

From Venice on the First of November 1642,

Your Most Humble and Most Devoted servant,

Giovanni Felice Sances

Giovanni Felice Sances, *Salmi a 8 voci concertati* (1643)
Dedicated to Ferdinand III's brother Archduke Leopold Wilhelm

ALTEZZA SERENIS[SI]MA

Stillerei non che questi languidi e morti inchiostri, il sangue più puro, e piú vivo dell'anima, nel glorioso servitio dell'Altezza Vostra Serenissima con quella prontezza, che à me prescrive il debito della mia humilissima servitù, se l'abilita, e l'ocasioni non fussero mancanti al mio ardentissimo desiderio; Pure astretto dalle gratie, che innumerabili ho sempre mai riceute dalla sua inefabile Clemenza; Dovendo comparire in facia del Mondo questi miei Salmi á Otto voci Concertati, non devo per tutti li respetti, tra lasciare di Consacrarli sotto l'Augustissimo suo Nome, si per essere eglino Materia confacevole all'animo suo sempre pio, si anco per provedersi di un protettore si grande come e l'A.V.S. Suplico per tanto restar servita di non indegnare la bassezza di questo tributo, con gl'eccessi della solita sua Magnanimità, rinovando l'esempio di quel Grande, che non rifiutò un picciolo sorso d'acqua, che da mano, benche povera, Devota però e fedele le fú presentato.

E mentre al gloriosissimo merito di V.A. Ser. auguro sempre prosperi, e furtunatissimi avvenimenti, humilissimamente me l'inchino bramandole felicità perpetua per servitio della sua Augustissima casa.

Venetia di Primo Giugno 1643
Di V.A. Serenissima
Humilissimo servo
Gioan Felice Sances

On the last page of each partbook, after the Tavola:

A Benigni Lettori e virtuosi

Perche ho pensato che questi miei Salmi à 8. voci potriano riuscir assai fiachi, e deboli di spirito nelli Ripieni, Però per comodità d'ogn'uno, che n'havesse gusto, ho pensato di farla presente fatica, con il segnar per ciascheduna parte questo segno di S. R. volendo significar che il segno S. vol dir quando la parte canterà concertata o sola, & il segno R. significarà quando la parte entrerà nel Ripieno. Onde nel segno S. si lascierà sempre cantar ad una voce sola, fin tanto che troverà il segno R. che sarà tutto Ripieno, sino al segno S & cosi sempre con questo ordine. potendosi agionger nelli ripieni per ciascheduna parte, altre parti cosi di voci come d'instrumenti.
       & vivete lieti.

TO THE MOST SERENE HIGHNESS
I would pour forth not only these languid and dead inks but also my purest blood and the liveliest spirit of my soul in the glorious service of Your Most Serene Highness with that readiness that is required from me by the debt of my most humble service, if the ability and the opportunity were not lacking from my most ardent desire. Even filled with the favors that I have always received innumerable times from your ineffable Clemency, needing to make known to the World these, my Psalms for Eight Concertato voices, I should not, with all due respect, forget to consecrate them under your Most August Name, both because they are Matter suitable for your always pious soul, and also in order to provide myself with a protector as grand as Your Most Serene Highness. I beg you to make worthy the baseness of this tribute with the excesses of your usual Magnanimity, following the example of that Great one [Jesus] who did not refuse a tiny sip of water presented to him by a Devoted and faithful, although poor, hand.[4]

And while for the most glorious merit of Your Most Serene Highness I wish always for prosperity and most fortunate events, most humbly do I bow down, yearning for the fortunate perpetuity of serving your Most August house.
Venice, the First of June, 1643
Your Most Serene Highness's
Most Humble servant,
Giovanni Felice Sances

To the Kind and virtuous Readers,
Seeing as I thought that these, my Psalms for 8 voices, could turn out very feeble and weak of spirit in the Ripienos, but to accommodate everyone who would enjoy them, I thought of making the present effort of indicating in each and every part the sign of S. and R., wanting to signify with the sign S. when the part is to be sung concertato or solo, and with the sign R. when the part will enter in the Ripieno. Thus, under the sign S. one is to leave the singing always to one solo voice, until one finds the sign R., which will be for the entire Ripieno, until the sign S., and so on always in this way. It is possible to augment in the ripienos for each and every part, other parts along with the voices, such as instruments.

And live happily.

---

[4] A reference to the Gospel story of the Samaritan woman at the well (John 4).

Giovanni Felice Sances, *Salmi brevi a 4 voci concertate* (1647)
Dedicated to Ferdinand IV

SACRA REAL MAESTÁ
Essendo i Prencipi Simolacri di Dio in Terra, all'hora si rendono maggiormente simili à quello, quando con virtù, & attioni heroiche, procurano d'imitarlo. Il ricever un'atto di ottima volontà in luogo dell'effetto di essa, è proprio del la Divina Bontà, e l'esser gradita dalla M.V. la sincera, & humil espressione dell'animo mio divoto, in queste Musicali Compositioni per quel più, che da me se le deve, sarà un'effetto proportionato all'innata benignità di Lei, che si accosterà al Divino. Con tal fiducia l'hò io dedicate à V.M. e sotto la di lei protettione le hò manda te alla stampa, & hora riverente gliele presento.

Prego in tanto S[ua] D[ivina] M[aestá] che si come anco nelle attioni humane si è compiacciuta di farla esser nel Mondo simile à sestessa, cosi doppo lunga serie di felicissimi anni, si compiaccia concederle una perfetta unione con essa medesima nell'Eternità. E qui alla M.V. profondissimamente m'inchino.
D.V. Sac. Real Maestà
Humilissimo & obligatissimo servo
Gioan Felice Sances

TO YOUR SACRED ROYAL MAJESTY
Being that Princes are the Image of God on Earth, they therefore make themselves more similar to Him when with virtue and heroic actions they seek to imitate Him. It is proper for Divine Goodness to receive an act of good will as a consequence of its own goodness, and because Your Majesty appreciates the sincere and humble expression of my soul's devotion in these Musical Compositions that should come to me from you, the fact that you appreciate them will be an effect proportionate to Your innate goodness, which approaches the Divine. With such faithfulness I have dedicated them to Your Majesty, and under your protection I have sent them to the press, and now I reverently present them to you.

I pray in the meantime that His Divine Majesty [God], seeing that He was so pleased to see in human actions one in the World so similar to Him, after a long series of most happy years may be happy to grant to you a perfect union with Himself for Eternity. And now to Your Majesty I most profoundly bow.

Your Sacred Royal Majesty's
Most Humble and most obliged servant,
Giovanni Felice Sances

Giovanni Felice Sances, *Antiphonae Sacrae B.M.V. per totum annum una voce decantandae* (1648)
Dedicated to Anton Spindler von Hofegg, Abbot of the *Schottenkirche*

REVERENDISSIMO NOBILI ET AMPLISSIMO DOMINO DOMINO ANTONIO SPINDLER Celeberrimi MNR ij Ad Scotos Abbati Vigilantissimo S: S: Theologiae Doctori Sac: Caes: Maiestatis Consiliario & Patrono Meo Colendissimo.

 Ea est Reverendissimae Dominationis tuae in Divam Virginem pietas, animique devotissima propensio, ut hascè ab Ecclesia Christi Sponsa eius honori concinnatas laudes, & à me modulis harmonicis innexas Tuae Amplitudini dicandas accederit.

 Novi quo amoris in eandem feraris affectu, & maximè cum eius musicus laudum sonus in Sacris Aedibus tuas demulcet aures.

 Tum enim mihi quodam modo videris persimilis fonti illi Regionis Alesiae, de quo Solinus in Mundi Mirabilibus qui licet mirifice placidus, quietusque decurrat ubi tamen vocem harmonicam, citharaeque sonum persenserit, mox festivo quodam modo exilit, seseque erigens intumescit, ita ut è suo lectulo; septisquae exire velle videatur. Talis omnino est placidissimus ille animus tuus, qui non alio impulsore, quam Dei, Matrisque ipsius laudibus de sua quasi statione dimonetur, & ita quidem, ut è corpore, amoris impetu, nescio qua ratione exiliat, & in hac quoque aerumnosa vita beatam faelicitatem delibet. Cuius dulcedinem, ut & imposterum degustare pergas, Praesul Reverendissime, harum Virginearum laudum praeconia, meae erga te humillime servitutis, ac subiectionis symbolum, ac monimentum, laeta fronte, eoque animo accipe, quo omnes tibi devotos pro innata tibi facilitate ac benignitate complecti consuevisti.

 Benevolentia haec tua mihi fuerit stimulus, imposterum maiori obsequio, ac devotione tuam gratiam, favoremque quo ad vixero demerendi. Precor interim DEUM ter Optimum terque Maximum, ut Dominationem Tuam Reverendissimam ad suam propagandam gloriam, plurimarumquae animarum salutem, saluam incolumemque annis quam plurimis conservet. Vale
Reverendissimae & amplissimae Dominationis tuae
Addictissimus servus
Ioannes Felix Sances

TO THE MOST REVEREND, NOBLE, AND MOST DISTINGUISHED LORD, ANTON SPINDLER, most celebrated MNR and most Vigilant Abbot of the Schottenkirche, Most Sacred Theological Doctor, Counselor to His Sacred Imperial Majesty, and My Most Honored Patron.

It is characteristic of your Most Reverend Lordship's piety for the Divine Virgin, and of the most devoted inclination of your mind that it would embrace these praises of its honor from the Church, Bride of Christ, which have been entwined by me with unworthy harmonies and are of necessity dedicated to Your Greatness.

May you be borne away by that affection of new love for the Virgin, especially when the musical sound of her praises caresses your ears in Sacred Halls.

Thus indeed do you seem to me in a certain way very similar to that stream of the Region of Alesia, about which Solinus wrote in his *Mundi Mirabilia*: granted that it is marvelously calm and quiet, it nevertheless hurries down where it perceives the harmonious voice and sound of the cithara, and soon in a certain lively way it springs forth and, raising itself up, swells so that it seems to want to leave its bed and its banks. Altogether so great is your most placid mind that it is moved from its convictions by no other instigation than the praises of God and his Mother, and indeed in such a way that it may somehow spring forth from the body by the force of its love and may taste a little blessed happiness in this life of suffering. Most Reverend Religious Leader, that you may also continue to taste this sweetness in the future, accept the proclamations of these praises for the Virgin (which are the labors of my most humble servitude toward you, both the symbol and the monument of my subjection) with kindly countenance and with that disposition with which you became accustomed to embracing all things devoted to you in accordance with your innate good nature and benevolence.

This your benevolence to me shall have been an incentive for greater allegiance and devotion in the future, until I shall have come to life in gaining your grace and your favor. I pray meanwhile that GOD, thrice Highest and Best, may preserve safe and unharmed for as many years as possible Your Most Reverend Lordship for the increase of his glory and the salvation of many souls. Be well.
your Most Reverend and most distinguished Lordship's
Most Devoted servant
Giovanni Felice Sances

Giovanni Antonio Rigatti, *Messa e salmi, parte concertati* (1640)
Dedicated to Ferdinand III

SACRA CESAREA MAESTÀ
Per averzar questi sacri componimenti à salire in Cielo, hò destinato d'inalzarli nelle mani di V.M. che in questo mondo siede nel supremo Trono del merito, e della Gloria. Sono parti deboli, tutta vianoso come meglio dichiararmi humilissimo servo della M.V. senon col dedicarle ciò che composi per la maestà di Dio.

 Ella che fràtutti i Prencipi dell'Universo cosi bene lo rapresenta in ogni virtù, non sdegni di ricever come magnanimo una tenue oblatione, e compatire come benigno un ardire divoto:
 Ed io mentre auguro dal Cielo Vittorie alla sua destra, grandezze al suo scettro, e felicità à suoi Regni, humilmente me le inchino.
Venetia il Primo Ottobre 1640
Di V. Sacra Cesarea Maestà
Humilissimo et divotissimo servo.
Gio: Antonio Rigatti

TO THE SACRED IMPERIAL MAJESTY[5]
To make these sacred compositions ascend to Heaven, I have decided to elevate them into the hands of Your Majesty who in this world sits on the highest throne of merit and glory. They are poor pieces, but I do not know how to make myself better known to Your Majesty as your most humble servant if not by dedicating to you what I composed for the majesty of God.

You, who among princes of the universe represents Him so well in each virtue, may not disdain to receive as a generous person a trifling offering, and to suffer graciously an ardent devotee.

And while I supplicate from Heaven victories to your right hand, greatness to your scepter, and happiness to your reign, I bow humbly before you.
Venice, the First of October 1640
Your Sacred Imperial Majesty's
Most Humble and most devout servant,
Giovanni Antonio Rigatti

---

[5] Translation from Giovanni Antonio Rigatti, *Messa e salmi, parte concertati*, ed. Linda Maria Koldau, RRMBE, vols 128–30 (3 vols, Middleton, 2003), vol. 1, p. 3.

Claudio Monteverdi, *Selva morale et spirituale* (1641)
Dedicated to Elenora Gonzaga

SACRA CESAREA MAESTÀ
Havendo io cominciato á consacrare alle glorie della Serenissima Casa GONZAGA la mia riverente servitù, all'hora quando compiacquesi il Serenissimo Sig. Duca VINCENZO Genitore della Sacra MAESTA Vostra (felice record.) di ricevere gli effetti della mia osservanza, quali nella mia verde età cercai con ogni diligenza, & co 'l mio talento della Musica per lo spatio di anni vintidue continui di mostrarli affettuosi, non hà mai potuto l'interpositione della terra, & del tempo ecclissare pure un minimo raggio del mio ossequio, per non essere mai restati oppressi dall'oblivione gli honori ricevuti, si dàlli Serenissimi Precessori, come anche dalla Maestà Vostra, má più tosto da essi sempre più io sono stato all'occasione cortesemente ravvivato sino à questa mia matura età. La onde ho preso ardire di dare alle luci questa Selva morale, e spirituale, dedicandola á V.M. acciò sul frontespitio tenendo il Suo Sacro Nome, vada d'ogni intorno sicura publicando al Mondo la mia obligata divotione. Per lo che supplico la Maestá Vostra con ogni humiltà possibile á degnarsi di riceverla, ancorche ella non sia forse in quel grado di perfettione, ch'io desidererei, ch'ella fosse, ma sarà un picciol testimonio da riverente affetto che humilmente, & prontamente la dedico & consacra alla Maestà Vostra, con pregarle da Dio il colmo d'ogni consolata prosperità.
Di Venetia il Primo Maggio 1641
Di V. Sacra M.C.
Humilissimo & obligatissimo servitore
Claudio Monteverde

TO THE SACRED IMPERIAL MAJESTY[6]

Having begun to consecrate my reverent servitude to the glories of the Most Serene House of GONZAGA when the Most Serene Lord Duke VINCENZO (of happy memory), father of Your Sacred MAJESTY, was pleased to receive the results of my service, which in my green age I sought with all diligence and with my talent for music to demonstrate loving to him for the space of 22 continuous years, the interposition of space and time has not been able to eclipse the slightest ray of my regard, so that the honors received, from your Most Serene predecessors as from Your Majesty, will never be covered in oblivion, but rather I have always on occasion been courteously revived by them until this my mature age. Whence I have dared to publish this *Selva morale, e spirituale*, dedicating it to Your Majesty so that bearing Your Sacred Name on the title page it may go secure everywhere, making public to the world my obliged devotion. For which I beg Your Majesty with all possible humility to deign to receive it, even if it is perhaps not in that state of perfection that I would desire it to be, but it will be a small testament of reverent affection that I humbly and readily dedicate and consecrate to Your Majesty, together with praying for you to God the height of all consoling prosperity.

From Venice, the First of May 1641
Your Sacred Imperial Majesty's
Most Humble and most obligated servant
Claudio Monteverdi

---

[6] Translation by Robert R. Holzer.

Teatro musicale de concerti ecclesiastici a due, tre, e quattro voci di diversi celebri, e nomati autori (1649)
Dedicated to Cardinal Francesco Peretti di Montalto

Emin[entissi]mo Sig[no]re
DA i communi applausi di questa Patria per l'arrivo felicissimo di Vostra Emin. risvegliate le Muse, havendo formato questo Musico Theatro, non altrove meglio collocar lo potevano, che vicino all'ombre amenissime del suo MONT'ALTO, sotto gli influssi amorevoli delle sue STELLE PERETTE. Che se l'armonioso concento di quel famoso Canto Thebano potè di modo dar moto alle pietre, & animare le felci, che da se stese, senza mano d'artefice, le mura d'una Città si fabricorono: qual maraviglia sia adesso, che all'aspetto giocondissimo di V.Em. animate le Muse habbiano potuto l'edificio di questo Theatro, quasi che d'improviso formare. Sò, che per pompa d'Imperiale grandezza fù ammirato da Roma quel superbo Theatro di Domitiano, che nello spatio di pochi giorni parve quasi in un medesimo tempo e disegnato, e fabricato. Sò, che Selimo gran Signore de Turchi soleva ne suoi viaggi portar su gl'homeri de Cameli così gran copia de legni lavorati, che con essi fin ne' più ermi deserti faceva d'improviso nascere le Città. Sò, che Henrico Rè d'Inghilterra dovendo abboccarsi in campagna con Francesco Primo Rè di Francia, fece in una notte fabricare così sontuoso Palaggio, che ad onta de cittadini edifitii vedeansi fra ori, & argenti spiegarsi ricche le Gallerie, diffundersi vaste le sale, allargarsi in lunga serie attapezzate le camere. Mà queste maraviglie hà osservato in questi giorni la nostra Città, quanto avezza già a vagheggiare le pomposissime gale, e superbissimi apparati fatti ad honore della Maestà Augustissima della Regina N. Signora, vidde all'improviso comparire V.Em. con sì nobile arredo, che sembrolle di mirare trasferite in Milano le magnificenze di Roma. Possono ben pregiarsi i secoli andati d'haver visto alle preghiere d'un Thaumaturgo trabalzata da un luogo all'altro una Montagna di marmo: che noi con più stupore habbiam visto, volar da Roma i MONTI d'oro: Che se quel potentissimo Rè Xerse per tragittare felicemente da Grecia in Asia le sue grossissime armate, spianò i Monti facendo caminar le onde, ove sorgeano le Isole: Gloria maggiore è del Nostro Potentissimo Monarca, che per condurre felicemente in Ispagna la sua dilettissima Sposa, faccia caminar su'l Mare i MONTI stessi. Così auguro a V.Em. felicissima la navigatione; e se ad Ansione, che dolcemente suonando navigava, quasi per secondargli il corso dell'onde, gli formavano attorno un bel Theatro i Delfini, anch'io per addolcirle, e prosperarle il suo viaggio, le invio d'innocenti Sirene un Musicale Theatro. Supplico V.Em. à gradirlo, alla quale faccio humilissma riverenza. Dalle mie Stampe li 12. Luglio 1649.
Di Vostra Eminenza
Humilissimo, e Devotissimo Servitore
Giorgio Rolla

Most Eminent Sir

The Muses, awakened by the communal applause of this Country at the most felicitous arrival of Your Eminence and having formed this Musical Theater, could not place it any better than near the most pleasant shadow of your HIGH MOUNTAIN, under the loving influences of your PERETTE STARS. If the harmonious song of that famous Theban Singer [Amphion] could move all the stones and animate the ferns; if on their own, without the hand of the craftsman, the walls of a city had built themselves: why would it now be a marvel that at the most joyful appearance of Your Eminence the Muses could have animated the edifice of this Theater, as if it were formed unexpectedly. I know that through the pomp of Imperial greatness that superb Theater of Domitian (which in the space of a few days seemed at the same time to be designed and built) was admired by Rome. I know that Selim, the great Lord of the Turks, was in the habit of carrying in his travels on the backs of the Camels such a great copy of wood carvings, that with it, as far as the more isolated deserts, he made Cities rise unexpectedly. I know that Henry [VIII], King of England, needing to meet in the field [of the Cloth of Gold] with Francis I, King of France, had constructed in one night such a sumptuous Palace that despite the town buildings, one could see the riches of the Galleries spreading out among gold and silver, the vastness of the halls, and the chambers spreading over a long series of upholstered rooms. But our City has observed these marvels in these days; as much as it already used to long for the most pompous splendor and most superb machinery made in honor of the Most August Majesty our Lady the Queen, it has seen Your Eminence unexpectedly appearing with such noble fittings that the magnificence of Rome seemed to be transferred to Milan. The past ages can well be pleased to have seen a Mountain of marble moved from one place to another by the prayers of a miracle worker: with more astonishment we have seen these MOUNTAINS of gold flying from Rome. If when that most powerful King Xerxes, in order to successfully cross his most large army from Asia to Greece, leveled the Mountains by making the waves walk where the Islands rose: Our Most Powerful Monarch has greater Glory in that, in order to fortunately accompany his most delightful Spouse to Spain, he can make the MOUNTAINS themselves walk upon the Sea. Thus I wish for Your Eminence a most felicitous journey; and like the Dolphins who, as if to favor the course of the waves, formed a beautiful Theater around Ansione, who used to sweetly play music while sailing, I too, in order to sweeten and make prosperous your voyage, send to you a Musical Theater of innocent Sirens. I beg Your Eminence, in front of whom I most humbly bow, to accept it. From my Publishing House, the twelfth of July 1649.
Your Eminence's
Most Humble and Most Devoted Servant
Giorgio Rolla

Andreas Rauch, *Currus triumphali muisici, Imperatorum Romanorum Tredecim ex Augustissima Archiducali Domo Austriaca* (1648)
Dedicated to Ferdinand III

SERENISSIMO, POTENTISSIMO, INVICTISSIMOQUE PRINCIPI AC DOMINO, DOMINO FERDINANDO TERTIO,
Electo Romanorum Imperatori semper Augusto, ac Germaniae, Hungariae, Bohemiaeque &c. Regi, Archiduci Austriae, &c. Domino meo Clementissimo, Iusto, Pio, Pacifico,

Triumphum, vitam, aeternitatem.

Quemadmodum, Augustissime Caesar, nullum unquam in orbe bellum exarsit, cujus flammas tandem non restinxisset Pax, humanae felicitatis apex; ita eandem postliminio reducem cumulatissimo semper celeberrimorum encomiorum, hymnorum & triumphorum honore omnis merito aetas condecoravit. Spe igitur fretus, fore, ut in nostra quoque diu jam furores Martis perperssa Patria; sagum togae, oleae gladius jam tandem cederet, Sacratissimae Caes: Regiaeque Majestati Vestrae, inter (de quo non dubito) plurimos alios ego minimus Currum hunc Triumphalen Cantionibus sacris concinnatum (utinam artis simplicitate titulo haud indignum) devotissima mente adornare ausus sum. Verum hunc bellissimum belli finem auspicatissimis Imperatorialium Nuptiarum solemnibus, Divina providentia, antevertentibus, prodromi instar subsecuturae Pacis, non dubitavi ad Augustissimos Thoros Thalamosque Sacratissimae Caesareae Regiaeque Majestatis Vestrae eundem demississime gratulabundus provehere, humillimis precibus contendens, dignetur Sacratissima Caesarea Regiaque Majestas Vestra tenues has infirmi[7] sui subditi Musas sereno innatae Clementiae vultu suscipere, meque sub umbra excelsarum alarum suarum protegere.

Deus Ter Opt. Max. Majestatum Vestrarum Augustissimo Consortio voto majorem prosperitatem aeternum largiatur,
Sacratissimae Caes: Regiaeque Majestatis Vestrae,
Humillimus & subjectissimus subditus,
Andreas Rauch, Civis Semproniensis

---

[7] Spelled "infimi" in the print.

TO THE MOST SERENE, MOST POTENT, MOST INVINCIBLE EMPEROR AND LORD FERDINAND III,
Elected Roman Emperor, always August; and King of Germany, Hungary, Bohemia, etc.; Archduke of Austria, etc.; My Most Clement, Just, Pious, Peace-making Lord,

may there be Triumph, life, eternity.

Most August Emperor, just as no war has ever flared up in the world whose flames Peace (the summit of human happiness) has not finally extinguished, thus every age adorned the restored Peace upon its return with the well-deserved and overabundant honor of encomiums, hymns, and triumphs for the most famous men. Trusting, therefore, in the hope that in our age our Fatherland will have already endured the furies of Mars to the greatest extent possible, that the military uniform has finally yielded to the toga and the sword to the olive branch, I, the least significant among many others (which I do not doubt), have with a most devoted mind dared to adorn for Your Most Sacred Imperial and Royal Majesty this Triumphal Chariot clad in sacred songs (if only it were worthy of such a simple title for the art). Indeed, with the most auspicious celebration of the Imperial Nuptials anticipating (with the help of Divine Providence) the most beautiful end of the war, the image of a prelude to the soon-to-arrive peace, I did not hesitate to most humbly present, offering my congratulations, this same Chariot before the Most August Marriage Bed of Your Most Sacred Imperial and Royal Majesty, hoping with most humble prayers that Your Most Sacred Imperial and Royal Majesty may deem these slender Muses of your feeble servant worthy of acceptance by the serene countenance of your innate Clemency, and may think me worthy of protection under the shadow of your exalted wings.

I pray that God, Thrice Highest and Best, lavish increasing and eternal good fortune upon the Most August Consort of Your Majesties,
Your Most Sacred Imperial and Royal Majesty's
Most Humble and lowest servant,
Andreas Rauch, Citizen of Sopron

Bibliography

Manuscript and Archival Sources

Archivio di Stato, Mantua.
    Seria E.VI.3, busta 554, fasc. Atto Melani—1653.
Benediktinerstift, Kremsmünster.
    L14.
    ser. C, fas. 15, no. 715.
Biblioteca Estense e Universitaria, Modena.
    ms. ital. 33.
Haus-, Hof- und Staatsarchiv, Vienna.
    Familienarchiv, Familienkorrespondenz A, Karton 11.
Hofkammerarchiv, Vienna.
    Niederösterreichische Herrschaftsakten, W61/A/32.
Österreichische Nationalbibliothek, Vienna.
    Cod. 9894.
    Cod. 9931.
    Cod. 11540.
    Cod. 12590.
    Cod. 12592.
    Cod. 13182.
    Cod. 13242.
    Cod. 13244.
    Cod. 13258.
    Cod. 13275.
    Cod. 13278.
    Cod. 13281.
    Cod. 13284.
    Cod. 13285.
    Cod. 13309.
    Cod. 13310.
    Cod. 13341.
    Cod. 13347.
    Cod. 13349.
    Cod. 13352.
    Cod. 13359.
    Cod. 13555.
    Cod. 13556.
    Cod. 13557.

Cod. 13911.
Cod. 13923.
Cod. 16202.
Cod. 16207.
Cod. Ser. n. 4270.
Cod. Ser. n. 4450.
Mus. Hs. 16042.
Mus. Hs. 18707.
Suppl. mus. 2451.
Suppl. mus. 2503.
Ratsbücherei, Lüneburg.
  Mus. ant. pract. K.N. 28.
  Mus. ant. pract. K.N. 206.
Statens Musikbibliotek, Stockholm.
  Musik Rar.
Státni Zámek a Zahrady, Kromé íž.
  Historicko-Umelecké Fondy. Hudební Archiv II-56 (A230).
  Historicko-Umelecké Fondy. Hudební Archiv II-64 (A236).
Wiener Stadt- und Landesarchiv, Vienna.
  Hs. A 41/16, Kirchenmeisteramtsrechunungsbuch, Jg. 1648.

Printed Primary Sources (Including Modern Editions)

Adler, Guido (ed.), *Musikalische Werke der Kaiser Ferdinand III., Leopold I. und Joseph I.* (2 vols, Vienna, 1892; reprint, Westmead: Gregg International, 1972).

Attione da rappresentarsi in musica nel giorno natalitio di S. Maestà Cesarea Ferdinando III. a 13. Luglio 1651 (Vienna: Cosmerovius, 1651).

[Avancini, Nicholas], *Theodosius Magnus Justus et Pius Imperator* (Vienna: Cosmerovius, 1654).

Avancini, Nicholas, *Poesis dramatica*, 4 vols (Cologne: Friessem, 1675–79).

Balduin, Christian Adolph, *Poetische Entdeckung der Ehren-Pforte* (Regensburg: Fischer, 1653).

Bastianschiz, Matthias, *Oliva Pacis, sive Virgo sine macula concepta* (Vienna: Cosmerovius, 1650).

Bendinelli, Cesare, *Tutta l'arte della trombetta* (1614); facsimile ed. Edward H. Tarr, Documenta Musicologica, vol. 2:5 (Kassel: Bärenreiter, 1975).

———, *The Entire Art of Trumpet Playing*, trans. Edward H. Tarr (Nashville: Brass Press, 1975).

Bucelinus, Gabriel, *Germania topo- chrono- stemmato-graphica sacra et profana* (2 vols, Ulm: Görlin, 1655–57).
Carafa, Vincenzo, *Fascetto di mirra, overo considerationi sopra le piaghe di Christo* (Vienna: Gelbhaar, 1638).
Collurafi, Antonino, *L'aquila coronata overo la felicita sospirata dall'universo* (Venice: Ginammi, 1637).
Czerwenka, Wenceslaus Adalbert, *Annales et acta pietatis augustissimae ac serenissimae Domus Habspurgo-Austriacae* (Prague: Störitz, 1694).
de Wael, Guillaume, *Corona Sacratissimorum Jesu Christi Vulnerum XXXV. Considerationibus* (Antwerp: Cnobbarus, 1649).
Der Röm. Kayserl. Mayest. FERDINANDI III. Wie auch Der Röm. Königl. Mayest. FERDINANDI IV. Hoff-Stat: Wie sich derselbe in Jahren 1653. und 1654. uff dem Reichstag zu Regenspurg eingefunden (Frankfurt: Serlin, 1654).
Dueller, Thomas, *Oesterreichischer Phoenix oder Ferdinandus Quartus ... nebest allgemeinen Wehemut diser Welt abgestorbem ... Durch gegenwertige Klag Rede beweinet* (Vienna: Cosmerovius, 1654).
Eigentliche Beschreibung deß den 24. May Anno 1654 Ihrer Kayserlich und Königlicher Mayestätten zu Wienn beschehenen Einzugs (Vienna: Cosmerovius, 1654).
Extra-Ordinari Mittwochs Postzeittungen (Vienna: Cosmerovius, 1645–98).
Falck, Georg, *Idea boni cantoris ...* (Nuremberg: Endter, 1688).
Fantini, Girolamo, *Modo per imparare a sonare di tromba, tanto di guerra quanto musicalmente in organo, con tromba sordina, col cimbalo, e ogn'altro istrumento* (Frankfurt: Vaustch, 1638); facsimile in *Collezione di trattati e musiche antiche edite in fac-simile* (Milan: Bollettino Bibliografico musicale, 1934).
_____, *Method for Learning to Play the Trumpet in a Warlike Way*, trans. Edward H. Tarr (Nashville: Brass Press, 1975).
Ferdinand III, *Poesie diverse composte in hore rubate d'Academico Occupato* (n.p., n.d.).
Ferrari, Benedetto, *L'Inganno d'Amore* (Regensburg: Fischer, 1653).
Froberger, Johann Jakob, *Lamentation faite sur la mort tres douloureuse de Sa Majestè Imperiale, Ferdinand le troiseme; et se joue lentement avec discretion. An. 1657*, in *Orgel- und Clavierwerke 3*, ed. Guido Adler, Denkmäler der Tonkunst in Österreich, vol. 21 (Vienna: Astoria, 1903).
Gabrielli, Diamante, *Theti* (Vienna: Cosmerovius, 1656).
Gentilotto, Cornelius, *Maria Virgo sine macula concepta Ferdinando III. Romanorum Imperatori in arcu coelesti repraesentata ipso die Immaculatae Conceptioni Sacro, dum primum Antiq. et Celeber. Universitate Viennensi solenniter hoc festum celebrante in Basilica*

D. Stephani, Sacra Maiestas Augustissimam sua praesentia reddidit solennitatem (Vienna: Cosmerovius, 1649).

Hill, Robert (ed.), *Vienna, Österreichische Nationalbibliothek, Musiksammlung, Mus. Hs. 18707 (Froberger Autographs)*, Seventeenth-Century Keyboard Music, vol. 3 (New York: Garland, 1988).

Jacobus, Matthias, *Arma virtutum quae Serenissimo, Potentissimo, et Invictissimo Principi ac Domino, Domino Ferdinando Tertio ...* (Breslau: Baumannianus, n.d.).

Khueffstain, Gotthulphus, *Maria Virgo sine macula concepta Ferdinando III. Romanorum Imperatori in speculo repraesentata* (Vienna: Cosmerovius, 1651).

Lapide, Cornelius a, *Commentarii in Canticum Canticorum* (Antwerp, 1638; reprint, Antwerp: Meursius, 1657).

Leopold Wilhelm, *Diporti del Crescente, divisi in rime morali, devote, heroiche, amorose* (Brussels: Mommartio, 1656).

Le quattro Relazioni seguite in Ratisbona nelli tempi sotto notati. Prima dell'Elettione del Rè de Romani à 22. Decembre 1636 in Persona di S. M. Ferdinando III. Re d'Ungaria e Boemia. Seconda della Incoronatione dell'istessa Maestà li 30. Decembre 1636. Terza del Balleto fatto nella Casa del Consiglio di detta Città li 4. Gennaro 1637. Quarta della Incoronatione della Regina de Romani à 7. detto (Vienna: Gelbhaar, 1637).

Lequille, Didacus, *Pietas Austriaca, secundo sibi Fortuna, ac suae fortunata Posteritati in Matrimonialium Foederum ingenuitate* (Innsbruck: Agricola, 1656).

_____, *De rebus Austriacis tomus tribus: Piissima atque augustissima Domus Austria* (Innsbruck: Wagner, 1660).

Lindelauf, Johannes Ernestus, *Maria Virgo sine macula concepta, in rosa repraesentata* (Vienna: Cosmerovius, 1653).

Lotichus, Johann Peter, *Austrias Parva: id est, gloriae Austriacae, et belli nuper Germanici, sub divo Matthia, Ferdinandis II. et III. Impp. gesti, compendaria* (Frankfurt: Schönwetter, 1653).

Lünig, Johann Christian, *Theatrum Ceremoniale historico-politicum*, vol. 2 (Leipzig: Wiedemann, 1720).

Manzoni, Luigi, *Applausi festivi fatti in Roma per l'elezzione di Ferdinando III al Regno de' Romani* (Rome: Facciotti, 1637).

Maria Virgo sine macula concepta Ferdinando III. Romanorum Imperatori in columba repraesentata (Vienna: Cosmerovius, 1650).

Merlo, Jacob (ed.), *Paradisus animae christianae* (Cologne: Kinchi, 1644).

Monteverdi, Claudio, *Selva morale et spirituale* (Venice: Magni, 1641).

_____, *Madrigals, Book 8: Madrigali guerrieri et amorosi*, ed. Gian Francesco Malipiero and Stanley Appelbaum (New York: Dover, 1991).

Motetti a voce sola de diversi Eccelentissimi Autori (Venice: Gardano, 1645).

Musart, Carolus, *Sunamitis Christiana, sive affectus pii, quibus exemplo mulieris sunamitidis Elisaeum Hospitio recipientis, Anima disponitur ad rite, et magno cum fructu suscipiendum Christum, in Venerabili Eucharistia* ... (Vienna: Rixin, 1637).

_____, *Nova Vienensium peregrinatio a templo Cathedrali S. Stephani per septem Christi patientis stationes ad s. sepulchrum in Hernals* ... (Vienna: Cosmerovius, 1642).

Ordentlichen Zeittungen (Vienna: Formica, 1625–39).

Pallantius, Albertus, *Serenissimo, Potentissimo Principi, ac Domino, Domino Ferdinando III. ... cum Rex Romanorum eligeretur, inauguraretur et coronaretur Panegyricus* (Cologne, 1637).

Paullus, Gualterius, *Affectus Eucharistici Pietati Ferdinandi Tertii Imperatoris* (Vienna: Formica, 1640).

Persiani, Horatio, *Lo Specchio di Virtù* (Vienna: Gelbhaar, 1642).

Phosphorus Austriacus de Gente Austriaca libri tres, in quibus gentis illius prima origo, magnitudo, imperium, ac virtus asseritur, et probatur (Louvain: Coenestenius, 1665).

Plati, Guglielmo, *La Gloria, Panegirico per le Grandezze di Ferdinando III. Re de' Romani eletto* (Milan: Gariboldi, 1637).

Princeps in compendio, hoc est puncta aliquot compendiosa, quae circa gubernationem reipublicae observanda videntur (Vienna: Gelbhaar, 1632; reprint, Vienna: Cosmerovius, 1668).

Priorato, Galeazzo Gualdo, *Historia di Ferdinando Terzo Imperatore* (n.p., 1656; reprint, Vienna: Cosmerovius, 1672).

Profe, Ambrosius (ed.), *Ander Theil geistlicher Concerten und Harmonien* (Leipzig: Köhler, 1641).

_____, *Erster Theil geistlicher Concerten und Harmonien* (Leipzig: Köhler, 1641).

_____, *Corollarium geistlicher Collectaneorum* (Leipzig: Ritzsch, 1649).

Promptuarii musici, sacras harmonias sive motetus V. VI. VII. et VIII. vocum ... pars altera (Strasbourg: Kieffer, 1612).

Rauch, Andreas, *Concentus votivus ... ad Comitia Semproniana ingressum solemnem et auspicatissimum, incliti senatus eiusdem loci, jussu et voluntate decantatus, anno MDCXXXIV, die 18. Decembris* (Vienna: Gelbhaar, 1635).

_____, *Currus triumphalis musici, Imperatorum Romanorum Tredecim ex Augustissima Archiducali Domo Austriaca* (Vienna: Rickhes, 1648).

Regiae virtutis, et felicitatis XII symbola ... Ferdinando III ... cum Rex Romanorum inauguraretur, coronaretur ... in humillimae gratulationis, venerationis, et gratissimi animi argumentum offerebat Collegium Societatis Jesu Dilinganum (n.p., 1637).

Regiae Virtutes, seu Initia Regni Salomonis Pietate et Justitia, Consilio et Industria, Duce Sapientia semper felicia (Vienna: Kürner, 1656).

Reliquiae sacrorum concentum Giovan Gabrielis, Johan-Leonis Hasleri, utriusque praestantissimi musici (Nuremberg: Kauffmann, 1615).

Rigatti, Giovanni Antonio, *Messa e salmi, parte concertati*, ed. Linda Maria Koldau, Recent Researches in the Music of the Baroque Era, vols 128–30 (3 vols, Middleton: A-R Editions, 2003).

Ruzola Dominicus [Dominicus a Jesu Maria], *Argumenta psalmorum ad utiliorem divini officii recitationem* (Rome: Zannetti, 1623).

Sances, Giovanni Felice, *Cantade ... a doi voci ... libro secondo, parte seconda* (Venice: Magni, 1633).

———, *Cantade ... a voce sola ... libro secondo, parte prima* (Venice: Magni, 1633).

———, *Il quarto libro delle cantate, et arie a voce sola* (Venice: Magni, 1636).

———, *Motetti a una, due, tre, e quattro voci (1638)*, ed. Steven Saunders, Recent Researches in the Music of the Baroque Era, vol. 126 (Middleton: A-R Editions, 2003).

———, *Motetti a voce sola* (Venice: Magni, 1638).

———, *Antifone e litanie della Beatissima Vergine a più voci* (Venice: Magni, 1640).

———, *Motetti a 2, 3, 4, e cinque voci (1642)*, ed. Andrew H. Weaver, Recent Researches in the Music of the Baroque Era, vol. 148 (Middleton: A-R Editions, 2008).

———, *Salmi a 8 voci concertati, con la comodità de suoi ripieni per chi li desiderasse* (Venice: Magni, 1643).

———, *Salmi brevi a 4 voci concertate* (Venice: Gardano, 1647).

———, *Antiphonare Sacrae B.M.V. per totum annum una voce decantandae* (Venice: Gardano, 1648).

———, *Capricci poetici* (Venice: Gardano, 1649).

———, *Trattenimenti musicali per camera* (Venice: Gardano, 1657).

Saunders, Steven (ed.), *Fourteen Motets from the Court of Ferdinand II of Hapsburg*, Recent Researches in the Music of the Baroque Era, vol. 75 (Madison: A-R Editions, 1995).

Sebald, Martin, *Novum Romanum breviarum* (Mainz: Albinus, 1622).

Schmelzer, Johann Heinrich, *Lamento sopra la morte Ferdinani III*, ed. Wolfgang Gamerith (Graz: Akademische Druck- und Verlagdanstalt, 1975).

Schnoebelen, Anne (ed.), *Solo Motets from the Seventeenth Century: Facsimiles of Prints from the Italian Baroque* (10 vols, London: Garland, 1987–88).

Schünemann, Georg (ed.), *Trompeterfanfaren, Sonaten und Feldstücke, nach Aufzeichnungen deutscher Hoftrompeter des 16./17. Jahrhunderts* (Kassel: Bärenreiter, 1936).
Schütz, Heinrich, *Gesammelte Briefe und Schriften*, ed. E.H. Müller von Aslow (Regensburg, 1931; reprint, New York: Olms, 1976).
Slavata, Vilem, *Maria virgo immaculate concepta: Publico voto Ferdinandi III. Rom. Imp. in Austriae patronam electa* (Vienna: Cosmerovius, 1648).
Strozzi, Barbara, *Arie ... Opera Ottava* (Venice: Francesco Magni detto Gardano, 1664); facsimile edn in Barbara Strozzi, *Cantatas*, ed. Ellen Rosand, The Italian Cantata in the Seventeenth Century, vol. 5 (New York: Garland, 1986).
Teatro musicale de concerti ecclesiastici a due, tre, e quattro voci di diversi celebri, e nomati autori (Milan: Rolla, 1649).
Valentini, Giovanni, *Messa, Magnificat et Iubilate Deo a sette chori concertati con le trombe* (Vienna: Formica, 1621).
_____, *Sacri concerti a due, tre, quattro et cinque voci* (Venice: Vincenti, 1625).
_____, *Ragionamento sovra il Santissimo* (Vienna: Cosmerovius, 1642).
_____, *Santi Risorti nel Giorno della Passione di Christo* (Vienna: Cosmerovius, 1643).
_____, *La Vita di Santo Agapito* (Vienna: Cosmerovius, 1643).
_____, *O felix Maria*, ed. Konrad Ruhland, Musica pretiosa, vol. 14 (Niederaltaich: Cornetto, 1997).
_____, *Cantate gentes*, ed. Andrew H. Weaver, Web Library of Seventeenth-Century Music, vol. 9 (December 2007), http://sscm-wlscm.org
Vernulz, Nikolaus, *Virtutum augustissimae gentis Austriace libri tres* (Louvain: Zeger, 1640).
Vimina, Alberto, *La Gara* (Vienna: Rickhes, 1652).
Wadding, Lukas, *De definienda controversia Immaculatae Conceptionis B. Virginis Mariae* (Louvain: Hastenius, 1624).
Wassenberg, Everhard, *Commentariorum de bello inter invictissimos imperatores Ferdinandos II. et III. et eorum hostes, praesertim Fredericum Palatinum, Gabrielem Bethlenum, Daniae, Sueciae, Franciae reges liber singularis* (Frankfurt: Hummius, 1638).
_____, *Panegyricus, Sacratiss. Imperatori Ferdinando III. dictus* (Cologne: Kolkhoff, 1647).
_____, *Theatrum gloriae, Serenissimo Principi Leopoldo Guilielmo, Archiduci Austriae ... post expeditionem Belgicam anni 1649 ab Everhardo Wassenbergio, ejusdem Archiducis Bibliothecario et Historiographo, extractum et consecratum* (Brussels: Mommartius, 1650).

Weaver, Andrew H. (ed.), *Motets by Emperor Ferdinand III and Other Musicians from the Habsburg Court*, Collegium Musicum: Yale University, second series (Middleton: A-R Editions, in press).

Werdenhagen, Johannes Angelius, *Germania supplex, Divo Ferdinando III. Caesari invictissimo, et Imperii Romano-Germanici semper Augusto, omnem sceptri beatifilicitatem cum pace saluberrima optans* (Frankfurt am Main: Merrian, 1641).

Secondary Sources

Aber, Adolf, *Die Pflege der Musik unter den Wettinern und wettinischen Ernestinern von den Anfängen bis zur Auflösung der Weimarer Hofkapelle 1662* (Bückenburg and Leipzig: C.F.W. Siegel, 1921).

Adel, Kurt, *Das Wiener Jesuitentheater und die europäische Barockdramatik* (Vienna: Österreichischer Bundesverlag, 1960).

_____, "Handschriften von Jesuitendrama in der Österreichischen National-Bibliothek in Wien," *Jahrbuch der Gesellschaft für Wiener Theaterforschung*, 12 (1960): 83–112.

Aercke, Kristiaan P., *Gods of Play: Baroque Festival Performances as Rhetorical Discourse* (Albany: State University of New York Press, 1994).

Álvarez-Ossorio, Antonio, "The Ceremonial of Majesty and Aristocratic Protest: The Royal Chapel at the Court of Charles II," in Juan Josè Carreras and Bernardo García García (eds), *The Royal Chapel in the Time of the Habsburgs: Music and Ceremony in the Early Modern European Court*, trans. Yolanda Acker, English version ed. Tess Knighton, Studies in Medieval and Renaissance Music, vol. 3 (Woodbridge: Boydell, 2005).

Antonicek, Theophil, "Italienische Akademien am Kaiserhof," *Notring Jahrbuch* (1972): 75–6.

_____, "Die italienischen Text-vertonungen Kaiser Ferdinands III.," in Alberto Martino (ed.), *Beiträge zur Aufnahme der italienischen und spanischen Literatur in Deutschland im 16. und 17. Jahrhundert*, Chloe, vol. 9 (Amsterdam and Atlanta: Rodopi, 1990).

_____, "Musik und italienische Poesie am Hofe Kaiser Ferdinands III.," *Mitteilungen der Kommission für Musikforschung*, 42 (1990): 1–22.

Asch, Ronald G., *The Thirty Years' War: The Holy Roman Empire and Europe, 1618–48* (New York: St. Martin's, 1997).

Attanasio, Wendy Maria, "Fiery Art: Festival Decorations for the Election of Ferdinand III as King of the Romans in 1637" (M.A. thesis, University of California Riverside, 1999).

Beissel, Stephan, *Geschichte der Verehrung Marias im 16. und 17. Jahrhundert* (Freiburg, 1910; reprint, Nieuwkoop: B. de Graaf, 1970).
Benecke, Gerhard, "The Practice of Absolutism II: 1626–1629," in Geoffrey Parker (ed.), *The Thirty Years' War*, 2nd edn (London and New York: Routledge, 1997).
Benedikt, Erich, "Ein altes Noteninventar (kurz nach 1700) der Klosterkirche der Barmherzigen Brüder in Wien," *Studien zur Musikwissenschaft*, 47 (1999): 35–52.
Bernstein, Jane A., *Print Culture and Music in Sixteenth-Century Venice* (Oxford: Oxford University Press, 2001).
_____, "Publish or Perish? Palestrina and Print Culture in 16th-Century Italy," *Early Music*, 35 (2007): 225–35.
Bianconi, Lorenzo, and Thomas Walker, "Production, Consumption and Political Function of Seventeenth-Century Opera," *Early Music History*, 4 (1984): 209–96.
Bierther, Kathrin, *Der Regensburger Reichstag von 1640/1641* (Kallmünz: Lassleben, 1971).
Bireley, Robert, *Religion and Politics in the Age of the Counterreformation: Emperor Ferdinand II, William Lamormaini, S. J., and the Formation of Imperial Policy* (Chapel Hill: University of North Carolina Press, 1981).
_____, *The Counter-Reformation Prince: Anti-Machiavellianism or Catholic Statecraft in Early Modern Europe* (Chapel Hill and London: University of North Carolina Press, 1990).
_____, "Ferdinand II: Founder of the Habsburg Monarchy," in R.J.W. Evans and T.V. Thomas (eds), *Crown, Church and Estates: Central European Politics in the Sixteenth and Seventeenth Centuries* (London: Macmillan, 1991).
_____, "Confessional Absolutism in the Habsburg Lands in the Seventeenth Century," in Charles W. Ingrao (ed.), *State and Society in Early Modern Austria* (West Lafayette: Purdue University Press, 1994).
_____, *The Jesuits and the Thirty Years War: Kings, Courts, and Confessors* (Cambridge: Cambridge University Press, 2003).
Blackburn, Bonnie J., "The Virgin in the Sun: Music and Image for a Prayer Attributed to Sixtus IV," *Journal of the Royal Musical Association*, 124 (1999): 157–95.
Bohn, Emil, *Bibliographie der Musik-Druckwerke bis 1700 welche in der Stadtbibliothek, der Bibliothek des Academischen Instituts für Kirchenmusik und der Königlichen und Universitäts-Bibliothek zu Breslau aufbewahrt werden: Ein Beitrag zur Geschichte der Musik im XV., XVI., und XVII. Jahrhundert* (Berlin: Albert Cohn, 1883; reprint, Hildesheim: Olms, 1969).

_____, *Die musikalischen Handschriften des XVI. und XVII. Jahrhunderts in Stadtbibliothek zu Breslau: Ein Beitrag zur Geschichte der Musik im XVI. und XVII. Jahrhundert* (Breslau, 1890; reprint, Hildesheim: Georg Olms, 1970).

Bonney, Richard J., "France's 'War by Diversion,'" in Geoffrey Parker (ed.), *The Thirty Years' War*, 2nd edn (London and Boston: Routledge, 1997).

Brady, Thomas A., Jr., "Confessionalization: The Career of a Concept," in John M. Headley et al. (eds), *Confessionalization in Europe, 1555–1700: Essays in Honor and Memory of Bodo Nischan* (Aldershot: Ashgate, 2004).

Braun, Werner, "Musik in deutschen Gelehrtenbibliotheken des 17. und 18. Jahrhunderts," *Die Musikforschung*, 10 (1957): 241–50.

_____, "Monteverdis große Baßmonodien," in Ludwig Finscher (ed.), *Claudio Monteverdi: Festschrift Reinhold Hammerstein zum 70. Geburtstag* (Laaber: Laaber-Verlag, 1986).

Bryant, Lawrence M., *Ritual, Ceremony and the Changing Monarchy in France, 1350–1789* (Farnham: Ashgate, 2010).

Burke, Peter, *The Fabrication of Louis XIV* (New Haven: Yale University Press, 1992).

Bussmann, Klaus, and Heinz Schilling (eds), *1648: War and Peace in Europe* (3 vols, [Münster]: Veranstaltungsgesellschaft 350 Jahre Westfälischer Friede, 1998).

Cantú, C., "La Pompa della solenne entrata fatta nella città di Milano dalla Serenissima Maria Anna Austriaca," *Archivio storico lombardo*, 14 (1887): 341–57.

Carter, Tim, "Resemblance and Representation: Towards a New Aesthetic in the Music of Monteverdi," in Iain Fenlon and Tim Carter (eds), *Con che soavità: Studies in Italian Opera, Song, and Dance* (Oxford: Clarendon, 1995).

_____, *Music, Patronage and Printing in Late Renaissance Florence* (Aldershot: Ashgate, 2000).

_____, "The Venetian Secular Music," in John Whenham and Richard Wistreich (eds), *The Cambridge Companion to Monteverdi* (Cambridge: Cambridge University Press, 2007).

Cenzato, Elena, "La festa barocca: La real solenne entrata di Maria Anna d'Austria a Milano nel 1649," *Archivio storico lombardo*, 112 (1987): 47–100.

_____, and Luisa Rovaris, "'Comparvero finalmente gl'aspettati soli dell'Austriaco cielo': Ingressi solenni per nozze reali," in Annamaria Cascetta (ed.), *Aspetti della teatralità a Milano nell'età barocca*, Comunicazioni sociali, vol. 16 (Milan: Vita e Oensiero, 1994).

Chafe, Eric, *Monteverdi's Tonal Language* (New York: Schirmer, 1992).

Chesler, Robert Douglas, "Crown, Lords, and God: The Establishment of Secular Authority and the Pacification in Lower Austria, 1618–1648" (Ph.D. diss., Princeton University, 1979).
Clark, Jane, "Les folies françoises," *Early Music*, 8 (1980): 163–9.
Coreth, Anna, *Pietas Austriaca*, trans. William D. Bowman and Anna Maria Leitgeb (West Lafayette: Purdue University Press, 2004).
Cowart, Georgia J., *The Triumph of Pleasure: Louis XIV and the Politics of Spectacle* (Chicago: University of Chicago Press, 2008).
Culley, Thomas D., *Jesuits and Music, vol. 1, A Study of the Musicians Connected With the German College in Rome During the Seventeenth Century and of Their Activities in Northern Europe* (Rome: Jesuit Historical Institute; St Louis, St Louis University Press, 1970).
Dallett, Joseph B., "The Mystical Quest for God," in Gerhart Hoffmeister (ed.), *German Baroque Literature: The European Perspective* (New York: Frederick Ungar, 1983).
de Bin, Umberto, "Leopoldo I. imperatore e la sua corte nella letteratura italiana," in *Bolletino del Circolo Accademico Italiano, 1908–09* (Trieste: Caprin, 1910).
de Hoop Scheffer, Dieuwke, George S. Keys, and K.G. Boon (eds), *Christoffel van Sichen I to Herman Specht*, Hollstein's Dutch and Flemish Etchings, Engravings and Woodcuts, ca. 1450–1700, vol. 27 (Amsterdam: Van Gendt, 1983).
Dixon, Graham, "The Origins of the Roman 'Colossal Baroque,'" *Proceedings of the Royal Musical Association*, 106 (1979–80): 115–28.
_____, "*Concertato all romana* and Polychoral Music in Rome," in Francesco Luisi et al. (eds), *La scuola policorale romana del seisettecento: Atti del Convegno internazionale di studi in memoria di Laurence Feininger* (Trent: Provincia Autonoma di Trento, 1997).
Donin, Ludwig, *Die marianische Austria*, 3rd edn (Vienna: Mayer, 1884).
Duhr, Bernhard, *Geschichte der Jesuiten in den Ländern deutscher Zunge* (4 vols, Freiburg: Herder, 1907–28).
Duindam, Jeroen, *Vienna and Versailles: The Courts of Europe's Dynastic Rivals, 1550–1780* (Cambridge: Cambridge University Press, 2003).
Ehalt, Hubert Christian, *Ausdrucksformen absolutischer Herrschaft: Der Wiener Hof im 17. und 18. Jahrhundert*, Sozial- und Wirtschaftshistorische Studien, vol. 14 (Munich: R. Oldenbourg, 1980).
Ehrenpreis, Stefan, "Konfessionalisierung von unten: Konzeption und Thematik eines bergischen Modells?" in Burkhard Dietz and Stefan Ehrenpreis (eds), *Drei Konfessionen in einer Region: Beiträge zur Geschichte der Konfessionalisierung im Herzogtum Berg vom 16. bis zum 18. Jahrhundert* (Cologne: Rheinland-Verlag, 1999).
Enggass, Robert, and Jonathan Brown (eds), *Italy and Spain, 1600–1750: Sources and Documents* (Englewood Cliffs: Prentice-Hall, 1970).

Erhardt, Tassilo, "A Longevous Cycle of Introits from the Viennese Court," in Tassilo Erhardt (ed.), *Sakralmusik im Habsburgerreich 1570–1770* (Vienna: Austrian Academy of Sciences, 2011).

Evans, R.J.W., *The Making of the Habsburg Monarchy, 1550–1700: An Interpretation* (Oxford: Clarendon, 1979).

Eymer, Wenzel, *Gutachten des Fürsten Gundacker von Liechtenstein über Education eines jungen Fürsten und gute Bestellung des Geheimen Rates* (Leitmeritz, 1905).

Fagiolo dell'Arco, Maurizio, *Bibliografia della festa barocca a Roma* (Rome: Antonio Pettini, 1994).

Fellerer, Karl Gustav, "Ein Musikalien-Inventar des fürstbischöflichen Hofes in Freising aus dem 17. Jahrhundert," *Archiv für Musikwissenschaft*, 6 (1924): 471–83.

Fidlerová, Alena et al. (eds), *Repertorium rukopisů 17. a 18. století z muzejních sbírek v Čechách* (2 vols to date, Prague: Karolinum, 2003–).

Fiedler, Joseph (ed.), *Die Relationen der Botschafter Venedigs über Deutschland und Österreich im siebzehnten Jahrhundert* (2 vols, Vienna: Kaiserlich-Königliche Hof- und Staatsdruckeri, 1866–67).

Fisher, Alexander J., *Music and Religious Identity in Counter-Reformation Augsburg, 1580–1630* (Aldershot: Ashgate, 2004).

Flemming, Willi, *Geschichte des Jesuitentheaters in den Landen Deutscher Zunge*, Schriften der Gesellschaft für Theaterwissenschaft, vol. 32 (Berlin: Selbstverlag der Gesellschaft für Theatergeschichte, 1923).

Forster, Marc R., *The Counter-Reformation in the Villages: Religion and Reform in the Bishopric of Speyer, 1560–1720* (Ithaca: Cornell University Press, 1992).

———, "The Thirty Years' War and the Failure of Catholicization," in David M. Luebke (ed.), *The Counter-Reformation: The Essential Readings* (Oxford and Malden: Blackwell, 1999).

———, *Catholic Revival in the Age of the Baroque: Religious Identity in Southwest Germany, 1550–1750* (Cambridge: Cambridge University Press, 2001).

———, "Catholic Confessionalism in Germany after 1650," in *Confessionalization in Europe, 1555–1700: Essays in Honor and Memory of Bodo Nischan* (Aldershot: Ashgate, 2004).

Frandsen, Mary, *Crossing Confessional Boundaries: The Patronage of Italian Sacred Music in Seventeenth-Century Dresden* (Oxford: Oxford University Press, 2006).

Gabriëls, Nele, "Reading (Between) the Lines: What Dedications Can Tell Us," in Ignace Bossuyt et al. (eds), *"Cui dono lepidum novum libellum?": Dedicating Latin Works and Motets in the Sixteenth Century*, Supplementa Humanistica Lovaniensia, vol. 23 (Leuven: Leuven University Press, 2008).

Genette, Gérard, *Paratexts: Thresholds of Interpretation*, trans. Jane E. Lewis (Cambridge: Cambridge University Press, 1997).

Göhler, Albert, *Verzeichnis der in den Frankfurter und Leipziger Messkatalogen der Jahre 1564 bis 1759 angezeigten Musikalien* (Leipzig, 1902; reprint, Hilversum: Knuf, 1965).

Goloubeva, Maria, *The Glorification of Emperor Leopold I in Image, Spectacle, and Text* (Mainz: von Zabern, 2000).

Greve, Werner, *Braunschweiger Stadtmusikanten: Geschichte eines Berufstandes 1227–1828* (Braunschweig: Stadtarchiv and Stadtbibliothek Braunschweig, 1991).

Gruber, Gernot, *Das Wiener Sepolcro und Johann Joseph Fux, 1. Teil* (Graz: Johann Joseph Fux Gesellschaft, 1972).

Guthrie, William P., *Battles of the Thirty Years War: From White Mountain to Nordlingen, 1618–1635* (Westport: Greenwood, 2002).

_____, *The Later Thirty Years War: From the Battle of Wittstock to the Treaty of Westphalia* (Westport: Greenwood, 2003).

Hagenow, Elisabeth von, *Bildniskommentare: Allegorisch gerahmte Herrscherbildnisse in der Graphik des Barock: Entstehung und Bedeutung* (Hildesheim: Georg Olms, 1999).

Hammond, Frederick, *Music and Spectacle in Baroque Rome: Barberini Patronage under Urban VIII* (New Haven and London: Yale University Press, 1994).

Hammond, Susan Lewis, *Editing Music in Early Modern Germany* (Aldershot: Ashgate, 2007).

Harness, Kelley, *Echoes of Women's Voices: Music, Art, and Female Patronage in Early Modern Florence* (Chicago and London: University of Chicago Press, 2006).

Hawlick-van de Water, Magdalena, *Der schöne Tod: Zeremonialstrukturen des Wiener Hofes bei Tod und Begräbnis zwischen 1640 und 1740* (Vienna: Herder, 1989).

Hintermaier, Ernst, "Musikpflege und Musizierpraxis an Kollegiatstiften des Erzbistums Salzburg im 17., 18. und 19. Jahrhundert," in Ladislav Kačic (ed.), *Musik der geistlichen Orden in Mitteleuropa zwischen Tridentinum und Josephinismus* (Bratislava: Slavistický kabinet SAV, 1997).

Höbelt, Lothar, *Ferdinand III. (1608–1657): Friedenskaiser wider Willen* (Graz: Ares, 2008).

Hofmann, Ulrike, "Die Accademia am Wiener Kaiserhof unter der Regierung Kaiser Leopolds I.," *Musicologia Austriaca*, 2 (1979): 76–84.

Holzer, Robert, "'Ma invan la tento et impossibil parmi,' or How *guerrieri* are Monteverdi's *madrigali guerrieri*?" in Francesco Guardiani (ed.), *The Sense of Marino* (New York, Ottawa, and Toronto: Legas, 1994).

Ingrao, Charles W., and Andrew L. Thomas, "Piety and Patronage: The Empresses-Consort of the High Baroque," *German History*, 20 (2002): 20–43.

Johnson, Trevor, *Magistrates, Madonnas, and Miracles: The Counter Reformation in the Upper Palatinate* (Aldershot: Ashgate, 2009).

Jung, Hans Rudolf, "Zur Pflege der Figuralmusik in Goldbach bei Gotha im 17. und 18. Jahrhundert," in Reinhard Szeskus (ed.), *Johann Sebastian Bachs Traditionsraum*, Bach-Studien, vol. 9 (Leipzig: Breitkopf & Härtel, 1986).

Jürgensmeier, Friedhelm, "'Multa ad pietatem composita': Continuity and Change in Catholic Piety, 1555–1648," in Klaus Bussmann and Heinz Schilling (eds), *1648: War and Peace in Europe* (3 vols, [Münster]: Veranstaltungsgesellschaft 350 Jahre Westfälischer Friede, 1998).

Kalinayová, Jana, *Musikinventare und das Repertoire der mehrstimmigen Musik in der Slowakei im 16. und 17. Jahrhundert* (Bratislava: Musaeum Musicum, 1995).

Kanduth, Erika, "Italienische Dichtung am Wiener Hof im 17. Jahrhundert," in Alberto Martino (ed.), *Beiträge zur Aufnahme der italienischen und spanischen Literatur in Deutschland im 16. und 17. Jahrhundert*, Chloe, vol. 9 (Amsterdam and Atlanta: Rodopi, 1990).

Kapner, Gerhardt, *Barocker Heiligenkult in Wien und seine Träger* (Vienna: Verlag für Geschichte und Politik, 1978).

Kellner, Altman, *Musikgeschichte des Stiftes Kremsmünster: Nach den Quellen dargestellt* (Kassel: Bärenreiter, 1956).

Kendrick, Robert L., "'Sonet vox tua in auribus meis': Song of Songs Exegesis and the Seventeenth-Century Motet," *Schütz-Jahrbuch*, 16 (1994): 99–118.

Kim-Szacsvai, Katalin, "Dokumente über das Musikleben der Jesuiten: Instrumenten- und Musikalienverzeichnisse zur Zeit der Auflösungen," *Studia musicologica Academiae Scientiarum Hungaricae*, 39 (1998): 283–366.

King, John N., "Henry VIII as David: The King's Image and Reformation Politics," in Peter C. Herman (ed.), *Rethinking the Henrician Era: Essays on Early Tudor Texts and Contexts* (Urbana: University of Illinois Press, 1994).

Kinsey, Laura, "The Habsburgs at Mariazell: Piety, Patronage, and Statecraft" (Ph.D. diss., University of California, Los Angeles, 2000).

Kolbuszewska, Aniela, *Katalog zbiórów muzycznych legnickiej biblioteki księcia Jerzego Rudolfa 'Bibliotheca Rudolphina'* (Legnica: Legnickie Towarzystwo Muzyczne, 1992).

Koldau, Linda Maria, *Die venezianische Kirchenmusik von Claudio Monteverdi* (Kassel: Bärenreiter, 2001).

Körndle, Franz, "'Ad te perenne gaudium': Lassos Musik zum 'Vltimum Judicium,'" *Die Musikforschung*, 53 (2000): 68–71.
Kromm, Jane, "The Bellona Factor: Political Allegories and the Conflicting Claims of Martial Imagery," in Cristelle Baskins and Lisa Rosenthal (eds), *Early Modern Visual Allegory: Embodying Meaning* (Aldershot: Ashgate, 2007).
Krummacher, Friedhelm, *Die Überlieferung der Choralarbeitungen in der frühen evangelischen Kantate: Untersuchungen zum Handschriftenrepertoire evangelischer Figuralmusik im späten 17. und beginnenden 18. Jahrhundert* (Berlin: Merseburger, 1965).
Krummel, D.W., "Venetian Baroque Music in a London Bookshop: The Robert Martin Catalogues, 1633–50," in Oliver Neighbor (ed.), *Music and Bibliography: Essays in Honor of Alec Hyatt King* (New York: Saur, 1980).
Kurtzman, Jeffrey, *The Monteverdi Vespers of 1610: Music, Context, Performance* (Oxford: Oxford University Press, 1999).
Kurz, Josef, *Zur Geschichte der Mariensäule am Hof und der Andachten vor derselben* (Vienna: Heinrich Kirsch, 1904).
Lavin, Irving, "Bernini's Image of the Ideal Christian Monarch," in John W. O'Malley et al. (eds), *The Jesuits: Cultures, Sciences, and the Arts, 1540–1773* (Toronto: University of Toronto Press, 1999).
Ledel, Eva-Katharin, "Private Briefe Kaiser Ferdinands III. an Erzherzog Leopold Wilhelm 1640–1643, 1645: Eine Studie" (Diploma-Arbeit, University of Vienna, 1995).
Leopold, Silke, *Al modo d'Orfeo: Dichtung und Musik im italienischen Sologesang des frühen 17. Jahrhunderts*, Analecta Musicologica, vol. 29 (Laaber: Laaber-Verlag, 1995).
Lewis, Mary S., "Introduction: The Dedication as Paratext," in Ignace Bossuyt et al. (eds), *"Cui dono lepidum novum libellum?": Dedicating Latin Works and Motets in the Sixteenth Century*, Supplementa Humanistica Lovaniensia, vol. 23 (Leuven: Leuven University Press, 2008).
Lorenz, Hellmut, "The Imperial Hofburg: The Theory and Practice of Architectural Representation in Baroque Vienna," in Charles W. Ingrao (ed.), *State and Society in Early Modern Austria* (West Lafayette: Purdue University Press, 1994).
Lotz-Heumann, Ute, "The Concept of 'Confessionalization': A Historiographical Paradigm in Dispute," *Memoria y Civilización*, 4 (2001): 93–114.
Louthan, Howard, *Converting Bohemia: Force and Persuasion in the Catholic Reformation* (Cambridge: Cambridge University Press, 2009).
Mannocci, Lino, *The Etchings of Claude Lorrain* (New Haven and London: Yale University Press, 1988).

Marcocchi, Massimo, "Spirituality in the Sixteenth and Seventeenth Centuries," in John W. O'Malley (ed.), *Catholicism in Early Modern History: A Guide to Research* (St Louis: Center for Reformation Research, 1988).

Matsche, Franz, *Die Kunst im Dienst der Staatsidee Kaiser Karls VI.: Ikonographie, Ikonologie und Programmatik des "Kaiserstils"* (2 vols, Berlin and New York: Walter de Gruyter, 1981).

Mayberry, Nancy, "The Controversy over the Immaculate Conception in Medieval and Renaissance Art, Literature, and Society," *Journal of Medieval and Renaissance Studies*, 21 (1991): 207–24.

Mayr-Deisinger, "Wassenberg, Eberhard," in *Allgemeine Deutsche Biographie*, vol. 41 (Leipzig: Dunker & Humblot, 1896).

McCabe, William H., *An Introduction to the Jesuit Theater: A Posthumous Work*, ed. Louis J. Oldani (St Louis: The Institute of Jesuit Sources, 1983).

McGinn, Bernard, *The Presence of God: A History of Western Christian Mysticism* (4 vols to date, New York: Crossroad, 1991–).

Melton, James Van Horn, "From Image to Word: Cultural Reform and the Rise of Literate Culture in Eighteenth-Century Austria," *Journal of Modern History*, 58 (1986): 95–124.

Mettenleiter, Johann Georg, *Musikgeschichte der Stadt Regensburg: Aus Archivalien und sonstigen Quellen bearbeitet* (Regensburg: J. Georg Bössenecker, 1866).

Mielke, Ursula, and Tilman Falk (eds), *Johann Schnitzer to Lucas Schnitzer*, Hollstein's German Engravings, Etchings, and Woodcuts, 1400–1700, vol. 46 (Rotterdam: Sound & Vision, 1999).

Mikanová, Eva, "Hudební kultura v České Lípě a okolí v 17. století: Příspěvek k dějinám hudby v severních Čechách," in Marie Vojtíšková (ed.), *Sborník příspěvků k době poddanského povstání roku 1680 v severních Čechách* (Prague: Tisková, edicní a propagační služba místního hospodářství, 1980).

Möller, Eberhard, "Die Weimarer Noteninventare von 1662 und ihre Bedeutung als Schütz-Quellen," *Schütz-Jahrbuch*, 10 (1988): 62–85.

Montrose, Louis, *The Subject of Elizabeth: Authority, Gender and Representation* (Chicago: University of Chicago Press, 2006).

Muir, Edward, *Ritual in Early Modern Europe*, 2nd edn (Cambridge: Cambridge University Press, 2005).

Müller, Johannes, *Das Jesuitendrama in den Ländern deutscher Zunge vom Anfang (1555) bis zum Hochbarock (1665)* (2 vols, Augsburg: B. Filser, 1930).

Müller, Joseph, *Die musikalischen Schätze der Königlichen- und Universitäts-Bibliothek zu Königsberg in Preußen* (Bonn, 1870; reprint, Hildesheim: Georg Olms, 1971).

Murata, Margaret, "'Quia amore langueo' or Interpreting 'Affetti sacri e spirituale,'" in Paola Besutti et al. (eds), *Claudio Monteverdi: Studi e prospettive* (Florence: Olschki, 1998).

Neubacher, Jürgen, *Die Musikbibliothek des Hamburger Kantors und Musikdirektors Thomas Selle (1599–1663): Rekonstruktion des ursprünglichen und Beschreibung des erhaltenen, überwiegend in der Staats- und Universitätsbibliothek Hamburg Carl von Ossietzky aufbewahrten Bestandes* (Neuhauen-Stuttgart: Hänssler, 1997).

Nirenberg, David, "The Historical Body of Christ," in James Clifton (ed.), *The Body of Christ in the Art of Europe and New Spain, 1150–1800* (Munich and New York: Prestel, 1997).

Nussdorfer, Laurie, "Print and Pageantry in Baroque Rome," *Sixteenth-Century Journal*, 29 (1998): 439–64.

Orso, Steven N., *Art and Death at the Spanish Habsburg Court: The Royal Exequies for Philip IV* (Columbia: University of Missouri Press, 1989).

Ossi, Massimo, *Divining the Oracle: Monteverdi's "Seconda Prattica"* (Chicago: Chicago University Press, 2003).

Paces, Cynthia, "The Fall and Rise of Prague's Marian Column," *Radical History Review*, 79 (2001): 141–55.

Parker, Geoffrey (ed.), *The Thirty Years' War*, 2nd edn (London and Boston: Routledge, 1997).

Pass, Walter, "Die Bregrenzer Musikalieninventare von 1609 und 1638," in Elmar Vonbank (ed.), *Musik im Bodenseeraum um 1600: Katalog der Ausstellung* (Bregenz: Vorarlberger Landesmuseum, 1974).

Pausz, Josef, *Andreas Rauch: Ein evangelischer Musiker, 1592 bis 1656* ([Vienna]: Evangelischer Pressverband in Österreich, 1992).

Piesch, Herma, "Domina Austraie," in Josef Stummvoll (ed.), *Die Österreichische Nationalbibliothek Festschrift: Herausgegeben zum 25 jährigen Dienstjubiläum des Generaldirektors Uni.-Prof. Dr. Josef Bick* (Vienna: Bauer-Verlag, 1948).

Piringer, Kurt, "Ferdinand des Dritten Katholische Restauration" (Ph.D. diss., University of Vienna, 1950).

Rabb, Theodore K., *The Struggle for Stability in Early Modern Europe* (Oxford and New York: Oxford University Press, 1975).

Reinhard, Wolfgang, "Reformation, Counter-Reformation, and the Early Modern State: A Reassessment," *The Catholic Historical Review*, 75 (1989): 383–404.

Renton, Barbara Ann, "The Musical Culture of Eighteenth-Century Bohemia, with Special Emphasis on the Music Inventories of Osek and the Knights of the Cross" (Ph.D. diss., City University of New York, 1990).

Repgen, Konrad, "Der päpstliche Protest gegen den Westfälischen Frieden und die Friedenspolitik Urbans VIII.," *Historisches Jahrbuch*, 75 (1955): 94–122.

_____, "Ferdinand III., 1637–1657," in Anton Schindling and Walter Ziegler (eds), *Die Kaiser der Neuzeit, 1519–1918: Heiliges Römisches Reich, Österreich, Deutschland* (Munich: Beck, 1990).

_____ (ed.), *Das Herrscherbild im 17. Jahrhundert*, Schriftenreihe der Vereinigung zur Erforschung der Neueren Geschichte, vol. 19 (Münster: Aschendorff, 1991).

Riedel, Friedrich W., *Kirchenmusik am Hofe Karls VI. (1711–1740): Untersuchungen zum Verhältnis von Zeremoniell und musikalischen Stil im Barockzeitalter* (Munich and Salzburg: Katzbichler, 1977).

Rietbergen, Peter, *Power and Religion in Baroque Rome: Barberini Cultural Policies* (London: Brill, 2006).

Roche, Jerome, *North Italian Church Music in the Age of Monteverdi* (Oxford: Clarendon, 1984).

_____, "Monteverdi and the *Prima Prattica*," in Denis Arnold and Nigel Fortune (eds), *The New Monteverdi Companion* (London and Boston: Faber and Faber, 1985).

_____, "Cross-Currents in Milanese Church Music in the 1640s: Giorgio Rolla's Anthology *Teatro Musicale* (1649)," in Alberto Colzani et al. (eds), *La musica sacra in Lombardia nella prima metà del Seicento: Atti del convegno internazionale di studi Como, 31 Maggio–2 Giugno 1985* (Como: Antiquae Musicae Italicae Studiosi, 1987).

Rosand, Ellen, *Opera in Seventeenth-Century Venice: The Creation of a Genre* (Berkeley: University of California Press, 1991).

Rose, Stephen, "The Mechanisms of the Music Trade in Central Germany, 1600–40," *Journal of the Royal Musical Association*, 130 (2005): 11–37.

Ruppert, Karsten, *Die kaiserliche Politik auf dem Westfälischen Friedenskongreß (1643–1648)* (Münster: Aschendorff, 1979).

Salzer, Elisabeth Charlotte, "Le grandi rappresentazioni del teatro italiano a Vienna barocca," trans. L. Cavalcoli, *Revista italiana del dramma*, 3 (1939): 155–90.

Sandberger, Adolf (ed.), *J.K. Kerll: Ausgewählte Werke, Erster Teil*, Denkmäler der Tonkunst in Bayern, vol. 2/2 (Leipzig: Breitkopf & Härtel, [1901]).

Saunders, Steven, "Sacred Music at the Hapsburg Court of Ferdinand II (1615–1637): The Latin Vocal Works of Giovanni Priuli and Giovanni Valentini" (2 vols, Ph.D. diss., University of Pittsburgh, 1990).

_____, "The Hapsburg Court of Ferdinand II and the *Messa, Magnificat et Iubilate Deo a sette chori concertati con le trombe* (1621) of Giovanni

Valentini," *Journal of the American Musicological Society*, 44 (1991): 359–403.

_____, *Cross, Sword and Lyre: Sacred Music at the Imperial Court of Ferdinand II of Habsburg (1619–1637)* (Oxford: Clarendon, 1995).

_____, "New Light on the Genesis of Monteverdi's Eighth Book of Madrigals," *Music & Letters*, 77 (1996): 183–93.

_____, "The Emperor as Artist: New Discoveries Concerning Ferdinand III's Musical Compositions," *Studien zur Musikwissenschaft*, 45 (1996): 7–31.

_____, "The Antecedents of the Viennese Sepolcro," in Alberto Colzani et al. (eds), *Relazioni musicali tra Italia e Germania nell'età barocca: Atti del VI convegno internazionale sulla muisca italiana nei secoli XVII–XVIII* (Como: Antiquae Musicae Italicae Studiosi, 1997).

_____, "Der Kaiser als Künstler: Ferdinand III and the Politicization of Sacred Music at the Habsburg Court," in Max Reinhart (ed.), *Infinite Boundaries: Order, Disorder, and Reorder in Early Modern German Culture*, Sixteenth-Century Essays and Studies, vol. 40 (Kirksville: Thomas Jefferson University Press, 1998).

Schaal, Richard (ed.), *Die Musikhandschriften des Ansbacher Inventars von 1686* (Wilhelmshaven: Heinrichshofen, 1966).

Schering, Arnold, "Die alte Chorbibliothek der Thomasschule in Leipzig," *Archiv für Musikwissenschaft*, 1 (1918–19): 275–88.

Schilling, Heinz, "Confessionalisation in Europe: Causes and Effects for Church, State, Society, and Culture," in Klaus Bussmann and Heinz Schilling (eds), *1648: War and Peace in Europe* (3 vols, [Münster]: Veranstaltungsgesellschaft 350 Jahre Westfälischer Friede, 1998).

_____, "War and Peace at the Emergence of Modernity: Europe Between State Belligerence, Religious Wars and the Desire for Peace," in Klaus Bussmann and Heinz Schilling (eds), *1648: War and Peace in Europe* (3 vols, [Münster]: Veranstaltungsgesellschaft 350 Jahre Westfälischer Friede, 1998).

_____, "Confessionalization: Historical and Scholarly Perspectives of a Comparative and Interdisciplinary Paradigm," in John M. Headley et al. (eds), *Confessionalization in Europe, 1555–1700: Essays in Honor and Memory of Bodo Nischan*, ed. (Aldershot: Ashgate, 2004).

Schmidt, Ernst, *Die Geschichte des evangelischen Gesangbuches der ehemaligen freien Reichsstadt Rothenburg ob der Tauber* (Rothenburg ob der Tauber: Peter, 1928).

Schmidt, Heinrich Richard, "Sozialdisziplinierung? Ein Plädoyer für das Ende des Etatismus in der Konfessionalisierungsforschung," *Historische Zeitschrift*, 265 (1997): 639–82.

Schorn-Schütte, Luise, "Konfessionalisierung als wissenschaftliches Paradigma?" in Joachim Bahlcke and Arno Strohmeyer (eds),

Konfessionalisierung in Ostmitteleuropa: Wirkungen des religiösen Wandels im 16. und 17. Jahrhundert in Staat, Gesellschaft und Kultur (Stuttgart: Steiner, 1999).

Schütz, Karl, "The Collection of Archduke Leopold Wilhelm," in Klaus Bussmann and Heinz Schilling (eds), *1648: War and Peace in Europe* (3 vols, [Münster]: Veranstaltungsgesellschaft 350 Jahre Westfälischer Friede, 1998).

Schwarz, Henry Frederick, *The Imperial Privy Council in the Seventeenth Century* (Cambridge, MA: Harvard University Press, 1943).

Sebastian, Wenceslaus, "The Controversy over the Immaculate Conception from after Scotus to the End of the Eighteenth Century," in Edward Dennis O'Connor (ed.), *The Dogma of the Immaculate Conception: History and Significance* (Notre Dame: University of Notre Dame Press, 1958).

Sehnal, Jiří, and Jitřenka Pešková (eds), *Caroli de Liechtenstein-Castelcorno Episcopi Olomucensis operum artis musicae collectio Cremsirii reservata*, Artis Musicae Antiquioris Catalogorum, vol. 5 (2 vols, Prague: Biblioteca Nationalis Rei Publicae Bohemicae Editio Supraphon Praha, 1998).

Sehnal, Jiří, and Svatava Přibánová, *Průvodce po archívních fondech: Ústavu dějin hudby Moravského musea v Brně* (Brno: Moravského musea Brně, 1971).

Seifert, Herbert, *Die Oper am Wiener Kaiserhof im 17. Jahrhundert* (Tützing: Schneider, 1985).

_____, *Der Sig-prangende Hochzeit-Gott: Hochzeitsfeste am Wiener Hof der Habsburger und ihre Allegorik 1622–1699*, Dramma per musica, vol. 2 (Vienna: Musikwissenschaftlicher Verlag, 1988).

_____, "Ein Gumpoldskirchner Musikalieninventar aus dem Jahr 1640," *Studien zur Musikwissenschaft*, 39 (1988): 55–61.

_____, "Akademien am Wiener Kaiserhof der Barockzeit," in Wolf Frobenius et al. (eds), *Akademie und Musik* (Saarbrücken: Saarbrücker Druckerei und Verlag, 1993).

_____, "The Beginnings of Sacred Dramatic Musical Works at the Imperial Court of Vienna: Sacred and Moral Opera, Oratorio, and *Sepolcro*," in Paola Besutti (ed.), *L'oratorio musicale italiano e i suoi contesti (secc. XVII–XVIII): Atti del convegno internazionale, Perugia, Sagra musicale umbra, 18–20 settembre 1997* (Florence: Olschki, 2002).

Seiffert, Max. "Die Chorbibliothek der St. Michaelisschule in Lüneburg zu Seb. Bach's Zeit," *Sammelbände der Internationalen Musik-Gesellschaft*, 9 (1907–1908): 593–621.

Seipel, Wilfried (ed.), *Kunsthistorisches Museum Wien: The Picture Gallery*, trans. Gitta Holroyd-Reece (Innsbruck: Alpina, 1996).

Silver, Larry, *Marketing Maximilian: The Visual Ideology of a Holy Roman Emperor* (Princeton: Princeton University Press, 2008).
Sharpe, Kevin, "Representations and Negotiations: Texts, Images, and Authority in Early Modern England," *Historical Journal*, 42 (1999): 853–81.
_____, "'So Hard a Text'? Images of Charles I, 1612–1700," *Historical Journal*, 43 (2000): 383–405.
_____, "Sacralization and Demystification: The Publicization of Monarchy in Early Modern England," in Jeroen Deploige and Gita Deneckere (eds), *Mystifying the Monarch: Studies on Discourse, Power, and History* (Amsterdam: Amsterdam University Press, 2006).
_____, *Selling the Tudor Monarchy: Authority and Image in Sixteenth-Century England* (New Haven and London: Yale University Press, 2009).
Shimp, Susan, "The Art of Persuasion: Domenico Mazzocchi and the Counter-Reformation" (Ph.D. diss., Yale University, 2000).
Simpson, Michael, "The Chariot and the Bow as Metaphors for Poetry in Pindar's Odes," *Transactions and Proceedings of the American Philological Association*, 100 (1969): 437–73.
Smither, Howard E., *A History of the Oratorio, Volume 1: The Oratorio in the Baroque Era, Italy, Vienna, Paris* (Chapel Hill: University of North Carolina Press, 1977).
_____, "The Function of Music in the Forty Hours Devotion of Seventeenth- and Eighteenth-Century Italy," in Carmelo P. Comberiati and Matthew C. Steel (eds), *Music from the Middle Ages through the Twentieth Century: Essays in Honor of Gwynn McPeek* (New York: Gordon and Breach, 1988).
Somerset, H.V.F., "The Habsburg Emperors as Musicians," *Music & Letters*, 30 (1949): 204–15.
Sommervogel, Carlos (ed.), *Bibliothèque de la Compagnie de Jésus* (10 vols, Brussels: Oscar Schepens; Paris: Alphonse Picard, 1890–1909).
Spielman, John P., *The City and the Crown: Vienna and the Imperial Court, 1600–1740* (West Lafayette: Purdue University Press, 1993).
Sponheim, Kristin M., "The Anthologies of Ambrosius Profe (1589–1661) and the Transmission of Italian Music in Germany" (Ph.D. diss., Yale University, 1995).
Steensgard, Niels, "The Seventeenth-Century Crisis," in Geoffrey Parker and Lesley M. Smith (eds), *The General Crisis of the Seventeenth Century*, 2nd edn (London: Routledge, 1997).
Stein, Beverly, "Between Key and Mode: Tonal Practice in the Music of Giacomo Carissimi" (Ph.D. diss., Brandeis University, 1994).
Steude, Wolfram (ed.), *Die Musiksammelhandschriften des 16. und 17. Jahrhunderts in der Sächsischen Landesbibliothek zu Dresden*,

Quellenkataloge zur Musikgeschichte, vol. 6 (Wilhelmshaven: Heinrichshofen, 1974).

Straková, Theodora, "Rajhradský hudební inventář z roku 1725: Příspěvek k poznání hudební kultury na Moravě v 1. pol. 18. století," *Časopis Moravského Musea. Acta Musei Moraviae,* 58 (1973): 217–46.

Stratton, Suzanne L., *The Immaculate Conception in Spanish Art* (Cambridge: Cambridge University Press, 1994).

String, Tatiana C., *Art and Communication in the Reign of Henry VIII* (Aldershot: Ashgate, 2008).

Strong, Roy, *Art and Power: Renaissance Festivals, 1450–1650* (Berkeley and Los Angeles: University of California Press, 1984).

Szarota, Elida Maria, *Geschichte, Politik und Gesellschaft im Drama des 17. Jahrhunderts* (Bern and Munich: Francke, 1976).

––––– (ed.), *Das Jesuitendrama im deutschen Sprachgebiet: Eine Periochen-Edition,* vol. 2, *Tugend- und Sündensystem* (2 vols, Munich: Wilhelm Fink, 1980).

Tanner, Marie, *The Last Descendant of Aeneas: The Hapsburgs and the Mythic Image of the Emperor* (New Haven and London: Yale University Press, 1993).

Taylor, Ralph McDowell, Jr., "Georg Falck's *Idea boni cantoris* ...: Translation and Commentary" (Ph.D. diss., The Louisiana State University and Agricultural and Mechanical College, 1971).

Telesko, Werner, "Barocke Thesenblätter in der Sammlung von Prof. Adolf Karl Bodingbauer, Steyr, II. Teil," *Jahrbuch des Oberösterreichischen Musealvereines,* 147 (2002): 205–21.

Tipton, Susan, "'Super aspidem et basiliscum ambulabis ...': Zur Entstehung der Mariensäulen im 17. Jahrhundert," in Dieter Breuer et al. (eds), *Religion und Religiosität im Zeitalter des Barock* (2 vols, Wiesbaden: Harrassowitz, 1995).

Tomek, Ernst, *Kirchengeschichte Österreichs* (3 vols, Innsbruck and Vienna: Tyrolia, 1935–59).

Tomlinson, Gary, *Monteverdi and the End of the Renaissance* (Berkeley: University of California Press, 1987).

Treadwell, Nina, *Music and Wonder at the Medici Court: The 1589 Interludes for* La Pellegrina (Bloomington: University of Indiana Press, 2008).

Turba, Gustav, *Die Grundlagen der Pragmatischen Sanktion* (2 vols, Leipzig and Vienna: Denticke, 1911–12).

Udris, Zane, "Tenuis musa: The Response of Propertius and Ovid to the Literary Views of Callimachus" (Ph.D. diss., Yale University, 1976).

Urbanek, Elisabeth, "Giovanni Valentini als Messenkomponist" (Ph.D. diss., University of Vienna, 1974).

Valentin, Jean-Marie, "Programme von Avancinis Stücken," *Literaturwissenschaftliches Jahrbuch der Görres-Gesellschaft*, N.F. 12 (1971): 1–42.

———, "Zur Wiener Aufführung des Avancinischen '*Sosa Naufragus*' (1643)," *Humanistica Lovaniensia*, 26 (1977): 220–27.

———, *Le théâtre des Jésuites dans les pays de langue allemande (1554–1680): Salut des a mes et ordre des cités* (3 vols, Bern: Peter Land, 1978).

———, "Gegenreformation und Literatur: Das Jesuitendrama im Dienste der religiösen und moralischen Erziehung," *Historisches Jahrbuch*, 100 (1980): 240–56.

———, *Le théâtre des Jésuites dans les pays de langue allemande: Répertoire chronologique des pièces représentées et des documents conservés (1555–1773)* (2 vols, Stuttgart: A. Hiersemann, 1983–84).

———, *Theatrum Catholicum: Les jésuites et la scène en Allemagne au XVIe et au XVIIe siècles; Die Jesuiten und die Bühne im Deutschland des 16.–17. Jahrhunderts* (Nancy: Presses Universitaires de Nancy, 1990).

———, *Les Jésuites et le théâtre (1554–1680): Contribution à l'histoire culturelle du monde catholique dans le Saint-Empire romain germanique* (Paris: Éditions Desjonquères, 2001).

Vloberg, Maurice, "The Iconography of the Immaculate Conception," in Edward Dennis O'Connor (ed.), *The Dogma of the Immaculate Conception: History and Significance* (Notre Dame: University of Notre Dame Press, 1958).

Vocelka, Karl, and Lynne Heller, *Die private Welt der Habsburger: Leben und Alltag einer Familie* (Graz, Vienna, and Cologne: Styria, 1998).

Wainwright, Jonathan P., *Musical Patronage in Seventeenth-Century England: Christopher, First Baron Hatton (1605–1670)* (Aldershot: Scolar Press, 1997).

Waldner, Franz, "Zwei Inventarien aus dem XVI. und XVII. Jahrhundert über hinterlassene Musikinstrumente und Musikalien am Innsbrucker Hofe," *Studien zur Musikwissenschaft*, 4 (1916): 128–47.

Walter, Rudolf, "Kirchenmusik-Inventar einer schlesischen Gebirgsstadt," in Axel Beer, Kristina Pfarr, and Wolfgang Ruf (eds), *Festschrift Christoph-Hellmut Mahling zum 65. Geburtstag* (Tutzing: Hans Schneider, 1997).

Wandruszka, Adam, "Ein Freskenzyklus der 'Pietas Austriaca' in Florenz," *Mitteilungen des Österreichischen Staatsarchivs*, 15 (1962): 495–9.

Warner, Marina, *Alone of All Her Sex: The Myth and Cult of the Virgin Mary* (New York: Knopf, 1976).

Weaver, Andrew H., "Piety, Politics, and Patronage: Motets at the Habsburg Court in Vienna During the Reign of Ferdinand III (1637–1657)" (Ph.D. diss., Yale University, 2002).

_____, "Music in the Service of Counter-Reformation Politics: The Immaculate Conception at the Habsburg Court of Ferdinand III (1637–1657)," *Music & Letters*, 87 (2006): 361–78.

_____, "Divine Wisdom and Dolorous Mysteries: Habsburg Marian Devotion in Two Motets from Monteverdi's *Selva morale et spirituale*," *Journal of Musicology*, 24 (2007): 237–71.

_____, "The Rhetoric of Interruption in Giovanni Felice Sances's *Motetti a voce sola* (1638)," *Schütz-Jahrbuch*, 32 (2010): 127–47.

Webhofer, Peter, *Giovanni Felice Sances, ca. 1600–1679: Biographisch-bibliographische Untersuchung und Studie über sein Motettenwerk* (Rome: Pontificio Istituto di Musica Sacra, 1964).

Weil, Mark S., "The Devotion of the Forty Hours and Roman Baroque Illusions," *Journal of the Warburg and Courtauld Institutes*, 37 (1974): 218–48.

Weiß, Franz M., "Das Musikalien- und Instrumenteninventar des Servitenklosters Maria Luggau in Oberkärnten aus dem Jahre 1689," *Kirchenmusikalisches Jahrbuch*, 82 (1998): 105–21.

Wellesz, Egon, "Einige handschriftliche Libretti aus der Frühzeit der Wiener Oper," *Zeitschrift für Musikwissenschaft*, 1 (1918–19): 278–81.

Welter, Friedrich, *Katalog der Musikalien der Ratsbücherei Lüneburg* (Lippstadt: Kistner & Siegel, 1950).

Werner, Arno, "Die alte Musikbibliothek und die Instrumentensammlung an St Wenzel in Naumburg a.d.S.," *Archiv für Musikwissenschaft*, 8 (1927): 390–415.

West, M.L., *Indo-European Poetry and Myth* (Oxford: Oxford University Press, 2007).

Whenham, John, *Monteverdi: Vespers (1610)* (Cambridge: Cambridge University Press, 1997).

Winkelbauer, Thomas, "Finanznot und Friedensehnsucht: Der Kaiserhof im Jahre 1645," in Lorenz Mikoletzky et al. (eds), *"Wir aber aus unsern vorhero sehr erschöpfften camergeföllen nicht hernemben khönnen …": Beiträge zur Österreichischen Wirtschafts- und Finanzgeschichte vom 17. bis zum 20. Jahrhundert* (Vienna: Berger, 1997).

Wolfsgruber, P. Cölestin (ed.), *Die Correspondenz des Schottenabtes Anton Spindler von Hofegg* (Vienna: Kirsch, 1893).

Zirnbauer, Heinz, *Der Notenbestand der Reichsstädtisch Nürnbergischen Ratsmusik: Eine bibliographische Rekonstruktion* (Nuremberg: Fränkische Verlagsanstalt, 1959).

Zulauf, Ernst, *Beiträge zur Geschichte der Landgräftlich-Hessischen Hofkapelle zu Cassel bis auf die Zeit Moritz des Gelehrten* (Kassel: Döll, 1902).

Index

Page numbers in bold refer to items in figures or music examples; page numbers in italics refer to items in tables.

anti-Machiavellianism 9, 51–4, 56–7, 133, 167–8, 191, 257, 260, 262
Avancini, Nicholas 86–7, 88–93, 94–7, 251–2, 261
   works by
      Curae Caesarum pro Deo pro populo (1644), 89, 261
      Fiducia in Deum, sive Bethulia liberata 88, 94
      Fortunae Tragoedia, sive Emmanuel Sosa naufragus 88, 92
      Jason 89
      Pax Imperii, sive Joseph a Fratribus recognitus 90, 94, 97, 251–2
      Sanctus Franciscus Xaverius (1651) 91
      Saxonia Conversa, sive Clodoaldus Daniae Princeps 89
      Suspicio, sive Pomum Theodosii 88
      Theodosius Magnus Justus et Pius Imperator (1654) 91, 94–7, **96**, 261
      Zelus, sive Francisus Xaverius Indiarum Apostolus (1640) 86–7, 88

ballet 15–16, 33, 34, 72, 74–6, 78, 80–82, 84–5, 97, 131, 254, 262
St Bernard of Clairvaux 215
Bernini, Gian Lorenzo 262
Bertali, Antonio 75–6, 108, 115, **117**, 132, 144, 146–8, 185–88, *186*, 191, 199, 200, 215, 251, 262
   motets by
      Ab aeterno ordinata 144

Anima surge 200
Exultate et cantate 115, **117**, 147, 185–7, *186*, 191
Hic est panis 200
Jesu dulcis amor meus 200, 215
O admirabile convivium 200
Quis loquetur potentias Domini 200
Sospiro pro te 200, 215
Te Deum "della Pace" 251
   operas by
      Inganno d'Amore, L' 75, 79, 82, 261
      Theti 76, 81–2, 262
Bonarelli, Prospero 72, 77, 78
Bonacossi, Francesco 73
St Bonaventure 205–6, 213–14, *214*
Bonvicino, Valeriano 15–16, 72
Botero, Giovanni 51–4, 57
Bratislava (Preßburg) 70, 74, 141
Breslau, *see* Wrocław
Bruynel, Jacob **96**
Burnacini, Giovanni 80
Burnacini, Lodovico Ottavio 81

Carafa, Vincenzo 206–7, 211–12
Carissimi, Giacomo 146, 190
Cecilia Renata, sister of Ferdinand III 15–16, 78
Charles V, Holy Roman Emperor **150**, 224
Charles VI, Holy Roman Emperor 102, 178
St Charles Borromeo **117**, 147, 185, *186*
Collurafi, Antonino 25, **26**
colossal baroque 108–10, 128, 149, 151, 252
confessionalization 9, 54–6, 99, 226

318   INDEX

Corpus Christi, *see* Eucharist
Czerwenka, Wenceslaus Adelbert 49,
    194, 224

da cappella 108, 137, 174
David, Old Testament King *89*, 94,
    161, 166, 178, 191–2, 198
Defenestration of Prague (1618) 38,
    137
Diets
    of Regensburg (1640–41) 33–4, 36,
        72–3, 78
    of Regensburg (1653–54) *75*, 78,
        82, 94, 102, 179, 257–61
Dueller, Thomas 52–3
durus 11–12, *12*, 174, 181, 231–3,
    235

edicts 48, 151
    Edict of Restitution (1629) 33, 45
Eucharist 10, 49, 193–203, 214–15,
        221, 224, 236, 239, 251
    as civic cult 196–203
    Corpus Christi, feast of 87, *88–90*,
        93, 94, 101, 194, 196–99, 203,
        261
    forty hours devotion 197
    motets for 199–201, *200–201*,
        202, 215
    processions in honor of 101,
        198–9, 203, 261
St Eustachius 194–6

Ferdinand I, Holy Roman Emperor
    150, **259**, 260
Ferdinand II, Holy Roman Emperor
    1–3, 15–17, 29, 44–6, 50,
    57–60, 80, 97, 100, 103, 105,
    109, 128, 145, **150**, 151, 168,
    195, 204, 206–11, 224–6, **259**,
    260, 266–7
Ferdinand III, Holy Roman Emperor
    as composer 59–60, 63, 69, *74*,
        111–15, **112, 113, 114**, 199,
        200, 242
    crisis of representation of 34–42

cultivation of Italian culture by
    59–61, 256–7, 262–3
as General of Imperial army 17–31,
    18, 19, 21, 22, 23, 24, 39, 254
images of
    engravings 20–22, **23, 24**, 36,
        46, **47**, 57–8, **58**, 61, **62**,
        96, **96**, 179, **180**, 236, **237**,
        254, **255**, 256–7, **258**
    medals 20, **22**, 34, 46, 252, **253**
    paintings 17–20, **18, 19, 21**,
        34, **35**, 49, 57, 256
Italian poetry by 59, 226–7, 263
legacy of 1, 11, 263–4
letters by 32, 43, 59, 63–4, 84, 197
library of 25, 161, 206, 211, 224
musical works by
    Ave maris stella 242
    Deus misereatur nostri
        112–15, **114**
    drama musicum 69, *74*
    Excita furorem et memento
        belli (author of text) 147,
        185, *187*, 188–91
    Humanae salutis sator 111–12,
        112, 113, 115
    Jesu Redemptor omnium 111,
        115
    Pange lingua 199, *200*
panegyrics about 25–9, **26, 28**, 36,
    38–40, 188–9, 264
as patron of Italian literary
    academy 59, 262–3
political policy of 50–57
piety of 9–10, 16, 25–9, 31, 37–41,
    44–9, 100, 160, 166, 171, 191,
    193–204, 211–21, 224, 226–7,
    229–36, 242–3, 246–8, 257–60
reception of public image of 9,
    139–42, 263–4
represented as Jove 80–82, 254–6,
    255
represented as King David 161,
    166, 178, 191–2, 198
represented as King Solomon 57–8,
    178–80, **180**, 182, 192, 257,
    264

represented as peacemaker 149–51, 251–60
Ferdinand IV, King of the Romans 39, 52–3, 78, 81, 85, 87, *89–91*, 93, 95, 96, **96**, 98, 109, 118, 121, 133–4, 179, 196, **255**, 256–7, 261–2, 278–9
Ferdinand, Cardinal-Infante of Spain 18, **18**, **19**, 20
Ferrari, Benedetto 75, 82, 261
St Francis Xavier 86, *88*, *91*
Froberger, Johann Jakob 121, 263
Frommer, Michael **62**

Gabrieli, Giovanni 173–4
Gabrielli, Diamante 76, 262
Gans, Johannes 44, 238–9
Gonzaga, Eleonora (wife of Ferdinand II) 15–16, 59, 132–5, 138, 143–5, 262, 270–71, 284–5
Gonzaga, Eleonora (wife of Ferdinand III) 59, *90–93*, 96, **96**, 98, 178, **255**, 256
Gonzaga, Vincenzo 145, 284–5
Graz 109, 223
Gregory XV, Pope 225

Hoecke, Jan van den 34, **35**
Holy Roman Empire 2, 6, 16, 27, 31–3, 45, 50, 56, 151, 194, 251–2
  government of 3, 6

St Ignatius Loyola *91*, 98
Immaculate Conception 10–11, 105, 138, 144, 166, 206, 224–48, **237**, **240**; *see also Mariensäule am Hof*
  as civic cult 242–3, 246–8
  history of 225
  iconography of 228, 241
  motets for 138, 144, 166–7, 227, 229–36, **232**, **233**, **234–5**, 242–8, **245**, **246**, **247**
  processions in honor of 236–9, **237**, 241–2

Jacobus, Matthias 27, **28**
Jesuit drama 10, 44, 86–98, *88–93*, **96**, 105, 178–9, 197–8, 251–2, 261; *see also* representation, role of Jesuit drama in individual works; *see also* Avancini, Nicholas
  Amor et Timor Eucharistiae 88
  Arma Austriaca Eucharistica, sive Lapis David de Goliath victor 89, 94, 97, 178, 198
  Bacchanalia fortunae aulicae 90
  Belisaurius, sive Speculum utriusque Fortunae 89
  Bertulphus 91
  Christus Eucharisticus Portus Afflictorum 90
  David sitiens 88
  Felix Annus 1644 89, 97–8
  Fortuna Eucharistico-Austriaca Pietati et Justitiae 90, 97–8, 197–8, 251
  Franciscus Fernandus Japonia Rex Animatus defensus sublevatus 89
  Hymenaeus Theandri et Psyches 92
  Increata et incarnata Dei Sapientia 90
  Liga Pietatis Austriacae cum Consilio et Industria contra arma invidiae 91, 97–8
  Morandus Cultu Eucharistico 90
  Pax in Passione Christi 92
  Phlebotomia languentis Jesu 91, 97–8
  Regiae Virtutes, seu Initiae Regni Salomonis 92, 97, 178–9
  Sacrificium Pacificum Melchisedech Regis Salem 90
  SS. Eucharistia, Certum Piis in necessitate subsidium 89, 97, 198

Zelus Ignatianus a divini nominis et gloriae zelo accensus 91, 98
Jesuits, *see* Society of Jesus
St John Nepomuk 184
St John of the Cross 205–6, 211
joyous entries 4–5, 20, 102, 148–9, 179, 257–61
  Ferdinand III into Regensburg (1652), 179, 257–60, **258–9**
  Ferdinand III into Vienna (1654) 261
  Maria Anna into Milan (1649) 148–9, 286–7

Kaiserstil 57
Kilian, Wolfgang **180**, 257, **258–9**
Kremsmünster 201

Lapide, Cornelius a 227–8
Leopold I, Holy Roman Emperor 1–2, 31, 39, 40, 44, 46, **47**, 52, 59–60, 67–8, 71, 79, 81, 87, 89–93, 127, 132, 144, 178–9, 238–9, 241–2, 244, 251, **255**, 256, 262–4
Leopold Wilhelm, brother of Ferdinand III 15, 32, 34, 38–9, 43, 52, 59–61, 63, 71, **75**, 78, 84, 102, 133–4, 197, **255**, 256, 262–3, 276–7
Lequille, Didacus 49, 195–6
Lipsius, Justus 51
Litany of Loreto 109, 132, 146, 172, 238–9, 243–4, 246; *see also* Sances, Giovanni Felice
Louis XIV, King of France 1–3, 5, 99, 264
Lünig, Johann Christian 199, 238–9, 243
Luyckx, Frans 20, **21**, 40

Magni, Bartolomeo 131, 139, 142, 145–6, 152
Manzini, Luigi 27–9
Margarita Teresa, wife of Leopold I 75, 79, 253

Maria Anna, daughter of Ferdinand III 89, *93*, 148–9, 286–7
Maria Leopoldine, wife of Ferdinand III 70, *93*, 149, 252, 288–9
Maria of Spain, wife of Ferdinand III 15, 73–4, 78, 84, **88**, *93*, 132–4, 143, 197, **237**, 238, 272–3
Mariensäule am Hof 10–11, 58, 109, 236–48, **237**, **240**, 263
  as representation of Ferdinand III 242–3
  compared with Bavarian Marian column 239–41
  imitations of 241–3, 263
  music composed for 242–8, *245*, **246**, **247**
  processions related to 236–9, **237**, 241–2
  significance of 241–3, 247–8
Mary, Blessed Virgin 10, **19**, 20, 32, 46, **47**, 49, 57, **58**, 77, 102, 115–17, **116**, 119, 133–4, 138, 143, 147, 166, 171–2, 185–7, *186*, 194, 224–48, **237**, **240**, *245*, 263, 272–3, 280–81; *see also* Immaculate Conception; *Mariensäule am Hof*
Maurizio of Savoy, Cardinal Protector of the Holy Roman Empire 27–9
Maximilian I, Duke of Bavaria and Elector 15, 33, 80, *92*, 179, 239
Maximilian I, Holy Roman Emperor 89, 97, **150**, 161, 195, 198, 203, 255
Melani, Atto 109
Milan 25, 146–9, 286–7
Mildert, Peter Paul van **96**
modal–hexachordal system 11–12, *12*, 115, 174, 180–81, 230–36
mollis 11–12, 115, 174, 181, 232, 236
Montalto, Alessandro 130, 148
Montalto, Francesco Peretti di 148–9, 286–7

Monteverdi, Claudio 29–31, 40, 69, 125, 131, 142–6, 205, 266–7, 284–5
  musical works by
    Ab aeterno ordinata sum 143–4
    Altri canti d'Amore 30
    Ballo (Book 8) 30
    Lamento d'Arianna 144
    Ogni amante è guerrier 30, 144
    Pianto della Madonna 144
  prints by
    Madrigali guerrieri, et amorosi (Eighth Book of Madrigals, 1638) 29–31, 40, 125, 143–6, 266–7
    Selva morale et spirituale (1641) 125, 142–5, 284–5
    Vespers (1610) 125, 143
Musart, Carolus 103, 196
mystical theology 10, 203–21, 230, 247
  in motets 205–21, *208*, *209*, *214*, 229–30, 236, 247
  vulnus amoris 205–6, 211, 213, 215–16

newspapers 101, 105, 197, 199
  Extra-Ordinari Mittwochs Postzeittungen 199
  Ordentliche Zeittungen 101, 197, 199

Ödenburg, *see* Sopron
Olomouc (Olmütz) 32
opera 2, 6–7, 10, 29, 34–6, 41, 67–82, 72–7, **80**, 84–6, 94–7, 99, 104–6, 122–3, 127, 129–30, 132, 253–4, 261–3; *see also* Bertali, Antonio; Ferdinand III, Holy Roman Emperor; representation, role of opera in; Sances, Giovanni Felice
  individual works
    Ariadne abbandonata da Theseo 73, 82
    Armida e Rinaldo (untitled) 35–6, 72, 82
    Attione da rappresentarsi in musica 74, 82, 253–4
    Dafne in Alloro 75, 82, 84
    Faneto, Il 72, 78
    Gara, La 75, 78–82, **80**, 253–4
    Specchio di Virtù, Lo 34, 71, 73, 82, 94
  oratorio 35, 72–5, 77, 83–4, 196; *see also sepolcro*; Valentini, Giovanni
Ordentliche Zeittungen, *see* newspapers

Padua 130
Palestrina, Giovanni Pierluigi da 108
Pallantius, Albertus 29
paratexts 8, 42, 121–4, 128, 132–7, 139, 142–3, 147–9, 151, 159, 171, 188, 244, 266–89
  dedications 22–3, 25, 29, 42, 60–61, 77, 84, 93, 109, 122–6, 128, 130, 132–7, 139, 142–5, 147–9, 151–2, 159–60, 196, 206, 227, 238, 241, 244, 252, 255–6, 266–89
  frontispieces 25, **26**, 46, **47**, 57, **58**, 61, **62**, 121, 124, 149, 179, 238, 252, 256
  rubrics 42, 122, 124, 141, 143, 147, 188, 214–15, 244
  title pages 38, 92–3, 122, 124, 135, **136**, 139, 151, 171
Paul V, Pope 225
Paullus, Gualterius 194–6
peace treaties, *see* Thirty Years' War
Persiani, Horatio 34, *73*
Pestsäule 241–2, 263
Philip IV, King of Spain 38, 79, 148
Pietas Austriaca 9, 49–50, 56, 101, 138, 143, 147, 193–204, 224–36, 263
pilgrimages 42, 100, 102–3, 204, 224–5, 242
  to Hernals 102–3, 204
  to Holy House of Loreto 224
  to Mariazell 102, 225
Plati, Guglielmo 25

Prague 2, 17, 32, 39, 50, 70–71, 77, 137, 241, 243
Preßburg, *see* Bratislava
Princeps in compendio 51–3
processions 5–6, 42, 98–9, 101–2, 111, 197–9, 203, 236–8, 237, 241–4, 246, 261; *see also* Eucharist; Immaculate Conception; joyous entries; *Mariensäule am Hof*
Profe, Ambrosius 126, 139–40
Psalms, book of *90–91*, 98, 101, 125, 128, 133, 137–8, 143, 160–61, 164–5, 167–9, 178, 185, *186*, 187, 190, 192, 229–31, 249, 251, 276–9

Rauch, Andreas 61, **62**, 109–10, 124, 149–52, **150**, 252, 255–6, 288–9
re-Catholicization 1, 45–50, 53–6, 135, 225, 248
Regensburg 15, 17, 20–22, **24**, 31, 33–4, 36, 39, 72–3, 75, 78, 80, 82, 85, *93*, 94–5, 97, 102, 131, 141, 179, **180**, 199, 257–61, **258–9**, 264; *see also* Diets; joyous entries
representation
  role of court in 7
  role of Jesuit drama in 86–98, 178, 198, 251–2, 261
  role of liturgy in 98–106
  role of opera in 34–6, 68–82, 253–4, 262
  role of print in 122–8
  role of printed music in 29–31, 123–8, 132–9, 143–52, 166–7, 171–2, 182, 184, 221, 227, 230, 244, 247–8
  role of ritual in 99–100
  role of sacred music in 41–42, 106–19
  theories of 3–9, 22–5, 31, 37
Riccioni, Carlo Benedetto 244
Rigatti, Giovanni Antonio 142–6, 148, 282–3

Rolla, Giorgio 146–9, 152, 184, *186*, 191, 286–7
Rome 27–9, 95, 129–30, 146, 239, 254–5, 260, 286–7
Rubens, Peter Paul 17–18, **18**, 20, 59
Rudolph I, Holy Roman Emperor 49, 97, 101, **150**, 194–6, 198, 203–4, 224, 252
Ruzola, Dominicus 161, 169, 185, 187

Sances, Giovanni Felice 8, 10, 70, 74, 108, **116**, 126, 128–42, **136**, 144–8, 152–3, 160–78, **162–3**, **165**, **175–7**, **181**, **182–8**, **184**, *186–7*, **188–9**, 191, *200–201*, 211–21, *214*, **216–19**, 227, 229–36, **232–5**, 238, 244–7, *245*, **246–7**, 257, 262–3, 268–81
  biography of 129–32
  motets by
    Alma Redemptoris Mater (1642) 172
    Ardet cor meum 138–40, 167, 230–36, **232–5**
    Audi Domine 172–82, **175–7**, **181**, 185, 246
    Audite me divini fructus 138
    Ave maris stella 141
    Caro mea 200, 215
    Conditor caeli 139, 169–71
    Domine ne memineris 167
    Domine quid multiplicati sunt 168–9
    Dominus possedit me 144
    Dulcis amor Jesu 213–15, *214*, **216**
    Excita furorem et memento belli 147, 185, *187*, **188–91**, **189**
    Honestum fecit 182–4, **184**
    Judica me Deus 160–64, **162–3**, 166–9
    Laetamini in Domino 139–40, 164–70, **165**, 183, 187, 231
    Lauda Sion Salvatorem 200

Laudemus viros gloriosos 167–8
Litanies "per l'Assunta alla Collonna" 244
Litany of Loreto (1642) 172
Miserere servorum tuorum 147, 185–7, *186*, **188**, 191, 247
O bone Jesu (1642) 115, **116**
O Crux benedicta 211–12, 215, **217**
O Domina gloriae 244–8, *245*, **247**
O Domine guttae tui sanguinis 211–12, 215, **218**
O Domine Jesu 216–21, **219**
O Domine Jesu Christe 200
O dulcis Virgo 244–6, *245*, **246**
O Jesu mi 213, *214*
O quam dellactabile 200
O quam speciosa 227, 229
O vos omnes 115, **116**
Pianto della Madonna 138–9, 144
Plagae tuae Domine 140, 211–14
Psallite Domino 167
Salve Regina (1638) 138
Salve Regina (1642) 172
Si criminum 141
Tota pulchra es 227, 229–30, 232
Vulnerasti cor meum 227, 229–30
  operas by
    Ermiona 130–31
    Trionfi d'Amore, I 70, 74, 78, 82, 132
  prints by
    Antifone e litanie della Beatissima Vergine a più voci (1640) 129, 132–4, 138, 140, 272–3
    Antiphonare Sacrae B.M.V. per totum annum (1648) 129, 135, 137–8, 140–41, 244, 280–81
    Cantade … a doi voci (1633) 130–31, 140
    Cantade … a voce sola (1633) 130–31, 140
    Capricci poetici (1649) 130, 257
    Motetti a 2, 3, 4, e cinque voci (1642) 129, 134–8, **136**, 141, 171–2, 182–4, 200, 215–16, 274–5
    Motetti a una, due, tre, e quattro voci (1638) 128, 132–3, 137–41, 160–71, 211–14, *214*, 227, 229–30, 268–9
    Motetti a voce sola (1638) 129, 132–5, 137–40, 144–5, 168–9, 270–71
    quarto libro delle cantate, et arie a voce sola, Il (1636) 131
    Salmi a 8 voci concertati (1643) 129, 133–4, 137–8, 140, 276–7
    Salmi brevi a 4 voci concertate (1647) 129, 133–4, 137, 141, 278–9
    Trattenimenti musicali per camera (1657) 257
Sances, Lorenzo 129, 133, 270–71
Sandrart, Joachim von **255**, 256, 260
Schmelzer, Heinrich 199, 200–201, 263
  musical works by
    Inquietum est cor meum 200
    Lamento sopra la morte Ferdinandi III 263
    Sileat misericordium tuam 200
Schnitzer, Lucas 20, **23**, **83**, 85, 254
Schut, Cornelius 18–20, **19**, 49, 57, **58**
Schütz, Heinrich 137
Sebald, Martin 161, 169, 185, 187, 190
sepolcro 83–4
Slavata, Vilem 135–7, **136**, 238, 243–4, 274–5

Society of Jesus 27, 29, 44–6, 49,
    52–3, 86, 103, 129, 196–7,
    199, 206, 211, 224, 227, 238,
    261; *see also* Jesuit drama
  Collegio Germanico 27, 129–30
  universities 44, 95, 239, 241–2
Solomon, Old Testament King 57,
    173–4, 178–80, **180**, 182, 192,
    257, 260, 264
Sompel, Pieter van 36
Song of Songs, book of 88, 220,
    227–30, 232, 249
Sopron (Ödenburg) 149, 151, 288–9
Spindler, Antonio 137, 244, 280–81
Steen, Franciscus van den **255**, 256

Te Deum 87, 109, 166–7, 192, 249,
    251–2; *see also* Bertali, Antonio
St Teresa of Avila 206, 211
Thirty Years' War
  battles of
    Allerheim (1645) 223
    Breitenfeld (Second Battle of,
        1642) 32, 37, 63, 94, 133–4
    Chemnitz (1639) 32
    Jankov (1645) 39, 223
    Nördlingen (1634) 1, 17–22,
        18, **19**, **21–3**, 25, 29, 31,
        32, 37, 39, 49, 51, 254
    re-conquest of Regensburg
        (1634) 17, 20–22, **24**, 31,
        39
    Rheinfelden (1638) 32
    White Mountain (1620) 1, 39,
        45, 204, 225
    Wittstock (1636) 17
  involvement of France in 2, 17,
    31–3, 223, 252, **253**
  involvement of Sweden in 17,
    31–3, 39, 60, 63, 94, 137, 178,
    182, 198, 223, 248, 252, **253**
  peace treaties
    Peace of Prague (1635) 1–2,
        17, 50
    Peace of Westphalia (1648) 2,
        11, 33, 50, 56, 79, 147–9,
        191, 198, 223, 248, 251–2,
        253, 256, 288–9
Trautmannsdorf, Maximilian von 223
triumphal arches 5, 20, 102, 179, **180**,
    257–61, **258–9**, 264
trumpets 15, 22, **24**, 60, 79, 87,
    111–15, 117–18, 126, 128,
    149, 183, 188, 198–9, 243–4,
    251–2, 261

Urban IV, Pope 194
Urban VIII, Pope 225–6
Urllmayr, Georg **47**

Valentini, Francesco 196
Valentini, Giovanni 35, 63, 72–4,
    84–5, 109, 117–19, 128,
    131–2, 196, **200**, 201, 206–12,
    215, 220
  musical works by
    Cantate gentes 118
    *Deus qui pro redemptione
        mundi* 206–12, 209
    O felix Maria 117, 119
    Mensa sacra 200, 201, **202**
    Missa non erit finis 117–19
    Salve tremendum 206–11, *208*,
        210, 215
  oratorios by
    *Ragionamento sovra il
        Santissimo* 73, 84, 196
    *Rime sovra la Colonna,
        Flagello, Corona di Spine,
        Croce, e Lancia di Christo*
        73, 84
    *Santi Risorti nel Giorno della
        Passione di Christo* 35, 73,
        84
    Vita di Santo Agapito, La 35,
        74, 84
  prints by
    *Messa, Magnificat et Iubilate
        Deo a sette chori concertati
        con le trombe* (1621) 109,
        128
    Sacri concerti (1625) 206–7,
        220

Venice 25, 68, 130, 139, 142–6, 238, 266–7, 274–7, 282–5
Verdina, Pietro 63–4
Vienna 2, 6, 10–11, 17, 31–2, 58, 61, 72–7, 78, 82, 86–7, 88–92, 94–5, 101, 105, 109, 131, 138, 142, 148, 151–2, 178, 195–9, 206, 223, 225, 236–41, 248, 251, 261, 268–73
- churches
  - Augustinian church 105, 197, 238, 243
  - Dominican church 105, 199
  - *Hofburgkapelle* 72–3, 75, 77, 104–5
  - Jesuit church *am Hof* 92, 95, 197, 199, 238–9
  - *Jesuitenkirche* 95, 206
  - *Karlskirche* 58
  - St Stephen's Cathedral 42, 105, 197, 199, **237**, 238–9, 241
- *Schottenkirche* 236–8, **237**, 244, 280–81
- Hofburg 7, 72–6, 85, 105, 196–7, 236, 238
- Kunsthistorische Museum 18, 59
- Österreichische Nationalbibliothek 141, 241
- *Platz am Hof* 11, 58, 238–9, 241, 243

Vimina, Alberto 75, 79–81, 254
Vorsterman, Lukas 58
vulnus amoris, see mystical theology

Wael, Guillaume de 211–12
Wallenstein, Albrecht von 17
Wassenberg, Everhard 38–40, 188–9, 264
St Wenceslaus 184
Wideman, Elias 254
Władysław IV, King of Poland 38, 70–71, 72, 78
Wrocław (Breslau) 140